Humanistic Management in Practice

Humanism in Business Series

The Humanistic Management Network is an international, interdisciplinary, and independent network that promotes the development of an economic system with respect for human dignity and well-being.

The Humanistic Management Network defends human dignity in face of its vulnerability. The dignity of the human being lies in its capacity to define autonomously the purpose of its existence. Since human autonomy realizes itself through social cooperation, economic relations and business activities can either foster or obstruct human life and well-being. Against the widespread objectification of human subjects into human resources, against the common instrumentalization of human beings into human capital and a mere means for profit, we uphold humanity as the ultimate end and principle of all economic activity.

In business as well as in society, respect for human dignity demands respect for human freedom. Collective decision-making, in corporations just as in governments, should hence be based on free and equal deliberation, participation or representation of all affected parties. Concerns of legitimacy must, in economics like in politics, precede questions of expediency.

We believe that market economies hold substantial potential for human development in general. To promote life-conducive market activities, we want to complement the quantitative metrics which hitherto define managerial and economic success with qualitative evaluation criteria that focus on the human dignity of every woman and every man.

As researchers, we work towards a humanistic paradigm for business and economics, trying to identify and facilitate corporate and governmental efforts for the common good.

As a think-tank, we set out to spread intellectual tools for culturally and ecologically sustainable business practices that have the human being as their focal point.

As teachers, we strive to educate, emancipate, and enable students to contribute actively to a life-conducive economy in which human dignity is universally respected.

As practitioners, we act toward the implementation of a humanistic economy on an individual, corporate, and governmental level.

As citizens, we engage our communities in discourse about the benefits of a human-centered economy.

Titles include:

Ernst von Kimakowitz, Michael Pirson, Heiko Spitzeck, Claus Dierksmeier, and Wolfgang Amann (*editors*)
HUMANISTIC MANAGEMENT IN PRACTICE

Humanism In Business Series
Series Standing Order ISBN 978–0–230–24633–1

You can receive future title in this series as they are published by placing a standing order. Please contact your bookseller or, in case of difficulty, write to us at the address below with your name and address, the title of the series and the ISBN quoted above.

Customer Services Department, Macmillan Distribution Ltd, Houndmills, Basingstoke, Hampshire RG21 6XS, England.

Humanistic Management in Practice

Edited by

Ernst von Kimakowitz
Michael Pirson
Heiko Spitzeck
Claus Dierksmeier
and
Wolfgang Amann

palgrave
macmillan

First published 2011 by
PALGRAVE MACMILLAN

Palgrave Macmillan in the UK is an imprint of Macmillan Publishers Limited, registered in England, company number 785998, of Houndmills, Basingstoke, Hampshire RG21 6XS.

Palgrave Macmillan in the US is a division of St Martin's Press LLC, 175 Fifth Avenue, New York, NY 10010.

Palgrave Macmillan is the global academic imprint of the above companies and has companies and representatives throughout the world.

Palgrave® and Macmillan® are registered trademarks in the United States, the United Kingdom, Europe and other countries.

ISBN: 978-0-230-24632-4 hardback

This book is printed on paper suitable for recycling and made from fully managed and sustained forest sources. Logging, pulping and manufacturing processes are expected to conform to the environmental regulations of the country of origin.

A catalogue record for this book is available from the British Library.

A catalog record for this book is available from the Library of Congress.

10 9 8 7 6 5 4 3 2 1
20 19 18 17 16 15 14 13 12 11

Printed and bound in Great Britain by
CPI Antony Rowe, Chippenham and Eastbourne

Contents

List of Tables   vii

List of Figures   viii

List of Exhibits   ix

Acknowledgments   x

Notes on Editors and Contributors   xi

1   Introducing This Book and Humanistic Management   1
    Ernst von Kimakowitz, Michael Pirson, Claus Dierksmeier,
    Heiko Spitzeck, and Wolfgang Amann

2   ABN AMRO REAL – A New Bank for a New Society   13
    Patricia Palacios and Michael Pirson

3   AES Corporation – Serving People and Society   28
    Burcu Rodopman

4   Humanistic Business via the Integral Enterprise:
    The Case of Broad Air Conditioning, China   42
    Alexander Schieffer and Ronnie Lessem

5   bracNet: Bridging the Digital Divide – Covering
    Bangladesh with Wireless Broadband Access   62
    Michael Pirson

6   Cascades Inc. (1959–2009): Some Lessons
    from a Resilient Organization   76
    Emmanuel Raufflet and Pierre Batellier

7   Dialogue-Based Leadership Style As Part of Humanistic
    Organizational Cultures: The Case of dm in Germany   92
    Wolfgang Amann and Shiban Khan

8   Grameen Danone Foods – A Case of a Social
    Business Enterprise   103
    Doris John

9   Entrepreneurship, Humanistic Management and Business
    Turnaround: The Case of a Small Chinese Private Firm   119
    Fang Lee Cooke

v

10 Level Ground Trading Ltd – Fair Trade Coffee As
a Front for Social Justice 131
Will Low and Eileen Davenport

11 The Best Inputs for Maximizing Your Output:
Humanistic Practices at Micromatic Grinding 147
Rakesh Kumar Agrawal

12 Mondragon: Could Something Like
This Be in Our Future? 170
Terry Mollner

13 Novo Nordisk – Making a Difference in
Diabetes Treatment 185
Patricia Palacios, Michael Pirson, and Bradley H. Bader

14 SEKEM – Humanistic Management in
the Egyptian Desert 204
*Clemens Mader, Gerald Steiner, Friedrich M. Zimmermann,
and Heiko Spitzeck*

15 What Is Your Calling? SEMCO's Invitation to
Participatory Management 215
Carlos Largacha-Martínez

16 Triple Bottom Line Management at Sonae Sierra 231
*Pedro Teixeira Santos, Miguel Pina e Cunha,
Arménio Rego, and Miguel Pereira Lopes*

17 Can Business and Humanism Go Together?
The Case of the Tata Group with a Focus on Nano Plant 247
Radha R. Sharma and Shoma Mukherji

18 TerraCycle – A Business Founded for Societal
Benefit Generation 266
Heiko Spitzeck

19 Wainwright Bank and Trust Case Study – Humanistic
Management in Practice 277
Christine Arena

20 Zipcar Incorporated: Do We Really Need to Own Our
Automobiles? 290
Janet L. Rovenpor

21 Concluding Remarks 307
*Michael Pirson, Ernst von Kimakowitz, Claus Dierksmeier,
Heiko Spitzeck, and Wolfgang Amann*

Index 325

Tables

2.1	AMRO REAL's new business model	24
7.1	Leadership principles over time	101
13.1	Revenue and income increases	198
14.1	Year, company, main business activity	209
16.1	Areas of impact	234
16.2	2007 and 2008 awards	240
16.3	Evolution of the key performance indicators from 2005 to 2007	242
18.1	The crisis ... and the consequences	271
19.1	Humanistic management in the banking industry	288
20.1	Zipcar incorporated's growth from 2000 to 2008	291

Figures

2.1 Bank of value concept   15
4.1 An archetypal view on the four worlds and
    their dominant expressions   44
4.2 Fourfold structure of the integral organization   46
4.3 Local identity & Global integrity   47
4.4 Broad's knowledge cycle   53
4.5 The fourfold of broad   58
4.6 Broad – Integrally linking of the internal
    and societal perspective   59
6.1 Production, expansion, and consolidation processes   77
11.1 Management philosophy at Micromatic Grinding   154
13.1 Paradigm shift   187
13.2 The Novo Nordisk way of management   188
13.3 The learning curve   192
13.4 Focusing on the patient behind the disease   194
14.1 Principles of decision making by Dr. Ibrahim
     Abouleish (Mader, 2009)   205
14.2 Structure of SEKEM network (Mader, C., 2009)   208
15.1 SEMCO's renunciation   220
16.1 Corporate responsibility governance structure   239
18.1 Business-as-usual scenario (1961–2100)   272

Exhibits

8.1	Objectives of the Grameen Bank	104
8.2	Tenets of an SBE	107
8.3	Mission and objectives of Grameen Danone	108
11.1	Vision of MGT	148
11.2	MGT's mission	149
11.3	Highlights in the growth of MGT	151
11.4	Organizational structure of MGT	152
11.5	Organizational values of Micromatic Grinding	155
11.6	Statements recorded on a panaboard during a "No Agenda" meeting	158

Acknowledgments

First and foremost, we wish to thank the contributors to *Humanistic Management in Practice*, who graciously submitted to a competitive case selection as well as a lengthy review process. While the final evaluation of this book can only come from its readers, we believe that they have written some very inspiring, deeply telling and thoroughly researched case examples. In having done so, they allow us to complement theoretical arguments on humanistic management approaches with proof of concept, demonstrating managerial choices that put people first while laying a solid foundation for sustaining success in a competitive market environment.

Second, we wish to thank those entrepreneurs, managers and business leaders who dare to depart from the beaten track and allow for values-based decisions to supersede opportunistic, short-sighted profit seeking; it is these men and women who demonstrate true business leadership and we hope that they will be an example for many more.

With this book being the first in the newly established *Humanism in Business Series* at Palgrave Macmillan we want to thank everyone involved in the editing and production process. We greatly appreciate their expertise and experience in helping us turn academic insight into published books.

We also wish to send a warm-hearted thank you to the many supporters of the Humanistic Management Network. Through their intellectual and logistical support they not only facilitate our work and leverage our impact but also inspire us to further our efforts to promote a more humane economic and social order for all. Last but certainly not least, we would like to thank our readers for accompanying us on our intellectual journey towards a humanistic business paradigm for the world we collectively inhabit.

The Humanistic Management Network

Editors and Contributors

Editors

Wolfgang Amann heads, as director of executive education, the open enrollment and custom programs at Goethe Business School in Frankfurt, and teaches on a variety of strategy and governance topics. He was previously the principal leader of the project to turn the European Business School into a fully integrated university with multiple disciplines and faculties. He has also been vice-director of the executive school of the University of St Gallen.

Claus Dierksmeier is Professor of Philosophy at Stonehill College, Easton, USA with a special interest in the theory of freedom and the history of liberal thought in Europe and in North and South America. He has published several books on legal, political, and religious philosophy, and is currently working on topics of globalization ethics and Corporate Social Responsibility.

Michael Pirson is Assistant Professor at Fordham Graduate School of Business in New York, as well as a research fellow and lecturer at Harvard University. Before receiving his PhD, Michael worked in international management consulting for several years. He also gained experience in the political arena while working on Hillary Clinton's Senate campaign. Michael currently serves on the board of three social enterprises.

Heiko Spitzeck is Professor at Fundação Dom Cabral, Brazil. Previously he was a lecturer at Cranfield University's Doughty Centre for Corporate Responsibility in the UK. He obtained his PhD in Business Ethics at the University of St Gallen in Switzerland, and has held visiting scholar positions at the University of California at Berkeley and Fordham University in New York.

Ernst von Kimakowitz holds an MSc from the London School of Economics, UK, and an award-winning PhD from the University of St Gallen, Switzerland, where he is also teaching as a guest lecturer. Following several years in the strategy practice of a large management consulting firm, he is now working as an independent professional, providing consulting, advisory, and executive coaching services in the Corporate Responsibility arena to both private and public sector clients.

Contributors

Rakesh Kumar Agrawal is an Associate professor at the Institute of Management Technology (IMT), Ghaziabad, India. He takes keen interest in exploring and comprehending human behavior, especially in relation to spirituality and higher principles of life, and seeks to relate these to management and management education. He holds an engineering degree from IIT Bombay, an MTech in Behavioral and Social Sciences from IIT Delhi, and a PhD in Humanities and Social Sciences from IIT Roorkee.

Christine Arena is an award-winning author, syndicated blogger and corporate strategist. Her books, *The High-Purpose Company* (Collins, 2007) and *Cause for Success* (New World Library, 2004), as well as her "Case in Point" blog, separate the strategies and companies that make a positive difference from those that don't. Her website is: http://christinearena.com

Bradley H. Bader is Teaching Fellow in the Department of Organismic and Evolutionary Biology at Harvard University. He assists in designing and teaching general education courses for undergraduates on global health, with attention to the impact of genomics on healthcare delivery in the developing world. He received his undergraduate degree from Harvard in Psychology.

Pierre Batellier is Sustainability Coordinator, responsible for the Specialized Graduate Diploma (DESS) in Management and Sustainability, and teaches corporate social responsibility (CSR) at HEC Montréal. He has worked as a sustainability consultant for various organizations. He has written numerous business cases on CSR and has coedited *Responsabilité sociale de l'entreprise: enjeux de gestion et cas pédagogiques* (Presses Universitaires Internationales Polytechnique Montréal, 2008).

Fang Lee Cooke is Professor of HRM and Chinese Studies and Deputy Head (Research and Innovation) of the School of Management, RMIT University, Australia. Previously, she was a chair professor at Manchester Business School, University of Manchester, UK. Her research interests are in the area of employment relations, gender studies, strategic HRM, knowledge management and innovation, outsourcing, and Chinese MNCs. Fang is the author of *HRM, Work and Employment in China* (2005), and *Competition, Strategy and Management in China* (2008).

Eileen Davenport completed her BA at Exeter, and MA and MPhil degrees at Nottingham Trent. She has been an independent consultant for 15 years, specializing in community development. Recent clients include Oxfam International, Catholic Relief Services, and WFTO. She has published in *Strategic Marketing, Sustainable Development* and *Journal of Business Ethics*.

Doris John is a Faculty at Chennai Business School in India. She has specialized in developing case studies as pedagogical tools for management education and has more than 200 publications on the European Case Clearing House (ECCH). She was the first runner-up in the case-writing competition on CSR conducted by the British Council and was also one of the finalists in the Annual Case Study Development Initiative 2009 coducted by London Business School's Aditya Birla India Centre. She was involved in academic publishing with Icfai, and has also handled client servicing and PR assignments.

Shiban Khan's expertise is in theories and cultural implications of CSR. She is a visiting tutor at the Henley Business School, UK, and has been visiting scholar at the Indian Institute of Management, Bangalore and Hosei University, Tokyo. Shiban holds a Master's in Environmental Studies from the University of Pennsylvania and a Doctorate from the University of St Gallen, Switzerland.

Carlos Largacha-Martínez (PhD) is Provost for Research at Universidad EAN in Bogotá, Colombia. He received his doctorate from the University of Miami (Coral Gables, FL) in international studies and quantum sociology. His main research interests are quantum humanism and humanistic management. His most recent book participation is a chapter on "Quantum mechanics and the humanities" in *Globalization and the Prospects for Critical Reflection* (Aakar Books). He is also the editor of "Aproximaciones a la Gerencia Humanista" (EAN, 2010).

Ronnie Lessem is the Co-founder of TRANS4M Four World Center for Social Innovation (Geneva). He is a graduate from Harvard Business School and London School of Economics. Zimbabwean by birth, and UK Citizen by choice, he spent the past 25 years of his life in developing educational and research curricula and programs, which led to social and economic transformation, for London's City University, the University of Buckingham and others. He is the author of over 20 books on the development of self, business and society, among them, together with Alexander Schieffer, *Transformation Management: Towards the Integral Enterprise, Integral Research and Innovation* as well as Integral

Economics. He is together with Alexander Schieffer, the series editor of *Transformation and Innovation Series* of Gower Ashgate.

Will Low joined Royal Roads University in 2006 as leader for courses in sustainable business practice. Trained as an economist at UBC and LSE, he has taught in Canada, the UK, New Zealand, and Australia. The main focus of his research is sustainable consumption and the fair trade movement.

Clemens Mader graduated in Environmental System Sciences and finished his PhD with an emphasis on Innovation and Sustainability Management as well as Regional Sciences at the University of Graz, Austria. His research focuses on sustainability leadership and processes. He is Center Chair and Senior Researcher at the University of Graz and Guest Lecturer at Hiroshima University and University of Novi Sad.

Terry Mollner is Chair of Stakeholders Capital, Inc., a socially responsible wealth management firm in Amherst, MA; since 1972, Founder, Chair, and Executive Director of Trusteeship Institute, Inc., which promotes Mahatma Gandhi's theory of economics; and a founder and member of the board of trustees of the Calvert Social Investment Funds and Calvert Foundation. He is also on the board of Ben & Jerry's Homemade, Inc., and author of a forthcoming book on personal and social maturation entitled *The Love Skill: Welcome to the Relationship Age!*

Shoma Mukherji is currently pursuing an Executive Fellowship Program in Management at the Management Development Institute, Gurgaon, India. She has completed a Master's in International Management from the American Graduate School of International Management, USA, and has been a HR practitioner for 15 years. She currently works as a consultant in HR, Brand Development, Sales Administration, and Training. Her research interests are Leadership Communication, Gender Issues, Emotional Intelligence, and Corporate Social Responsibility.

Patricia Palacios obtained her MBA degree at the University of St. Gallen. She has a master's degree from Harvard University, where she also worked as a research assistant in the areas of sustainability, employee engagement and stakeholder trust. She has held several positions at UBS AG in wealth management and is currently working at the Consumer Goods Business Department of Daniel Swarovski Corporation.

Miguel Pereira Lopes is Visiting Assistant Professor and postdoctoral researcher at FEUNL. He holds a PhD in Applied Psychology from Universidade Nova de Lisboa. He has published papers in journals such as *Journal of Enterprising Culture, International Public Management Review, Journal of Positive Psychology, Organization,* and *Public Management Review.*

Miguel Pina e Cunha is Professor at the Faculdade de Economia, Universidade Nova de Lisboa. He has a PhD from Tilburg University. His research focuses mainly on emergent organizational processes and positive and negative organizing.

Emmanuel Raufflet (PhD McGill) is Associate Professor in Management at HEC Montréal. He has co-edited *Responsabilité sociale de l'entreprise: enjeux de gestion et cas pédagogiques* (Presses Universaitaires Internationales Polytechnique Montréal, 2008), *The Dark Side: Cases in the Down Side of Business* (Grenleaf, 2009) as well as two other books. His work has been published in the *Journal of Business Ethics, Journal of Corporate Citizenship, Management International,* and in *International Studies in Management and Organization.* He has won several case awards including the Emerson Award for best case in Business Ethics (2005 and 2007) and the Best Workshop Case Award (2008) at NACRA (North American Case Research Association).

Arménio Rego is Assistant Professor at the Universidade de Aveiro. He has a PhD from ISCTE and has published in journals such as *Applied Psychology: An International Review, Creativity Research Journal, Journal of Business Ethics, Journal of Business Research,* and *Journal of Occupational Health Psychology.* His research deals with positive organizational behavior.

Burcu Rodopman is Assistant Professor in the Management Department at Boğaziçi University, Istanbul, Turkey. She completed her doctorate in Industrial and Organizational Psychology at the University of South Florida and her Master's in Management at Harvard University. She has published work on mentoring, citizenship, and counterproductive work behaviors.

Janet L. Rovenpor is Louis F. Capalbo Professor of Business at Manhattan College. She teaches courses in Introduction to Management, Human Behavior in Organizations, and Strategic Management, and is the author of numerous articles in academic journals. Dr Rovenpor's research has focused on business ethics, managerial values, women in management, e-commerce, and organizational crises.

Alexander Schieffer is Co-founder of TRANS4M Four World Center for Social Innovation (Geneva). A graduate of the University of St. Gallen, Switzerland, where he still lectures, he wrote his PhD on leadership and personality development. After working in various industries in Europe and Asia, where he ran his own publishing company in Singapore, Alexander found his passion in turning education and research into vehicles for social and economic transformation and innovation. He has published a large variety of articles and books, among them, together with Ronnie Lessem, *Integral Research and Innovation, Transformation Management: Towards the Integral Enterprise and Integral Economics*. He is also, together with Ronnie Lessem, series editor of the *Transformation and Innovation Series* of Gower Ashgate.

Radha R. Sharma is a Professor of Organizational Behavior and Human Resource Development at the Management Development Institute (MDI), Gurgaon, India. She has completed research projects supported by the World Health Organization (WHO); UNESCO; McClelland Centre for Research and Innovation; IDRC, Canada; and Government of India.

Gerald Steiner is Associate Professor of Systemic and Sustainability Management at the Institute of Systems Science, Innovation and Sustainability Research (ISIS) at the University of Graz. His research fields include systems sciences, innovation and sustainability research, entrepreneurship, and industrial design, with special consideration of transdisciplinary creative problem-solving processes.

Pedro Teixeira Santos is Teaching Assistant at Faculdade de Economia, Universidade Nova de Lisboa. He is currently pursuing his PhD in Management and his interests are organizational rhythm, organizational design, change and sustainability.

Friedrich M. Zimmermann is Professor and Chair, Institute of Geography and Regional Science, University of Graz. Former Vice-President for Research and Knowledge Transfer, currently on the Supervisory Board of the University of Klagenfurt, Austria. Research focuses on regional development and tourism planning, using sustainable approaches to study rural and urban areas. International affiliations as professor at the University of Munich, Germany, and in the US (Pennsylvania and Oregon).

1
Introducing This Book and Humanistic Management

Ernst von Kimakowitz, Michael Pirson, Claus Dierksmeier, Heiko Spitzeck, and Wolfgang Amann

It seems virtually impossible today to open a newspaper without finding articles about corporate predators stalking the planet with unethical and sometimes bluntly illegal acts. Companies are involved in human rights violations, environmental degradation, bribery, excessive executive compensation, misleading corporate communication, and spying on employees or competitors; the examples are too numerous to list. Have corporations become more ruthless in the means they use to seek ever-greater profits, or have society and the media become more sensitive to corporate misconduct? While the truth may well lie in between, the number of publicized cases that undermine what we believe to be ethically sound corporate conduct has reached unprecedented levels.

Making corporate misdemeanor public should be welcomed, as it allows consumers, business partners, employees, and other stakeholders to make better informed decisions on where to spend their money, who to do business with, where to work, or how to appraise a corporate citizen.

There is one risk from the vast publicity corporate misdemeanor currently receives, though: some people may be led to believe that such are the ways of business, that is, that companies and executives have no alternative but to compete on questionable grounds, since it's a competitive, dog-eat-dog world out there. Companies that are exposed for unethical behavior are really only doing what everybody else does; they were just unlucky enough to get caught, but they're no different from the rest, one might think.

However, such a view is not only rather cynical, it is also wrong – on two counts. First, it would mean that executives have little responsibility for misconduct under their reign, for one cannot be held responsible for actions to which there is no alternative. Managers do have choices, though; our economic activities follow man-made rules, not laws of

1

nature, which is why managers should be perceived and act as *decision-makers*. For the most part, managers do have occasion to evaluate the ethical content of their decisions – even if, at times, they seem to lack an inner compass to guide them in evaluating the ethical dimensions of their business decisions.

Second, this view fails to recognize that the vast majority of the world's business activities are conducted in line with what is ethically justifiable; some companies even excel at ensuring that their business is aligned with societal aims. From telegraphy to mobile telephony, from the automobile to every step towards emission-free individual mobility, from book printing to personal computing, and from coal-fired power plants to renewable energy generation, in many cases great business leaders and inspired entrepreneurs have stood at the helm of developments that have greatly benefited humanity. Some of the companies providing us with innovative products and services go even further: they also focus on *how* they produce what they offer, paying close attention to how they interact with and impact on all of their stakeholders.

This book aims to unearth accounts of businesses that excel at doing well and doing good. They make products and services that address genuine human needs and they do so in ways that equally respect all stakeholder concerns. This book also follows the *Humanistic Management Network's* previous book, *Humanism in Business*,[1] in which we laid the theoretical foundations for a more life-conducive role of business in society. The book you are now holding in your hands provides concrete examples – proof of concept, as it were, that business success and societal benefit can very well go hand in hand.

What you can expect from this book

We set out to collect evidence of businesses that stand out by demonstrating that managerial freedom includes the option to align societal purpose and business success. We wanted to demonstrate that it is not only possible for companies to earn healthy profits when putting people first, but that those who do, deliver outstanding results to their owners *and* to society.

The *Humanistic Management Network* has selected 19 case examples of companies from around the globe, in a variety of industries, and with different ownership structures and sizes. These cases explore the principles of humanistic management and examine its theoretical merits by assessing its practical feasibility. They show how businesses can unite social value generation with financial success. One general prerequisite for managing a business along humanistic principles is the emancipation from a sole focus on maximizing profits. What these companies share is that they are managed as an integrated and responsive part of society by:

- Seeing that their organizational raison d'être includes the promotion of social benefit, for which business methods and market mechanisms are a means to support a specific end, rather than an end in itself.
- Submitting to the necessity of earning at least a sufficient income to be a self-sustaining organization but without succumbing to profit maximization as a normative criterion.
- Maintaining the liberty to opt out of the application of market rationality where this would conflict with or decrease the social benefits the organization seeks to create.

All these cases, which we present alphabetically, are independent accounts. You may choose the order in which you want to read them, and the following table provides a handy overview of the cases.

Company	Location	Size	Industry
1 ABN Amro Banco Real	Latin America (Brazil)	Big / National	Services
2 AES Corporation	North America (USA)	Big / Global	Industrial goods
3 Broad Air Conditioning	Asia (China)	Big / Global	Industrial goods
4 Brummer and bracNet	Asia (Bangladesh)	Small / National	Services
5 Cascades Pulp and Paper	North America (Canada)	Big / Global	Industrial goods
6 dm	Europe (Germany)	Big / National	Services
7 Grameen Danone	Asia (Bangladesh)	Small / National	Consumer goods
8 Hongfei Metal Limited	Asia (China)	Small / National	Industrial goods
9 Level Trading	North America (Canada)	Small / National	Consumer goods
10 Micromatic Grinding Technologies	Asia (Based in India)	Big / National	Industrial goods
11 Mondragon	Europe (Spain)	Big / National	Conglomerate
12 Novo Nordisk	Europe (Denmark)	Big / Global	Consumer goods

13 Sekem	Afrika (Egypt)	Small / Regional	Consumer goods
14 Semco	Latin America (Brazil)	Big / National	Conglomerate
15 Sonae Sierra	Europe (Portugal)	Big / Global	Industrial goods
16 Tata Group	Asia (India)	Big / Global	Conglomerate
17 TerraCycle	North America (USA)	Small / National	Consumer goods
18 Wainwright Bank and Trust	North America (USA)	Small / National	Services
19 Zipcar	North America (USA)	Small / National	Services

In the concluding observations we then revisit the cases and provide a brief reminder of their central messages followed by an examination of what can be learned from these examples. The lessons we suggest are, on the one hand, of a general nature and relate closely to the guiding principles of humanistic management as outlined on the following pages. On the other hand, we deduct more concrete lessons by looking at how the examples in this book demonstrate that humanistic practices can generate managerial success. In doing so, we trust that we can assist other companies that are seeking to adopt more humanistic practices.

We hope that these cases will stimulate alternative perceptions of managerial and organizational success, of what makes a company a corporate citizen that one would want as a neighbor. Enjoy the read! We trust that you will find these accounts thought-provoking and inspirational.

What is humanistic management?

We understand humanistic management on the basis of three inter-related dimensions. First, that unconditional respect for the dignity of every person is the foundation for interpersonal interaction, including any interactions taking place in business contexts. Second, that ethical reflection must form an integrated part of all business decisions. Third, that seeking normative legitimacy for corporate activities is crucial for assuming corporate responsibilities. This third dimension, which is to be understood as the dialogical extension of ethical reflection on corporate conduct, allows for the aligning of good intentions with activities that have the potential to produce good outcomes. Taken together, these three dimensions promote human flourishing through economic activities that are life-conducive and add value to society at large. Submitting business decisions to these three guiding principles is what we call humanistic management.

Unconditional respect towards human dignity

Part of what makes us human is our shared vulnerability. Investigating humanistic management is therefore based on the fundamental acceptance that the *conditio humana* entails our shared need for protection of our human dignity. Respecting every human being, in all its depth and complexity, as individually unique and collectively worthy of unconditional protection against exploitation is a shared endeavor of societies and all their institutions. As Immanuel Kant noted, every human must always be seen as an end in itself, and never as a mere means:

> Everything has either a price or a dignity. Whatever has a price can be replaced by something else as its equivalent; on the other hand, whatever is above all price, and therefore admits of no equivalent, has a dignity. But that which constitutes the condition under which alone something can be an end in itself does not have mere relative worth, i.e., price, but an intrinsic worth, i.e., a dignity. (Kant, 1785)

This presents a challenge to how we generally define managerial tasks. Managing is traditionally viewed as the task of achieving predefined objectives effectively and efficiently. Effectiveness is attained when the objective is achieved (i.e., output-oriented), and efficiency is attained when the objective has been achieved without wasting resources (i.e., input-oriented). This input–output orientation entails a tendency to objectify human beings (as human resources); managers influence the managed in favor of predefined objectives, thus turning them into a means to achieve an end, reducing people to little more than the equivalent of a piece of machinery.

If humanism demands seeing every individual as an end in itself, while managing people implies turning people into means, instrumental to achieving predefined objectives, is *humanistic management* even possible? Is it not an oxymoron?

The problem is that, for as long as we continue to base the manager's role on utilizing *human resources*, as which people are merely a means of production rather than embraced as ends in themselves, humanistic management is not possible, as it remains fraught with contradictions. Humanistic management is, therefore, much more than just a checklist for treating employees or other stakeholders *nicely*; it demands a fundamental paradigm shift away from the objectification of human beings within economic activities.

Yet, surely, people need to be instrumental in production processes in order for a business to thrive; they need a place in the organization and to fulfill specific tasks. This is undisputed. Within humanistic management, though, people need to autonomously assume their roles as a result of a self-determined process. Only then are they not *instrumentalized* in their human capacity; instead, they are themselves *assuming an instrumental role* within their job. They are then offering their working hours, creativity, and commitment to achieve certain goals, to produce certain goods and services.

The utilization of people in humanistic management must therefore always be limited to the role a person assumes, never to the person himself or herself. It must result from the autonomous will of an individual to be instrumental, to turn himself or herself into a means. Within this understanding, people will only become instruments within businesses which they consider aligned with their personal values and congruent with what they perceive to be worthy of being instrumental to. A person will not autonomously choose to become a means to an end that is profoundly inconsistent with his or her values and aims.

The distinction between turning oneself into an instrument by assuming a certain role and being seen and defined as instrumental through the objectification of the whole persona is therefore more than mere semantics: it lays the foundation that allows the alignment of business goals and societal aims by respecting each person as an end.

Integrating ethical concerns into managerial decisions

The need for respecting people as ends in humanistic management leads us to the impact it has on the economy and society as a whole. In its broader context, humanistic management is based on the insight that claims of assuming corporate responsibility remain mere rhetoric without the integration of ethical evaluation into business decisions. If one follows through on unconditional respect for the dignity of all persons, one must accept that decisions that impact others must be examined in terms of their consequences for all those affected.

Humanistic management criticizes one-dimensional managerial objectives such as profit maximization. Economic rationality becomes incompatible with protecting human dignity whenever it leaves no room for the balancing of interests of stakeholders based on the quality of the arguments articulated. When factual power overrides argumentative power – as any paradigm that proclaims the maximization of particular interests demands – those interests that cannot enforce their consideration are excluded and suppressed. This leads to situations where the interests of weaker stakeholders are disregarded and their vulnerability exploited. Therefore, we must formulate economic success criteria that no longer exclude respect for human values but are inclusive of them.

When one considers the role the private sector has been assigned in society, one finds such descriptions as: to supply goods and services that people want and/or need; or to generate employment opportunities and thereby sustainable livelihoods within an economy; or to be a source of innovation and creative solutions to existing problems.

It is, however, hard to find convincing arguments that define the role of business in society as an instrument to maximize monetary returns on investments for financiers or owners of businesses. Even the most hard-nosed proponents of shareholder value maximization ultimately argue that defining the raison d'être of a business organization through the maximization of monetary returns to its investors is right *because* it provides the greatest welfare gains for society overall. This argument presupposes that growing national incomes equal public welfare gains, which is not supported by either empirical findings or normative arguments. In addition, proponents of shareholder value generally remain silent on what findings support the view that maximization of financial returns to one stakeholder group automatically generates the highest welfare gains for *all*, as such views on public welfare are, by and large, blind to distributional questions.

Unsurprisingly, attempts to assign normative character to shareholder value maximization resonate strongly from many businesses and Wall Street agents that seek to *make money* rather than *make goods and services*. Unfortunately, this turns the underlying rationality about the role of business in society on its head. One-dimensional profit maximization is indifferent to the idea of businesses serving the interest of society and rewarding those people who chip in their money with a decent return for the risks they have taken. Instead businesses must strive to maximize the return for their financiers, and therefore need to offer goods and services for which they can generate demand. The difficulty with this reversed rationality is that different ends lead to different means.

A company driven by the maximization of financial returns is not overly concerned as to whether the needs it serves are genuine, as long as it can find a way to generate profitable demand. Such a company is unlikely to have the capability for self-restraint when pursuing a growth opportunity means turning a blind eye to ethical or environmental concerns, for example. Nor can a purely profit-maximizing company afford to accept and act upon legitimate claims from weaker stakeholders if the result might be reduced earnings. It is therefore not difficult to find examples where market forces and societal gains are at odds, leaving little room to claim that shareholder value maximization is the best way to promote societal gains.

In short, a company that maximizes profit will not be able to integrate ethical considerations into all business decisions, as the maximization of the interests of one stakeholder group, superseding all others, excludes equal respect for other stakeholders. However, equally respecting all stakeholders is a necessary precondition of the unconditional respect for the dignity of all persons affected by a company's activities.

Therefore, it clearly *does* make a difference whether the role of a business is to maximize return on investment or to create value for society. While the latter includes responsibilities towards financiers, it also includes responsibilities towards other stakeholders. Without an inclusive relationship between ethical reflection and business decisions, humanistic management is simply unachievable, as managers would be precluded from equal respect for all stakeholders.

The dialogical extension of managerial ethical reflection

The integration of ethical reflection into business decisions alone can be seen as a monological process in which the decision-maker might, in all sincerity, fail to see the concerns of others, leading to what we may call honest mistakes. Therefore, the third guiding principle – seeking normative legitimacy – is necessary to ensure that the outcomes of (monological) ethical reflection are tested by entering into a dialogue with those who may challenge any aspect of a business's conduct. The solitary managerial decision about whether a certain action is ethically sound is thereby transferred to the "moral site" of stakeholder dialogue, where the manager shares the responsibility with the stakeholder to embark on a course of action that is acceptable to both parties. This is how businesses gain normative legitimacy.

Legitimacy can be considered the general recognition of an entity's conduct as desirable or apposite within a system of norms and values. This definition leaves much room for interpretation.

In management studies, legitimacy is most widely seen as bestowed by self-interested, calculating stakeholders who legitimize an organization on the basis of their perception of receiving some kind of utility gains. For the company, this instrumental or pragmatic understanding translates into a desire to be regarded as legitimate (only) by key stakeholders, since transactional processes depend on trust, and trust will only arise when an organization is perceived as legitimate. Consequently, pragmatic legitimacy is all about the "business case" for legitimacy, encouraging organizations to manage legitimacy by providing certain stakeholders with tangible rewards as a lubricant for building trust.

Such a view is incompatible with unconditional respect for human dignity, as it turns legitimacy into a profit-enhancing resource to be obtained from society based on a cost–benefit analysis. Such a view seeks to substitute the need to gain legitimacy from all stakeholders with a reductionist concept of wanting to be perceived as legitimate only by those stakeholders powerful enough to cause harm to a business. In this view, even those stakeholders that are the putative beneficiaries, those upon whose trust a company depends, are effectively instrumentalized as a means for that company's profit-oriented aims. The moment the cost of obtaining legitimization from certain stakeholders exceeds the benefits the company derives from it, these stakeholders will cease to be seen as worthy of the company's efforts to gain their legitimization.

In contrast, humanistic management bestows legitimacy if the normative evaluation of an organization and its activities results in the perception that it is "doing the right thing." This clearly differentiates *normative legitimacy* from *pragmatic legitimacy*, as the former is based on values and reason rather than mere self-interest and strategic business calculus. Arguments that create legitimacy must be normative; they must be able to ethically justify why a certain course of conduct is considered desirable or apposite.

Legitimacy that equally respects all stakeholders thus cannot be gained if ethical reasons for justifying corporate conduct cannot be established. As Max Weber pointed out, seeking legitimacy helps determine the choice of means for an exercise (Weber, 1978, p. 214).

The sincere seeking of legitimacy therefore forces a company to continuously assess its conduct, to rationally justify its behavior and compare it to expectations and the desirability of its impact on society, which is best achieved in a dialogue between all those affected.

In short, humanistic management is the pursuit of strategies and practices that seek to create sustainable human welfare. Humanistic management derives its legitimacy from preserving human dignity in business through submitting its practices to societal critique. By engaging in an open dialogue about the values that should serve business as criteria to assess managerial success, corporate decision-makers realize that the value proposition of business is ultimately to serve people rather than to make money. The shift from one-dimensional profit maximization towards a multidimensional and value-integrative understanding of corporate success is as necessary today as it is imminent.

Why humanistic management is the way forward

The fundamental reason why humanistic management is beneficial to all stakeholders is that it has a profoundly liberating effect on a company and, consequently, on all – internal as well as external – stakeholders.

The debate about corporate responsibilities is primarily framed as a sacrifice that companies should make in order to be good corporate citizens. This proceeds along the lines that a company would be better off without all those less desirable stakeholders who demand proper conduct but do not generate revenue. These stakeholders have gained sufficient power, though, to seriously harm a company, so it must pay attention to how it is perceived by the public; it must invest in gaining and maintaining an image of moral integrity.

While this view confirms that a negative image can cost a company dearly, its reasoning is flawed. In this view, ethical corporate conduct is an investment in reputational risk avoidance in order to steer clear of the costs that may result from a negative image; it is not motivated by normative, ethical evaluation or the outcome of stakeholder dialogue; it is not rooted in wanting to do what is right.

Humanistic management means getting the priorities right from the outset and emancipating the company, first, from the restraints of a one-dimensional goal set – profit maximization – and, second, from the permanent apprehension of being exposed to the harsh public response that may follow losses of legitimacy.

Freedom from a one-dimensional goal set

The strict application of economic rationality as foundation for the share-holder value – the profit-maximizing objective function – undermines sustained business success. Shareholder value is a resultant benefit of providing products and services that address genuine needs, and producing them in ways worthy of normative legitimization. In other words, *shareholder value is not a strategy*. Companies that fail to see this will find their employees disengaged, their customers disloyal, and their public reputation at risk. Most stakeholders regard shareholder value maximization as inherently opportunistic, and with good reason, for it is normatively wrong. While those stakeholders that could pose a threat to a company's financial success receive great attention, all others are neglected, regardless of the ethical weight of their concerns. The translation of economic rationality into the profit-maximizing company creates a situation in which rational arguments can be stonewalled by company power.

The profit-maximizing objective function inevitably leads to situations in which asymmetric power relations between a company and its weaker stakeholders result in disrespect for weaker stakeholders' moral right to have their human dignity protected.

Humanistic management acknowledges these shortcomings and enables managers to remove the blinkers that make their vision one-dimensional; it lets *human rationality* prevail over *market rationality*. Humanistic management thus enables managers to maintain their personal integrity, employees are free from working in companies whose primary aims they do not share, and all stakeholders are liberated from corporate citizens that, ultimately, follow the logic of "might is right."

Freedom from losses of legitimacy

Humanistic management substitutes *maximized profits* with *legitimized profits*. Moral or normative legitimacy thus becomes a *pre*condition for profit-oriented goals. A company is enabled to share responsibility with its stakeholders, as the balancing of conflicts is transferred from the (monological) executive decision to the (dialogical) "moral site" of stakeholder dialogue.

The commercial risks of losing legitimacy are clear from the possible repercussions of a negative public image on a business. The real reason for seeking moral legitimacy is not commercial risk avoidance, though, but its normative foundation. A company must seek legitimacy to ensure that it does not act against the moral rights of others, that it does not exploit human vulnerability or instrumentalize people following profit-enhancing aims. Thus, gaining legitimacy is a *pre*condition for all company activities, an end in itself rather than a means. The commercial benefits that may result from bestowed legitimacy are a bonus for having done what is right, rather than the reason for seeking legitimacy in the first place.

Kant's principle of *publicity* (1795), according to which an action that affects the rights of others is wrong if its maxim cannot be declared publicly, provides the ground rule for principled openness for engagement with all stakeholders. This is how a company obtains its "public license to operate," and, if it understands stakeholder dialogue as an ongoing form of legitimizing corporate conduct firmly embedded in the organizational culture, it renews this "license" continuously – free from the constant pressure to manage reputational risks and strategically influence public perceptions.

In return, internal as well as external stakeholders can derive meaning from and find purpose in a company's activities that create value for society, making them loyal customers, engaged employees, long-term-oriented investors. Stakeholders are then also more forgiving if things do occasionally go wrong. In humanistic management, normative legitimacy becomes the decisive source of societal acceptance while simultaneously enabling managers to maintain their personal integrity as well as the organization's.

Humanistic management thus frees the company from the constant pressure of losing legitimacy and the need to manage reputational risks, as it has made moral legitimacy the unconditional platform of activities within the market environment. Humanistic management makes moral legitimacy the yardstick for measuring the right or wrong of its conduct.

Kant's definition of enlightenment as "man's leaving his self-caused immaturity" (Kant, 1784) serves to describe the emancipation from a profit-maximization focus and an instrumental view of legitimacy. In Kant's definition, immaturity is the incapacity to use one's intelligence without the guidance of another. For managers, enlightenment is being freed from a restrictive economic rationality as the source of indisputable guidance that prevents them from exercising their intelligence. Therefore, managerial enlightenment is the emancipation of managers from self-imposed restraints that curtail the intuitive scope and the moral depth of their rationality.

Note

1. Spitzeck, H., Pirson, M., Amann, W., Khan, S. and von Kimakowitz, E. (eds) (2009). *Humanism in Business*. Cambridge: Cambridge University Press.

Bibliography

Kant, I. (1784). Beantwortung der Frage: Was ist Aufklärung? *Berlinische Monatsschrift*, Vol. 4, 481–494.
Kant, I. (1785). *Groundwork of the Metaphysic of Morals*. Koenigsberg.
Kant, I. (1795). *Zum Ewigen Frieden*. Königsberg.
Weber, M. (1978). *Economy and Society: An Outline of Interpretive Sociology*. Berkeley, CA: University of California Press.

2
ABN AMRO REAL – A New Bank for a New Society

Patricia Palacios and Michael Pirson

> Succeed by doing the right things, the right way.
>
> Value Proposition ABN AMRO REAL

"Two roads diverged in a wood, and I – I took the one less traveled by and that has made all the difference," said Robert Frost in his poem "The road not taken" in 1918 (Frost, 2002, p. 270). The road not taken leads to the unexplored; a pathway that usually involves taking higher risks. At the same time, these risks can present opportunities; competitive advantages that can reposition an organization and place it in an entirely new spectrum. ABN AMRO REAL, one of Brazil's top five largest privately owned banks, is among those leading financial institutions to have chosen a distinct pathway by placing corporate social responsibility at the center of all their business activities. Their business model has revolutionized the South American banking industry, demonstrating to others how an organization can be profitable while maintaining an ethical attitude. In 2008 the bank was declared "the most sustainable bank of the year" by the Financial Times and the International Finance Corporation (IFC) (IFC Press Release, 2008). This case study will illustrate how ABN AMRO REAL became successful by placing corporate social responsibility at the center of their business activities and the lessons that can be learned from their management practices.

Envisioning a new bank for a new society

ABN AMRO REAL traces its roots to Banco da Lavoura de Minas Gerais, a financial group in Belo Horizonte Brazil founded with the aim of providing farmers with financing opportunities. In 1925 Banco da Lavoura de Minas Gerais moved its head office to São Paulo, where it assumed the name Banco Real. From that time, Banco Real expanded its operations until it had the biggest branch network in the country in 1975. In 1998, the bank was acquired by ABN AMRO S.A., the Brazilian subsidiary of a Dutch financial group, which had begun its activities in 1917 as Banco Holandês da America do Sul. ABN AMRO REAL, the merged bank, had over two million retail customers and employed over 17,000 employees in 1998.

Fabio C. Barbosa, the president of FEBRABAN, the Brazilian banking association, and newly appointed head of ABN AMRO REAL, faced the challenge of integrating the merger after the acquisition. At a time when several other acquisitions were taking place in the banking sector, competition was strong. Many of their bigger competitors did not only have a better technological infrastructure, but also stronger brand recognition. At the same time, poverty combined with a poor infrastructure, a high level of income disparity, and increasing environmental deficiencies afflicted the country, although Brazil was defined as one of South America's leading emerging economies. Mr Barbosa believed "there is limited value in succeeding in a country which does not enjoy the same success itself" (Barbosa, 2006). Given the competitive landscape in the industry and the huge societal problems, he knew it was possible to establish a new bank; a bank that would not only be distinguished from its competitors, but, most importantly, would have a new identity that could transform the society. Such a bank would be respected and admired by all its stakeholders, not only its investors.

Inspired by the vision of creating "a new bank for a new society," Mr Barbosa and other senior executives of the bank believed they could succeed by "doing the right things, the right way." "The right way" meant placing corporate social responsibility at the center of their business activities to make an impact. They wanted to move beyond mere philanthropy, and intended to demonstrate that it was possible to be profitable and at the same time create value for the society. Their emphasis on "value creation" led them to introduce the *bank of value* concept in 2001 (Figure 2.1).

The *bank of value* concept was developed by a group of senior executives of ABN AMRO REAL, including Mr Barbosa, Jose Luiz Majolo, COO, and Maria Luiza de Oliveira Pinto, Executive Director of Sustainable Development. Underlying this new concept was the belief that, by having an ethical approach to business, the bank could achieve total customer satisfaction, and, ultimately, all stakeholders would benefit. It was a business model in which everyone would win. Embedded in the group's business model was their mission: "To be an organization renowned for

Figure 2.1 Bank of value concept
Source: ABN AMRO REAL website.

providing outstanding financial services to our clients, achieving sustainable results and the satisfaction of individuals and organizations, who together with us contribute to the evolution of society" (ABN AMRO REAL Website, 2008). However, merely being satisfied was not enough for the bank. It strove for total customer satisfaction, which was considered an unending mission and implied a continuous improvement process (Banco Real Sustainability Report, 2003–2004, p. 29).

Placing sustainability at the center of their business activities

While the *bank of value* concept was applauded by many, some executives were skeptical of the new business model, mostly because they did not consider the idea of "everyone a winner" to be feasible. Like most unexplored pathways, this one was also filled with many uncertainties. Nevertheless, although there was some initial resistance, most senior executives, including Mr Barbosa and Ms Pinto, stuck to the new way of doing business, as they believed this was the "right thing to do." This was contrary to the old way, which emphasized transactions, while the new way meant focusing more on the type and quality of customer relationships.

For their vision to be successfully implemented, the relevant senior executives knew it was crucial to establish an internal team dedicated to ensuring that corporate social responsibility would be ingrained in all their business activities. Consequently, a committee was appointed to discuss and develop ways that could bring about the desired change, while work groups from various areas of the bank carried out the implementation of the projects. In 2002, the committee created under the *bank of value* concept was divided into three committees: management, market, and social action. While the management committee was responsible for eco-efficiency, employee diversity, and suppliers, the market committee was focused on the products, customers, and credit risk analysis. The social action committee was accountable for social investment and community involvement.

A crucial step had been taken by appointing committees that would serve to integrate the bank's new business model. However, before aiming to transform the outer world, the management knew they had to change the company from within. The bank's business processes were therefore analyzed and redesigned to make them more socioenvironmentally sustainable. In 2001, ABN AMRO REAL introduced their "3Rs" eco-efficiency program (*reduction, reutilization, and recycling*). Most of the bank's efforts to reduce its environmental footprint were primarily focused on reducing water and energy consumption, and the usage of recycled resources, such as paper, batteries, and ink used for their printing devices. Through these initiatives, energy consumption was reduced by 12 percent during the last three years; currently, approximately 90 percent of all the paper used is derived from recycled paper (ABN AMRO REAL Website, 2008). As a way of compensating for their emissions generated by travel, the executives introduced the "Floresta Real" program – an initiative targeted at the reforestation of the Atlantic Forest, which mainly follows the course of the Juquiá River in the interior of São Paulo. Since this area of São Paulo ranks among the lowest in terms of sanitary conditions, education, and development, the harvest generated by these plantations would help generate income that would improve living conditions in the community.

Although these initiatives helped the bank become more eco-efficient, the management knew that placing corporate social responsibility at the center of all their business activities meant much more. A key determinant to creating "a better bank for a better society" was to mobilize others to adopt more sustainable practices. The management knew that they could not be as successful alone, but, by sharing corporate social responsibility with others, they could come closer to making their vision a reality. This meant, for example, that the bank would only engage with those customers who shared the same principles, otherwise those principles would be meaningless. Consequently, the bank screened out those customers whose activities would pose high socio-environmental risks. This process generated much resistance at first, as many managers thought the bank would lose a significant client base and their assets would decline.

Nevertheless, the bank executives stuck to their principles and developed a socio-environmental risk department in 2002 to better screen and monitor their commercial clients' socio-environmental risks. Among the main areas assessed were safety and medical care in the workplace, outsourcing hazardous and polluting processes, and child or forced labor (ABN AMRO REAL Website, 2008). In addition, periodical compliance checks via questionnaires were required for companies in certain industries, such as agriculture and the transportation of hazardous chemical products. Thereafter, the socio-environmental department carefully assessed these questionnaires. The exclusion of clients only followed if they were engaged in certain sectors, such as the manufacturing of weapons, whose nature would not comply with ABN AMRO REAL's corporate principles, or if the company had failed to adopt the bank's suggestions regarding more sustainable measures.

Of the 2,112 credit applications received in 2003, 11 were refused for non-compliance with ABN AMRO REAL's socio-environmental obligations. Between 2004 and 2007, another 36 credit applications were rejected (Sustainability Reports, 2003–2004, 2005–2006, 2007). Although, in the end, the number of credit applications rejected represented only a small percentage of the total number of applications received, it was a crucial step to demonstrate to all that the bank's principles went beyond their financial pursuits (Mansur, 2008). At the same time, ABN AMRO REAL was among the ten initial banks in 2003 to have voluntarily adopted the Equator Principles, which are a set of guidelines established by a group of financial institutions to ensure that the projects they finance are structured in a socially responsible way and reflect sound socio-environmental management practices (The Equator Principles Website, 2008).

Engaging their staff to make a difference

To further succeed in its mission, management conceived the initial structure to ensure that corporate social responsibility was incorporated at all levels of the organization. The buy-in of ABN AMRO REAL's staff was most important for the continued implementation of the vision. Senior executives of the bank believed that a more engaged and motivated workforce, proud to work for ABN AMRO REAL, would independently enact responsible business decisions. The staff would then provide a better service to their customers, who would in turn be more satisfied. In order to develop a culture that reflected the values and principles of the bank, its staff's level of socio-environmental awareness had to be raised. Education was considered the best method to achieve this. Consequently, the senior management decided to form a directorate of education and sustainable development by temporarily unifying the sustainability and education departments in 2003. The main goal of this unified department was to train the staff on the topic of sustainability and to ensure that it was also incorporated in all the training programs at ABN AMRO REAL. In the following years, the bank also partnered several training specialists from other organizations to enhance the training experience of its staff. Later, other technological methods, such as online education programs, were also introduced to reach a greater audience. Once senior management considered the task accomplished and the staff sufficiently trained on sustainability, they decided to dismantle the directorate of education and sustainable development in 2007 and again form two separate departments.

Training was essential to mobilize the employees to implement the bank's vision, as was their engagement. ABN AMRO REAL encouraged and supported its staff to work towards finding solutions that could enhance their socio-environmental performance. This has given rise to some innovative projects that have not only demonstrated remarkable results in terms of profits and enhancing their socio-environmental performance, but have also increased employee engagement and motivation. Among the projects that were introduced was the Escola Brazil Project, which was founded and run by a group of employees (ABN AMRO REAL Website, 2008). This volunteer program was primarily aimed at improving the quality of public school education in Brazil and at helping these institutions adopt more sustainable practices. Later in 2002, the Amigo Real Project was also introduced and run by a group of staff members. Like the Escola Brazil Project, the Amigo Real Project was designed to strengthen the community's service systems and improve the lives of those children and adolescents in need (ABN AMRO REAL Website, 2008). This program became very successful. It has been calculated that between 2002 and 2005 the Amigo Real Project collected 22 million Reals (approx. USD 9.4 million) for children and adolescents in need. ABN AMRO REAL's efforts to engage their employees have brought formidable results: according to an internal study, employee satisfaction increased from 68 percent in 2004 to 91 percent in 2006 (ABN AMRO REAL Website, 2008). The Great Place to Work for Institute also ranked ABN AMRO REAL among the top ten best companies in Brazil for camaraderie and employee pride in 2008 (Mansur, 2008).

Bringing sustainable solutions to the market

ABN AMRO REAL did not only introduce several initiatives to enhance its socio-environmental performance, but also strove to have an even greater impact through product stewardship. It introduced new sustainable solutions by actively interacting with external parties (Hart, 2007). In 2001, ABN AMRO REAL launched its Ethical Fund, an equity fund aimed at obtaining high returns by investing money in companies demonstrating exemplary sustainable business practices. As one of Latin America's pioneer funds addressing socio-environmental needs, the Ethical Fund registered a 163 percent rate of return between 2001 and 2004 in comparison to São Paulo's average Stock Exchange (Bovespa) rate of 131.6 percent for the same period (Sustainability Report, 2003–2004, p. 44). According to Bloomberg Financial Information Services, of the 210 socially responsible investment funds they monitored worldwide, ABN AMRO REAL's ethical fund performed best in 2004. Their remarkable success led others in Brazil to become interested in launching similar funds. That same year, for example, Banco Itaú launched its Fundo Itaú Excelência Social (Itaú Social Excellence Fund) (Bovespa Corporate Social Sustainability Index, 2010).

Example: Among the companies to have benefited greatly through the support of ABN AMRO REAL was DryWash, a Brazilian company founded in 1994 that has revolutionized the cleaning industry (ABN AMRO REAL Website, 2008). By using Carnaúba wax, which is derived from the Carnaúba palm, an indigenous plant, the company introduced a new method of "washing" cars that did not require the usage of water or harmful chemicals, while efficiently removing dirt from vehicles without damaging their surface. As a way of helping the company to enhance its infrastructure and product line, ABN AMRO REAL financed some of their activities and helped them gain access to a socio-environmental credit line provided by the International Finance Corporation (IFC). Over the first ten years, DryWash was able to save 450 million liters of water through their innovative technology, and their revenues exceeded their expectations, reaching USD 2.7 million in 2005 (World Resources Institute, 2006). When choosing to open an account with ABN AMRO REAL, the company considered "sustainable conduct" as one of the main criteria. "If a bank has sustainable practices, then the likelihood that the institution really cares about the client is higher," said Lito Rodriguez, founder and president of DryWash (Portal Exame, 2006). By supporting DryWash to introduce sustainable products that could be of benefit to society, ABN AMRO REAL not only contributed to the success of the company, but it also gained a valuable customer.

ABN AMRO REAL decided to provide financing options with special conditions for their commercial clients interested in improving their socio-environmental performance. These credit options were made available to corporate clients provided they were targeted at enhancing the clients' socio-environmental performance.

Financing projects to help its corporate clients introduce more sustainable measures proved to be extremely lucrative for the bank, helping it increase its customer base with those who shared the same values. By 2007, ABN AMRO REAL's corporate portfolio amounted to 34,337 million Reals (approx. USD 19,354 million), indicating an increase of 32 percent compared with the previous year. At the same time, its number of current accounts increased by 32.5 percent between 2001 and 2007 (Sustainability Report, 2007). Like DryWash, several other companies benefited greatly through the bank's support. These special credit options were another way in which ABN AMRO REAL could demonstrate how everyone could benefit.

With all the costs that went into assessing credit line options to support companies' socio-environmental development and the expenditure on training the bank's credit analysts, many stakeholders were skeptical and questioned whether the bank would benefit from the socio-environmental risk assessment in the end. After analyzing several companies, many of the bank's experts came to the conclusion that companies with socio-environmental problems are also most likely to have financial problems (Sustainability Report, 2005–2006). Christopher Wells, head of the bank's socio-environmental risk department in Latin America, explained that, by avoiding loans to those poor-performing companies, and even turning them down when necessary, it could outperform banks that did not consider environmental issues when lending to companies (Schneider, 2009). These benefits are partially reflected in the bank's insolvency rate, which is comparatively lower than the market average. For example, in December 2007, ABN AMRO REAL had an insolvency rate of 2.8 percent compared with the 4.3 percent market average (Sustainability Report, 2007). In addition, it would gain by increasing its brand attractiveness and, consequently, the bank would gain more customers who shared the same values and principles.

The bank did not, however, limit its support to corporate clients, but also helped those at the base of the pyramid. Together with Acción International, an NGO with vast experience in microfinance, ABN AMRO REAL created a joint venture called "Real Microcredito" in 2002. It was founded before the Brazilian government started investing in microcredit incentives and before Muhammed Yunus won the Nobel Peace Prize (Sustainability Report, 2005–2006, p. 55). Micro-lending (small loans provided to the poor) was intended to spur economic growth by financing productive activities that would help the low-income community generate income. The bank's first micro-lending project was in Heliópolis favela, the biggest low-income community in São Paulo (Metaonginfo, 2002). To gain access to these loans, those in need were not required to go to the bank itself. Ten representatives were sent to work at the Heliópolis favela to contact those interested, while various other volunteers also contributed to making this project successful. Over time, the number of microcredit clients increased, from 85 in 2002 to 53,421 in 2007 (Sustainability Reports, 2002–2003, 2007).

ABN AMRO REAL's consistency and transparency in incorporating corporate social responsibility in all its business activities quickly led to its gaining credibility from its stakeholders. The International Finance Corporation (IFC) was among those impressed by the bank's social commitment. In 2004, ABN AMRO REAL was granted 51 million Reals (approx. USD 21.6 million) to support its sustainability investments – an amount rarely approved by a financial institution (IFC Sustainable Report, 2004). With this funding, the bank could expand its sustainability portfolio basis for an even greater impact. It was also the first time a bank enjoyed complete autonomy to perform its socio-environmental risk analysis with the funds granted – a task that was generally done by the IFC.

Shortening the journey by sharing best practices

Over time, other companies could no longer overlook the fact that, in order to remain competitive in the market, they had to contribute to societal goals. For many, however, the challenge remained finding new sustainable solutions to enhance their socio-environmental performance. ABN AMRO REAL, however, knew that by collaborating with its stakeholders and sharing best practices it could be of help. More than being merely supportive of others, ABN AMRO REAL knew that alone it could not accomplish much, but, together with its clients, could achieve much more and shorten the journey to make a real difference. Consequently, the bank introduced the "Espaço Real de Prácticas em Sustentabilidade" – a program designed for the public, and especially for companies, supporting them in rethinking and redesigning their business processes in a lucrative and innovative manner, integrating financial results with corporate social responsibility. Companies would benefit not only by sharing best practices with a leading financial institution that had successfully integrated sustainability into its business processes, but also by exchanging experiences with other participants.

The "Espaço Real de Prácticas em Sustentabilidade" program offers events, which are open to the public, that promote reflection and debate on topics pertaining to sustainability. Some of the meetings are specifically designed for the public to ask questions and to learn from the views of renowned specialists from around the world. Among the leaders to have participated in these events in the past were Stuart L. Hart, author of "Capitalism at the Crossroads" and Eduardo Gianetti, Brazilian economist and author of "O Valor do Amanhã" ("The Value of Tomorrow"). ABN AMRO REAL has expanded the offices previously used for training its employees to offer free introductory sessions to all who are interested in gaining knowledge of sustainability. For those who are unable to attend these events in person, ABN AMRO REAL has introduced video chats and online courses to extend its best practices to a wider audience. As a way of further engaging its stakeholders and of keeping these practices vivid, the bank has appointed a council comprised of leaders in their respective areas, such as Alexandre Hohagen, general director of Google Inc. in Brazil.

The examples above illustrate how ABN AMRO REAL has taken a greater leap forward towards developing a more sustainable world by engaging its stakeholders. In much the same way, the bank also encourages others to engage their stakeholders to have a greater impact. ABN AMRO REAL has therefore created the "Practica de Engajamento com Stakeholders," a guide for companies to support them in the development and creation of initiatives that help engage others. At the end of this guide, the bank provides a checklist that allows companies to diagnose and reflect on their management practices in order to find better ways of enhancing their stakeholder engagement.

Several of the bank's initiatives have also been targeted at the sharing of its best practices with its suppliers. For example, it created an Internet portal to foster communication and to nurture the relationship with its suppliers. A document called "Parceria de Valor" ("Partnerships of Value") was created to foster the exchange of best practices. In addition, in all its supplier contracts ABN AMRO REAL has stipulations that specifically prohibit any actions or business practices that do not comply with its corporate principles, such as discrimination, child labor, and slavery.

Acting today, thinking of tomorrow

ABN AMRO REAL had made significant steps towards enhancing its socio-environmental performance. At the same time, the number of employees engaged either fully or partially in sustainability increased over the years. In 2007, there were 407, mostly due to the microcredit expansion (Sustainability Report, 2007, p. 94). But the road ahead was a long journey. The bank executives knew that strong leadership from the top was not enough. For the initiatives to endure and the bank to continue its long journey, it was crucial to build and train effective leaders across all departments; leaders who could drive sustainability in the future, not only within the company itself but also beyond the boundaries of the bank. With this in mind, in 2007 they launched the Sustainability Development Leadership program, which was aimed at amplifying the bank's product and service line to stimulate the innovation of new, sustainable business solutions. Initially 2,200 managers were trained, but the bank later expanded this program to encompass other 130 leaders of other functional areas, such as the corporate communication department (Jornada Real, 2007). After successfully completing the program, the leaders applied the knowledge gained in their respective functional areas and proactively looked for future solutions that would help them take a greater leap forward towards enhancing their financial as well as their socio-environmental performance.

For ABN AMRO REAL, leadership meant also forecasting future trends and making them a present need. Since its financial products for sustainability increased from 217 million to 825 million Reals (approx. USD 122 million to 465 million) in 2007 – reflecting a total growth increase of about 280 percent – the bank knew there was a high likelihood that the demand for sustainable products would increase in the coming years. At the same time, post-secondary education in Brazil was experiencing a high drop-out rate due to high tuition fees. Acknowledging the adage that "every social problem is a business opportunity in disguise," ABN AMRO REAL saw this as an opportunity to tap a new market and create a new sustainable product solution (Cooperrider, 2008, p. 1). Together with the IFC, the bank set up a student lending facility for 50 million Reals (approx. USD 21 million), from which students can borrow money to attend a participating university and repay the loan after their graduation (IFC, 2008). Taking into account Brazil's high demand for university graduates, this initiative seems very promising. According to Guy Ellena, IFC director for health and education, it is the first time one of Brazil's large banks has developed products to exclusively support university students, establishing a distinct market segment (IFC, 2008).

The idea was not just to help university students; educating future generations and increasing their awareness of sustainability was seen as a part of the mission. This is why ABN AMRO REAL created an entertaining website for children aged between five and 12 called "Brincando na Rede" (Playing on the Net). This tool was aimed at triggering children's interest in learning to navigate the Internet, thus contributing to their education and raising their awareness of sustainability.

The road less traveled that made all the difference

Looking back at the road traveled, ABN AMRO REAL's new business model (Table 2.1) had proved successful. As demonstrated below, its net income and assets grew steadily between 2002 and 2007. In comparison with 2002, its net income had grown by approximately 80 percent to USD 1,677 million. Since 1998, the bank's investments in training, technology, and the re-engineering of its business processes, as well as the rising number of clients, have enabled it to increase its efficiency significantly. From 68.3 percent in 2002, its efficiency ratio decreased to 49.2 percent in 2007.

In 2007, the bank's surveys revealed that 74 percent of its clients were satisfied, including 36 percent who were totally satisfied (ABN AMRO

Table 2.1   AMRO REAL's new business model

	2002	2003	2004	2005	2006	2007
Net Income (USD in millions)	341	392	467	616	958	1,677
Total Assets (USD in millions)	10,431	19,090	23,184	32,455	56,503	89,931
Efficiency Index	63.8%	58.1%	60.0%	57.3%	50.9%	49.2%

Source: Adapted from ABN AMRO REAL Social Sustainability Report, 2007. All USD/Real conversions reflect the exchange rate on December 31 that year.

REAL Website, 2008). The number of employees grew to approximately 27,000, and their satisfaction level was estimated to be well over 90 percent between 2005 and 2007 (ABN AMRO REAL Website, 2008). The bank went from number 11 in the list of the greatest places to work for in Brazil in 2006, to number 6 in 2008 (Great Place to Work For Website, 2008). The bank also received recognition for its efforts. In 2006 alone, the bank won a total of 49 awards, including the Eco 2006 Award from the American Chamber of Commerce (ABN AMRO REAL Website, 2008).

Several factors contributed to the bank's success. Behind the integration of the new business model was a strong leadership that mostly originated from the senior bank executives. Among those leaders were Mr Barbosa and Ms Pinto, who had had the vision and power to ingrain corporate social responsibility and place it at the center of all their business activities. Mr Barbosa was admired by the public and regarded as a role model for his social commitment.

Success Factors:

- Strong leadership by senior executives
- Sharing best practices to have a greater impact
- Engaging others to increase their sustainability portfolio
- Education on sustainability to ensure that the bank's vision was carried out throughout the organization

---

In addition, by sharing best practices that allowed others to benefit from its learning journey, the bank could accelerate the adoption of more sustainable practices by others – a catalyzing effect that facilitated the bank's greater impact. The bank's ability to engage others in its road to sustainability and to focus on innovation to increase its socio-environmental performance likewise contributed to its success.

At the same time, the bank faced several challenges. In sharing its best practices externally, and considering that many of its competitors had adopted more sustainable practices over time, many feared the bank would lose its dominant position as a sustainability market leader. In addition, when launching so many different initiatives, the problem was how to keep track of their progress and measure their impact over time.

In 2007, Grupo Santander acquired ABN AMRO REAL, making it the fourth largest Brazilian bank. Other mergers followed as part of the Brazilian financial consolidation wave: Banco Itaú merged with

Unibanco to form Brazil's and Latin America's largest bank, while Banco do Brazil acquired Nossa Caixa (Latin American Herald Tribune, 2009). Competition remained strong and the challenge was how these banks could strengthen their brand differentiation to uphold their leading position. Once again, Mr Barbosa – now the head of Santander Brazil – was faced with the challenge of integrating two merging organizations. Many wonder how the integration is going to be carried out and, most importantly, whether sustainability will remain at the center of all their business activities. As Mr Barbosa looks ahead, there are many roads, which all lead in different directions, but fundamentally the right one is clear. This road could imply choosing a distinct direction away from the others. Nevertheless, this road could again be the one that could make all the difference in future.

Lessons learned:

- Educate and build leaders who can drive sustainability in the future
- Forecast future trends and make them a present need
- Engage staff to increase the innovation of sustainable solutions
- Share best practices with stakeholders to have a greater impact

---

Bibliography

ABN AMRO REAL Website (2008). http://www.bancoreal.com.br/sustentabilidade/?clique=Geral/Frame_Superior/Menu_Institucional/Sustentabilidade [accessed December 9, 2008].

Barbosa, F. (2006). *Integrating Sustainable Development Into The Bank's Business.* Presentation World Business Award: May 9, 2006. http://www.iccwbo.org/WBA/id7029/index.html [accessed December 10, 2008].

Bovespa Corporate Social Sustainability Index (2010). http://www.ifc.org/ifcext/media.nsf/Content/IFC_Launches_Brazils_Sustainability_Index [accessed October 10, 2010].

Cooperrider, D. (2008). *Sustainable Innovation.* BizEd. July/August.

Equator Principles Website (2008). http://www.equator-principles.com/principles.shtml [accessed December 11, 2008]

FNV Company Monitor (2006). *Banco Real / ABN AMRO Brazil.* http://www.redpuentes.org/pais/holanda/centro-de-documentos/company-monitor-abn-amro-brazil-summary [accessed December 11, 2008]

Frost, R. (2002). *The Road Not Taken: A Selection of Robert Frost's Poems.* 2nd ed. New York: Holt Paperbacks.

Great Place to Work for Institute (2008). *Greatest Places to Work for in Brazil.* http://www.greatplacetowork.de/best/list-br-2008.htm [accessed December 9, 2008]

Hart, S. (2007). *Capitalism at the Crossroads.* 2nd ed. Pennsylvania, PA: Wharton School Publishing.

IFC (2008). *IFC Partners with Banco Real to Set up Innovative Student Loan Program in Brazil.* http://www.ifc.org/ifcext/media.nsf/content/SelectedPressRelease? OpenDocument&UNID=00F30D69DB8D7AE285257404006A0DB1 [accessed December 14, 2008].

IFC Press Release (2008). *IFC and FT Announce Sustainable Banking Awards Winners.* http://www.ifc.org/ifcext/media.nsf/Content/IFC_FT_Awards_ June08 [accessed December 10, 2008].

IFC Sustainable Report (2004). http://www.ifc.org/ifcext/sustainability.nsf/ Content/Publications_Report_Sustainability2004 [accessed December 10, 2008].

Jornada Real (2007). http://www.relatoriodesustentabilidade.com/jornada_real/ index.php?ano=2007 [accessed March 26, 2009].

Latin American Herald Tribune (2009). *5 Largest Banks hold 65.72% of Brazil's Assets.* http://www.laht.com/article.asp?ArticleId=324759&CategoryId=14090 [accessed January 6, 2009].

Mansur, A. (2008). *A empresa verde é um caminho sem volta. Entrevista Fabio Barbosa.* Revista EPOCA: São Paulo, Brazil. http://revistaepoca.globo.com/Revista/ Epoca/0,,EMI6303-15295,00-FABIO+BARBOSA+A+EMPRESA+VERDE+ E+UM+CAMINHO+SEM+VOLTA.html [accessed December 14, 2008].

Metaonginfo (2002). *Banco Real ABN AMRO Bank lança microcrédito para moradores de favela.* http://www.newventures.org/?fuseaction=content&IDdocume nto=250 [accessed December 14, 2008].

Portal Exame (2006). *Um banco e seus princípios.* http://portalexame.abril.com. br/static/aberto/gbcc/edicoes_2006/m0117609.html

Schneider, Ivan (2009). *Lessons from Brazil: How to Incorporate Environmental and Social Factors into Lending.* EcoTech. http://www.ecotech.financetech.com/ blog/archives/2009/03/lessons_from_br.html [accessed March 26, 2009].

Sustainability Reports (2002–2003; 2003–2004; 2005–2006; 2007). ABN AMRO REAL Website. http://www.bancoreal.com.br/sustentabilidade/?clique=Geral/ Frame_Superior/Menu_Institucional/Sustentabilidade [accessed December 14, 2008].

World Resources Institute (2006). *Rising Ventures.* New Ventures March 2006 – July 2006. http://www.newventures.org/?fuseaction=content&I Ddocumento=250 [accessed December 9, 2008].

3
AES Corporation – Serving People and Society

Burcu Rodopman

> The purpose of business is not to maximize profits for share-holders but to steward our resources to serve the world in an economically sustainable way.
>
> Dennis Bakke, former AES CEO, 2005

> We broke all the rules. No overtime. No bosses. No time records. No shift schedules. No assigned responsibilities. No administration. And guess what? It worked!
>
> Oscar Prieto, AES director of Light Servicios de Electricidade, Brazil, 1998

The AES Corporation (formerly Applied Energy Services, Inc.) is a large-scale multinational corporation, which operates as an independent producer of electrical power. AES was established by Roger W. Sant and Dennis W. Bakke in 1981 in Arlington, Virginia. After building its first power plant in 1985 in Texas, AES expanded initially in the US, and then broadened its operations globally in the early 1990s to achieve its mission of "providing electricity worldwide." The company operates mainly in two segments: Generation and Utilities. The Generation segment generates and sells power to wholesale customers. The Utilities segment distributes, transmits, and sells electricity to end-user customers in the residential, commercial, industrial, and governmental sectors. The company generates electricity from various resources, including coal, gas, fuel, oil, and biomass, as well as hydro, wind, and solar. In 2008, the AES Corporation owned a portfolio of electricity generation and distribution facilities with generation capacity of approximately 43,000 megawatts and distribution networks serving approximately 11 million people in 29 countries. In 2009, the company had 3,000 MW of power plants under development in ten countries. AES has a global workforce of 25,000 employees in facilities located in North America, Latin America, Asia, Europe, and Africa.

AES experienced high financial and operating performance during the 1990s and became one of the top-performing companies in the stock market, with assets of USD 37 billion in 2001. It was listed among the companies with fastest-growing and best returns to shareholders in *Fortune* and *Washington Post* lists. This was surprising, because AES never stated profitability as a primary performance indicator. In 2002, AES went through a major retrenchment to deal with challenges due to the Californian power crisis in 2001, changing risk perceptions after the Enron crisis, the meltdown of the Argentine economy, and uncertainties after the September 11, 2001 terrorist attacks. AES had lost more than 90 percent of its stock value and joined the many other companies that suffered in 2001 – the so-called "90 percent club." As a result of a turnaround in management over more than 5 years in 2008 AES reported USD 16,070 million in sales and was included in the Fortune 500 (ranked 158), Standard & Poor's 500, and Dow Jones Utilities listings. AES Corporation's Corporate Governance Quotient, which evaluates the strengths, deficiencies, and risks of a company's corporate governance practices and board of directors, was better than 34 percent of S&P 500 companies and 49.5 percent of Utilities companies.

From its foundation, AES was conceived as a humanistic company marked by its business rationale of "stewarding the resources to meet needs of society" (Bakke, 2005). This objective was supported by its core values, which shaped its management practices and redefined the roles of stakeholders, leaders, and employees. The founders, Sant and Bakke, identified the purpose of AES to serve people, to serve all stakeholders, not only shareholders, by adhering to shared values of integrity, fairness, fun, and social responsibility.

Business rationale: Meeting a need in society

The AES founders believed that a business should exist to "meet a need in society" and to improve people's lives. AES fulfills this mission by supplying electricity and power, which are essential to human progress and to advancing economic growth, public health, and security, wherever it operates. As Bakke states, "The most socially responsible thing we can do is to do a really good job of fulfilling our business mission, which is to provide clean, reliable, safe, low-cost electricity around the world" (Wetlaufer, 1999). According to Sant and Bakke, profits and social responsibility were not mutually exclusive, but they believed that, if the company did a good job of meeting a need in society, profits would likely follow. In other words, money is a natural and inevitable by-product of the firm's shared values and of its operations that contribute to society. In line with the idea of stewarding resources to serve the society, AES holds a holistic view of the constituency of the company. Accordingly, AES does not serve only the interests of shareholders, but also those of their employees, the customers, the communities that host AES plants, suppliers of services, and governments of countries where AES operates.

AES is an example of an achievement that couples financial success with a commitment to humanistic practices. AES generates revenues and profits, while simultaneously conducting business in a socially responsible way. The business philosophy at AES emphasized "good business" as opposed to mere profits. The founders recognized that profits are essential to pay the shareholders the returns for their investment, but profits were neither an end in themselves nor the chief reason for the firm's existence. Bakke states in one article:

> Where do profits fit? Profits...are not any corporation's main goal. Profits are to a corporation much like breathing is to life. Breathing is not the goal, but without breath, life ends. Similarly, without turning a profit, a corporation too, will cease to exist...At AES we strive not to make profits the ultimate driver of the corporation. My desire is that the principles to which we strive would take preeminence. (Bakke, 1996, p. 5)

AES values and guiding principles

From the time Sant and Bakke decided to create AES, they knew they wanted to make it a different type of organization. Having worked in government and private business before, they knew well the downsides of corporate America. As a values-driven, humanistic company, AES founders embraced corporate values, which render the company its unique character and its humane touch. The four values at the heart of AES are integrity, fairness, social responsibility, and having "fun" at work (Bakke, 2005; Waterman, 1994). According to the corporate charter:

- **Integrity** means achieving a "wholeness" in which "the things AES people say and do in all parts of the company fit together with truth and consistency." By carefully weighing all factors – ethical concerns, stakeholder interests, and societal needs – AES strives to act with integrity in all of its activities.

- **Fairness** refers to being fair in the company's relations with all stakeholders including employees, customers, suppliers, stockholders, governments, and the communities in which it operates. On the one hand, fairness captures the belief that it is not right to "get the most out of" each negotiation or transaction to the detriment of others. On the other hand, fairness is not necessarily "treating everybody equally;" rather, it involves treating everybody in a just manner depending on his or her circumstances.
- **Social responsibility** is based on the belief that AES has a responsibility to be involved in projects that provide social benefits, such as lower costs to customers, a high degree of safety and reliability, increased employment, and a cleaner environment.
- **Having fun** entails providing a work environment in which people can flourish in the use of their gifts and skills. People have fun when they enjoy the work they do through empowerment, participation in decision-making, continuous development, and improvement.

These four values were chosen because they allowed the founders to create a humanistic organization which included the principles of serving society's needs, fair conduct with stakeholders, and active employee empowerment. It is not that these values are new, but the extent to which AES is committed to them was not common. Ironically, the US Securities and Exchange Commission (SEC) considered the adherence to these values a risk factor for investors. Therefore, it required the following statement to be inserted under the heading of investment risks in the prospectus for AES's initial public offering in 1991:

> An important element of AES is its commitment to four major "shared" values: to act with integrity, to be fair, to have fun and to be socially responsible ... AES believes that earning a fair profit is an important result of providing a quality product to its customers. However, if the company perceives a conflict between these values and profits, the Company will try to adhere to its values – even though doing so might result in diminished profits or forgone opportunities. Moreover, the Company seeks to adhere to these values not as a means to achieve economic success, but because adherence is a worthwhile goal in and of itself. (AES, 1991, p. 12)

AES also faced situations in which its core values conflicted with the profit-focused mindset. For example, AES employees in Indonesia decided that paying a bribery "tax" to a member of the Suharto family did not fit with the values of fairness and integrity. Although the project promised significant revenues, they opted for not taking on any projects in Indonesia at all. AES also willingly engaged in planting trees in Guatemala at a cost equal to its annual profits. In sum, drawing from its core values, AES applies guiding principles in all business dealings with all its stakeholders to fulfill the responsibilities of a socially responsible company. The AES statement announces that each and every employee commits to:

> *Put Safety First.* We will always put safety first – for our people, contractors, and communities.
> *Act With Integrity.* We are honest, trustworthy, and dependable. Integrity is at the core of all we do – how we conduct ourselves and how we interact with one another and all of our stakeholders.
> *Honor Commitments.* We honor our commitments to our customers, teammates, communities, owners, suppliers, and partners, and we want our businesses, on the whole, to make a positive contribution to society.
> *Strive For Excellence.* We strive to be the best in all that we do and to perform at world-class levels.
> *Have Fun Through Work.* We work because work can be fun, fulfilling, and exciting. We enjoy our work and appreciate the fun of being part of a team that is making a difference. And when it stops being that way, we will change what or how we do things. (AES, 2001)

These principles serve as guidelines to operate AES as a company that is honest, treats people fairly, and provides safe, clean, inexpensive energy worldwide. There has been controversy over the extent to which these values can be instilled in other countries and cultures (e.g., traditional Islamic societies such as Pakistan, or countries with a socialist history such as China and Ukraine), which may be very different from those in the US. Surprisingly, AES was able to maintain its company culture because the values proved to be universal enough to be embraced by employees worldwide, even though the implementation of them differed according to regional context.

Social responsibility: Environment and community

AES constitutes an example of a company that successfully combines profitability with social responsibility. AES's basic mission is to provide electrical power in a way that is safe, clean, reliable, and cost-efficient. However, AES has gone beyond simply providing electricity to serve society. As a corporate citizen, AES also strives to conserve the environment and contributes to the other needs (e.g., employment and education) in the communities in which it operates.

Environment. AES commitment to social responsibility has been linked to environmental sustainability. Roger Sant has long been involved with environmental sustainability in his role as vice chairman of the World Resources Institute, chairman of the World Wildlife Fund, and a board member of other leading environmental organizations. AES leaders underscore the belief that corporate citizens have the same responsibility as private citizens in committing resources to better the world, which includes the stewardship of environmental resources.

As part of its efforts to reduce greenhouse gases, AES established a consulting arm, AES Greenhouse Offset Group, to help other electric power companies to be environmentally responsible and progressive. In recognition of these efforts, Harvard University honored AES in 1994 with its George S. Dively Award for Corporate Public Initiative. Sant voiced AES concern for the environment as an important principle.

> Electricity – or more accurately the services that electricity provides – bears about the highest correlation of any product or service to economic well-being... Dennis Bakke and I started AES with the goal of supplying competitive power in the most socially beneficial way. And that meant an abiding concern for the environment. So why coal? Because coal is so abundant around the world, and because technology has all but eliminated coal pollution as society had traditionally measured it. (Paine, 2000, p. 3)

From early on, AES took steps to eliminate coal pollution as society had traditionally measured it; that is, to minimize three types of emissions: sulfur dioxide (SO_2), nitrous oxide (NO_x), and particulates. To this end, AES has started to use circulating fluidized bed (CFB) boilers, which were superior to standard boilers in reducing SO_2 and NO_x emissions at selected plants. In other plants, AES used supplemental pollution control technology including "scrubbers" and low-NO_x burners to reduce SO_2 and NO_x emissions, respectively. When global warming became an issue in the mid-1980s, AES committed itself to a tree-planting and preservation program, whereby the company agreed to plant or preserve enough trees to offset the carbon dioxide emissions from its power-generating facilities. In 1989, the company launched a USD 7 million CO_2-offset program that included agro-forestry, forest preservation, and sustainable use. AES committed itself to planting more than 52 million trees in Guatemala over roughly a ten-year period. The number of trees was selected based on estimates of the number required to absorb the entire amount of carbon dioxide produced in a plant during its anticipated 40-year lifespan. AES Executive Vice-President stated that "making electric power historically has had a relatively high level of environment impact. We are not planting trees as part of our strategy to make us a more valuable company, we are doing it because we think it's a responsible thing to do." In fact, the project cost the company an estimated USD 2 million, an amount that reportedly nearly equaled AES profits for that year. Similar company efforts to plant and preserve trees, woodlands, and forests followed, included giving a grant to preserve 144,000 acres of forest in Paraguay and a USD 3 million effort undertaken in conjunction with Oxfam America to preserve 3.7 million acres of South American forest. AES also promoted a private property-rights approach to environmental protection by helping indigenous peoples in South America establish ownership rights to their territorial homelands. This also involved developing land-management programs that would help keep this land in good condition for decades to come. In 2006, AES made a significant investment in a greenhouse gas emission offset project, AES AgriVerde. Through this initiative, AES plans to generate 34 million tons of greenhouse gas emissions offsets annually by 2012. Lately, AES has also looked for new ways to reduce and offset greenhouse gas emissions by alternatives such as solar power and wave technologies. For example, AES invests in environmental upgrades such as biomass conversions and environmental retrofits to maximize the protection of the environment.

Community. Social responsibility at the community level involves providing social benefits to societies in which AES has its operations. At AES, giving back to the community is regarded as an important part of the work, and includes a full range of activities from donations to active participation in educational programs. In 2005 alone, AES businesses donated more than USD 40 million to support various programs worldwide, from public safety initiatives in Ukraine to sponsoring underprivileged children to attend school in Pakistan. The tree planting project In Guatemala put 40,000 farmers to work and increased the welfare of local people. AES activities are intended to help the surrounding community meet its needs. AES supported local community programs that tie into its business, such as building medical centers in Kazakhstan. AES also funded and constructed a USD 1.5 million public elementary school in Panama, Oklahoma. AES's Shady Point plant contributed USD 1.5 million for the development of an urgently needed elementary school in that suburb. Furthermore, AES sponsors gift-matching programs worldwide, which enable employees to send AES's philanthropic dollars to improve lives.

During these efforts to provide social benefits, AES thrives on a community-based approach, which also enables AES to adapt quickly to new business environments (Gluski, 2007). For example, in Brazil, AES managers interviewed local leaders to understand the problems related to energy theft. Then, AES pilot tested many different approaches to offering a formal electricity service, including installing group meters in areas with a strong sense of community, training local representatives in leadership courses, and employing them to distribute bills and collect payments. The most successful programs were implemented in the entire region. As a result, losses from energy theft were reduced by USD 35 million in 2006 and overall customer satisfaction improved. AES also encourages the plants to conduct a "social benefits analysis" of their projects and to concentrate their efforts on the areas that maximize social benefits. For example, while AES in North America focused on environmental issues, some plants in Pakistan and China decided to engage in building schools.

As a socially responsible company, AES holds safety to be of the utmost importance. AES monitors the dangers inherent to the industry and tries to take preventative measures worldwide. It holds an annual AES Safety Action Forum that brings together leaders and key personnel from AES businesses around the world to take on specific issues and share ideas on how to improve safety. Confirming AES's commitment to safety, CEO Bakke stated that "if there is one accident, everyone's bonus is cut by 25 percent, two accidents means a 50 percent cut, and by the third, there is no bonus for anyone" (Wetlaufer, 1999). As a result of AES efforts, the reliability and safety levels of AES's plants exceed industry averages. In addition to ensuring safety at its plants, AES also initiated programs to promote electrical safety within their various communities. In Latin America, AES employees themselves provided people there with basic training on the dangers of electricity. As a part of such an initiative in Ukraine, AES produces a magazine, "The ABCs of Electric Safety," which provides tips on how to avoid accidents involving electricity and the dangers of electrical theft. Ukraine's Department of Education and Science adopted the magazine for use in preschool and elementary classes throughout the country. Similar programs were initiated worldwide, including such places as El Salvador and Kazakhstan.

AES leaders and AES people

To be able to run the company in such a manner, AES relied on its specific AES style of management. AES considers individuals as 1) creative, intelligent, capable of learning and making decisions; 2) trustworthy, responsible – can be held accountable; 3) unique and deserving respect and special treatment; 4) fallible; 5) oriented to teamwork; and 6) eager to make a contribution (Pfeffer, 1997). This view of human nature, coupled with AES values, especially the value of "fun," has resulted in AES-unique leadership style and management practices.

AES leaders work hard to show their commitment to the core values by striving to instill them in every employee, by rewarding adherence to them, and by exercising the principles themselves. AES provides values training for 3 or 4 months to all employees at all levels when a new plant is set up. Employees view videos of Sant and Bakke explaining the corporate philosophy and values within the first few weeks on the job. Within a year, new employees and their spouses also attend an orientation at corporate headquarters, where again the corporate values are discussed with corporate leaders. In addition to values training, each year's Letter to Shareholders reports on AES performance on shared values in addition to plant operations, assets, and sales backlogs. An annual survey is administered to all employees to evaluate the commitment to AES values and to identify areas of disagreement, miscommunication, and dissatisfaction. A Founder's Award is given annually to employees who stand out as practitioners of AES values, as well as a President's Award for Technical Achievement. Furthermore, a portion of the CEO's compensation is tied to the board's assessment of his effectiveness in upholding the value system. For example, after an incident of employee fraud in the Shady Point plant in 1992, Bakke, as the most senior person responsible for adherence to AES values, took a 30 percent pay cut. Other executives also took pay cuts ranging from 10 to 20 percent. AES took measures to make it easy for people to act in accordance with AES values. Employees were encouraged to discuss them and their applications in regular meetings. In recognition of ethical conflicts that may arise, AES leaders are available as advisers to help employees with concerns. AES also provided a helpline that is available 24 hours, 7 days a week, and employees can access it anonymously and confidentially.

Organizational structure. AES thrives on the principle that strong businesses are built on trust, accountability, and an environment that allows people to reach their full potential. AES founders state that "the people in AES are not principally economic resources. We are not tools of the corporation. Rather we hope the corporation is structured to help individuals make a difference in the world that they could not otherwise make" (Wetlaufer, 1999). To this end, AES utilizes a "honeycomb" system of organizational structure, with a highly decentralized and non-hierarchical organization that minimizes bureaucracy. The honeycomb system of employee management revolves around a web of worker families who form small autonomous teams, which govern their own state of affairs. It encourages shared responsibility, the reduction of hierarchy, and democratic control of the environment. AES has a flat organizational structure, and few layers of management separate an AES entry-level employee from the firm's plant supervisor.

The honeycomb system was put to the test in an incident in the Shady Point plant in Oklahoma in 1992. Upon the discovery of employee fraud in falsifying emission levels, it was suggested that the honeycomb system might not be appropriate for every organization and at every stage. Following the announcement, the price of AES stock fell from USD 26.50 to USD 16.50, reducing the company's market value by USD 400 million. After the incident, workers revised the organizational structure, creating specific human resources, technical, environmental, and operations functions, and adding a new layer of supervision. This was a major blow, because introducing more control conflicted with AES's fundamental principles. Eventually, however, after much discussion, employees at Shady Point decided to go back to the honeycomb system.

No functional departments. AES has no centralized company-wide departments for human resources, operations, purchasing, or public relations. All these functions are managed at plant level. To be specific, the plants do their own hiring and a worker-led committee participates in the allocation of merit-based bonuses. Decisions are made by empowered employees and teams. The few company officers assigned to these functional areas act typically as remote in-house advisers to the plant project management team responsible for a given project rather than making decisions at the top level. In an interview (Wetlaufer, 1999), Bakke confirms that "the modern manager is supposed to ask his people for advice and then make a decision. But at AES, each decision is made by a person and a team. Their job is to get advice from me and from anybody else they think it is necessary to get advice from. And then they make the decision. We do that even with the budget. We make very few decisions here (indicating the headquarters office). We affirm decisions." For plant financing, for example, in one year CFO Barry Sharp raised less than 10 percent of the estimated USD 3.5 billion needed for AES's first ten power plants; most of the necessary financing was raised by each plant's own project team, composed of a broad cross-section of AES employees. Accordingly, leaders mainly serve as chief guardians of the principles, chief accountability officers inside and outside AES, or chief encouragers. By giving employees a greater sense of involvement and responsibility for their actions, this eccentric system has led to positive outcomes, including high employee satisfaction and low turnover, and to perceptions of a growth-oriented and very desirable work environment.

Employee engagement and empowerment. As for the experience of employees, Sant and Bakke intended to create a company in which people have "fun" – engaging experiences – on a daily basis (Markels, 1995). Having fun implies that people who work at AES are fully engaged. Bakke suggested that "The struggle before a deal... the challenge and the creativity required to make it work, taking risks, even sleepless nights. Believe it or not, those things are really fun because they engage people – heart, mind, and soul" (Wetlaufer, 1999). To provide full engagement, work is structured in such a way as to give people full experience of how everything operates. For example, as opposed to many companies in the industry, operations and maintenance functions were kept within each team, with the attitude "You run it; you keep it up; you fix it." In the absence of functional departments, people are given the power to make important decisions, to engage with their work as "business people," not as cogs in a machine. The AES approach also emphasizes employee responsibility for decisions and accountability for results. For example, in Uncasville, Connecticut, the maintenance team volunteered to invest the USD 12 million cash reserve held at the plant. The crew of 15 employees did not have prior experience in investing short-term money in the market, so they hired a teacher who told them what a spread was, who to call on Wall Street to get the process going, and so forth. After a few weeks of studying, the team started calling up brokers and looking for the best vehicles for investing. By the third month, they were earning better returns than the people who were investing at the headquarters. Bakke and Sant agree that lack of specialization may hurt efficiency and may increase mistakes, but they believe that the trade-off is well worth it. According to them, the sense of control and total responsibility that people feel when they really own their decisions is crucial for them to become better businesspeople.

Internal measurement and information sharing. At the foundation of good decisions lie knowledge sharing and open communication. To support individual and collective excellence, AES promotes an open environment, in which employees volunteer information, share knowledge, give and take advice. Although personal compensation issues are confidential, for everything else there is free and frequent information flow. The company publishes its monthly financial reports in the corporate newsletter. AES makes information from internal measurement and assessment available to everyone to improve management and operating practices. The plant policy and planning sessions are open to all employees regardless of rank and tenure. For SEC purposes, every one of our people is considered an "insider" for stock trading.

Employee Development. At AES, "fun" at work is associated with personal and professional development, which also enables people to become better business people. Empowerment necessitates commanding better skills and knowledge. This objective is achieved with job rotation, mentoring, and opportunities for continuous improvement.

Through job rotation programs, AES tries to promote generalists instead of specialists. In that way, every person understands all aspects of the operations and the economy in which AES works, and can keep the good of the whole company in mind when he or she makes decisions. In fact, the career of Pete Norgeot, starting in the fuel-handling team in Thames, Connecticut, moving though many different teams and then ending up as plant manager in Wales, is common rather then exceptional (Wetlaufer, 1999).

To promote employee development, AES offers traditional academic programs at the University of Virginia's Darden Graduate School of Business Administration, as well as online training and mentoring programs, to develop the leadership skills of its employees. The AES Learning Center program is built around the concept of "leaders teaching leaders." AES offers tuition reimbursement and has created a comprehensive set of online self-directed "how-to" courses in conjunction with General Physics Corp., which cover a wide range of topics in the energy area and provide instruction on running a power plant, from the latest emissions scrubbing technologies down to the nuts and bolts of how to repack a valve. Upon the program's success, AES also set up similar programs in Ukraine, Cameroon, Kazakhstan, and Brazil in cooperation with leading local universities.

AES also encourages its employees to benefit from mentoring, which aids with work adjustment and career development. AES provides all its businesses with a framework that includes training for mentors and protégés, as well as guidelines for structuring such relationships. AES has adopted the Harvard Business School's "ManageMentor" online training program, which is available in different languages. This program gives access to modules addressing the full range of daily management responsibilities – from running a meeting and leading teams to strategy development and finance essentials. Therefore, this program allows AES employees to become businesspeople and gain leadership skills by providing both conceptual information and practical advice.

In addition to online exercises, AES also has a formal mentoring program to increase the socialization of new employees. Each MBA hire is given an AES leader as a mentor, and together they forge a unique relationship guided by best practices, collaboration, trust, and mutual commitment.

Lessons from AES's experience

It is challenging to imitate AES's experience and to maintain its value-driven practices. Still, we can learn valuable lessons from AES's successful implementation of a value-based system, which underscores attaining financial success by adhering to important humanistic values that promote justice, welfare, and goodwill.

1. Businesses can achieve objectives for profits and social responsibility at the same time. In the case of AES, a value-based system (integrity, fairness, social responsibility, and fun at work) with universal principles enabled AES to achieve both objectives.
2. A company can contribute to the world by meeting a need in society, by being socially responsible and environment-friendly. As a collective entity, businesses, with their services and operations, can make a difference beyond what individuals and governments can do to improve people's lives.
3. Empowering employees will contribute to a company's success. Companies may better utilize the skills and knowledge of their employees when they regard them as businesspeople and give them opportunities for participating in autonomous teams and in decision-making.

Bibliography

AES Common Stock Offering Prospectus, 1991.

AES Corporation, 10K submission to the Securities and Exchange Commission for 2001.

AES Corporation website, http://www.aes.com [accessed October 7, 2010].

Bakke, Dennis W. (1996). Erecting a grid for ethical power. *The Marketplace*, May/ June.

Bakke, Dennis W. (2005). *Joy at Work*. Seattle: PVG.

Bakke, Dennis W. and Sant, R. (1997). Annual Letter to Shareholders, *1997 AES Corporation Annual Report*.

Gluski, Andres (2007). Turning consumers into customers. *EnergyBiz*, September/ October, 136–137.

Markels, Alex (1995). A power producer is intent on giving power to its people. *Wall Street Journal*, July.

Paine, Lynn Sharp (2000). AES global values. *Harvard Business School*, 1–20.

Pfeffer, Jeffrey (1997). *Human Resources at the AES Corporation: The Case of the Missing Department*. Stanford Graduate School of Business, 1–26.

Waterman, Jr, Robert H. (1994). Values from the start: Culture is strategy at the AES Corporation, in *What America Does Right*. New York: Penguin Books, 111–136.

Wetlaufer, Suzy (1999). Organizing for empowerment: An interview with AES's Roger Sant and Dennis Bakke. *Harvard Business Review*, January–February, 111–123.

4
Humanistic Business via the Integral Enterprise: The Case of Broad Air Conditioning, China

Alexander Schieffer and Ronnie Lessem

Problem: The problem of disintegration

Over the past 5 years we have been developing an approach to social and economic transformation that builds on an *integral* perspective. Through this approach we aim to integrate, on the one hand, individual, organization, and society, and, on the other, the four societal (organizational) dimensions of nature (animate), culture (civic), politics (public), and economics (private/business) (Lessem and Schieffer, 2009). It is an approach that is equally rooted in the four corners of our world (South, East, North and West) (Lessem and Palsule, 1996), which means that we root an enterprise or community in its local context, while also drawing upon global knowledge from other cultures.

We purposefully talk, in that integral respect, about transformation, not about change. Take, as an illustration, the case of the butterfly: here, transformation is the process of a caterpillar transforming gradually into a butterfly, arriving at a totally different stage. Change, to stay with this metaphor, is the small caterpillar growing into a big one. We argue that mere change – a bigger caterpillar, as it were – is not enough. Rather, we need to work towards a new organizational and societal form, in which the formerly fragmented perspective of organization, individual, or society on the one hand, or the sectoral fragmentation into either economics (private business), politics (public), culture (civic), or nature (animate) on the other hand, is altogether overcome. As a result of both, the very functioning of the enterprise is transformed.

All too often today, there is a tendency to use the terms "economy" and "society" as equivalent terms, which means overlooking the other equally important aspects of society: its environment (nature), its culture (civic sector), its public (political) sector, and, of course, its economic (private) sector. This widespread oversight is a clear indication of how far we have come in defining ourselves, our organizations, and our societies in purely economic terms.

Finally, we suffer from a fragmented perspective on the world as a whole, where the West, at least in the past few 100 years, has taken the lead. The result is a totally unbalanced globalization that is dominated mainly by the West and chiefly by economics. We are also painfully aware, especially today, that we are missing out in relation to our environmental, cultural, and political dimensions. Huntington's "Clash of Civilisations" (Huntington, 1993) is only one of the scenarios that seem to have become all too true.

We urgently need to develop a more integral perspective to show that it is not conceptual beauty that drives us, but that there are farsighted organizations all over the world that lead the way along an integrated path and, by doing this, deliver extraordinary results.

So far, we have not come across a major organization in China that clearly represents a fully integrated perspective. China impresses the world with its economic prowess; it is, however, worrying to witness the exploitation and pollution of its environment, social inequity, suppression of minority rights, and a seemingly one-sided economic approach to the future. Altogether, this gives the impression that China is disconnected from its extraordinary cultural heritage.

China's development is of significance for the entire world. It is of enormous importance that "the Chinese get it right," and do not, with their large population leverage, repeat the mistakes of the West, especially in polluting their environment. Where, we ask for example, is the strong relationship to nature that the Chinese culture has built over 3,000 years? Chinese philosophies are filled with deep wisdom regarding how to live in balance with nature, Lao Tsu's Tao Te Ching being only one of the most prominent exemplars. The Daoist Principle of Yin and Yang is perhaps the most powerful and well-known example from a philosophical perspective that aims to balance opposing forces in order to create a dynamic balance between them. According to Daoism, the world is made up of two energies: there is the male (Yang) and the female (Yin), the day (Yang) and the night (Yin). These two energies are opposite forces, but have a deep reliance on each other.

With Broad Air Conditioning we have identified a powerful case of an organization that strives to stay in balance with its different inner and outer dimensions, in an organizational (micro) context, as well as in a societal (macro) context. It shows that, if an organization builds on its local wisdom, and is rooted in local nature and culture, it can contribute strongly to sustainable development not only of its economy, but of society as a whole.

We shall now introduce our integral approach to organizations in more depth (part II) before we turn to our case (part III).

Approach: From disintegration to integration via the integral enterprise

In our approach we build on the fourfold aspects of nature (the animate sector), culture (the civic sector), politics (the public sector), and economics (the private sector); further, we regard this as a kind of fourfold that each institution and society needs to reflect within itself.

Broadening this perspective for a moment, we can see that this fourfold has its roots in the universal archetype of the four worlds. In this archetypal "picture" it is the South that is most closely related to nature, specifically to human nature, as well as the intersubjective perspective. In Figure 4.1 this is represented by humanism. The East is home of the

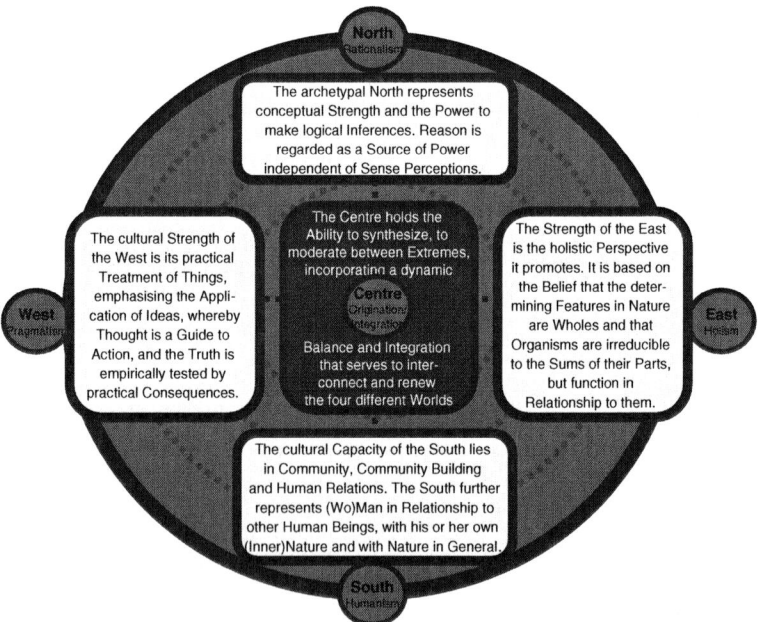

Figure 4.1 An archetypal view on the four worlds and their dominant expressions

civic, evolutionary dimension of man (holism), while the North hosts man's rational dimension. And it is the West that holds the pragmatic dimension, which is only of value if it embodies and thereby stays connected to the other three dimensions. It is surprising to note that in all kinds of different cultures all over the world one can find variations of this archetypal perspective (Angeles, 1993; Stevens, 1994).

While we are not saying that, for example, humanism is only rooted in the South (hence in Africa), or, for example, holism is only rooted in the East (hence in countries such as Japan and China), we argue that, over time, each world region has evolved one inner dimension that seems to be more strongly developed than the others. The East has arguably the longest and deepest tradition in the area of holism, spirituality, and non-material aspects, while, for example, the West has developed an enormous capacity for the pragmatic and material elements. Of course, you find all aspects in every society, in every organization, in every individual. And we argue that it is ultimately necessary to differentiate and integrate these four dimensions within the fields of the individual, the organization, and the society. The pragmatic West needs not only the rational northern dimension, but also the holistic eastern dimension and the humanistic (people and community-orientated dimension) of the South. Each dimension needs the others in order to be truly meaningful and effective. In fact, when one dimension is isolated from the others it degenerates; so, for example, pragmatism degenerates into materialism, and humanism into nepotism.

If you regard this as too far-fetched, then carefully examine the current state of our so-called globalized world, with the one-sided domination of a) economic principles that b) developed in a heavily dominating West. It is this fragmented and one-sided perspective that, in our view, is one of the core reasons for many of the problems that the world community currently faces, including the current financial and economic crisis.

And, yes, there are significant efforts to overcome this fragmentation, which, as many believe, is rooted in the rational, analytical, and dualistic worldview identified as Descartian ("Cogito Ergo Sum"). There are efforts to acknowledge the existence of other sectors (e.g., the private sector acknowledges the existence of the civil sector; this finds its contemporary expression in the concepts of CCR and Corporate Citizenship), but, we argue, this is mere mutual acknowledgement by the dimensions, not building on each other, and therefore certainly not integration. CSR activities are mostly actions by which organizations do good in society. These actions are, however, mainly disconnected from their own core orientation, Microsoft and Bill Gates being a prominent case in point. We argue that a private company should first be deeply rooted in nature and culture (which ideally comes *before* the public and the private anyway, not afterwards), and hence its engagement in society ought to be in relation to its own product focus. If this does not happen, we will not overcome the existing fragmentation between the different sectors. Based on our argument, our generic perspective of an integrally transformed organization looks as follows (Figure 4.2). Specifically, marketing builds on nature and community, thereby becoming community-building; human resources builds on culture and spirituality (conscious evolution); operations builds on science and technology (and evolves into knowledge creation); and finance builds on economics and management, whereby it is transformed into sustainable development. The full argument of the transformation of the core enterprise functions is laid out in our work on "Transformation Management" (Lessem and Schieffer, 2009).

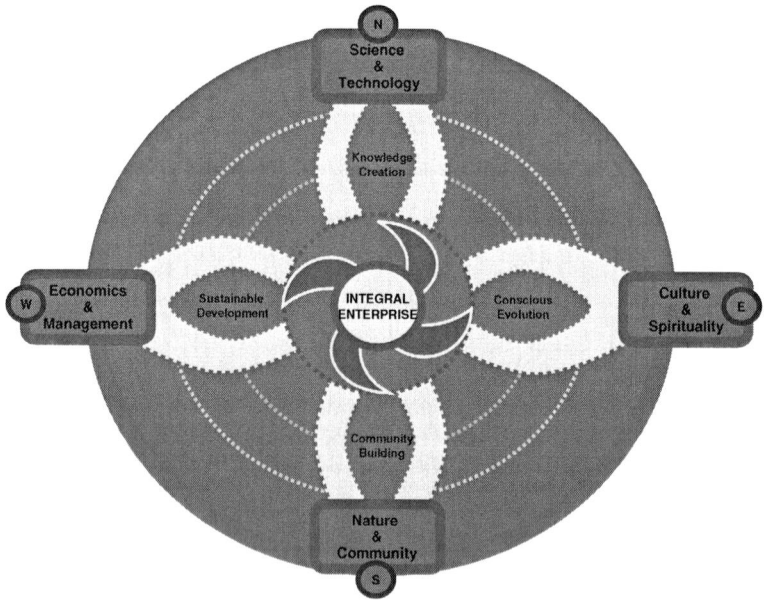

Figure 4.2   Fourfold structure of the integral organization

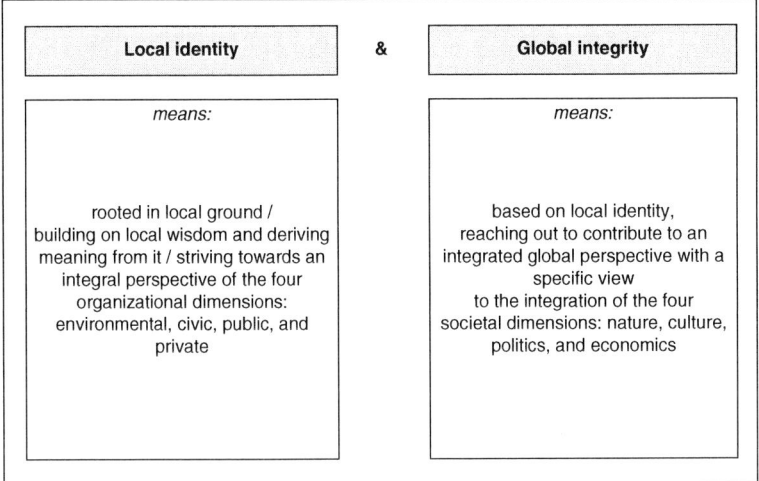

Figure 4.3   Local identity & Global integrity

It is with this orientation to the animate–civic–public–private four-fold that the organization also contributes to an integral transformation of society as a whole, and the natural–cultural–political–economic fourfold of society. The integrated fourfold is the core expression of the identity of the organization, and also of society.

With a view to global processes and to globalization, we regard it as important that an institution, or indeed a society, first develops its local identity in order to subsequently contribute to global integrity (see Figure 4.3).

For a practical understanding of our approach, we take you now on a journey with Broad in China. Broad is a good example of an organization striving for an integral perspective, anchoring itself clearly and expressively in its Chinese identity, while simultaneously striving to contribute to global integrity.

Case: The integral enterprise in action – the case of Broad Air Conditioning

Broad Air Conditioning Co. Ltd ("Broad") in Changsha in China's Hunan Province is a rare case. In this section we explore the dynamics behind Broad's simultaneous development of its private (economic/business), public (political, public engagement), civic (social and cultural engagement), and natural (environmental protection / bio-organic farming etc.) activities.

Broad Air Conditioning: Company overview

Broad is the world's largest and most technologically advanced absorption chiller manufacturer. Established in 1988, Broad is a privately owned company, with current assets of approximately USD 2.2 billion and around 1,800 employees. Broad's growth has been internally funded, and the company claims to have been debt-free since 1995. Broad has operations in more than 30 cities in China and overseas subsidiaries in Paris and New York. Broad's domestic offices are located in more than 20 cities in China.

> The company was established in 1988 by the Zhang Brothers and had developed quickly...It grew from a "family" company in 1992 to a "nationwide" company in 2002. (Zhi and Beamish, 2004)

Broad's systems, centrally controlled from a high-tech monitoring station in Changsha, are found in more than 25 countries. The Company's headquarters has recently been shifted to Beijing, while the manufacturing base is still situated in Changsha.

Broad's "Nomen est Omen": the Chinese word for Broad is composed of two syllables, meaning "far and big," or "designed to last long" and "designed to grow." Its founder and CEO, Zhang Yue, is a former teacher who started designing environmentally friendly air conditioners in his own garage before founding Broad. By now Broad is one of China's most successful private companies, and an important player in raising China's environmental awareness, as we shall see later.

Broad's natural and communal "animate" functioning: From Changsha to the United Nations

The local perspective of Broad's natural dimension

Broad's technology has a strong environmental impact. The company specializes in manufacturing absorption chillers and heaters, using lithium bromide and water, respectively, as the refrigerant agent. Absorption chillers use heat rather than mechanical energy to provide cooling and are considerably more energy-efficient than traditional mechanical air conditioning systems.

Broad's products have saved over 400 tons of standard oil for its customers, saved over RMB 100 billion investment on electricity for global society and protected thousands of square kilometers of green land from desertification. Broad has won a number of awards for its contribution to the protection of the environment, including China's Gold Medal for ozone protection. Broad has also been China's first environmental protection case listed and read at Global Compact Learning Forum (United Nations).

The estate where the company is located is called Broad Town, reflecting that the estate is not only built for people to work; they are part of a community. Every employee has a place on campus to stay overnight, with houses for men and women. This is not an obligation, but an option. Most people stay overnight during the working week and only go home to their families for the weekend. Broad's CEO also lives on the campus with his family.

In addition to accommodation, the company also provides a number of other basic staff needs, including clothing and food. All employees wear uniforms during working hours. While workers are all dressed in blue, office workers are all dressed in black trousers or skirts and white shirts or blouses. Free meals are provided in the staff canteen. Staff can buy further items in the company-owned supermarket. There is a till, but no cashier in the supermarket. Employees pay cash-free, using their employee tag, and scanning all items themselves at the electronic cashier. This system is therefore fully based on trust. In various interviews employees highlighted the significance of "trust and honesty" within the Broad Community. A vital expression of this attitude is that the private rooms of the employees are not locked. There is not even a locker. If convicted of stealing, an employee would lose his or her job immediately.

The sense of community comes alive in a number of ways. For example, while everyone has a clear job description and responsibility, all employees are encouraged to support others wherever possible. In the company's brochure on its values, it is stated: "In an era of indifferent interpersonal relationships, unbalanced economic ecosystem, and money worship, Broad has focused on creating more values for customers, caring for employees, and being fair to partners. Love is more important than anything else."

Broad's entire business premises (360,000m² or 89 acres) is a green campus, rather than a typical industrial estate. The cleanness of the entire area is surprising. Cars are hardly used on the estate. Employees walk or use bicycles. Visitors are driven around in electric golf carts.

Recycling plays an important role. One example is that packaging materials based on wood are recycled into floors and other housing construction parts.

One will, however, also notice the fleet of luxury cars reserved for prominent visitors, as well as the on-site helicopter. Furthermore, among the company achievements of the year 1997, Broad also proudly listed that it was China's first company to have its own business jet.

Broad is also engaged in bio-organic farming. Various types of vegetables are grown on the campus or on nearby fields. "Company-owned" pigs are fed with rice straw from Broad's own rice fields. The dung from the pigs is used as fertilizer. These vegetables are served in the company canteen.

Broad tries to reduce waste in a large variety of ways. This can be observed, for example, by looking at the company documentation. Paper space is used very efficiently; many documents, including the company profile, are limited to one page only.

Another example is package waste, which is used, wherever possible, as construction material for Broad's facilities. For example, the floor in the employees' restaurant is made of the wooden packaging of equipment parts. Many similar cases can be found in Broad Town. People deeply understand the importance of recycling and of using waste creatively to improve the environment of Broad Town.

The global reach of Broad's natural and communal dimension

Broad's environmental engagement is not limited to the scope of the company. In December 2003 the United Nations Environment Programme (UNEP) held its Global Environmental Forum in Broad Town. The meeting brought together government officials, scientists, members of the business community, and environmentalists from ten countries.

Broad has submitted an environmental proposal in which it states its viewpoint on environmental protection (Broad, 2005). Here it states: "No matter where you live, China or India, the US or Switzerland, Nigeria or Brazil, we must work together to protect our world." In this paper a large variety of suggestions are made on how each individual can contribute to a cleaner environment; in particular factory workers, farmers, architects and building designers, product designers, scientists, teachers, journalists, commuters, mayors, and parents are addressed. The statement ends with the following pledge: "Today we at Broad Town, Changsha, China make this proposal to people all over the world: for the sustainability of an earth that has existed 4 billion years, and for the sustainability of all the plants and animals that depend on this earth, and for the sustainability of mankind, let's make a joint pledge: We will protect our environment – everyone of us will play his or her role – we will all start now."

Next to the entrance of Broad Town, a large replica of an Egyptian pyramid will surprise any visitor. Recalling one of the most ancient and long-lasting civilizations of the world, the pyramid is built to host an environmental museum. This museum will be open to the public. It is one of Broad's contributions to creating awareness of environmental protection in Chinese society.

Broad's cultural and spiritual "civic" functioning: Evolving its own workforce and educating society

The local aspect of Broad's cultural dimension

Broad seems to take the issue of developing its employees very seriously and provides (on campus) ample opportunities for individual and group development. There are extensive learning facilities at Broad Town. In the lobby of the staff education center, visitors are greeted by Leonardo da Vinci's quote: "Whatever others can do, I can do, too." On a Sunday night, at 10:00 pm, the center is filled with employees attending classes, studying in small groups or alone. The standard is high and jobs at Broad are very sought after. In 2001 and 2002 Broad was listed among the top 20 most admired companies in China.

Perhaps the most astonishing building on the campus is the newly built management school, which, although the architect included architectural elements from other epochs and cultures, strongly reminds us of a small version of the famous castle of Versailles. It is meant not only to become the home of a recognized management school, bringing teachers from all over the world to develop Broad's staff, but also to offer courses open to the public.

But what kind of management development is Broad pursuing? Asked what kind of qualities he is looking for in Broad's managers, Zhang Yue answers: "Fast reaction, the ability to take in information quickly, a high EQ, and, most importantly, a clear long-term view. When tackling a problem, a person should have the 'big picture' in mind, considering the long-term objectives and the overall benefits. The details are important when things are going smoothly, but when the details and the overall scheme conflicted with each other, the small benefits should be put in second place." It was indeed the focus on the long term that Zhang stressed most, an attitude that clearly relates to Zhang's and Broad's overall long-term perspective on the natural and social environment. Zhang felt that his philosophy had played an important role in the formation of his earliest workplace values. Zhang himself offers a metaphor from nature when describing his perspective on management. He believes in the principle of farming. That is, management of an enterprise involves first paying and then gaining. When confronted with the unfamiliar, Zhang's attitude is not to take on anything he cannot manage.

The global reach of Broad's cultural dimension

The company's entire business premises is a most astonishing composition of global architecture. As mentioned, one can find a replica of an Egyptian pyramid next to a replica of the Chateau of Versailles. The green areas between the buildings are filled with bronze sculptures of outstanding individuals, from Aristotle, Alexander the Great, Diogenes, Confucius and Zhang Heng, through Robespierre, Adam Smith, Napoleon Bonaparte, Jean Jacques Rousseau, Leonardo da Vinci, Franz Schubert, Honoré de Balzac, Charles Darwin, Thomas Edison, and Abraham Lincoln, up to contemporary figures such as Deng Xiaoping, Peter Drucker, and Jack Welch.

There are personalities from all disciplines, cultures, and times: from science, politics, arts, business, and the military, from all times and from many different cultures and nations. Among the scientists on display, one finds Rachel Carson, one of the founding spirits of the global environmental movement, whose famous book "Silent Spring," according to his own account, enormously influenced Zhang Yue's own environmental engagement. The upper and middle management of Broad still have to read Carson's book, and some of them mentioned in interviews that even the workers mimic verbal distillations by the engineers. In this context Zhang mentioned that, according to his perspective, China has forgotten much of its deep knowledge on the preservation of nature in the past 100 years, and needs to relearn this knowledge from the West.

Broad's scientific and technological "public" functioning: creating new internal knowledge and engaging with new public regulations

The local perspective of Broad's public and knowledge dimension

Broad itself has developed all technologies, with over 70 patented rights, and the company claims never to have copied any other manufacturers. All Broad's absorption chillers are CE market, UL and ETL listed and ASME certified; they are CCMS approved, including TÜV-ISO9001 of Germany, SGS-ISO14001 of Switzerland.

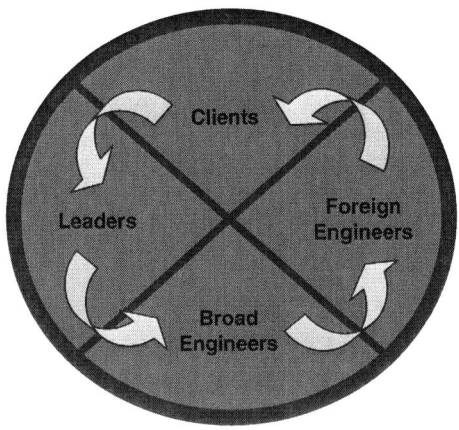

Figure 4.4 Broad's knowledge cycle

The list of Broad's achievements in creating new knowledge is long. The company continues to develop innovative technologies. Selected successes are:

- 1999: Development of the world's first power heat recovery exhaust chiller
- 2001: Development of the world's first multi-energy direct-fired chillers
- 2001: Development of the world's first two-stage solar chiller

Zhang Yue has a clear view on how Broad will continue to create innovative products and will stay ahead of the industry. He introduced his "new knowledge cycle" (see Figure 4.4), starting with Broad's own engineers, who are in constant interaction with engineers from all over the world, most of them based with clients. They will then work with the clients in order to develop products that will exactly meet their needs. The clients themselves are in constant touch with the top management of Broad, and vice versa, to improve cooperation and explore the need for new products, which are then internally discussed and explored at Broad.

Zhang also mentioned that he still feels that Broad's innovations do not have enough impact on the world as a whole. He stressed the enormous potential of energy saving. His goal is to produce better and better products, until it becomes evident to businesses and politicians all over the world what impact on energy consumption they can have with the right kind of energy. In his metaphor, he sees himself as the fire in the middle of the knowledge cycle, keeping it turning. In conversations Zhang uses cyclical images over and over again: he speaks about knowledge cycles, value and life cycles, as well as of recycling.

The global reach of Broad's public and knowledge creation dimension

Zhang Yue has more than once addressed the issue of Intellectual Property Rights. In his speeches, in China and abroad, he takes a firm stand against the violation of IPR and urges Chinese government officials to ensure these rights for Chinese as well as for foreign investors.

The company regularly publishes on matters relevant to society, with Zhang Yue initiating most of the publications. He writes and regularly speaks on environmental issues, CSR, and other societal issues.

In 2004 Broad published a brochure called "A Green Perspective" (a book on culture, architecture, airport design, urban planning, waste, sewage, energy strategy, and district cooling and heating). The bilingual (English and Chinese) brochure is directed at mayors, architects, airport planners, HVAC designers, energy experts, and young readers. This brochure underlines the fact that Broad tries to look beyond its own borders and make an impact on society.

Broad's economic and managerial "private" functioning: committed to sustainable economic development and promoting it globally

The local perspective of Broad's private (business) dimension

While acknowledging the wide-ranging animate–civic–public reach of Broad, one should not overlook its commitment to economic success. Broad has clearly spelled out in one of its principles, which it calls "Hard and High," that it wants to be market leader in its field: "Striving to be the No.1: We bear in mind constantly we were No.1, this is not self-complacent but a self-encouragement. No.1 is the most beautiful word in human languages. It is the most shining part of Broad corporate culture, which reflects our staff's wisdom, the company's dignity, our social responsibility and our client's values. This lights the road ahead of us and encourages us to overcome our failings and always strive to be the No.1."

In its outspoken striving for success, Broad always tries to get the balance right. At the entrance of the main office building one can read one of Broad's "Golden Rules," formulated by Zhang Yue: "We are dedicated to provide the most perfect products and services in the world, not only for the purpose of gaining market or making high profits, but also to serve the purpose of satisfying the expectations and gaining the support from the customers of Broad. If we have disfigurement, which is caused by our carelessness, our benefits and dignity would be damaged and more seriously our dear friends' heart could get hurt."

Broad understands environmental protection as one of its guiding principles. "In an era of global warming, environmental degradation, and ozone depletion, Broad specializes in absorption chillers powered by clean and recyclable energies. Broad chillers also use non-polluting refrigerant. The company has a continual goal of enhancing energy efficiency and minimizing pollution. Protecting our future is more important than profit" (*Broad Values*, internal publication).

Many Chinese companies still grow and invest in a highly opportunistic way. It is interesting to notice that Broad has fully stuck to its core business until now. In fact, Broad explicitly declares that it deliberately sticks to what it is good at. "In an era when most companies are diversifying at frenzied pace and purely focused on size, Broad has stuck with what it is good at. … Excellence is more important than growth." Even within its own product line the company has refused to expand for opportunistic reasons.

This attitude is illustrated by the following example:

Since 1992, the production and sales of air conditioners powered by heat sources had rapidly increased in China. This was because such products could meet the needs created by the electricity shortages during the summers. In 1996, gas air conditioners became the leading product in China's central air conditioner market, and Broad was set to be the market leader on the direct-fired absorption segment … In 1997, with many newly built electricity stations beginning to work, and the decreasing needs of industrial electricity, the supply and demand of electricity had reached equilibrium in China. Then, in 1999, due to the regulation of China's energy policy, the electricity supply was greatly developed. Without the limitation of electricity usage, the market volume of electric refrigeration increased rapidly. … Broad's direct-fired heater production had been directly limited. The highest sales had peaked USD 247 million, around

1996–1997, but since 1999 had hovered around USD 140 million. Every year some Broad employees, mostly in the Sales Department, recommended that management should consider producing electric air conditioners. Some of the sales employees even left Broad, thinking that the company was going in the wrong direction. (Zhi and Beamish, 2004)

Broad could easily have expanded into the field of electric air conditioners, but refused to do so for environmental reasons, and it took years before China's economic surge and the accompanying energy shortages created new growth opportunities for Broad.

The global reach of Broad's private (business) dimension

Zhang had announced in meetings that Broad would never make electric air conditioners, unless nobody else made them. However, people still need them in emergencies. "In that situation we will make them. But when the responsibility has a conflict with our benefits, I will put responsibility and the company's reputation first."

It is important to see that Broad's environmental vision unfolded gradually. Zhang himself stated in 2006 that it took him a number of years after Broad's foundation to see what an enormous environmental impact he could make, realizing more and more the problematic situation of China and the world in relation to energy resources.

Since 1996, Broad had gradually turned into a strong proponent of safe energy sources and environmental protection. The company attempted to influence and inform the government, electric companies, heat source companies, and end-users of air conditioners in society in general about the prospect of heat-source powered air-conditioners with regard to protecting the environment and improving the efficiency of resource utilization. Broad took great effort to find a way to harmonize the relationships between improving the quality of life, benefiting the company, and protecting the environment. (Zhi and Beamish, 2004)

Employees of Broad do not regard Zhang simply as their CEO. They see him as CEO, innovator, and artist at the same time. According to his perspective on management, introduced earlier on, Zhang constantly looks for a "broad perspective," for the "big picture." It is from this perspective that Zhang has also written a kind of fictitious plot, imagining the world in 2015 (Zhang, 2005).

In his play, Zhang takes a historical stance and delves deep into Chinese cultural heritage. From there he develops a future perspective on Chinese society, which by 2015 has been transformed into a "service economy." Here, for example:

- A Chinese housekeeping business is the largest business in the world, followed by a trash collecting and recycling company.
- An Energy Service Company becomes the most profitable in the world. This company also erected solar-energy heat collection machines for gas-fired air-conditioner users, or prepared methane generators to save the natural gas. It conducted transformation of the energy control systems of the buildings for the users so that the air-conditioner and ventilation can be adjusted to the temperature and demand changes and that lighting can suit the demand and sunlight changes. Therefore, the energy is saved and people feel more comfortable.
- Besides that the company also carries on business of 'management of the operation of buildings' air conditioning and energy system.
- With five thousands employees, this company earns an annual turnover of about 15 trillion Asian dollars, with net profits exceeding three trillion Asian Dollars. Who would have ever thought that so huge profits come from an invisible place – the energy leak inside the buildings?

Zhang has used all of his artistic and imaginative style, developed as a young art teacher, to introduce his vision of a sustainable society. An artist (and farmer), turned engineer and businessman, has written a political play (that comes close to a manifest for a politically, environmentally, economically, and culturally integrated society). Zhang as an individual represents here the four dimensions of nature, culture, politics, and economics, and allows himself and his organization as a whole to integrate all four dimensions.

Conclusion: The integral enterprise

Broad as an integral enterprise

Broad is a rare combination of conscious integration of achievements in business, culture, and ecology. The organization demonstrates how its animate, civic, public, and private dimensions are building on each other.

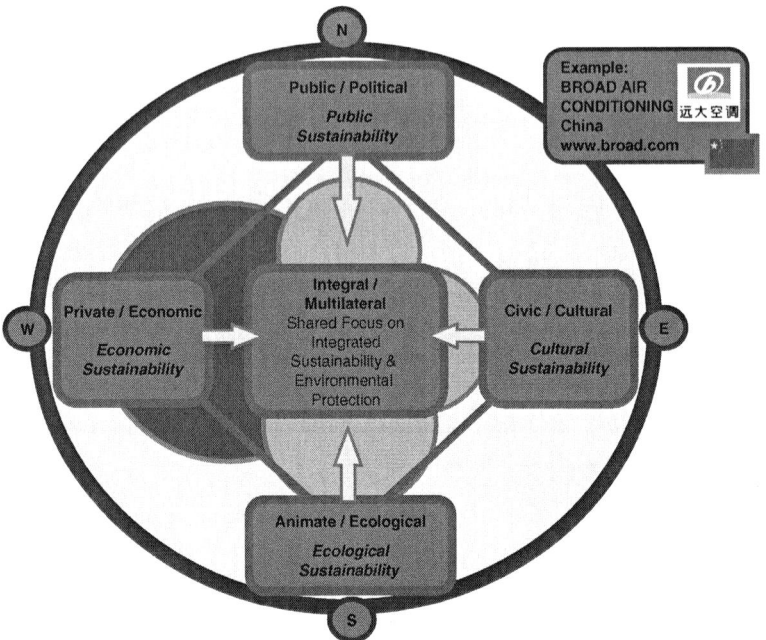

Figure 4.5   The Fourfold of broad

Sustainability and environmental protection are the core threads of Broad, and the main linkage between the various dimensions (see Figure 4.5). While environmental protection, and therefore environmental sustainability, seems to be the main focus of Broad, one can clearly recognize that Broad's understanding of sustainability reaches out in the civic/cultural/social dimension, in the public, political dimension, and, of course, in the private, business-oriented dimension.

In summary, the ecological, cultural, and public or technological engagement of Broad within and beyond the company borders are all in direct relation with its business. That makes it a strong case for an Integral Enterprise. Figure 4.6 summarizes the core internal and external aspects of Broad as an Integral Enterprise.

Guiding questions for "becoming an integral enterprise"

We conclude this paper by offering a set of guiding questions for enterprises committed to transcending a singular "one worldly" economic

Broad: Elements of an integral enterprize		
Local activities **Rooted in China**	**&**	**Global activities** **Reaching out to the world**
Environmentally friendly technology / Broad town / Green campus / Bioorganic farming / Company song, linking the evolution of employee & customer (self), community, society, and planet Earth	**Nature** **&** **community**	Public environment museum (Egyptian pyramid style) Hosting of UN environmental programme / Broad environmental proposal
Creation of a learning environment / Broad management school	**Culture** **&** **spirituality**	Integrating global architecture / Building on global art and wisdom
Continuous creation of internal knowledge (New knowledge cycle)	**Science** **&** **technology**	Engagement for IPR-regulations and execution in China / Bringing new knowledge to society
Strong commitment to be market leader (No.1) / However, no compromise to guiding principle: Environmental protection	**Economics** **&** **management**	Broad as strong proponent for Chinese and global industry of environmentally friendly technology / The world in 2015 (an integrated political, cultural, economic, and environmental manifest) / towards a 'service economy'

Figure 4.6   Broad – Integrally linking of the internal and societal perspective

perspective and moving towards a more integral "four worldly" one; a perspective that balances the economic (private), ecological (environmental), cultural (civic), and knowledge (public) dimensions. In reflecting on these questions, the reader might be inspired by the path that Broad and its Chairman, Zhang Yue, have taken. However, and we regard this as crucial, by starting with one's own nature and community (southern perspective) and one's own Eastern culture and spirituality (eastern perspective), the outcome is inevitably a very different one:

- To what extent can our organization combine public, private, civic, and environmental functioning in a way that all dimensions mutually reinforce each other, thereby making the organization on the whole more sustainable?
- How can we draw explicitly upon nature and culture, while also building on science and technology and economics and management?
- In what way do you see such an "integral enterprise" as being more suitable to contribute more meaningfully to the evolution of the society in which it is situated?
- How do we bring the arts – poetry, music, sculpture, painting and so on – purposefully into our enterprise?
- In what way is our enterprise rooted in our own culture; in what way does it reach out to the world?
- Altogether, how does that make our enterprise a more "human" one?

Bibliography

Abouleish, I. (2005). *Sekem – A Sustainable Community in the Desert*. Edinburgh: Floris.

Angeles, A. (1993). *The Fourfold Way*. San Francisco: Harper.

Broad (2005) (ed.). *Thinking of Our Future: The Broad Environmental Proposal*. Unpublished Discussion Paper. Changsha.

Broad Values: Internal (unpublished) Publication of Broad Air Conditioning.

Carson, R. (2002). *Silent Spring*. New York: Mariner Books.

Hock, D. (2002). *Birth of the Chaordic Age*. San Francisco: Berrett-Koehler.

Hock, D. (2006). *From One to Many*. San Francisco: Berret-Koehler.

Huntington, S. (1993). *The Clash of Civilisations*. Foreign Affairs.

Kaku, R. (1997). The Path of Kyosei. *Harvard Business Review*, July–August.

Koopman, A. (1991). *Trans-Cultural Management*. Oxford: Blackwell.

Tsu, L. (1996). *Tao Te Ching*. Translation by Brian Walker. New York: St. Martin's Griffin.

Lessem, R. and Palsule, S. (1996). *Managing in Four Worlds.* Oxford: Blackwell.

Lessem, R. and Schieffer, A., (2009). *Transformation Management: Towards the Integral Enterprise.* Aldershot: Gower Ashgate.

Schieffer, A., Lessem, R. and Al-Yaoussi, O. (2008). Corporate governance: Impulses from the Middle East. *Transition Studies Review,* August.

Stevens, A. (1994). *On Jung.* Harmondsworth: Penguin.

Yunus, M. (1999). *Banker to the Poor.* New York: Public Affairs.

Zhang, Y. (2005). *The World in 2015.* Unpublished Play.

Zhi, Y.H. and Beamish, P. (2004). *Broad Air Conditioning and Environmental Protection.* Unpublished Case Study. Richard Ivey School of Business, The University of Ontario.

5
bracNet: Bridging the Digital Divide – Covering Bangladesh with Wireless Broadband Access

Michael Pirson

Khalid Quadir sipped on his coffee at Crema Café near Harvard Square. He had just returned from a long trip around the world, meeting with potential business partners, and now, back in Cambridge, MA, he was reflecting on how it all started. He had founded bracNet 4 years ago with the mission of bringing broadband wireless internet access to his native Bangladesh. bracNet had made much progress since, but much more remained to be done. It still sounded very bold that a country which barely provided running water to all its citizens should soon possess comprehensive access to high-speed wireless internet. As he glanced over Cambridge, MA, he was reminded that this feat had not even been achieved here in the hub of technological development (near MIT and Harvard).

As he was waiting for his brother, Iqbal, with whom he had started a cell-phone venture now known as Grameenphone, he was thinking again about some of the statistics he had just heard regarding the digital divide. He was more convinced than ever that his approach to spreading internet access to the poorest of the poor was a crucial endeavor.

The Digital Divide

According to the non-governmental action group, Digital Divide.org, the world's most affluent 20 percent of citizens were garnering 85 percent of the wealth in 1990. By 2000 that figure had doubled (10 percent now owned 85 percent of the wealth), while the percentage of wealth held by the poor had been halved, from 8 to 4 percent. While the inequity gap is predicted to double again by 2010, Nobel laureate economist, Joseph Stiglitz, singles out digital technology as the main driver for this development. While internet access has become a mere commodity in the developed world, providing economic, educational, and social advancement, the digital divide is threatening developing nations with further exclusion from global trends and global trade, crucial in the fight against poverty and terrorism. Those without the appropriate tools (in terms of PCs and internet connectivity) and applicable skills are disadvantaged in terms of fewer employment opportunities, restricted access to information, and general support.[1] Bridging the digital divide creates social inclusion, which can, in turn, empower people to participate much more effectively in global, regional, and local communities. e-services, such as electronically supported health care delivery (e-health), internet based education (e-learning), technology-based agricultural sourcing, marketing, and learning (e-agriculture), are just a few of the services that are deemed to impact poverty reduction. Many experts thus consider closing the digital divide to be a precondition for reducing poverty and terrorism, as well as achieving sustainable world markets.[2]

Despite all the efforts made on behalf of governments (see, e.g., the US Telecommunications Act, passed in 1996), and international NGOs (such as the Open Society Institute), the digital divide continues to increase. In the early 1990s the Digital Divide issue was caught in an ideological friction between public and private sectors. Politicians argued that the private sector should pay the costs of bringing the poor into the information society. Companies, on the other hand, insisted that governments subsidize technological infrastructures and deregulate the telecom sector so that prices could drop. In the late 1990s, the big multinationals involved in the digital revolution dropped their defensive attitude and turned their philanthropic efforts to the matter of closing the Divide. The big multinational IT companies poured USD 2 billion a year into such philanthropic efforts in the late 1990s as their way of allaying the public's concerns and assuring wary government officials of their concern. Few such projects survived the dot.com bust of 1999. The crash in tech stocks enormously relieved public pressure on the companies, and most CEOs in advanced countries stopped making speeches expressing their concern about the digital divide.

A different approach was taken by a new breed of entrepreneurs, including Khalid, who applied their managerial skills to addressing the digital divide problem in a systematic way. One of the best-known stories is that of Grameenphone, which dramatically increased telephony access for people in Bangladesh from less than 1 percent (landline usage) to 25 percent. Grameenphone had relied on leapfrog wireless cell phone technology and innovative ways to bring it to the rural markets (e.g., phone ladies). However, internet access was still a luxury for most Bangladeshis, something Khalid Quadir aimed to change with his new venture, bracNet.

The Bangladeshi context

Bangladesh is located between India and Burma, with a population of over 158 million (2008) and a land area of 144,000 km², making it the ninth most populous nation in the world, with one of the highest population densities at 1,000 people/km². Approximately 25 percent of the country's population lives in urban areas, a figure expected to increase to 40 percent within 20 years. Despite continuous domestic and international efforts to improve economic and demographic prospects, Bangladesh remains a developing nation.[3] Total GDP was estimated at USD 299.9 billion and GDP per capita was ranked 175th out of 232 countries as per 2006 data. Its per capita income in 2006 was USD 2,300 (adjusted by purchasing power parity), compared with the world average of USD 10,200.[4] Approximately half of the population lives below the poverty line. Traditional business, therefore, seems very unattractive.

One of the major problems business is facing in Bangladesh is the continuing political instability. Formerly East Pakistan, Bangladesh came into being only in 1971, when the two parts of Pakistan split after a bitter civil war. After winning independence, Bangladesh spent 15 years under military rule and, although democracy was restored in 1990, the political scene remains volatile to this day. Political tensions have spilled over into violence and hundreds of people have been killed in recent years. As an Army-backed caretaker government took over, an emergency law was declared on January 11, 2007, and the election of January 22, 2007 was postponed indefinitely. In early 2009, a new democratically elected government took over again.

Another central impediment to economic growth, and a barrier to infrastructure investment, is recurring natural disasters: extreme monsoons and cyclones cause severe floods, which often destroy roads, energy, and communication infrastructure. With increased climate changes Bangladesh's problems are expected to become even more marked.[5]

It is unsurprising that Bangladesh is also one of the countries severely affected by the digital divide. Fewer than 1 percent of the population had access to telephony services in the mid-1990s. With the advent of wireless cell phone technology, roughly 25 percent now have access to telecommunication services.[6] With regard to internet services, though, there were only 500,000 internet users in Bangladesh by March 2008, which corresponds to 0.3 percent of the population (ITU figure).

Khalid Quadir

All in all, Bangladesh does not seem attractive to most businesses, and only a few people would put up with the challenges to aim specifically at bridging the digital divide. Despite the particular challenges outlined above, doing business in Bangladesh has become more attractive over time. According to the World Bank, the country has achieved an average annual growth rate of 5 percent since 1990. Bangladesh has also seen an expansion of its middle class, and its consumer industry has grown as well. In December 2005, 4 years after its report on the emerging "BRIC" economies (Brazil, Russia, India, and China), Goldman Sachs named Bangladesh one of the "Next Eleven," along with Egypt, Indonesia, Pakistan, and seven other countries.[7] So it did not seem entirely foolish to keep investing there.

Khalid Quadir was born and raised in Dhaka, the capital of Bangladesh. After finishing high school in Bangladesh he moved to the US to receive his college education. Thereafter he went to work on Wall Street and later gained expertise in private equity in the telecommunication sector. In 1997 he joined his brother, Iqbal Quadir, to start what is now known as Grameenphone,[8] the largest mobile phone operator in Bangladesh, serving over 22 million of its 150 million inhabitants. In 2003 Khalid left the board of Grameenphone and took a 2-year time-out at Stanford University. Khalid was committed to search for ways to provide Bangladesh with leapfrog technology in order to close the digital divide further. Doing business in Bangladesh was no easy task, but it was something he had committed himself to. To give you a better understanding of the context for business in Bangladesh, let's look at some basic facts.

bracNet's beginnings – the shared value creation strategy

Khalid knew that doing business at the base of the pyramid was challenging, but possible. When growing up in Bangladesh, he had had the feeling that his country was always depicted as being on the receiving end, depending on outside aid and benevolence. He was bothered by that, and always felt the need to demonstrate the capacity of his people to sustain themselves, without depending on benevolent donations. He felt that doing business profitably was in itself an act of empowerment, and, when business approaches could be used to promote general welfare, this should be done.[9]

The fellowship at Stanford allowed him to continue his search for ways to provide Bangladesh with leapfrog technology that could create digital inclusion. While he did not consider himself to be a technology expert, he thought that WiMAX[10] technology could be a good solution for a country like Bangladesh, which has a very flat topography and a dearth of landlines. In his own words:

> Knowing that wireless is a way to go for Bangladesh and broadband will be the means of any communication, I realized that WiMAX could be the ultimate modern communication solution to Bangladesh to lift it and connect it to the worldwide information super highway.

Even though WiMAX networks had not at this time been installed anywhere except for testing purposes, Khalid was inspired by their potential for Bangladesh. It was clear to him that his venture needed to address both social and financial needs, otherwise it would not work. First, the goal of his new organization needed to be the inclusion of the entire country, in order to successfully bridge the digital divide. This would have to include all rural areas of Bangladesh, some of which did not even have access to running water and canalization. Second, he did not want his venture to be government or NGO-based. He believed in the business's ability to provide real value to people. He viewed financial sustainability as a key factor for his success.

Thus, he put together a business plan for a venture he initially named gNet and which later became bracNet. This plan was intended to convince both the traditional investors and the potential local partners whom he needed to implement the social part of the agenda. It was a proposal for shared-value creation, not only shareholder value creation.

bracNet's humanistic business model

Quadir saw his task as economic and social development work, but he wanted to demonstrate a new model for development, one that was marked by cross-sector collaborations and for-profit opportunities. If bracNet had only been about building communications infrastructure, he argued that government should have been in charge. On the other hand, if his only target had been the rural population, perhaps bracNet should have been a non-profit organization. He explained:

bracNet has a social component which is a plus, but it is a clear for-profit venture. The idea is to have a viable project for development which is not based on charity or begging, where people from Bangladesh and others meet eye-to-eye not as dependent receivers...

The decision to be for-profit was also driven by concerns of financial sustainability. While he was confident that there was a market in rural areas, he counted on urban clients to fund the expansion to rural areas until they achieved financial sustainability themselves. Therefore, the target market for bracNet was both urban and rural. Pondering his motivations for seeking such a broad market, Quadir explained:

[W]ith the rural clients the social component enters the scene. Building infrastructure and thus developing the country, bracNet can also make profit – so it is a double-edge business.

With the backing of BRAC, currently the world's largest NGO based in Bangladesh, Khalid Quadir further refined his concept to attract not only socially minded investors, but also more traditional members of the investment community.

The plan was to build on the existing e-mail services already offered by BRAC and to target the largest urban areas first, starting with Dhaka. Broadband internet would be rolled out, including the first Bengali portal using local content. Quick wins in the urban areas were the cornerstone of financial viability, as one could expect to attract a significant number of customers quickly. The focus would initially be on four types of customers:

- Residential customers in apartment blocks;
- Small and medium enterprises (SMEs);
- Corporate customers requiring Service Level Agreements (SLA) and Quality of Service (QOS); and
- Resellers of internet services requiring broadband access service to serve their customers.

In a second wave, starting in years 2–3, the plan was to extend services in three main directions:

- web hosting and IP centrex services to corporations and SMEs;
- enhanced content, IP-telephony services, and mobile access solutions to residential and corporate/SME clients; and
- geographic coverage to new urban centers.

Humanistic-based partnerships – partnering for social impact
Quadir knew that he wanted to bring the most advanced technology to some of the most impoverished areas of the world in a way that would be financially sustainable. It was a social development task, something that was usually done by government or international development institutions such as the World Bank. Maybe it was too ambitious, but, when he reflected on potential local partners, he saw potential synergies and wanted to make it happen.

Quadir was looking at BRAC, a large NGO in Bangladesh, as a potential partner that could support his endeavor. In 1972, Fazle Hasan Abed founded BRAC (then known as the Bangladesh Rural Advancement Committee), with the mission of rebuilding the remotest villages which government aid was unable to reach. Conceived as a short-term emergency initiative, BRAC was then transformed into a long-term community development organization, focusing on agriculture, fishery, cooperatives, microcredit, rural crafts, adult literacy, health and family planning, vocational training for women, and construction of community centers. BRAC became heavily involved in institution-building, including functional education and training, credit operation, income and employment generation, and support service programs. Among the most recent programs are a dairy and food project, a university, and a bank. Today BRAC employs over 97,000 people and qualifies as one of the world's largest non-profit and non-governmental organizations. The ultimate goal of BRAC is social development.

BRAC's executive director, Abdul-Muyeed Chowdhury, had a grasp of technology and immediately understood the vision behind gNet. He championed a collaboration and convinced BRAC's management to engage with gNet. When reflecting on the importance of being connected to BRAC, Quadir mused:

> Having BRAC as a partner is extremely important. First for business reason[s], it is a very well regarded brand name in the country. It has a reach almost all over Bangladesh. All together it has 2500 local offices which would help the new venture to deploy its network. It is a clean organization with institutional integrity and transparency. Lastly and most importantly, the vision and mission of gNet partners matched with BRAC. We both wanted to build a financially sustainable and viable enterprise with a social development objective.

Before fully entering into a partnership, however, BRAC's leadership wanted to know more about how gNet could roll out internet connectivity to the rural areas.

The e-hut concept

To connect the rural population, Khalid created the concept of internet-enabled kiosks. He aimed at creating small information and communication technology centers that could be run by local entrepreneurs in the countryside. He named these centers "e-huts:"

> "E-huts" are little centers in rural areas, that can be compared to a KINKO's in the US. They provide technological solutions for small businesses and local people.

Quadir had the support of Greg Wolff, Vice President of Ricoh Innovation, to develop the first e-hut prototypes. Together with Stanford computer science professor, Terry Winograd, and a design school partnership between Stanford and Berkeley (the "D-school"), they built the "e-huts," which were then tested in the San Francisco Bay Area and in Bangladesh.[11] After a successful test, Khalid and BRAC's management team were confident that these e-huts could work in a rural environment, with the potential to become precursors of a dynamic domestic economy, providing market information, e-government, and directory services to local people.

The main goal of partnering with BRAC was to bring leapfrog technology, such as broadband internet, to Bangladesh. bracNet's overall mission, however, would go beyond technological advancement to focus on empowering people through access to information and entrepreneurship. In the words of Quadir:

> My view of empowerment is to provide wealth for the local entrepreneurs and their community. With the e-hut they become part of the productive sector.

In addition, local e-huts have the power to support various rural communities through e-services. The e-huts provide computer training to anyone interested, which in turn will support e-health, e-agriculture, e-government, e-business, and most of all e-learning opportunities. Many of those opportunities will be directly provided by BRAC, which was looking for a convenient way to reach out to even more people. The broadband internet infrastructure would be crucial to bringing higher levels of education, health care, and economic development to poverty-stricken areas.

Financing a humanistic business at the base of the pyramid

Of course, it was not easy to convince people to get on board. However, Quadir was able to meet several key figures that helped him make important contacts. DEFTA partners, an international venture capital firm, decided to sign up as lead investor in early 2005. Marubeni Corporation, a Japanese trading conglomerate which had already invested in Grameenphone, followed. Calvert, a socially responsible mutual fund based in the US, as well as Brummer & Partners, a Scandinavian hedge fund, signed on later. Thirty percent of the shares were bought by a range of private Japanese and American investors, and BRAC itself bought 40 percent of the shares. It is important to understand the governance implications of this move. An NGO now owned a major share of the business. In this way the social goal of bridging the digital divide was structurally supported by the governance and ownership structure. Khalid Quadir calls this a new way of leveraging -ectoral partnerships to solve some of the most pressing problems.

By September 2005 Khalid was able to close the first round of financing and registered the company as gNet DDH LLC in Delaware, US. brac-Net began its communication operations in November 2005 in Dhaka and Chittagong, with services to corporate clients and home users. The e-huts were launched in April 2006. By December 2007 its operations covered the three main cities of Bangladesh (Dhaka, Chittagong, and Shylet), where it also serviced part of BRAC's infrastructure of ten libraries and 20 offices, and established 35 e-huts in Dhaka, Norshingdi, Gazipur, Comilla, Munshigonj, and some other districts. By May 2008, 50 e-huts had been established and a total of 200 were to be set up by the end of 2008.

Why would traditional investors finance such a venture?

As mentioned before, one of the main investors in bracNet was Patrick Brummer and Partners, a Scandinavian hedge fund firm. Their main interest in funding ventures with a social and financial value creation was strategic. In their eyes, it made sense to clearly focus on social AND financial value creation, even from a financial investor's viewpoint; especially for ventures at the base of the pyramid. Brummer believed in the potential of bracNet, but also saw the engagement as a step towards a larger strategic move for the hedge fund. With bracNet, Brummer was testing the waters of investing at the base of the pyramid. With a mid-term perspective, a fund investing in technology ventures at the base of the pyramid seemed a viable idea for his clients and a way to create a competitive advantage for his company. As such, Brummer viewed his investment in bracNet as a learning experience as much as a real opportunity for financial gain. In fact, the success of bracNet so far had been lagging behind plans.

Challenges for business at the base of the pyramid

One reason for this was the government collapse. In January 2007 an army-backed caretaker government took over after riots erupted, contesting the election results. Prior contracts were therefore up for renegotiation. As of August 2007 the government effectively halted the addition of wireless communication towers, because it planned a revision of the wireless broadband infrastructure code. The initial expansion plan, by which a continuous addition of wireless towers with a 35-km aerial radio distance range would allow coverage of the whole country, came to a halt. While it had once seemed feasible to cover all BRAC's 2,500 offices and establish 1,000 e-huts within 2 years, hold-ups by the government crisis and a cash shortage led to a significant scaling-back. bracNet's leadership and its investors had to drastically reconsider their business plan and focus on growing in the existing urban areas.

While operational profitability had been achieved, an overall break-even had not yet been reached. One of the questions was whether and how bracNet could influence any of the governmental decisions yet to be made. Especially with regard to the corrupt environment, this seemed a tricky issue. Much of bracNet's success depended on the credibility and trustworthiness of the brand. Its reputation for integrity was therefore crucial. In the short term this could damage bracNet, since, unlike its competitors, it was unable to benefit from bribery. Since BRAC owns 40 percent of bracNet, and its name is a visible part of the venture, any kind of unethical behavior could hurt the whole of BRAC. There is a clear structural barrier preventing bracNet from succumbing to the cultural norms of bribery.

For instance, BRAC has long insisted that bracNet pay value added tax (VAT), even though most Internet Service Providers are not doing so. According to Quadir, *'The government is happy that we are a regular income paying company, that we are a cleaner company and have more open books than any other competitor.'* BRAC also insists that bracNet does not yet support any Voice over Internet Protocol (VOIP) services, despite their financial attractiveness. VOIP is illegal in Bangladesh, because the government does not want to endanger the profits of the state-owned telecom. bracNet's board continues to hope that the government will open up VOIP. Overall, Quadir believes that the presence and national reputation of BRAC give the business considerable advantage in terms of name recognition, and that it has won the much-needed trust of consumers as well as eased dealings with the government.

In addition, even though the first round of investors had already multiplied their investment on paper (the initial investment was USD 6 million), more funds were needed to secure the rural roll-out. To push the rural expansion, new funders were needed to raise USD 100 million. Strategic partners, such as Telecom companies, were needed in order to push the operational roll-out.

bracNet already has a diverse set of partners, and bringing in new partners could make it difficult to run the company. While financial viability was central to many of the investors in the first round, the social component of the business made them all "feel good." Only BRAC really strategically cared about the social mission. Most of the investors eventually signed on because of the promising financial prospects, even though they still considered it a high-risk investment. The risks led some investors, such as DEFTA, to adopt a very hands-on approach. Quadir recalled that they *"were often getting very operational, trying to almost run the business ... They have gotten better, the more established the company has gotten."* While the larger corporate investors relied on others to ensure monitoring, they wanted to learn about the new technologies and how they could be implemented at the base of the pyramid markets. Bringing in new, powerful partners, such as Telecom operators, could change that. However, any new partner needed to be in line with the dual value creation strategy, otherwise BRAC could opt out.

While the rural expansion is stalling, the competition has increased. Grameenphone has become bracNet's biggest competitor, as it too has moved into mobile internet connectivity. Other mobile phone providers also increasingly pursued opportunities in the broadband internet market. The existing internet providers, as well as the established cellphone operators, were hatching strategies to make use of these new opportunities. Being able to meet the competitive pressures was crucial for the long-term viability of bracNet.

The home users in urban areas were still untapped (approximately 6,000 had signed up by December 2007). The retail segment grew by

10 percent per month in December 2007 and was expected to continue growing steadily. bracNet needed to acquire more clients in this segment, mainly the upper middle class. The population of the three main cities is approximately 15–20 million,[12] of whom only 10 percent are considered upper middle class. It seemed, however, that the cell phone providers would soon also be targeting this market with upscale internet services. So bracNet had to move swiftly.

Individual businesses (Small Office, Home Office (SOHO)), and Small to Medium Enterprises (SME), were an additional client segment which could be expanded. Even though bracNet was serving larger corporate customers, comprised mainly of financial institutions, real estate companies, law firms, medical facilities, software developers, web-based businesses, and internet and application services providers (ISPs and ASPs), this market seemed saturated.

Since growth in the other key segment of resellers and e-hut franchisees largely depended on bracNet's ability to deploy new WiMAX transmission towers, investors pressured bracNet to increase the service provision. bracNet's portal was an important gateway, but not yet strategically used to generate value added services. As a consequence, bracNet's strategy moved from providing internet only to providing a triple service (voice+ data+ video) in 2007. In March 2008 it acquired SQUARE, a large Bengali telecommunication provider, purchased primarily for its telephone license. As a possible next step, bracNet's leadership envisioned providing content as well as other services such as cable television, fixed phone, and internet. To Brummer this made a lot of sense, even though it required a different level of expertise within bracNet.

Conclusion and takeaways

Business at the base of the pyramid is full of challenges. bracNet seems poised to take them on. It has been able to acquire much of the needed funding and has established important partnerships with telecommunication providers. With the new government in place, many obstacles are now being cleared away, and expansion is happening at a much faster rate. Overall, bracNet has been a success story so far, despite all the difficulties one can imagine. bracNet is a great example of how business techniques can be employed for the greater good. Profit is a necessary means to bridging the digital divide successfully, not an end in itself. As Porter and Kramer (2006) say with regard to corporate social responsibility: financial and social value creation need to be aligned to make strategic sense.[13] bracNet serves as a model for companies concerned with strategic corporate social responsibility. As such there are several takeaways for managers:

1. Business at the base of the pyramid is a viable business option that lends itself very well to strategic corporate responsibility;
2. Strategic corporate responsibility focuses on creating social value and uses financial value creation as its driver. Profit is the means to achieving a higher purpose;
3. Creating partnerships that make strategic sense is important. Having BRAC as a partner on board ensures the social mission is fulfilled, while the various other investors bring in their respective expertise. Creating the right partnerships and governance structures is important to keep priorities right. Creating partnerships across the three sectors also seems a very important aspect of creating a dual value business organization; and
4. Having a higher purpose helps a company generate societal trust that translates into customer preferences. bracNet is a strong market player because of BRAC's name recognition and trust.

As such, Khalid Quadir hopes to inspire many other businessmen and women to look beyond the traditional way of doing business, creating operations that satisfy several human and societal needs. Khalid Quadir handed over the CEO position of bracNet in 2007 and is now becoming a social venture capitalist, focusing on technology ventures able to bridge the digital divide.

Notes

1. Chris Fleetwood, http://dspace.dial.pipex.com/town/parade/hq69/Protected/ Features/Digital%20Divide.html [accessed February 8, 2009].
2. www.digitaldivide.org/dd/digitaldivide.html [accessed February 8, 2009]. For a good assessment of this issue, see the archive of World Development Reports of United Nations Development Programme, http://hdr.undp.org/ reports/. Also see International Telecommunications Union's reports on the subject, www.itu.int/ITU-D/digitaldivide).
3. "Reproductive Health and Rights is Fundamental for Sound Economic Development and Poverty Alleviation," United Nations Population Fund [accessed July 17, 2007].
4. http://en.wikipedia.org/wiki/Bangladesh [accessed June 7, 2008].
5. Climate Change and Bangladesh, Department of Environment, Government of P.R. Bangladesh (2007), http://www.climatechangecell-bd.org/ publications/13ccbd.pdf [accessed November 7, 2008].

6. https://www.cia.gov/library/publications/the-world-factbook/geos/bg.html
7. http://www2.goldmansachs.com/hkchina/insight/research/pdf/ BRICs_3_12–1-05.pdf [accessed July 7, 2008].
8. Grameenphone has been providing mobile communications in Bangladesh since 1997, and its network covers nearly 98 percent of the country's population. The village-phone (VP) program, administered by Grameen Telecom Corporation, enables rural people who normally cannot afford to own a telephone to avail themselves of the service while providing the VP operators an opportunity to earn a living.
9. See Ebrahim, A., Pirson, M. and Mangas, P. Patrik Brummer and the BracNet Investment, HBS case No 309065.
10. WiMAX is a telecommunications technology that provides wireless transmission of data using a variety of transmission modes, from point-to-multipoint links to portable and fully mobile internet access. The technology provides up to 72 Mbit/s symmetric broadband speed without the need for cables. The technology is based on the IEEE 802.16 standard (also called Broadband Wireless Access). The name WiMAX was created by the WiMAX Forum, which was formed in June 2001 to promote conformity and interoperability of the standard. The forum describes WiMAX as "a standards-based technology enabling the delivery of last mile wireless broadband access as an alternative to cable and DSL." [Wikipedia; accessed February 16, 2009].
11. Lia Steakley "Khalid Quadir: Distributing Documents in Developing Nations." Digital Vision Program Blog. September 1, 2004. http://rdvp.org/ archives/2004/09/01/khalid-quadir-distributing-documents-in-developing-nations/ [accessed May 22, 2008].
12. See http://en.wikipedia.org/wiki/Bangladesh and www.world-gazetteer.com [accessed June 5, 2008].
13. Porter, M. and Kramer, M. (2006) Strategy and society: The link between competitive advantage and corporate social responsibility. *Harvard Business Review*, 1.

6
Cascades Inc. (1959–2009): Some Lessons from a Resilient Organization

Emmanuel Raufflet and Pierre Batellier

Introduction

Kingsey Falls, 120 km west of Montreal, 1959 – Antonio Lemaire is unemployed. He uses a blender to recycle paper and fiber gathered around his village. Five years later, in 1964, his two older sons get a grant from their local credit union (*caisse populaire*) to refurbish and restart a local abandoned paper mill. They quickly transform the equipment to manufacture brown packaging paper from old recycled paper. These two components, namely (1) *production* of output using recycled paper – as opposed to virgin fiber from forests – and (2) *expansion* through the refurbishing, or "recycling," of old, idle production plants based on an on-the-ground knowledge of production processes, represent two key elements of their organizational model.

Kingsey Falls, 2009 – Headquartered in Kingsey Falls, Cascades Inc. employs close to 15,000 people working in 150 plants in six countries (Canada, the United States, France, Sweden, the United Kingdom, and Germany). One-third of its assets and employees are located in Québec. Its sales in 2006 amounted to CAD 3.5 billion.[1] Cascades Inc. has become a leader in its industry and is ranked as the fourth best producer of tissue and the eighth best producer of corrugated cardboard in North America (see Appendix 6.3). This relatively young company has evolved with ease in a mature industry, and is able to compete successfully with companies often a hundred years old on the economic, human resources, and environmental fronts. Since its inception, Cascades has often surpassed its industry's average performance, even despite the beginning of an industry-wide structural crisis in 2004. Cascades Inc. has been ranked several years in a row as one of Canada's best employers, and its environmental practices have been recognized and rewarded on several occasions (see Appendix 6.1 for more detailed information). The successful growth of this business model has been enabled by a third process, *consolidation*. Figure 6.1 maps these three interacting processes.

The purpose of this chapter is to explain the widely recognized economic, environmental, and social success of this company and to draw some lessons from its experience. Our analysis is based on the identification of three intertwined processes, namely production, expansion, and consolidation.

Each of these components encompasses policies and practices which have contributed to building this resilient organization. Thus, the production process consists of practices such as continuous product diversification and optimization of resources based on recycling. The expansion process is based on a strategy of acquiring assets at a low cost and "recycling" them based on a logic of product and geographical diversification. Finally, the consolidation process has been supported by a decentralized structure, reinforced by human resources practices, as well as by a family-like culture. The combination of these three processes has contributed to the sustained performance of the company.

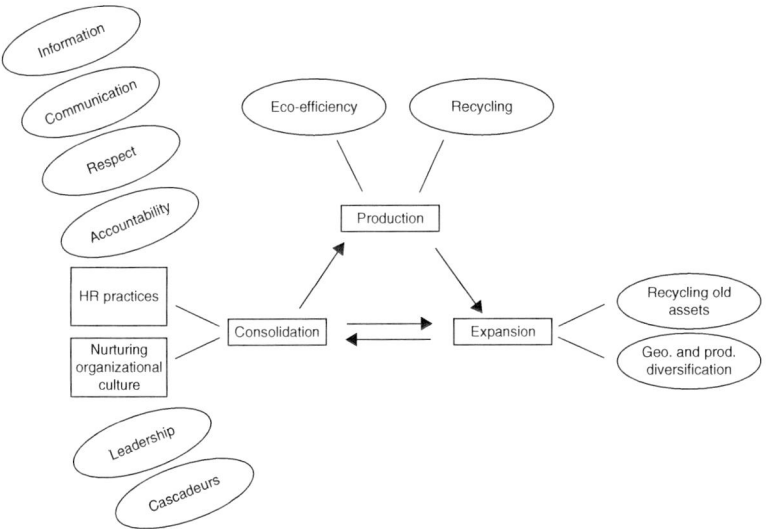

Figure 6.1   Production, expansion, and consolidation processes

Process 1: Production

Cascades has long defined itself as a strong production-driven company based on a quest for efficiency in the use of inputs (recycling) as well as in the production and transformation processes (resource and energy optimization).

Recycling – As mentioned above, Cascades innovated by using recycled fiber as raw material, as it lacked access to a source of virgin fiber in the 1960s. In 2008, recycled fibre accounted for 70 percent of Cascades' raw material, compared with about 40 percent for its competitors.[2] This choice has become a major source of competitive advantage, for several reasons. The first stems from the stable increase of fiber consumption in North America. Between 1960 and 1990, the increase in North American pulp and paper consumption, and the production of 20 to 35 million tons of waste paper per year, have provided Cascades with a constant supply of raw material – especially given that the market for recycled paper is more stable than that of virgin fiber, which is vulnerable to exchange rate fluctuations. The second reason is that the entire production line – from fiber recovery to pulp production and conversion into the finished product – takes place in plants located close to urban areas. Considering that the latter represent the main sources of supply of recycled fiber, as well as the main markets for finished products, this proximity holds numerous economic and environmental benefits. First, there is a reduction in transportation costs compared with the production of pulp and paper from virgin fiber, which needs to be transported from remote forested areas to urban locations. Cascades has set a policy that limits the distance between the supply of fiber and the transformation plant to 500 km. Second, reduced transportation translates into a reduction of greenhouse gas (GHG) emissions. By December 2009, Cascades was calculating its GHG emissions from transportation.[3]

Resource and energy optimization – Cascades' focus on resource optimization and innovative production processes has resulted, among other things, in maximum recovery and conversion rates of waste materials. For example, the company uses de-inking liquor waste as fuel, and resells the remaining de-inking sludge as fuel and fertilizer. Optimizing energy use processes, as well as developing closed-loop water systems, has also helped to improve energy efficiency – a major competitive advantage in an industry in which energy accounts for 25–35 percent of production costs. In fact, Cascades pays special attention to energy, whether it is through several efficiency programs, or through an interest in energy production. For example, Cascades has acquired 35 percent of Boralex – a company with around 300 employees in Canada, the US and France, specializing in the generation of renewable energy (wind, solar, hydro, and biomass).[4] The two companies created their first cogeneration plant of natural gas into electricity and steam, in order to supply pulp and paper plants. To complement this "green" energy production, Cascades promotes energy efficiency in the form of policies in its facilities, or via major innovations, such as the use of biogas produced by the controlled waste dumps of Ste-Sophie, north of Montreal, in the pulp and paper mill in St Jerome. Such energy innovations have provided cost savings for Cascades while reducing GHG emissions.

Process 2: Expansion

Cascades' expansion has consisted of geographical and product diversification based on the acquisition of brownfield plants.

Product and geographic diversification – Cascades is active in five inter-related market segments: (1) packaging, which relies on large agri-foods and consumer products clients; (2) containerboard, a more regional market; (3) specialty paper, which is sold to niches less sensitive to major economic cycles; (4) fine papers sold to retailers, who, in turn, sell to offices, the press, and the publishing industry; and (5) tissue papers, for which the main clients are retailers and consumers – a stable segment directly related to the overall economy (see Appendix 6.2 for a breakdown of sales). This product/segment diversification has been complemented by a progressive geographic expansion that began as early as 1983 in the north-eastern US, continued in Western Canada and Europe (France, Belgium, and Sweden) during the late 1980s, and, in the 1990s and 2000s, focused on the southern and western US. This growth strategy has relied on brownfields (the acquisition of existing plants) as opposed to greenfields (the construction of new production plants). The process has so far been successful: between 1982 and 2008, Cascades has acquired more than 100 plants in Canada, the US, and Western Europe; and its sales grew by 4,500 percent between 1985 and 1995.

Since 2000, the group has multiplied its acquisitions, extending to the west and south in the United States, in particular with the buyout of the 30-odd production and converting lines of the bankrupt American Tissue, which specialized in tissue papers.

At the end of 2002, to better manage this growth, Cascades Inc. was restructured into five independent operations.

This strong drive for expansion through brownfield acquisitions was guided by a corporate strategy that Bernard Lemaire, Cascades' CEO, summarizes as follows:

> Our acquisition policy is to prioritize the purchase of assets rather than shares in order to have a tangible asset with potential we can use, rather than the history and the problems of the old company[5]...Cascades has grown by buying assets from companies in financial difficulty at low cost. We were innovative, we changed things to enhance efficiency, and our management method ensured that our people were involved in the development process.[6]

Each plant acquisition follows a well-rounded recipe. Once a plant is purchased, Cascades sends a group of *Cascadeurs* to salvage the obsolete plant based on the experience inspired by the refurbishing of the first mill in Kingsey Falls in 1964. The *Cascadeurs* are managers and operators who have been with the company for a long time and who are brought in to manage the newly acquired plant and instill the Cascades culture. The usual trio of *Cascadeurs* brought in consists of a plant director, a financial controller, and a human resources supervisor.

The plant director is a hands-on type of entrepreneur, close to the workers and familiar with operations. Plant directors are given a lot of room to maneuver around the mandate to "fix it and run the plant" so that return on investment can be recouped within 3 to 5 years. Controllers enforce strict financial objectives during the restructuring and refurbishing processes of the old plant. Finally, the human resources supervisor works closely with the plant manager to incorporate Cascades' human resources approach and corporate culture in the newly acquired plant.

This entire process of acquiring brownfield plants leads to important cost savings for Cascades. By recognizing the value of old plants and acquiring them at low prices, the company extends the life cycle of the buildings, while reducing the construction of new plants, which requires considerably more financial and natural resources.

Process 3: Consolidation

The third process aims at supporting the production and expansion processes: it cements and unifies this fast-growing organization through internal structural, human resources, and cultural elements.

Making it work: organizational structure – Cascades' structure has long been based on a dialogue between corporate general management (headquarters), which defines the major corporate orientations, and the individual plants that enjoy operational autonomy. Located in Kingsey Falls, in rural Quebec, the 150-employee headquarters sets and monitors general corporate orientations. In addition, it has veto power over the five sector groups when it comes to financial planning, legal affairs, information technologies, accounting policies, internal control systems, and human resources management. Finally, the headquarters provides the individual plants with payable corporate services, such as communications, R&D, and energy management and environmental services. Whereas other North American pulp and paper companies often tend to have heavily populated headquarters,[7] Cascades' structure has remained simple. For Cascades managers, such simplicity is a "stroke of genius"[8] that emphasizes the idea that "orientations come from management, but initiatives come from the grassroots."

The plants, which vary in size from 20 to 300 employees, are highly diversified independent profit centers, with their own equipment, customers, and local operational environment. Plant directors are responsible first-hand for the day-to-day operations and the performance of their locations, as well as for developing action plans and setting production objectives. This autonomy is supported directly by the group's profit-sharing policy, which is linked to operations management and the financial performance of each plant.

Most of the profits generated in one unit are reinvested in this same unit. Profit-sharing is a key, non-negotiable aspect of Cascades' management policy. This autonomy pushes each plant to be innovative on its own, reduce its costs, and seek out new markets. The Lemaire brothers describe their company as "a group of distinct units that operate in different sectors and collaborate with each other to optimize synergies."[9] Another way the group is widely described internally is: "A company of 15,000 employees managed like a group of SMEs."

The creation of the five operational groups in 2002 triggered a major change in the direct relationship between the plants and headquarters. The purpose of this restructuring was to go beyond the limitations of a too decentralized model at a time when competitors and clients were consolidating. It stemmed from the need to foster synergies between plants with similar or complementary activities, and create a critical mass that could better rely on the size of the company when dealing with large suppliers, customers, and competitors. Thus, these five groups served from now on as intermediaries between the company's headquarters and the local plants, and were accountable for their own profits and losses. Each sector group was therefore equipped with a management team and a specific organizational structure, so that it could maintain operational autonomy and its technological and business expertise. These sector groups operated independently when it came to policies and budgets, operations management, hiring staff, sales, marketing, maintenance, new product development, and administration. But they also sometimes collaborated to increase their collective bargaining power vis-à-vis both suppliers and clients.

Human resources management: values and practices – Cascades has institutionalized five key human resources practices: internal communication, access to information, respect, responsibility and accountability, and profit-sharing. Each of these practices has contributed to the company's continuous selection by its employees as one of Canada's 100 best employers.

Internal communication and access to information – A constant concern for Cascades, despite its growth, is to remain a human-scale organization with open internal communication and easy access to information. These values are reflected in several practices that promote information-sharing and employee participation.

The principle of transparent and open internal and external communication has been promoted throughout the management succession of the three Lemaire Brothers, who have headed the company since 1964. In 2003, Alain Lemaire, then 57, took over from Laurent, who himself had inherited the position in 1995 from Bernard Lemaire, who had been at the helm of Cascades since 1964. "It is important that we maintain flexible and open relations between the various levels and units of Cascades, so that if necessary, each employee can have easy access to the leaders of his unit, its cluster, and even the parent company. In addition, leaders must take care to respect the authority of managers as part of their team or their business units." Thus, management views communication as including active listening, the willingness to consult with employees, who are in the best position to know where changes and improvements are required. This sustained practice of internal communication has, among other things, generated several innovations and cost-reduction opportunities in production processes.

Access to information – In order to encourage employee participation, access to higher management and information is made as easy as possible. This policy of transparency and open doors is viewed as a source of respect between management and employees and has proved a great asset: in fact, strong participation has made it possible for Cascades to bounce back more quickly during the structural economic downturns of the industry.

Respect – The other key element of the group's culture concerns the respect for each person (*respect de l'humain*). Concretely, Cascades promotes three dimensions of respect.[10] it considers its employees as business partners, it shows empathy towards each one of these partners, and, finally, it treats each partner with consideration, diplomacy, and humility.

Responsibility and Accountability – Given its autonomous business structure, Cascades has based its growth on the responsibility and accountability of both its local plants and each individual employee. While Cascades defines broad boundaries for its employees, it also expects them to remain rigorous about their actions.[11] In Cascades' philosophy, autonomy comes with responsibility and accountability, but also leaves more room for creativity. A manager summarizes this:

"The feeling of responsibility is the most powerful engine of motivation, value of work done and belonging." The concept of accountability is deeply integrated throughout the company, as each member is accountable for his work, results, and budget. For example, plant managers in other companies may share similar responsibilities as in Cascades – a significant difference being financial accountability. Within Cascades, plant managers determine and approve initiatives on their own before putting them into the financial plan. This tradition of financial accountability comes from the Lemaire Brothers' belief that it is always easier to spend other people's money. Other benefits of this practice include resourcefulness and ownership. As a manager puts it: "This obliges people in charge to be more imaginative and find the best possible solutions." This idea of responsibility and accountability is reinforced by the policy of profit-sharing.

Profit-sharing – Cascades has been a pioneer in Quebec with its system of profit-sharing. Historically, this tradition started when the Lemaire Brothers had a small company with limited financial resources to pay their employees. They then promised to share future profits. Laurent Lemaire explains:

> At the beginning, 40 years ago, our employees were paid CAD 1 an hour, half of the industrial wages then in effect. Cascades' management told them: 'At the moment we have no money. When the plant is profitable, we will improve your conditions and share profits together.' People trusted us. They have not regretted it.

This experience has since been embedded in Cascades' HR policies, and the policy of profit-sharing has been institutionalized. In 2008, EBDTA amounted to CAD 250 million, of which CAD 40 million was distributed as profit to the employees. Specifically, these amounts ranged between 3 percent and 30 percent of the employees' individual salaries. As profits are distributed in proportion to the profit realized in each unit, it has occurred in the past that plant managers have earned more in this profit-sharing system than presidents of business units positioned "higher" in the hierarchy. To counterbalance potential polarization between profit-making units – which are better enabled to attract and retain talented managers – and less profitable units, Cascades has established a mechanism to foster the transfer of skilled and talented managers and technicians from a profit-making unit to a less profitable one, thanks to an individually measured performance reward. In the words of a Cascades senior manager: "This system is not perfect, but so far this is the best we have been able to come up with."

The results of the Consolidation process: Building and
nurturing a culture through a management style

Cascades' consolidation process has resulted in a unique management style and culture that is reflected throughout the organization. The company's employees translate this culture through their everyday work and their career paths.

Management style: the role of the *"Cascadeurs"* – The vitality of the three Lemaire brothers, who still own 38 percent of Cascades shares, continues to permeate the culture and management style of the company. Their management philosophy has consolidated an organizational culture that values information-sharing and employee participation in decision-making through open dialogue, respect for people and for the communities in which the plants operate, and a risk-taking and entrepreneurial mentality for everyone. Since 2003, Cascades has been rated as one of the top 100 employers in Canada.[12] The Lemaire brothers are keen on maintaining the company's SME values despite its expansion.

In addition, the company's growth has facilitated promotion from within, thus leading to improved motivation of management and staff stability. Many of the current executives started out with the company when they were very young. For example, Suzanne Blanchet, President of CGT (Cascades Groupe Tissu), one of the five business units, was hired by Cascades in 1978 in accounting. She quickly moved up the corporate ladder, one rung at a time – controller, plant manager, and senior management positions – which led her to endorse her current position in 1997. As of 2009, she is the only female president of a paper company in Canada. Her unit sells more than CAD 1 billion worth of products a year.

Overall, the three processes – *production* with a constant focus on efficiency; *expansion* through the acquisition of brownfield plants; and *consolidation* through structuring, human resources, and cultural practices – have contributed to building an organization that has remained resilient in the fast-changing evolution of its industry. The first two processes are directly related to the company's production and business models, and have constantly defined the company's growth and change initiatives. By contrast, the third process has provided a solid backbone in the form of structures, human resources procedures, values, and culture, which has given a sense of continuity and stability to this fast-changing company.

Cascades Inc. at 50: The challenges ahead

Despite its successes and innovative business and organizational model, Cascades faces several challenges after 50 years of operation. First, the North American pulp and paper industry is currently going through the most critical period in its history. Since the beginning of the crisis in 2004, the industry has suffered hundreds of plant closures and numerous job losses.[13] This structural crisis is explained by several factors, including (1) rising energy costs in an energy-intensive industry; (2) market saturation in packaging in many industrialized countries (due to development of plastic substitutes and flexible packaging that are lighter to transport), in newsprint and in fine papers (due to digitization of documents, the internet, decrease in demand for newspapers). All these factors have led to a situation of overproduction and excess capacity in North America; (3) a growing number of retailers and other industrial customers increasing pressure on their paper suppliers to reduce costs; (4) the arrival of products from emerging countries such as China and Brazil; and (5) a disadvantageous economic context in Quebec due to the rising Canadian dollar compared with the US dollar (USD 0.62 to USD 0.91 between 1998 and 2006), which penalizes exports. This situation is further exacerbated by the low productivity of Quebec's plants relative to their US or Scandinavian competitors; and (6) the increased cost of fiber – among the most expensive in the world – as a result of having to go further into forests to harvest timber.[14] Together, these factors have increased competition in the industry and drastically reduced the profit margins of producers, putting them under extreme pressure to reduce costs. Until now, Cascades has resisted this crisis relatively well, due to its model based on recycled fibers and its strict focus on eco-efficiency. However, the difficulties of the pulp and paper industry remain a constant challenge to Cascade's future success.

In addition to this difficult environment, Cascades currently faces, according to its president Alain Lemaire, a real challenge in planning its succession and the development of a new generation of leaders. The company seems to be transitioning into a new demographic cycle. Until now, the *Cascadeurs*, the core management teams both in the headquarters and in the plants, have all had fairly similar career paths as operators who have worked their way up the corporate ladder and contributed to the success of the company. By far, most of the corporate managers and plant managers are French-speaking Quebecers, in their mid-fifties or older. They joined Cascades when they were young and the company was just starting out, have spent most – if not all – of their careers there, and are often linked to Kingsey Falls in one way or another. This homogeneity has been an asset for Cascades, cementing a very close-knit culture and having allowed the company to pull together internally and bounce back during slower economic cycles. However, this cohesion – to a certain extent a lack of cultural and background diversity – might limit the company's future growth. Indeed, Cascades might find its expansion into emergent markets with high and sustained growth, such as Brazil and China, challenging, as the company has limited access to human capital with the necessary knowledge and experience to enter these markets.

The third challenge Cascade is facing concerns the limits of its decentralized, entrepreneurial business model, in which its plants, and more recently its business units, enjoy wide autonomy. Although this structure has historically been a source of growth and profits, it now risks limiting the expansion of the company's resources, skills, and position in an increasingly consolidated market. Indeed, Cascades' competitors and customers have in recent years decreased considerably in numbers and scope, due to a combination of supply chain consolidation and product standardization, which have reduced the need for regional markets. In 1998, the three largest retailers in Canada represented 88 percent of sales; in 2004, they represented 98 percent.[15] In this context, remaining decentralized and small in the face of larger players is risky, since conducting business and negotiating with large players such as Wal-Mart does require tighter coordination in order to reach economies of scale and competitiveness. Cascades' 2002 internal restructuring aimed to address this, but, in the words of one of the heads of the business units, much more needs to be done in this direction.

Lessons from Cascades

Overall, the experience of Cascades offers an interesting insight for managers concerned with the integration of environmental sustainability within a business. Through its three processes of production, expansion, and consolidation, Cascades has been able to integrate "green" concerns within its operations and its business and strategic models in a resourceful and *sui generis* way. As such, this sustained economic achievement both reflects and reinforces the company's entrepreneurial and decentralized culture.[16] Cascades has so far been a leading organization in sustainability, while being fairly reluctant to standardize its environmental practices and policies through environmental norms. Standardization straightjackets and successful resourcefulness may not be compatible in all organizations (Bodiot and Raufflet, 2009). The lesson for managers interested in promoting sustainability in their organization may relate to this: start what could become a sustainability journey from what your organization is, that is, from its values, culture, and practices. It may be tempting to "adopt" a one-size-fits-all template. Reading about "best practices," trying them in one's organization, and imitating what competitors do may be a way to start learning about sustainability. However, attempting to integrate "sustainability" with little understanding or consideration for your organization's own culture, identity, strategy, and practices may be misleading. After all, gardeners teach us that not all plants are compatible with all soils.

Appendix 6.1

Recent recognition of Cascades' sustainability initiatives

- Cascades was awarded Quebec's *Phénix de l'environnement* for Enhancement of Residual Materials in 2002 and for overall environmental management in 2003.
- For the fourth year in a row, Cascades Fine Papers Group has been chosen as the official supplier to Canada's version of Earth Day, the world's largest environmental event. Cascades' contribution has grown since 2004, as the company also supplies Jour de la Terre, Quebec's version of Earth Day Canada.
- Cascades was named among the 100 Best Employers in Canada in 2004, 2005, and 2006. The study rated the company "above average" or "outstanding" in terms of quality of the work environment, social life, benefits, performance management, training, and commitment to the community.
- The Norampac Division in Vaudreuil received the *Grand Prix québécois de la qualité* 2005. This award recognizes the continual quest for improvement and excellence in quality and the processes leading to it.
- In receiving Green Seal certification, North River™ (Cascades tissue paper brand) became the brand holding the widest range of environmental certifications in the commercial and industrial tissue paper market.

- In 2005, Cascades was awarded the first FSC (Forest Stewardship Council) Recycled certification in Canada for fine papers made at the mill in Quebec. The award certifies a product's 100 percent post-consumer content from start to finish of the manufacturing process.
- The St Jerome unit is also one of only two mills in Canada to bear Environment Canada's EcoLogo™ mark.
- Greenpeace added Cascades tissue products to the positive "green" category of its Shopper's Guide to Ancient Forest Friendly Tissue Products.
- Cascades has been honored with awards from the Paperboard Packaging Council for the design and development of two innovative packaging solutions: Nestlé Sundae Cup 2™ and Unilever Marinades™.
- Under the auspices of the Canadian government's Energy Conservation Program, Cascades was recognized, in 2005, for its awareness and training program on energy efficiency in the workplace.

Appendix 6.2

Cascades business overview

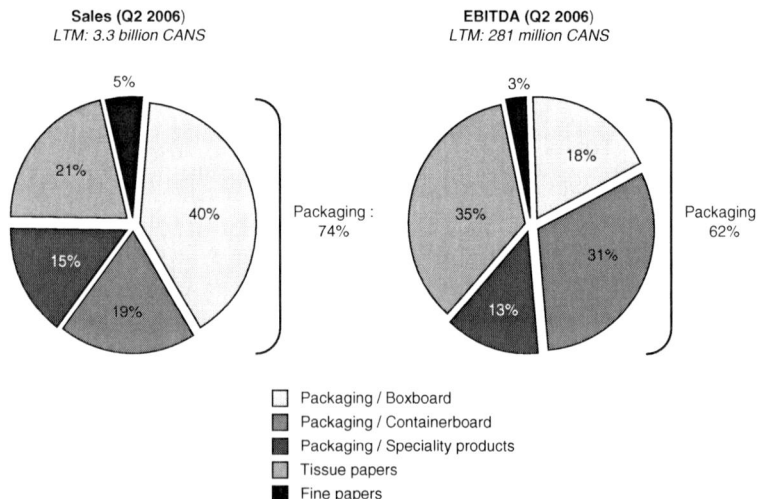

Source: Cascades: Sustainable packaging and tissue, Alain Lemaire, Cascades CEO, September 20, 2006, Presentation at the UBS GLOBAL PAPER & FOREST PRODUCTS CONFERENCE.

Appendix 6.3 Cascades' positioning in its four main markets in 2004

Top 10 North American tissue producers			Top 10 North American corrugated box		
Company	Capacity (000 tons)	Mkt share (%)	Company	Production share (%)	#Box plants
1 Georgia-Pacific	2,777	34.6	1 Smurfit-Stone Container	22.2	130
2 Kimberly-Clark	1,433	17.8	2 Weyerhaeuser	15.9	94
3 Procter & Gamble	1,154	14.4	6 Inland Paperboard	10.1	41
4 Cascades	550	6.7	5 Georgia-Pacific	8.1	46
5 SCA	537	6.7	4 International Paper	6.8	59
6 Kruger	311	3.9	3 Packaging Corp of America	5.5	68
7 Irving Tissue	196	2.4	7 Greif	3.0	27
8 CelluTissue	193	2.4	8 Norampac	2.3	26
9 Potlatch	163	2.0	9 BOX USA	2.0	19
10 MarcalPaper	142	1.8	10 Green Bay	1.8	11

Top 10 North American Containerboard Producers			Top 10 North American Boxboard Producers		
Company	Capacity (000 tons)	Mkt share (%)	Company	Capacity (000 tons)	Mkt share (%)
1 Smurfit-Stone Container	8,036	20.1	1 MeadWestvaco	2,540	17.5
2 Weyerhaeuser	5,638	14.1	2 International Paper	2,065	14.3
3 International Paperboard	4,520	11.3	3 Graphic Packaging	1,442	10.0
4 Georgia-Pacific	3,934	9.9	4 Sonoco Products	1,380	9.5
5 Temple-Inland	3,090	7.7	5 Caraustar	943	6.5
6 Packaging Corp of America	2,300	5.8	6 Rock-Tenn	928	6.4
7 Norampac	1,601	4.0	7 Newark Group	907	6.3
8 Longview Fibre	740	1.9	8 Cascades	865	6.0
9 Green Bay Packaging	735	1.8	9 Smurfit-Stone	725	5.0
10 Solvay Paperboard	730	1.8	10 Potlatch	566	3.9

Source: Paperloop & Cascades.

Notes

The authors are grateful to Hubert Bolduc, Cascades Inc. for providing detailed information on Cascades as well as to Miheala Stefanov for copyediting a previous version of this chapter.

1. All figures are in Canadian dollars. As of December 1, 2009, C\$ 1 = 0.92 US\$.
2. Cascades, 2008.
3. Source: Conversation with M. Hubert Bolduc, VP Communications, Cascades Inc., December 3, 2009.
4. For example, between 2001 and 2005 Cascades reduced its energy consumption by 7 percent, representing total annual savings of \$10–20 million, and this in the context of a substantial increase in energy prices.
5. Lemaire brothers, "Les valeurs qui nous guident," 2005, internal document.
6. Interview with B. Lemaire on *Téléjournal – Le Point* on Radio-Canada, September 28, 2004, marking Cascades' 40th birthday.
7. By way of comparison, *Maison Domtar*, Domtar's headquarters in Montreal, employs close to 400 people for a company with fewer employees than Cascades. Source: Domtar. Information obtained on April 20, 2006.
8. Lemaire brothers, "Les valeurs qui nous guident," 2005, internal document.
9. Lemaire brothers, "Les valeurs qui nous guident," 2005, internal document.
10. Source: Cascades' website, http://www.cascades.com/profil/philosophie
11. Source: Cascades' website, http://www.cascades.com/profil/philosophie
12. Mediacorp annual survey for *Maclean's* magazine.
13. 10,000 jobs were lost in the pulp and paper industry in Canada between April 1, 2005 and March 31, 2006 (source: NRCan).
14. *Revue Commerce*, November 2006, page 28.
15. Source: Nantel, Jacques, (2006), *L'effet Wal-Mart, une analyse du secteur du commerce de détail*, ASDEQ, February 22, 2006.
16. Cayer and Raufflet (forthcoming).

Bibliography

Batellier, P. and Raufflet, E. (2008). Cascades in 2006 at the crossroads, pp. 262–276, in Russo, M. (ed.) *Environmental Management: Texts and Cases*. Thousand Oaks, CA: Sage Publishing.

Bodiot, C. and Raufflet, E. (2009). L'évolution des motivations d'adoption de normes environnementales: l'expérience de quatre firmes canadiennes du secteur des pâtes et papiers (1996–2005), *Management & Avenir*.

Cascades (2008). Annual Report, Montreal.

Cayer, D. and Raufflet, E. (2009). *Culture organisationnelle et formation des politiques environnementales*. Working paper, HEC Montréal.

This case study is based on several interviews conducted between 2005 and 2008. The information of this case is mainly based on interviews of senior management and managers of Cascades at Cascades' headquarters in Kingsey Falls (Quebec) and in various Cascades business units in Canada and the United States.

Interviews carried out at Cascades' headquarters in Kingsey Falls or Montréal (Quebec):

• February 2005: Interview with M. Alain Lemaire, CEO of Cascades Inc., on Cascades' overall and environmental strategies.

- February 2005: Interview with M. Léon Marineau, Vice-president Environment, on environmental challenges and Cascades' environmental management.
- 2005–2006: Four interviews with M. Hubert Bolduc, Vice-President Communications and Public Affairs, on Cascades' strategy.
- April 2006: Interview with M. Léon Marineau, Vice-president Environment, on environmental challenges and Cascades' environmental management.
- April 2006: Interview with Mme Andrée Lavoie, Director of the Laurent Lemaire Information Technology Centre.
- April 2006: Interview with Mme Maryse Fernet, Corporate Director of Human Resources.
- October 2006: Interviews with Mme Blanchet, CEO CTG, Jocelyne Pinsonneault, VP Marketing, CTG, Daniel Gélineau, VP Production, CTG.

Visits of Business Units in the Cascades industrial complex of Kingsey Falls (Bois-Francs, QC, headquarters):

- February 2005: tissue paper plant and Formapak plant (specialized products).
- April 2006: tissue paper, Cascades plastics, boxboard and Norampac (containerboard).

Visits of Business Units and interviews with the plant managers outside Quebec (US and Ontario):

- July 2005: visit to three Cascades' tissue paper plants in the United States. Each visit included an interview with the director of the plant and other managers on the environmental strategy of the plant, daily management, Cascades corporate culture and the specific challenges of the plant.
  Northwest: St Helens (Oregon) – production and conversion plant.
  Southwest: Kingman (Arizona) – conversion plant.
  Southeast: Rockingham (North Carolina) – production and conversion plant.
- August 2005: visit of Cascades' boxboard production plant in Toronto, Cascades' biggest paper mill. Interviews with the director of the plant and other managers on the strategic challenges of the plant, especially those of environmental management.

Other data sources for the case:

- Cascades Website: www.cascades.com
- CASCADES Inc., Cascades Annual Report 2004 and 2005, Cascades CSR Report 2004.
- CASCADES Inc. (2005). *Mémoire sur le plan de développement durable du Québec et l'avant-projet de loi concernant la loi sur le développement durable, présenté au ministre du développement durable du Québec Monsieur Thomas J. Mulcair,* February 25, 2005.
- *Le Cascadeur*: Cascades house newsletter.
- Les 40 ans de Cascades, Les Affaires, Promoaffaires, May 2004.
- Interview with Bernard Lemaire at the Téléjournal – Le Point of Radio Canada, September 28, 2004, for the 40th anniversary of Cascades.
- Sectorial Data: Québec Forest Industry Council, Natural Resources Canada, Ressources Naturelles & Faune Québec.
- L'industrie forestière à bout de souffle, *Le Devoir*, December 10, 2005.

7
Dialogue-Based Leadership Style As Part of Humanistic Organizational Cultures: The Case of dm in Germany

Wolfgang Amann and Shiban Khan

Introduction

dm drogerie markt is a chain of drugstores that has been operating mainly in Germany since the company's inception in 1973. Over time, dm has expanded in other European countries as well. In 2008, Erich Harsch took over as CEO from Goetz Werner, who built a reputation for dm as being one of the most humanistic companies – an example for others to follow. Declining market conditions, comprising a marked price sensitivity, market concentration, and a slowing demand due to the burst subprime mortgage bubble would challenge Erich Harsch considerably, putting the sustainability and humanistic concepts instilled by his predecessor to the test. There is reason to believe that a humanistic orientation and humanistic practices at dm do not represent a cost to be minimized, but rather act as a key ingredient to leverage employee and customer satisfaction, as well as sustaining business success. dm enjoys a strong market position, but dm's current main rival, Schlecker, is still the market leader in Germany – with significantly different values, as will be outlined below.

dm's beginnings were as humble as its subsequent growth was spectacular. Goetz Werner opened his first outlet in 1973 in Karlsruhe, in south-west Germany, and steadily expanded the business over time. In 2008, dm generated 4.7 billion Euros with its 30,000 employees and 2,024 outlets. Since real growth to new levels was not possible in Germany due to the tough competition, dm started opening outlets in other countries. Currently, only half (1,024) of its outlets are in Germany; others serve Austria (354), the Czech Republic (150), Slovenia (61), Hungary (225), Croatia (104), Bosnia (17), Serbia (23), and Romania (7), and the market entry in Bulgaria was initiated in 2009.[1] Most of the company's profit still stems from Germany, where, based only on a gentlemen's agreement, the market was split for over 30 years. Its main competitor in its early days, Rossmann, primarily served the northern and eastern parts of Germany, while dm focused on the south. Since tough times call for tough measures, Rossmann – with additional funding from Hong Kong-based Hutchison Whampoa – entered southern territories and, in turn, dm started to open outlets in northern Germany. Competition has worsened ever since.

In 1986 dm started selling products under its own dm label, which now accounts for 30 percent of its product range. For the purpose of furthering company growth, Werner and Harsch added the distribution of pharmaceuticals to the services offered by dm. Since initial court rulings were in favor of the distribution of pharmaceuticals by dm, it is likely that more outlets will open in addition to the existing 86 outlets that distribute pharmaceuticals to customers. The distribution of pharmaceuticals was, in contrast to various other countries, strictly limited to pharmacies until a recent court ruling. dm has also responded to recent technological trends, now offering digital photo printing in its outlets and offering a service where customers can put together their own mp3 compilations in dm music shops. dm has thus evidenced adaptability in response to new opportunities over time.

As the head of the supervisory board, Werner continues to influence the company. Overall, having worked with Harsch for 27 years, he maintains the carefully built-up humanistic set-up. Harsch knows the organizational culture perfectly well. The company already enjoys the best reputation in the industry for its competence in health products, green products, and quality price value.[2] To name just a few examples, many branded products, such as Schauma shampoo, Meister Proper cleaning utensils, Fa shower gel, and Nivea crèmes, are substantially cheaper at dm than elsewhere.[3] This has by no means harmed the financial success of the company. On average, dm outlets, which are slightly bigger, generate some 270,000 Euros per month in contrast to Rossmann's 150,000 Euros and Schlecker's 45,000 Euros per outlet.[4]

Other indicators of success are equally significant. dm ranks first when it comes to employee satisfaction.[5] dm also scores highest on customer satisfaction, along with customer loyalty, when compared with its competitors. Additionally, dm has received the best ratings among the larger group of retail companies. Its long-term CEO, Werner, has received awards for business conduct,[6] product quality,[7] entrepreneurial achievements,[8] and so forth. In stark contrast, Anton Schlecker, the 60-year old CEO of dm's competitor carrying his name, has been a notoriously stingy employer and has paid employees so far below the industry standards that a court ruling was necessary to stop this practice. A specially bitter aftertaste resulted from the fraudulent attempt by Schlecker to feign that pay was in line with industry standards until employees stopped believing it. Spying on staff, as well as rapid dissolutions of contracts following minor incidents, only completes this list of misdeeds. Schlecker was also forced to pay a 1 million Euro fine, which went to charity.[9] Nevertheless, workers' councils continue to complain about the scandalous conditions at Schlecker. But what is it that really distinguishes dm from its arch-rival in terms of corporate practices?

The origins of dm's humanistic management approach

The uniqueness of dm's approach to leadership and its special organizational culture, as we shall outline throughout this text, were not entirely planned ex ante. dm built the ship while at sea. Concrete demands caused Werner and Armin Foell, with whom he opened the first store in 1973, to ask the key questions on how to lead on an ongoing basis. Opening the first few stores had its challenges, but these were more in the fields of marketing, logistics, and finances. After opening 30 to 40 subsidiaries, Werner aimed to professionalize leadership and governance. Over time, more leadership levels were introduced, starting with people in charge of smaller numbers of stores located in a delineated area. Later, a leadership layer was introduced to manage geographic regions. After a few years, Werner felt he might lose the overview of his rapidly expanding company and decided to organize substantive executive education for himself and his executives, including those in charge of regions and areas. He signed up for a seminar on organizational development, and several events started in 1978, with Hellmuth ten Siethoff as their primary coach. The participants soon realized that, after the pioneering phase of organizational development, more professional organizational efforts had to be carried out in the next life cycle stage. Based on role-play and theatrical play techniques, the portrayal of the situation revealed that the corporate structure and leadership were too top-down. Staff described superiors as merciless dictators with clubs in their hands and with their subordinates, playing themselves, on their knees on stage. This depiction of the current situation catalyzed the fundamental thought process of how the ideal situation should be.

Werner knew that this scenario was not what he wanted. Roles of lower levels, especially those of subordinates, were changed, along with communication and other aspects of leadership. In some instances, staff members unable to work in a dialogue culture had to be replaced to allow the rise of a dialogue-based leadership in the second life cycle stage as the company's requirements changed to accommodate larger numbers of employees and locations in the system.[10]

Management understood that previous governance structures had begun to fail. Some decisions were made on the subsidiary level, some on the area management level, and some on the regional management level. Preferences and priorities were becoming incongruent. The growing number of area managers and regional managers in the system did not make things easier. Lower levels were held accountable for results, while higher levels continued making top-down decisions for too long. Additional project leaders complicated operations, such as when cosmetics consultants toured the subsidiaries to recommend changes to foster their products. Especially in the early 1990s, change had to accelerate, as existing solutions had reached their limits. Werner admitted that he had also held onto initial principles for too long, such as the obligation of lower levels to adopt the values and ideas of higher levels, or a standardization mania, as he called it ex post.[11] Economic success lured him into holding on to this recipe before fundamentally thinking about how the system should be constructed in an ideal world in the future. An economic crisis and financial losses forced Werner to rethink the system. Economically, things had to get worse before they could improve and the dialogue-based leadership took off. Nevertheless, this phase, in which more subsidiaries were closed than were opened in the early 1990s, turned out to be extremely valuable for the company's future.

Lower levels of the organization now enjoyed more responsibility than ever before. Each management level is trained and held accountable for properly cascading this system down and overseeing its implementation at lower levels. If a local competitor started special promotions, the local subsidiary could react much faster. They could decide upon shelf space themselves, and they were given full transparency on financial figures so that they could also better steer initiatives. Subsidiaries were no longer falling victim to an area manager who insisted on changes one day and regional or special initiative promoters, such as cosmetics consultants, often demanding contradictory changes only a few days later. Top-down communication was replaced by dialogue to establish what would work best. Decentralization to the lowest level took place. The subsidiaries solved problems, rather than some remote central department too far away from relevant context information. Responsibility was embraced, and no longer rested on an area manager who had to take charge of too many subsidiaries. These changes penetrated all areas. Another case in point was HR management. In the past, because area managers recruited staff, any problem with an individual staff member was reported to the area manager. If, for example, someone wanted to work part-time, rather than full-time, this request would, in the past, have been referred to the area manager. From now on, the subsidiary dealt independently with such HR-related issues, and they are now solved more effectively by making use of alternatives unknown to upper management, leaving everybody better off. Substantial training was necessary, however, for individuals throughout the entire organization to fill the responsibility void that was suddenly opening up. Employees in subordinate positions in retail outlets and distribution functions had to learn how to operate the latest financial and IT systems. Key staff suddenly had to know all about innovations previously completely unknown at the subsidiary level, such as layout structure analysis, a tool to calculate the sales and success of individual sections on the shop floor to check on results and initiatives. Werner understood that no two stores could be run in exactly the same way. He realized the tremendous intelligence that there was in the system, and reorganized his company accordingly.

Unforeseen dynamics suddenly emerged throughout the organization. Subsidiaries in terms of individual outlets started to exchange insights regarding, for example, changes in the shop floor layouts or the success of payback card initiatives in the pre-Christmas season. Payback was a customer loyalty program and thus crucial for success. Hierarchies were effectively replaced by individual autonomy, horizontal communication, and cooperation. These dynamics surprised Werner, but he did whatever he could to facilitate them. He even fostered what he called constructive unhappiness – dissatisfaction with the status quo mobilized employees, and this would lead to a decentralized search for solutions. Disagreeing was constructively encouraged. Staff assumed ownership at all levels, instead of pushing problems to higher levels. The question was no longer whether the superior liked the situation, but whether the individual felt that his or her role was helpful. Henceforth, identifying goals in teams characterized decision-making processes, and it was this freedom to co-shape reality that unleashed motivation, ideas, and commitment among employees. In summary, failing organizational processes at the end of the first life cycle stage gave Werner a unique opportunity to construct the future dm, where he institutionalized the new leadership concept of dialogue-based leadership. The entire process needed more than two decades to fully deploy its potential and bear fruit.

Individualism as a principle

Deep at the core of dm's current organizational culture rests a strong belief in the intrinsic value of each individual, by far surpassing the view of retail employees as a a mere turnover-generating resource. Individuals count as an end in themselves.[12] Subsequently, leadership and organizational culture at dm aims to initially recognize the individuality of an employee, without, at first, having a specific goal in mind. Factoring in this individualism is thus the first principle in organizing a social setting.

According to Werner's view on society, there is a trend towards more individualism, more freedom for individuals to choose and influence more of their immediate environment. Individuals increasingly claim their right to think and act independently and to be responsible for their own actions. Customers and employees want to be taken seriously. As a consequence, Werner and dm became known for dialogue-based leadership. The latter is defined as an organizational culture in which employees take over and are granted exactly this responsibility. Employees contribute to the overall success of the organization as independently as possible. An employee is not regarded as a cog in a big machine, but is recognized as a contributor who is merely positioned at a certain level. Organizing such freedom, responsibility, and recognition is vastly different from empowerment. While empowerment is usually seen as something positive, dm takes an even more progressive and contrasting approach. At dm, empowerment is seen as something that is actually negative, because it is manipulative and even conceptually flawed. Werner takes the clear position that he wants more than empowerment. Empowerment, to him, relies on the mechanism of intentionally granting freedom to employees to strongly encourage them to motivate themselves. Empowerment thus tries to manipulate the motivation process. After consulting for dm for more than a decade, Dietz and Kracht (2007) stated: "If I am taking somebody seriously only because his or her reaction is exactly the benefit I aimed to draw out of the situation, then I have not taken the person seriously in the first place" (p. 15). While many employees in other organizations long for more empowerment for a variety of reasons, Werner set the standards higher at dm.

Simultaneously, Werner linked this individualism as a concept with economic thinking. According to him, economic settings and competition are merely a competition of free ideas. This is in stark contrast to classic hierarchical thinking, where people at the upper echelon of the organizational pyramid think they know what is best for everybody throughout the organization and therefore aim to homogenize the way people think at all levels.

The second guiding principle, next to this hierarchy of ideas, is to find a way for individuals to deal with one another in such a way that the best idea always wins. This extends the humanistic way of thinking by first taking each individual seriously and recognizing him or her as a source of ideas and as an expert when it comes to the implementation of these ideas. Senior staff who lead others must therefore be masters of understanding the individuality and unique potential of their colleagues. Senior staff have[13] to lead in such a way that any subordinate, or superior for that matter, feels comfortable with expressing his or her own ideas. Staff members must also be continually trained to ensure that necessary skills for communication and implementation are in place. Instead of drafting detailed plans for the future with rigid goals, superiors initially organize opportunities for subordinates to express and actualize themselves. In turn, subordinates must also possess and enhance comparable reading and comprehension skills so that they can understand how superiors operate and to ensure proper communication patterns.

Skeptics may object by pointing out that it is difficult to ensure that the different actions of all these individuals do not lead to chaos; rather, they must be aligned, since dm does, after all, operate in a competitive environment, and profit margins in the retail sector are too frequently razor-thin. dm takes a clear stance.[14] According to Werner, such points are fundamentally flawed, as he starts with a basic trust in everybody. Future action determines what this trust will become. Will it grow or wither away? dm believes in granting such trust, since it legitimizes superiors' expectations of their staff. Employees reach their full potential through being trusted and being allowed to responsibly fulfill their tasks, not by being commanded and imposed on. A command and control structure falsely assumes that individuals cannot be trusted, have wrong motives, lack brainpower, and are unable to act responsibly without being under constant control. dm assumes a different understanding of a human being, and therefore organizes around the individual, who is the company's center of attention.

Such an assumption regarding the nature of human beings also leads to strategies and plans that do not ignore but build on the individuality of staff members.[15] Such strategies and goals do not contradict the nature and desires of human beings. As a consequence, dialogues replace top-down instructions. Two individuals, both responsible for their actions, ought to meet for dialogue. They mutually respect each other, refraining from misusing one another. The given task is not something a superior dumps upon his or her subordinate; the task becomes their joint challenge. A prerequisite for such a system to work is that each person is recognized as an individual, and individuals are perceived differently. Each person is not recognized solely or primarily based on the role or function that he or she has to fulfill. Each staff member develops a special, individual relationship with his or her situation at work, acknowledging that the responsibility to provide good-quality work rests with each individual. Therefore, solutions may also be unique, and do not have to be fully standardized across all staff members in all subsidiaries in different countries. Each staff member shapes or co-shapes solutions instead of being given assignments, orders, or checklists without any room for discretion. Such independence is only possible if staff members are given enough context information. Consequently, there is an obligation to provide such information, within reason, of course. Dialogue-based leadership cannot be introduced as a system that is imposed on employees. Staff members have to agree to it, have to get used to it, and usually become better at practicing it over time. This turns dialogue-based leadership into a dynamic system. It is also brought to life differently in various parts of the organization. Dialogue-based leadership is, thus, both a stimulus for participation and a growth and learning opportunity for individuals to jointly develop better solutions. Finally, this also means that leadership does not necessarily change the individuals. Individuals lead themselves and subsequently lead and change the system. Individuals lead themselves to an extent with which they are comfortable. Organizational control is brought to life through self-control. The resulting climate is extremely open to new ideas, positive energy, and commitment.

dm proves that dialogue-based leadership is not a utopia. dm's priorities and assumptions on the way colleagues deal with one another are fundamentally different from traditional assumptions based on the

the *homo oeconomicus* model. As summarized by Frederick Taylor in his "scientific management approach," in contrast to Werner's and dm's belief system, *homo oeconomicus* assumes that humans basically, among other things:[16]

- are egoistic,
- are motivated primarily by money,
- pursue recognition,
- attempt to give in to their laziness,
- cannot control themselves.

Dialogue-based leadership as a social trend

As the organization gathered more experience with this new concept of organizing social interactions and became substantially better at it, many differences crystallized that had not previously been fully recognized. The fundamental differences are portrayed in the following figure. As Dietz and Kracht (2007) point out, when comparing dm's development with political developments, democracy had already replaced hierarchies around 700 BC, as groups were often better than kings at solving problems. In order to receive legitimization, elections were held and key tasks were subsequently delegated to the groups. Clear structures allowed the overcoming of arbitrary decision-making by an arbitrary ruler. People were enabled to have more clarification and expectations. The authors also question whether this emerging form of leadership brought out the best in all individuals, or whether this system pays enough attention to the idiosyncrasies of each individual. Instead of focusing on privileged groups that take charge, making all individuals the center of attention could represent an interesting way forward. Instead of groups, each individual should be listened to and given the opportunity to contribute, to deploy his or her own full potential if there is an interest in doing so. Nevertheless, new rules and patterns for value-creation are necessary. The plethora of ideas could grow significantly. It goes without saying that a prerequisite for such individualism lies in each individual's realization that he or she is part of a larger system and can contribute through initiatives and well-meant, voluntary cooperation. Individualism is not to be understood as a concept that competes with democracy, but rather as an extension or further development of it (Table 7.1).

Werner recognizes this focus on the individual as an accelerating trend in society. According to him, he implemented it in his company as one of the first of many firms who use this practice today. Werner regards it as the future of organizing firms. After seeing all the benefits,

Table 7.1 Leadership principles over time

	Decision-making unit	Process of expressing wills	Principle of cooperation	Social form
Hierarchy	One individual	Authority	Administration	Instruction
Democracy	The group	Coordination	Delegation	Structures
Individualism	Each individual	Initiative	Agreement and cooperation	Processes

Source: Based on Dietz and Kracht (2007), 131.

not only in economic terms, Werner launched a number of initiatives to spread his insights into individualism as a social concept for organizing not only companies, but also society in general. He subsequently compiled many publications on a just society and specific topics such as wage policies and individuals' responsibility. As outlined, he received many awards for his endeavors, such as "entrepreneur of the year," "fairness award," and even the German Federal Cross of Honor. Before more external pressure emerged for many firms, dm also embarked on becoming a sustainability leader in its field, running one of the greenest retail operations, evidenced, for example, by the Hanse Globe Award in 2008 acknowledging such outstanding achievements.[17] Additionally, dm's apprenticeship and training system has won awards, but Werner has long since shifted his focus to having an impact on society beyond his company.

Conclusion

Organizing in a way that puts individuals and their natures and interests at center stage can be done. More humanism in business is, therefore, not a utopia. It can work in practice without adversely affecting financial performance. Too frequently, one is interpreted as being possible only at the expense of the other. However, it is likely that dm has found a unique way of implementing a more respectful way of management. Its dialogue-based leadership and organizational culture have been brought to life and perfected over time – not top-down, but in a self-organizing system. Other companies will have to find their own ways. dm has also had its own triggers for substantially increasing its humanism in business. Triggers have included failing leadership and governance elements, and a somewhat self-inflicted economic crisis, which stimulated the company to rethink its management approach and corporate set-up, since it was, fortunately, particularly open to change at that time. Triggers have also included Werner's insight into organizational development and the need for training, the availability of a strong, humanistic coach in the person of Hellmuth ten Siethoff, and developing an understanding of what really matters most – the human being as the center of attention.

Notes

1. Source: Company information.
2. Cf. Expansion in der Zeit nach Götz Werner, *dpa / manager magazin*, May 9, 2008.
3. Cf. Kampf der Discounter, *stern*, No. 4, January 27, 2005.
4. Cf. dm will vor allem in Berlin wachsen, *Tagesspiegel*, October 19, 2007.
5. For a full review see, for example, Mercer Management Consulting (2006). *Kundenzufriedenheit im deutschen Drogeriesektor.*
6. Cf., for example, Sprenger, R. (2003). Fairness – Ehrenpreis 2003 an Götz Werner, http://www.fairness-stiftung.de/FS_PM0304.htm [accessed October 6, 2003].
7. A case in point is the Salute to Excellence Award by the Private Label Manufacturers Association (PLMA), awarded for the first time to a firm outside the US in 2008. Cf. http://www.dm-drogeriemarkt. de/dmDHomepage/generator/dmD/Homepage/Unternehmen/ Pressearchiv/2008/Internationale__Auszeichnung__Quama/Internationale_ 20Auszeichnung_20f_C3_BCr_20dm-Qualit_C3_A4tsmarken.html. [accessed January 23, 2009].
8. More specifically, the Ernst & Young Entrepreneur of the Year Award 2008.
9. Cf. Keun, Chr. and Langer, K. (2003). Knüppeln, knausern, kontrollieren. In: *Manager Magazin* online at http://www.manager-magazin.de/koepfe/unt ernehmerarchiv/0,2828,276910,00.html [accessed September 23, 2003].
10. Cf. Dietz and Kracht (2007). Dialogische Unternehmensfuehrung. *Grundlagen – Praxis. Fallbeispiel dm-drogerie markt*, pp. 27–29. Campus.
11. Dietz and Kracht (2007). Dialogische Unternehmensfuehrung. *Grundlagen – Praxis. Fallbeispiel dm-drogerie markt*, p. 121. Campus.
12. Cf. Pullig, K. (2000). *Innovative Unternehmenskulturen: Zwoelf Fallstudien zeitgemaesser Sozialordnungen.* Rosenberger.
13. Dietz and Kracht (2007). Dialogische Unternehmensfuehrung. *Grundlagen – Praxis. Fallbeispiel dm-drogerie markt*, pp. 72ff. Campus.
14. Dietz and Kracht (2007). Dialogische Unternehmensfuehrung. *Grundlagen – Praxis. Fallbeispiel dm-drogerie markt*, pp. 124ff, Campus.
15. Cf. for a fuller account Hage, S. (2006). Gegen den Strom, Artikel von Simon Hage. *Manager Magazin*, March.
16. Cf. Matthiesen, K. (1995). *Kritik des Menschenbildes in der Betriebswirtschaftslehre. Auf dem Weg zu einer sozialoekonomischen Betriebswirtschaftslehre*, p. 109. Haupt.
17. Cf http://www.dm-drogeriemarkt.de/dmDHomepage/generator/dmD/Homepage/ Unternehmen/Pressearchiv/2008/Hans__Globe__Nachhaltigkeitspreis/ Hans__Globe__Nachhaltigkeitspreis.html. [accessed January 23, 2009].

8
Grameen Danone Foods – A Case of a Social Business Enterprise
Doris John

On November 9, 2006, the famous French soccer player Zinedine Zidane inaugurated Grameen Danone Foods Limited (Grameen Danone), near Bogra, about 220 km from Dhaka. A 50:50 joint venture between the Grameen Bank of Bangladesh (Grameen Bank) and Groupe Danone of France (Danone), Grameen Danone was modeled as a "social business enterprise (SBE)." This unique concept was propounded by Prof. Muhammad Yunus, Nobel Laureate and founder of the Grameen Bank. A social business enterprise operates as a no-loss, no-dividend business enterprise, striving for social rather than financial gain. To achieve this end, Danone had innovated effectively to launch a project that would meet the social and economic needs of the local community. The plant at Bogra was built to be a prototype of similar SBEs in Bangladesh and around the world. Despite many challenges, Danone was committed to serve the poorest of the poor in Bangladesh and to succeed in its maiden effort to operate an SBE. Describing Danone's involvement in social businesses as not a "peripheral corporate social responsibility" project, Emmanuel Marchant, Managing Director of Danone Communities, said that such projects made business sense to the company. "This is not about charity for us. This is about business and building our brand,"[1] he said.

Social business – the Grameen way

The two partners of the venture – Grameen Bank and Danone – were pioneers in their own right. The Grameen[2] Bank was formed by Muhammad Yunus in 1983 in response to the need for micro-lending in Bangladesh. Moved by the abject poverty prevailing in his country, Yunus extended loans from his personal finances, on a small scale, to help basket-weavers escape the exorbitant interest charged by money-lenders. Yunus continued extending "micro-loans," much against the advice of traditional banks and the government, and later founded the Grameen Bank on "principles of trust and solidarity" (Exhibit 8.1). Starting with a $27 loan, the Bank had grown to include 7.84 million[3] borrowers, with 97 percent of its borrowers being women. With 2,554 branches, the Grameen Bank provided services in 84,237 villages, covering nearly all the villages in Bangladesh.[4]

Yunus reasoned that, if financial resources can be made available to poor people on reasonable terms, "these millions of small people with their millions of small pursuits can add up to create the biggest development wonder."[5] The Grameen Bank had reversed conventional banking practice by removing the need for collaterals and still boasted of a recovery rate higher than any other banking system. Borrowers were required to join a group with four other borrowers. Initially, loans were given only to two members of the group, and, based on their repayment, loans were extended to others in the group. Groups met weekly with a Grameen representative, and each member handed over the loan repayment in front of the others. Although members were not responsible for repaying each other's loans, such groups provided support and peer pressure. The Bank operated just like any other traditional bank – the majority of the bank's loanable funds were obtained from the central bank, financial institutions, the money market, and aid organizations. However, the repayment rates surpassed those of the traditional system.

Exhibit 8.1   Objectives of the Grameen Bank

The Grameen Bank Project came into operation with the following objectives:

- extend banking facilities to poor men and women;
- eliminate the exploitation of the poor by money lenders;
- create opportunities for self-employment for the vast multitude of unemployed people in rural Bangladesh;
- bring the disadvantaged, mostly the women from the poorest households, within the fold of an organizational format which they can understand and manage by themselves; and
- reverse the age-old vicious circle of 'low income, low saving & low investment', into virtuous circle of 'low income, injection of credit, investment, more income, more savings, more investment, more income'.

Source: A Short History of Grameen Bank, http://www.grameen-info.org/index.php?option=com_content&task=view&id=19&Itemid=114

The Cumulative Amount Disbursed (since inception) was USD 7,971.49 million and the Cumulative Amount Repaid (since inception) was USD 7,071.71 million.[6] Barring a few years of downturn, the bank reported consistent profits.

To address the social needs of its clientele, borrowers were asked to sign up in peer groups to "the 16 Grameen decisions," a range of pledges spanning from day-to-day activities such as vegetable-growing to more serious social issues such as "no dowries." Ninety percent of the Bank's shares are owned by its borrowers, while the remaining 10 percent are owned by the government. Yunus claims that 58 percent of Grameen borrowers had already crossed the poverty line, and his bank had Millennium Goals of reducing the number of poor people in Bangladesh by half by 2015. The Grameen model is applied in projects in over 58 countries, including poor, developing, and developed economies.

Following the success of its bank, Grameen branched into other ventures, providing facilities such as cell phones, clean drinking water, and hospitals to the poor. Operating under the Grameen Foundation, these ventures were conceived as "social businesses." Social Business Enterprises or SBEs are based on the benefit maximization principle. "So far, the main understanding of Business is only for Profit-Making. But no. There can be Business for doing good things also,"[7] Yunus said. According to him, human beings are multi-dimensional, with an urge to be useful and helpful to others. However, the capitalist framework of business did not accommodate this, and thus was born the "social business enterprise." "Profit-making business is ok... It is one door to take. I just created a new door. Everyone can choose,"[8] he said. He pointed out that the model was different from charity in that money recycled in a social business, but not in charity. "Some people may give thousands, millions, even billions. I am not talking about giving away. I am talking about investment. The money recycles. It never stops," he said. He referred to Warren Buffet's donation in 2006 to give USD 31 billion in shares to the Gates Foundation. "He could have set up a social business to fund health insurance for the 47 million in the US without it – and there are lots like him,"[9] Yunus said. "So far, at the end of the year, we ask – How much money did we make? In social business, we can ask – How many children did we get out of malnutrition?" he added.

Inspired by this concept, Franck Riboud, the Chairman and CEO of Groupe Danone, offered to collaborate with Muhammad Yunus to "to do something good." Danone (known as Dannon in the United States) is a French food products company based in Paris. It claimed global leadership position in fresh dairy products, the No. 2 position in bottled water and baby nutrition and the No. 3 position in medical nutrition. It is highly popular through its Danone/Dannon brand of yogurts and Volvic, Evian, and Badoit bottled water. Danone's own history was steeped in corporate social responsibility. Its employees were often reminded of the 1972 "Marseilles Speech," in which its founder, Antoine Riboud, said that "a company's responsibility does not end at the office door or the factory gate, since its action affects the community as a whole."[10] These sentiments have been reflected in Danone's activities, which have sought to combine business success and social progress. The main social cause for Danone was eradicating child malnutrition worldwide, besides other environmental and social issues.

Capitalizing on the sustainability model, Danone had launched operations in developing nations where hunger was a serious problem. "We have major businesses in Brazil, in Indonesia, and in China. Recently we have expanded into India. In fact, more than 40 percent of our business is in developing markets,"[11] Riboud told Yunus during their initial meeting over lunch in Paris in October 2005. It was at this meeting that Grameen Danone was born. "We don't want to sell our products only to the well-off people in those countries. We would like to find ways to help feed the poor," Riboud said, expressing his desire to expand markets. Yunus recalls making an impulsive offer to Riboud. "Your company is a leading producer of nutritious foods. What would you think about creating a joint venture to bring some of your products to the villages of Bangladesh? We could create a company that we own together and call it Grameen Danone. It could manufacture healthful foods that will improve the diet of rural Bangladeshis – especially the children. If the products were sold at a low price, we could make a real difference in the lives of millions of people," Yunus said. Riboud responded spontaneously by agreeing to the offer, saying, "Let's do it." A handshake followed and the deal was sealed. Riboud also agreed to operate the project as a Social Business Enterprise (SBE). "It's a business designed to meet a social goal. In this case, the goal is to improve the nutrition of poor families in the villages of Bangladesh. A social business is a business that pays no dividends. It sells products at prices that make it self-sustaining. The owners of the company can get back the amount they've invested in the company over a period of time, but no profit is paid to investors in the form of dividends. Instead, any profit made stays in the business – to finance expansion, to create new products or services, and to do more good for the world,"[12] Yunus elaborated (Exhibit 8.2: Tenets of an SBE).

"For us, the idea was completely new. So far, our sole objective and mission was to maximize shareholder value. Now, we completely had

Exhibit 8.2 Tenets of an SBE

Features of an SBE

- to be designed and operated to pass on all the benefits to the consumers.
- to be operated without incurring losses.
- to be operated competing with Profit Maximizing Enterprises (PMEs).
- making profit by an SBE shall be consistent and desirable
  - to generate enough surplus to pay back the invested capital to the investors as early as possible
  - to generate surplus for –
- Expansion.
- Improvement of quality.
- Increasing efficiency through introducing new technology.
- Innovative marketing to reach the deeper layers of low-income people and disadvantaged communities.
- Undertake research and experimentation to improve and diversify products and services.

Dividend Policy of SBE

- Investors' capital out of the profit will be paid back within a time period agreed upon by the investors.
- After the capital amount is paid back, SBEs may even give a nominal annual fixed dividend (not above 5 percent).
- Bottom line for an SBE will always be to deliver benefits to people, rather than to earn money for the investors.

Share Transfer

- If an investor wants to withdraw his investment from an SBE at any point of time, he may do so, provided he sells his shares to the existing shareholders, or to a new shareholder who accepts the philosophy, practice and conventions of a SBE.

Source: www.adbi.org/conf-seminar-papers/2007/07/03/2311.microfinance/ – 19k – [accessed October 11, 2010].

to change perspective. Profit was now a condition, a means – it was no more the end, no more the goal. This changed all the approach,"[13] said Emmanuel Faber, the chief of Danone's operation in Asia, who had been assigned to oversee operations of Grameen Danone. The 50:50 joint venture was established with an authorized capital of USD 3.67 million and a paid-up capital of USD 1.103 million, and registered under the Companies (Bangladesh) Act. The partnership was between Group Danone and four other companies of the Grameen Bank. The word "Grameen" was included in the name of the company to capitalize on the strong brand name Grameen had created for itself in Bangladesh.

Grameen had a presence in almost every village of Bangladesh and had become ubiquitous through its Grameen Telecom and other companies. There were nearly 30 Grameen companies, ranging from the country's biggest phone firm to a company supplying affordable health care. Grameen Danone was also supported by the Danone communities, a venture capital investment fund set up by Danone to "support the development of businesses with a strong and lasting social impact." A USD 70 million fund, the Danone communities channeled 90 percent of its investment into low-risk not-for-profit social ventures in developing countries and the remaining 10 percent into higher-risk social ventures. Being conceived as a social business, Grameen Danone was free from shareholder pressure demanding quick returns. The project, however, had to be self-supporting to generate funds for its operations. At the same time, maximization of social goals had to be achieved. With this in mind, the mission and objectives of Grameen Danone were chalked out after initial rounds of meetings involving both sides (Exhibit 8.3).

The Grameen Danone venture would produce and market yogurt that would provide poor Bangladeshi children with "a healthy and nutritious food that they can consume every day." Branded "Shoktidoi,"[14] the yogurt was designed to provide nutrients essential to the health of the Bangladeshi population, especially children. Reports indicated the following:

1. Fifty-six percent of Bangladeshi children under the age of five suffer from moderate to severe malnutrition.
2. Twenty-one percent of these children are significantly underweight.[15]

Exhibit 8.3   Mission and Objectives of Grameen Danone

Mission

"Reducing poverty by a unique proximity business model that will provide daily healthy nutrition to the poor."

Specific objectives

- Strong leadership by senior executives
- Sharing best practices to have a greater impact
- Engaging others to increase their sustainability portfolio
- Education on sustainability to ensure that the bank's vision was carried out throughout the organization

Source: http://www.danonecommunities.com/project/

To address these issues, Grameen Danone collaborated with GAIN (an NGO dedicated to fighting malnutrition around the world) to conduct a detailed analysis of their nutritional deficiencies. The results showed a deficiency in many nutrients, including vitamin A, iron, and so forth. The product, therefore, had to be enriched with these nutrients. Also, the price had to be affordable by the poorest of the poor, and hence manufacturing costs had to be kept at a minimal level (Annex 8.1: Some facts about Bangladesh). "We had never before found a model for really poor populations,"[16] says Emmanuel Marchant, managing director of Danone Communities.

The plant at Bogra – a challenge to innovation

Production

While the concept of a social business enterprise was highly appealing to Danone, its skills and capabilities were put to the test as never before. It had to evolve a model that optimized on all resources available, but still delivered on social, environmental, and economic fronts. For instance, the design of the factory to produce Shoktidoi had to be "diametrically opposed to all western management principles: very little automation and a large staff to help create jobs." Recounting his experience, Guy Gavelle, Danone's Director of Production, Quality and Food Safety for Asia, said that the project, the smallest he had built thus far, was in stark contrast to the large production facilities built to cater to larger markets.

> In Bogra it was easy. I just did the opposite of what I've been doing up to now! We built it in three months with only EUR 700,000. Normally, I work on facilities that are 50 to 100 times larger and fully automated. In Bogra, however, something less automated was needed that could accommodate more staff working at jobs for which most of them were not highly skilled. All in all, it was impossible to rely on existing plans or to use standard equipment, which was usually European. I had to find new Bangladeshi suppliers to provide us with appropriate solutions. This was a very exciting challenge for all of us. We also had to reduce operating costs as much as possible, have a positive environmental impact, and so on. For each problem, we had to come up with totally new solutions. What comes to mind is our use of gases from waste composting to light the factory. We even had to rethink the way in which we develop the product. Using sugar, for example, would have meant importing it, which would

have been expensive and not profitable for the local economy. We therefore chose to use date palm molasses. We also had to deal with the lack of a cold chain between the milk collection points and the factory: we tracked down the perfect product for preserving the quality of the milk during transport. All these constraints required us to be more inventive and to really keep challenging ourselves! Today, I know that some of these 'far-out' ideas will be applied elsewhere in the Danone group.[17] (Guy Gavelle)

To operate profitably, the Grameen Danone Foods joint venture would have to slash manufacturing costs to one-third the average cost per ton in other countries. The cost of Shoktidoi had to be kept to the barest minimum. With this in mind, Grameen Danone had introduced an optimized production process for manufacturing the yoghurt. The manufacturing unit was established on 800 sq. m of land in Banani Betgari, an area close to Bogra town. Although the factory, with an area of 7,500 sq. ft, was only about 1 percent of the size of most Danone plants, it was "more advanced than the huge plants I have designed in Brazil, Indonesia, China, and India," Guy Gavelle commented. The project had to conform to the social requirements:

- reduce raw material costs (no import tariffs, simplified logistical chain)
- minimize consumption of fossil fuels (less transport)
- promote the development of local communities and combat rural exodus.

Very little machinery, and wherever possible only simple equipment, easy to maintain and able to be operated by relatively unskilled workers, was used. To reduce cost, most of the equipment was purchased either locally or from China, while fully complying with the technical specifications laid down by Groupe Danone. In order to ensure adherence to the quality parameters, all other ingredients (apart from milk and date molasses), such as cornstarch and micronutrients (vitamins, iron, protein, and so forth), were imported and supplied by Groupe Danone itself. The production process at the Grameen Danone plant in Bogra had been optimized, bringing the cost of the plant to only 25 percent per ton, the normal cost in other Danone plants.

Milk was the main ingredient, and hence its uninterrupted supply at a reasonable cost was crucial. Also, 90 percent of the Bangladeshi milk market was unorganized. To ensure smooth supply and to avoid competing with other purchasers, Grameen Danone developed a series of micro-farms to which Grameen Bank offered micro-credit. Farmers would buy cows with the loan and supply milk to Grameen Danone at a guaranteed fixed price through the year.[18] Grameen Danone supported farmers by sending veterinary experts to help them improve yield and quality. Irregular monsoons affected milk production, so, to ensure consistent supply, the company organized cooperatives and set up refrigerated collection centers to deliver milk.

To sweeten the yoghurt, date molasses was used instead of sugar. A kind of syrup secreted naturally by date palms, date molasses was available locally and used in local dishes to add flavor. With a sweetening power approximately 70 percent that of sugar, date molasses was substantially cheaper. Grameen Danone planned to develop its existing farms to supply date molasses through micro-credit.[19]

As of 2007, the Bogra factory processed around 6,000 l of milk on a daily basis to produce 3,000 kg of yoghurt. It aimed to increase production up to 10,000 kg/day by the third year and beyond. The facility was manned by 35 employees, who were mostly from the local community.[20] After months of intensive research, scientists at Danone's research and design center developed a recipe that would be "inexpensive to produce and meet basic nutritional requirements, but still have a pleasant flavor and texture." Offered in a single flavor and priced at Tk 5 (approximately seven US cents) per 80 g cup, "Shoktidoi" provided 30 percent of a child's daily requirements of vitamin A, iron, zinc, and iodine.

Distribution

"Shoktidoi" was distributed through door-to-door sales and via local stores. Grameen Danone adopted a "proximity business model," which had both suppliers and consumers in close proximity to the plant. This helped maintain taste and acidity levels in the yoghurt, which required cooling until consumption. Since refrigerated storage and transport were not available, this proximity model was a feasible alternative. According to Yunus, "our distribution system had to be designed in such a way that it ensured a quick turnaround from factory to consumer, with yoghurt leaving the production line in the morning and ending up in children's stomachs within 48 hours. This would be the only way to ensure that the flavor, texture, and acid content of our yoghurt would be consistent."

"Shoktidoi" was transported using rickshaw vans to points of sale within 5 km of the plant. The lack of an expensive cold chain was overcome by substituting isothermal crates and ice packs. The door-to-door selling of the yogurt was done by "Grameen Ladies," local ladies who were recruited to carry on the sale. Nearly 300 of these women carried the yogurt in specially designed chilled and insulated bags and sold "Shoktidoi" to villages within a radius of 30 km. They sold the cups on a door-to-door basis and earned a commission of just over a cent on each container sold (Tk 0.5/cup).[21] On an average, each vendor sold around 60–70 cups per day, and through experience they had learnt how much stock they could sell every day, and thus order accordingly, to minimize wastage. They were trained to convey a nutrition-based message using visual aids developed in partnership with Danone and GAIN (Global Alliance for Improved Nutrition). Recruiting "Grameen Ladies" proved difficult, because Bangladeshis believed that people who go from door to door were beggars. To remove this stigma, the company launched a public information campaign in neighboring villages. Apart from door-to-door sales, "Shoktidoi" was distributed through small shops at Bogra. Dispensers were placed at these outlets, so that customers could also bring their own containers to buy the yoghurt. The dispensers at the shops were refilled every day by the company with fresh yoghurt. Later, 200 small shops were supplied with refrigerators.

To popularize the product, the marketing strategy developed was also tailored to the local context, and emphasized the importance of nutrition. Informative posters were displayed at the meeting centers used by the Grameen Bank borrower groups every week. Nearly 160,000 women met at these centers, and this was an ideal platform to target potential consumers.[22] Campaigns were also conducted at schools in Bogra.

Eco-friendly initiatives

In keeping with the objectives of the project, the Grameen Danone venture was designed to be eco-friendly in all possible ways. The plant had been designed to avoid wasting electricity wherever possible by using energy-saving lights, timers on light switches, and so forth. As a pioneering effort and the first of its kind in Bangladesh, a waste water treatment station was installed at the plant. The system produced biogas, which was used for lighting at the plant. A rainwater collection system and solar water heaters were also in place. The container in which the yoghurt was sold was made of cornstarch instead of plastic. Cornstarch was biodegradable and, if buried, was transformed into a nutrient-rich substance suitable as a fertilizer. The plant had a specially prepared pit for recycling used containers. At the behest of Yunus, the team at Grameen Danone was trying to design edible containers. "Well, it is poor people, and they have paid for it! Why pay for something they don't need?"[23] Yunus said.

Originally, Grameen Danone had set a short-term plan to set up two more plants by 2008 and a long-term plan to establish 50 more factories in the next ten years in various remote areas across the country. Apart from the employees at the Bogra plant, the door-to-door distribution system also provided employment for more than 300 women in the rural areas that surround the plant, with 400 farmers supplying the milk. In 2008, the Danone communities FCPR (French Risk Mutual Fund) announced that it would invest in Grameen Danone to increase the size of the Bogra plant and to build a second production unit near Dhaka. Once the Bogra factory had reached its full capacity, the project's social impact was bound to increase.[24]

The social business Enterprise – a challenging business proposition

Recognizing its social, ethical, and environmental performance, CSR Europe, a non-profit organization that supports companies in their CSR initiatives, named Grameen Danone Foods as one of the top five social responsibility solutions at an event organized in Brussels in November 2007. Danone expressed satisfaction about the project, but admitted that several challenges remained before the company could proceed to build similar factories in other poor communities. One of the chief concerns was that the sales efforts through the "Grameen Ladies" lacked professionalism. Also, due to the perishable nature of the product, distribution and marketing were a major issue.[25] Among other things, rising costs for basic agricultural goods were forcing Danone to raise prices on "Shoktidoi" by about one-third. The profit margin was only Tk 0.5/cup, and according to Danone the operation did not yield profit as yet. "We're still in the pilot phase," said Emmanuel Marchant, managing director of Danone Communities. Apart from operational challenges, the project faced culture incompatibility between the highly educated and experienced Danone professionals and the more laid-back and less skilled Bangladeshis of Grameen. However, it was the single-minded goal of creating a social business enterprise that kept these two disparate organizations together. Danone was continuously innovating the business model and implementing changes to counter these challenges.

Despite the challenges, Danone's involvement in the project seemed to have paid off well. It was argued that, for the US$ 1 million that

Danone had invested in the Bogra plant, a small amount for a company with revenues of nearly USD 17,656.7 million, the investment had earned significant returns that were hard to measure financially. Danone had learnt invaluable lessons. According to the company, it had "learnt how to cut energy and save money in its supply chain and how to sell the idea of nutrition to the poor in emerging markets. And then there is the reputation rub-off of being associated with Yunus, founder of the Grameen Bank..."[26] Yunus' book, "Creating a World Without Poverty: Social Business and the Future of Capitalism," opened with several pages on Danone's chief, Frank Riboud. The venture met with not only Danone's social objective of combating child malnutrition, but also the objectives of extending its brand in developing countries and maintaining its reputation for social responsibility. Riboud had described the venture as a win-win situation: "it is both emotional, and also a growth strategy for our company; with this we are building not only the image, but also the future of our company." At the opening ceremony of Grameen Danone, Riboud had expressed that "the strength in its [Grameen Danone's] success lies in the fact that it is a business (not a charity), and if it is a business, it is sustainable...and if it works, we plan to take it to Africa and other developing countries."[27] Danone had not ruled out the future possibility of doing business the conventional way in Bangladesh. It also reported that many NGOs had vied to be part of the project, and some had even offered to pay to be part of the venture. Danone commented that dialog with these NGOs would not have been possible if it had ventured into Bangladesh without the association with Grameen. Yunus' model of social business, however, did not seek just revenue but social returns, and returned the profits to the communities where the business operated.

In the case of the Grameen Danone project it was evident that the social goals the project was helping to achieve were varied.

- The nutritional profit[28]

According to Danone, with over 2 million units of yoghurt sold in 2008, mostly within a radius of 40 km around the plant in Bogra, representing a penetration rate of approximately 40 percent in villages in the area, the Grameen Danone project can have a real impact on the health of children living in the region.[29] This impact was being measured by the long-term study of 100,000 children undertaken by GAIN with assistance from the Johns Hopkins University. To increase the reach of its products, Grameen Danone had expanded its range with two new flavors. It was also reported that the live cultures of "Shoktidoi" reduced the intensity and length of diarrhea.

- The employment profit

Based on the proximity model, jobs had been created locally along the entire value-chain of the project – at the micro-farms, the factory, and the distribution channel. The "Grameen Ladies" had increased their income through the distribution of "Shoktidoi."[30] Also, the factory at Bogra had been designed to favor local employment rather than the use of sophisticated machinery, in order to create employment and avoid recurrent equipment maintenance problems. With increase in scale, local employment opportunities are bound to increase. Thus, with the development of local employment that does not compete with existing networks, Grameen Danone helps fight against rural exodus, which is a major challenge in Bangladesh. Furthermore, Grameen Danone plans to attract local investment and promote local entrepreneurs who will also have ownership of the project.[31]

- Eliminating negative impact on the environment

The project achieved these profits – nutritional and employment – without compromising on the third bottom line: environmental issues. Grameen Danone tried to implement eco-friendly policies in all its activities. It used biodegradable packaging, reduced energy use and recycled wherever possible. Even the rickshaw vans used in distribution did not use any natural gas or oil.

> If we can create this, the world will be a much better place. What if we lived in a world where companies didn't measure their performance only in terms of revenue and profitability? What if pharmaceutical companies reported on their bottom lines, along with those familiar figures, the number of lives saved by their drugs every quarter, and food companies reported the number of children rescued from malnutrition? What if companies issued separate stock based on social returns, and people could buy the shares of those that saved more lives than others, or sell the shares of energy companies that polluted more than their competitors? What if, by raising 'social capital' and investing it in sustainable businesses without a profit motive, companies could reach into new markets, expanding their core businesses at the same time they improved lives?[32] (Muhammad Yunus)

Danone was very committed to the project and would not have wanted to let the social business experiment fail. Drawing from the case of Grameen Danone, the critical success factors required for such projects are the:

- involvement and commitment of top management
- single-minded goal to succeed at all costs
- constant innovation to optimize resources to achieve the set social objectives and make the project self-sustaining.

Enthused by the progress of Grameen Danone and undeterred by recession, Danone announced new partnerships with social entrepreneurs in Senegal and Cambodia. According to Yunus, an SBE provided a whole new way of looking at business. "Once you take the profit-making glasses off, and ... the social business glasses on, all your thinking changes. From what I hear, this little plant has touched the hearts of all Danone employees worldwide. They think they should also have it in Brazil and China,"[33] Yunus said. With increasing collaboration between social entrepreneurs and private sector business, involving social profit-oriented shareholders, the number of SBEs is bound to increase.

Appendix 8.1 Bangladesh: Development indicators

Non-MDG

Population in millions	142.46	(2008)
Annual population growth rate (%)	1.3	(2006–2008)
Adult literacy rate (%)	26.7	(2007)
Percent of population in urban areas	26.7	(2007)
MDG		
Percent of population living on less than $1.25 a day	49.6	(2005)
Percent of population living below the national poverty line	40.0	(2005)
Under-5 mortality rate per 1,000 live births	61	(2007)
Percent of population using an improved drinking water source	80	(2006)

MDG = Millennium Development Goal.
Sources: ADB 2009 Basic Statistics 2009 Mania.
UNESCO 2009 Institute for statistics Data Centre.
World Bank 2009 World Development Indicators Online.

Notes

1. Black, Liam. Pots of gold, http://www.guardian.co.uk/society/2009/feb/18/liam-black-bangladesh. February 18, 2009.
2. Grameen means "rural" or "village" in the Bangla language.
3. Figures as of April 2009.
4. Introduction, http://www.grameen-info.org/index.php?option=com_content&task=view&id=16&Itemid=112. May 12, 2009.
5. http://www.grameen-info.org/index.php?option=com_content&task=view&id=16&Itemid=112
6. http://www.grameen-info.org/index.php?option=com_content&task=view&id=453&Itemid=527
7. Schneider, Eric. Muhammad Yunus Recounts Grameen Success Stories. http://www.pnyv.org/index.php?id=34&tx_ttnews[tt_news]=1568&tx_ttnews[backPid]=29&cHash=c8a27af195, 2008.
8. Schneider Eric. Muhammad Yunus Recounts Grameen Success Stories. http://www.pnyv.org/index.php?id=34&tx_ttnews[tt_news]=1568&tx_ttnews[backPid]=29&cHash=c8a27af195, 2008.
9. Grameen Bank began with a $27 loan. http://www.grameen-info.org/index.php?option=com_content&task=view&id=396&Itemid=199
10. http://dannon.com/pdf/2007DannonCSROverview.pdf
11. Excerpt from *Creating a World Without Poverty.* http://www.npr.org/templates/story/story.php?storyId=18008873
12. Excerpt from *Creating a World Without Poverty.* http://www.npr.org/templates/story/story.php?storyId=18008873
13. Schneider, Eric. Muhammad Yunus Recounts Grameen Success Stories. http://www.pnyv.org/index.php?id=34&tx_ttnews[tt_news]=1568&tx_ttnews[backPid]=29&cHash=c8a27af195, 2008.
14. "Shoktidoi" in Bengali means "that which builds strength."
15. Discover The Project. http://www.danonecommunities.com/en/grameendanonefood?detail=more [accessed October 11, 2010].
16. Danone innovates to help feed the poor. http://www.businessweek.com/globalbiz/content/apr2008/gb20080428_971498.htm
17. http://www.danonecommunities.com/project/
18. Ghalib Kamran Asad and Hossain Farhad. *Social Business Enterprises – Maximizing Social Benefits or Maximising Profits? The Case of Grameen-Danone Foods Limited.* http://papers.ssrn.com/sol3/papers.cfm?abstract_id= 1265652 [accessed October 11, 2010].
19. http://www.danone.at/fileadmin/template/Downloads/Presse/DP_GrameenDanoneFoods_GB.pdf
20. Ghalib Kamran Asad and Hossain Farhad. *Social Business Enterprises – Maximizing Social Benefits or Maximising Profits? The Case of Grameen-Danone Foods Limited.* www.bwpi.manchester.ac.uk/resources/Working-Papers/51-GhalibHossain-grameen_danone-abstract.pdf, July 2008.
21. Ghalib Kamran Asad and Hossain Farhad. *Social Business Enterprises – Maximizing Social Benefits or Maximising Profits? The Case of Grameen-Danone Foods Limited.* www.bwpi.manchester.ac.uk/resources/Working-Papers/51-GhalibHossain-grameen_danone-abstract.pdf, July 2008.

22. Ghalib Kamran Asad and Hossain Farhad. *Social Business Enterprises – Maximizing Social Benefits or Maximising Profits? The Case of Grameen-Danone Foods Limited.* www.bwpi.manchester.ac.uk/resources/Working-Papers/ 51-GhalibHossain-grameen_danone-abstract.pdf, July 2008.

23. Schneider, Eric. Muhammad Yunus Recounts Grameen Success Stories. http://pnyv.org/index.php?id=541&tx_ttnews%5Btt_news%5D=1568&tx_ ttnews%5BbackPid%5D=530&cHash=18dbdd8433, 2008

24. *Sustainability Report.* Groupe Danone, 2007.

25. Black, Liam. Pots of gold. http://www.guardian.co.uk/society/2009/feb/18/ liam-black-bangladesh. February 18, 2009.

26. Sustainability. www.svneurope.com/readarticle/312–23k

27. Ghalib Kamran Asad and Hossain Farhad. *Social Business Enterprises – Maximizing Social Benefits or Maximising Profits? The Case of Grameen-Danone Foods Limited.* www.bwpi.manchester.ac.uk/resources/Working-Papers/51- GhalibHossain-grameen_danone-abstract.pdf, July 2008

28. Muhammad Yunus. *Building Social Business Models: Lessons from the Grameen Experience.* HEC Paris – Working Paper 913, February 2009.

29. *Danone 08 Sustainability Report.* http://www.danone.com/images/pdf/ danone_rtdd_2008_en.pdf

30. *Danone 08 Sustainability Report.* http://www.danone.com/images/pdf/ danone_rtdd_2008_en.pdf

31. Muhammad Yunus. *Building Social Business Models: Lessons from the Grameen Experience.* HEC Paris – Working Paper 913, February 2009.

32. Prasso Sheridan. Saving the world with a cup of yogurt. http://www.sheridan- prasso.com/fortune_yunus_yogurt.htm [accessed October 11, 2010].

33. Schneider, Eric. Muhammad Yunus Recounts Grameen Success Stories. http://pnyv.org/index.php?id=541&tx_ttnews%5Btt_news%5D=1568&tx_ ttnews%5BbackPid%5D=530&cHash=18dbdd8433, 2008.

9
Entrepreneurship, Humanistic Management and Business Turnaround: The Case of a Small Chinese Private Firm

Fang Lee Cooke

Introduction

Aspirational managers around the world often look to business giants for recipes of success, but few organizations are able to remodel these success stories. Is being big essential to be successful? Do we have to employ the best and the brightest talent to create an innovative and high-performing workforce? Do we not live in a reality where over 90 percent of firms are of small and medium size, measured by the number of people employed? Is it not the case that the majority of the workforce, particularly those in less developed countries, are less than optimally educated and poorly equipped for a knowledge economy that is believed to be embracing the world? Can ordinary small firms have a successful story?

China's shortage of human capital, particularly in the form of management competence and entrepreneurship, has been widely reported.[1] This paper reports the process of business turnaround of a small Chinese manufacturing company that is privately owned. It examines how the combination of entrepreneurial leadership and a humanistic management approach has created a success story for a firm that employs primarily rural migrant workers with relatively low levels of education and skills. It must be acknowledged at the outset that this case study is drawn from work conducted by Miao and Yao,[2] who conducted the fieldwork with the company.

Background

Hongfei Metal Ltd (a pseudonym: hereafter Hongfei) was initially set up in the late 1980s as a small township-and-village enterprise (TVE) in a small town in Zhejiang Province, located on the eastern coast of China. Zhejiang is one of the most economically developed provinces, powered by the mushrooming growth of TVEs and private businesses run by farmer-turned entrepreneurs. Built from the "remnants of the disintegrating people's communes,"[3] TVEs have been praised as one of the wonders of the Chinese economic reform beginning in the late 1970s. A major economic strategy adopted by the Chinese government in the mid-1980s to combat the stagnating income from farming was to stimulate non-agricultural production. Consequently, TVEs have been encouraged to grow throughout the 1980s and 1990s to create jobs mainly for the labor force in rural China. Over the years, the number of people employed in TVEs has continued to grow. By 2006, the number of people employed by TVEs had reached 146.8 million, compared with 64.3 million employed by the state-owned sector, which was once the dominant employer.[4] TVEs have become the most vibrant part of China's marketizing economy, absorbing surplus rural labor, processing agricultural products, and diversifying production into a range of consumer goods and products for both the home market and export. Sources of their competitive advantages come mainly from favorable tax policies and the abundant availability of a highly mobile and flexible labor force.[5] Most TVEs are collectively owned by the local citizens or privately owned, but they may often be controlled by the local government. This tie with the government is important for gaining access to resources such as bank loans and bureaucratic approval.[6] Compared with state-owned enterprises, TVEs may be more innovative, proactive and risk-taking when they encounter an adversarial business environment.[7] The majority of TVEs are labor-intensive and operate with a low level of technology and low profit margin. Human resource management (HRM) practices in these firms have been typically informal, with little training provision beyond the immediate skill needs of the firm. Wage levels are relatively low, and employees tend to work long hours and overtime to make up for the low wages.[8]

It is in this context that Hongfei was set up and operated. Employing some 350 employees, it specializes in the production of small mechanical components such as wire bars and metal rings. Products are supplied to other manufacturing firms as part of their final products. In the mid-1990s, Hongfei was in deficit due to poor management by the previous

CEO, and wage payments were regularly delayed. In 1998, Mr Li Haitao was given the task by the local government, which owned Hongfei at the time, of taking over the company and turning it around. At that time, the products that Hongfei produced relied on labor-intensive work with no trade secrets. Market competition was fierce and chaotic due to the coexistence of a large number of TVEs that were engaged in similar business in the region. Nevertheless, Hongfei was one of the largest enterprises of the town, and its business performance had an important bearing on the economy of the town and the life of its people. It was an enterprise that had once been seen as the pride of the town.[9]

After taking over as the CEO of Hongfei, Li's first priority was to raise money to pay the wages owed to the workers. He did so in spite of the concern from his management team that the workers would not stay with the firm once they received their wages. Li held a meeting with all his workers and announced that those who wished to stay would be well treated, but those who wished to leave were most welcome to come back any time. It was reported that his sincerity touched the workers and the majority of them chose to stay. As part of the restructuring process, Hongfei changed its ownership from being a local government-invested TVE to a privately owned enterprise. The majority of the shares were held by the management team and a small proportion were held by the workers. Another of Li's priorities was to develop new products and identify new markets in order to lift the company out of the competition trap. After market research and analysis, Li led his workers to launch a new product component for electrical fan manufacturing firms. This proved to be a success, and Hongfei was beginning to break even. Li's business philosophy, according to his interview with Miao and Yao,[10] is that a business exists to benefit its people. And his subsequent business turnaround strategy and human resource practices seem to reflect this humanistic underpinning.

Embracing social responsibility

Investing in people – Li gave his workers a pay rise of 15 percent in the year when the business started to make a profit. This was followed by another pay rise of 20 percent in the following year. Within 2 years, Hongfei leapt from being the largest employer to the highest-paying employer in the town. In addition, the company spent over RMB 200,000 (approximately USD 30,000) to set up a recreational centre for its employees. The centre contains a fully equipped multifunctional singing and dance hall, a swimming pool of 250 m², table tennis and basketball facilities, and so forth. This heavy investment aimed at enhancing the staff's welfare and well-being has triggered negative remarks about Li outside the company. It was reported that some fellow businessmen held the view that Li should invest the money in business development instead of recreational pursuits. But Li believed, as he disclosed to Miao and Yao,[11] that it was more important to raise the morale and motivation of employees through work–life balance and social bonding activities. Only then will employees be committed to the company and perform effectively.

In the ensuing 3 years, Hongfei maintained a high level of investment in employees, including free lunch for employees (unlimited portions), providing basic housing for key technical and production staff, providing dormitory accommodation for non-local employees, and sending rural migrant workers to technical colleges for skill training for 6 months. Providing subsidized housing/accommodation arrangements for employees was a typical form of workplace welfare in the state sector during the state-planned economy period of Socialist China.[12] This welfare has diminished as a result of the state sector reform in the 1990s. By contrast, TVEs and privately owned factories that employ rural migrant workers continue to provide free or subsidized accommodation to their workers to compensate for low wages, to better utilize workers' productive time, and to facilitate the administrative control of migrant workers from local labor authorities.[13] It has been noted that this "dormitory labor"[14] regime is exploited by profit-hungry proprietors in order to maximize labor control and productivity through excessively long hours, which workers are often willing to work to increase their earnings. But exploitation, hidden or blatant, is not the motive of Hongfei, whose CEO is not the owner of the business and holds a management philosophy of "from the people, for the people, to the people." There is no compulsory overtime or restriction of movement of employees in their spare time. Unlike many foreign-funded sweatshop plants, where a dozen rural migrant workers share a small bedroom with poor sanitary facilities, Hongfei provided its migrant workers with spacious accommodation, where three workers shared one bedroom with a built-in bathroom. Employees who experienced family problems (e.g., serious illness or death of family members) or financial hardship were visited at home and provided with material and emotional support. According to the workers interviewed, the quality of life of Hongfei's employees had improved significantly by 2003. Staff turnover rate was low, as employees felt attached to the firm.

Business crossroads – Hongfei also invested heavily in quality assurance by employing two senior engineers from Shanghai and Suzhou city to oversee the quality of the products. As the product quality of TVEs was generally low in relative terms, this emphasis on quality differentiated Hongfei's products from its competitors. However, the company's long-term future was still vulnerable, as it was still trapped in its business profile of a small range of simple products. With electricity fan production reaching market saturation by early 2000s, Hongfei's business prospects were becoming less clear. Business loss and plant closure were never far away, just as in the case of many other small private firms in China. How should Hongfei make its next move? According to the employees interviewed, most employees became increasingly concerned, and were actively involved in giving suggestions for business redevelopment. Both management and workers went through months of anxiety without any sign of a solution. It was reported that the CEOs of other companies were making sarcastic comments in the community, such as "Li is more suitable to be a philanthropist than an entrepreneur" and "Hongfei will face closure sooner or later."

Product innovation through employee involvement – Li decided to take his management team abroad for an inspection and learning tour to gain ideas. This is a common practice in the state sector and large privately owned companies, but is much less common among small privately owned firms due to resource constraints. When the team returned, a very bold business proposal emerged – Hongfei would bid to make display shelves for Wal-Mart in China. The management team believed that, given Wal-Mart's rapid expansion in China since the 2000s, this would give the company a secure business source. Moreover, once Hongfei secured its supplier's position with Wal-Mart, other businesses would follow, due to Wal-Mart's prestige. The main challenge, however, was that numerous Chinese companies had aimed to become the shelving supplier to Wal-Mart, but had failed to meet its high technical specifications. A series of discussions and debates took place in Hongfei at various levels, although the main discussions were held among a core group of 12 to 15 or so technical staff and managers. Some staff were skeptical about Hongfei's capacity to meet the high specifications demanded, in view of their predecessors' failure to do so. Hongfei needed to make a heavy investment in new machinery in order to be able to produce the trial product. Technical and production workers also needed to develop their skills. If the bid failed, all investment would be lost. The management team became hesitant about whether this would be a wise move. But the employees' enthusiasm had overtaken events. Driven by the fear of business closure and job losses and the excitement of trying something new and groundbreaking, nearly 100 production workers, led by the core technical staff who were closely involved in the discussions, collectively signed a letter and presented it to the management – they were determined to have a go, and requested the support of the management team.

The management team made the decision to go ahead. A project team was subsequently formed consisting of around 15 managers, key technical staff, and production workers. During the next 124 sleepless days and nights, the project team members worked and lived in the factory together, led by the chief engineer. Li was closely involved throughout the problem-solving period, overseeing the project and providing moral support to the project team. After many failed attempts, they finally produced a product that met Wal-Mart's requirements, and became its supplier. Shortly after, Hongfei secured business orders with other multinational supermarket chains in China, including IKEA and Carrefour. In 2004, Hongfei reached another new milestone – from being the highest-paying employer to the most profitable enterprise in town.

Key success factors – The success of Hongfei was heavily influenced by a number of key factors, including the entrepreneurship and leadership of its CEO and his humanistic approach to people management. Many of Hongfei's HR practices demonstrate a strong Chinese culture, characterized by paternalistic care, collectivism, altruism, and a "can do" culture.

Entrepreneurial leadership – The entrepreneurship of Li has opened up new product markets for Hongfei on two occasions. The first was identifying the electrical fan market. This lifted Hongfei out of debt, and it became profitable. The second occasion was a path-breaking adventure for the firm, going from competing in an undifferentiated product market marked by low technology and low profit margins to being a niche product manufacturer with a string of foreign multinational giants as its clients. Li played the multiple roles of an entrepreneur, innovator, employer, and owner–manager. He used his management philosophy and astute business sense to shape the organizational behavior, human resource practices, and growth pattern of the firm. According to the workers interviewed, Li was a hands-on commander and led his troops from the front. He had a style of "I will not ask you to do what I will not do myself." He also retained the employees through paternalistic care and emotion bonding, or in Chinese *ganqing liuren*. As such, Li is highly respected as a CEO by his workers.

Li's leadership style and management philosophy feature the desired attributes of a good leader in China,[15] although his philosophy may not be endorsed by some of his fellow entrepreneurs. Chinese workers are known to prefer leaders who are modest and strategic, as well as hands-on and practical.[16] In other words, competent Chinese leaders should be visionary and competent workers who have worked their way up so that they are familiar with the business. At the same time, they should also be compassionate and prudent individuals who care for and are always ready to provide guidance to their subordinates. In addition, Chinese managers are typically collective-oriented and Confucianist in their outlook and management style, although it has been noted that the younger generation of Chinese managers are more willing to take risks in the pursuit of profits.[17] They also demonstrate a high level of moral character in their actions and decisions, reflecting the deep-rooted influence of Confucian values.[18] In the case of Li, he showed a high level of democracy by actively involving his employees in the company's decision-making and problem-solving. He also displayed a strong sense of Confucian humanism in his management philosophy (see below for discussion).

Humanistic and welfare-oriented HR practices – In China, taking care of employees, particularly when they are experiencing difficulties and hardships, is considered a moral duty and a social obligation of the employer. Employee welfare is one of the essential ingredients of organizational culture management.[19] It focuses on the material welfare and physical well-being of employees. Attention is paid to improving employees' quality of life by improving their living standards and working conditions, usually through bonuses, subsidized canteens, transportation to work, health care provision, and better working and living environments. Some firms also extend their welfare activities to sending employees birthday presents, visiting them when they get married or when there is a bereavement in the family, and providing hardship funds to employees whose families are going through difficult times. The objective of this is to alleviate employees' non-work-related worries and let them feel the warmth of the company so that they can concentrate on their work. Hongfei's high level of investment in its employees and the extensive provision of workplace welfare reflect this Chinese value with a humanistic orientation.

To some extent, the objective of the employee welfare programs adopted by Hongfei (and other Chinese firms) is similar to that of the Employee Assistance Programs (EAPs) developed in Western organizations. They are grounded in a humanistic paradigm and aimed to manage dysfunctional stressors originating from work and non-work sources. The main difference between the two is that EAPs provide a range of psychological services to help employees cope with emotional difficulties, family issues, financial problems, and so forth.[20] By contrast, employee welfare programs in China provide primarily material services with a lesser degree of emotional support. Professional psychological counseling remains rare, though it is slowly on the increase. Employee welfare programs are targeted at the whole workforce and not just those in need. It is expected that the psychological outcome (e.g., enhanced commitment, motivation, and morale) will be achieved through material support to satisfy their physiological and environmental needs. The emphasis on material provision to enrich employees' material and spiritual life is important in China because it is a relatively poor country and the majority of its workers can only earn enough for the most basic living.

Employee entertainment is another important component of organizational culture-building in China.[21] This takes the form of provision of a range of workplace entertainment. Examples include sports events, arts competitions, theatrical performances, local festive competitions, holiday trips, libraries, games rooms, literary clubs, match-making, and fashion shows. Again, these activities are aimed at enhancing the employees' quality of life in order to retain and motivate employees. Compared with the employee welfare activities, these activities are aimed at satisfying a higher level of employees' needs. Employee entertainment programs also fulfill a deeper social function. The Chinese culture is a collective and relationship-based culture. A workplace plays an important role in providing social bonding activities to develop and maintain a harmonious relationship among employees and between the firm and its workforce.

Hongfei's high investment in, and extensive welfare arrangements for, its employees reflect this traditional Chinese culture and prove highly effective, with congruent power. The workforce reciprocated with a high level of commitment and engagement when the firm was at the crossroads on two occasions. They took on the challenge and helped turn the company round. Two points need to be noted here. One is Hongfei's investment in training its workforce, partly subsidized by the local government. Providing skill training to employees not only imparts skills, but also sends a signal to the workforce that they are valued by the firm and worthy of investment. The educational level of rural migrant workers is generally low, with the majority of them educated to junior high school level only. Few have had vocational skills training. Although they are a highly flexible and mobile group in the labor market, they are the least marketable mass. They are also the group who are least likely to receive training from their employers beyond the immediate skills required.[22] Hongfei's investment in sending some of its rural migrant workers to technical colleges for training not only raised the skill level of its workforce, but also had a strong inspirational effect. In response to the Chinese government's drive to provide training to raise the skill level of its rural workforce, Hongfei was sharing its social responsibility. The other point is the effect of employee involvement through the employee ownership scheme. Although employees only owned a small proportion of the company's shares, this ownership did bind the workers' fate to that of the firm and enhanced their commitment.

All these factors led to Hongfei workers' devotion to the firm during the period of time when it was battling to overcome the technical difficulty in producing Wal-Mart's high-specification display shelves. Here, they exemplified the Chinese virtues of altruism, diligence, and a "can do" (perseverance) culture. Employees on the project team prioritized collective needs over their individual needs and those of their own family for the public good. They sacrificed their personal lives. This would be socially less acceptable in Western societies due to the encroachment into family space and the disruption of work–life balance. But, without this commitment and sacrifice, Hongfei's future could have been very different.

Shared views in Western and Oriental philosophies

This case shows that the traditional Chinese culture remains valuable in business management. There is, in fact, a high level of similarity between Chinese traditional values (Confucianism) and the humanistic approach advocated in Western philosophies and management theories. The influence of Confucianism has been profound in political thought, economic ideologies, social relationships, and education in China. In Confucianism, a human being is essentially a social being who is bound by five cardinal relationships, between: ruler and subject, parent and child, elder and younger brother, husband and wife, and friend and friend.[23] Individuals are expected to fulfill specific duties and obligations in their daily behavior and adherence to social norms, which leads to social harmony. According to Tu,[24] the main concern of Confucianism is the well-being of humanity. As such, Confucian values, as an alternative to Western liberalism, are universally applicable and are able to address many serious challenges in contemporary societies. Indeed, Confucian humanism as the foundation of human rights and economic ethics has had enduring influence in East Asian societies such as Japan, Korea, the People's Republic of China, Taiwan, and Singapore. The contemporary value of Confucian humanism is said to share similarity with the virtue ethics of the Greek philosopher, Aristotle.[25]

Inherent in the Confucian values of selflessness and altruism in social relationships is the notion of collectivism, which emphasizes the interdependence of human beings and therefore the importance of communal and social interests over and above those of the individual. Again, the notion of collectivism can find its shadow in Western philosophical thoughts, for example, in Auguste Comte's (1798–1857) ethical argument of altruism as a moral and social obligation of the individual for the sake of greater social good,[26] and in Jean-Jacques Rousseau's (1712–1778) discourse of social contract in the governance of political society.[27]

Transferability of good practices

In view of the above discussion, the divide between the West and East may not be as wide as it would seem. This is in spite of the fact that the humanistic values prevailing in the Confucian societies are founded on the basis of collectivism, whereas the humanistic ethos promoted in modern Western society tends to focus on the needs of individuals. Therefore, the practices found in Hongfei and those in China more generally may be transferable to less developed countries that share a collectivist culture similar to China's. They may also be suitable for firms in less developed areas in Western countries where local communities are closely bonded and the company plays an important role in the local economy and social life. Firms in developed and less developed countries alike that employ large numbers of migrant workers from less developed countries can also benefit from Hongfei's HR practices, which are characterized by extensive welfare provisions as well as satisfying employees' development needs. Migrant workers employed by factories often come from less developed areas. The need to make a living for themselves and their families is the main reason for them to be working away from home, many separated from their families. Employers are therefore the main source of their material and emotional support and play an important role in helping them integrate into the local community life.

Hongfei's story also tells us that business success is not the patent of well-resourced business giants. A humanistic approach to managing the workforce will be reciprocated by a high level of commitment and engagement that are essential to business success, regardless of the background of the workforce. This is what differentiates Hongfei from sweatshop plants, which employ primarily rural migrant workers who are low-skilled, low-paid, and highly replaceable.

Acknowledgement

The Hongfei story was adapted and expanded from one of the case studies (Haidun Ltd) reported in Miao and Yao[28] (in Chinese).

Notes

1. For example, Farrell and Grant, 2005; Wilson, 2008.
2. Miao and Yao, 2007.
3. Garnaut, 2001, 3.
4. *China Statistical Yearbook*, 2007.
5. Cooke, 2005; Saich, 2001.
6. Chang and Wang, 1994.
7. Luo et al., 1998.
8. Cooke, 2005; Ding et al., 2004.
9. Miao and Yao, 2007.
10. Ibid.
11. Ibid.
12. Cooke, 2005.
13. Cooke, 2004; Smith, 2003.
14. Smith, 2003.
15. See Fu and Tsui, 2003, for more detail.
16. Ibid.
17. Ralston et al., 1999.
18. Fu and Tsui, 2003.
19. Cooke, 2008.
20. Bhagat et al., 2007; Cooper et al., 2003.
21. Cooke, 2008.
22. Cooke, 2005.
23. Tu, 1993.
24. Ibid.
25. Ibid.
26. Campbell, 2006.
27. Rousseau, 1968.
28. Miao and Yao, 2007.

Bibliography

Bhagat, R., Stevenson, P. and Segovis, J. (2007). International and cultural variations in employee assistance programmes: Implications for managerial health and effectiveness. *Journal of Management Studies*, Vol. 44, 222–242.

Campbell, R. (2006). Altruism in Auguste Comte and Ayn Rand. *The Journal of Ayn Rand Studies*, Vol. 7, 357–369.

Chang, C. and Wang, Y. J. (1994). The nature of the township-village enterprise. *Journal of Comparative Economics*, Vol. 19, 434–452.

China Statistical Yearbook (2007). Beijing: China Statistics Publishing House.

Cooke, F. L. (2004). Foreign firms in China: Modelling HRM in a toy manufacturing corporation. *Human Resource Management Journal*, Vol. 14, 31–52.

Cooke, F. L. (2005). *HRM, Work and Employment in China*. London: Routledge.

Cooke, F. L. (2008). Enterprise culture management in China: An "insiders" perspective. *Management and Organization Review*, Vol. 4, 291–314.

Cooper, C., Dewe, P. and O'Driscoll, M. (2003). Employee assistance programs, pp. 289–304, in Quick, J. and Tetrick, L. (eds) *Occupational Health Psychology*. Washington, DC: American Psychological Association.

Ding, D., Ge, G. and Warner, M. (2004). Evaluation of organizational governance and human resource management in China's township and village enterprises. *International Journal of Human Resource Management*, Vol. 15, 836–852.

Garnaut, R. (2001). Twenty years of economic reform and structural change in the Chinese economy, pp. 1–18, in Garnaut, R. and Huang, Y. P. (eds) *Growth with Miracles: Readings on the Chinese Economy in the Era of Reform*. Oxford: Oxford University Press.

Farrell, D. and Grant, A. (2005). China's looming talent shortage. *The McKinsey Quarterly*, No. 4. http://www.mckinseyquarterly.com/article_page. aspx?ar=1685 [accessed March 3, 2007].

Fu, P. P. and Tsui, A. (2003). Utilizing printed media to understand desired leadership attributes in the People's Republic of China. *Asia Pacific Journal of Management*, Vol. 20, 423–446.

Luo, Y. D., Tan, J. and Shenkar, O. (1998). Strategic responses to competitive pressure: The case of township and village enterprises in China. *Asia Pacific Journal of Management*, Vol. 15, 33–50.

Miao, Q. and Yao, X. G. (2007). Employer branding and enterprise growth: An analysis of privately owned enterprises. *The Development and Management of Human Resources*, Vol. 6, 71–75 (in Chinese).

Ralston, D., Egri, C., Stewart, S., Terpstra, R. and Yu, K. C. (1999). Doing business in the 21st Century with the new generation of Chinese managers: A study of generational shifts in work values in China. *Journal of International Business Studies*, Vol. 30, 415–428.

Rousseau, J. (1968). *The Social Contract* (Translated and introduced by Maurice Cranston). Penguin Books.

Saich, T. (2001). *Governance and Politics of China*. Hampshire: Palgrave.

Smith, C. (2003). Living at work: Management control and the dormitory labour system in China. *Asia Pacific Journal of Management*, Vol. 20, 333–358.

Tu, W. M. (1993). The Third Epoch of Confucian Humanism, in his *Way, Learning, and Politics: Essays on the Confucian Intellectual*. Albany: State University of New York Press, pp. 141–159.

Wilson, B. (2008). Hidden Dragons. *People Management Magazine Online*, http://www.peoplemanagement.co.uk/pm/articles/2008/08/hidden-dragons.htm [accessed September 4, 2008].

10
Level Ground Trading Ltd – Fair Trade Coffee As a Front for Social Justice

Will Low and Eileen Davenport

Introduction

In November 2008, Stacey Toews, one of the founders of Level Ground Trading Ltd. (LGT), addressed business students at Royal Roads University in Victoria, BC. Educating young people about fair trade is something he often does, as it is part of Level Ground's mission. Stacey says: "you need to reach the under-20s who are anti-establishment ... and who will put pressure on their parents to buy fair trade."[1] But talking to business students represents a special challenge, because most do not necessarily think about business as a way of furthering social justice. Stacey's talk is often the first opportunity that business students have had to think about an alternative vision of business that is embedded in fair trade – one that is about improving the lives of marginalized producers in developing countries through trading partnerships that are more direct, more humane, and more personalized. The talk must have been thought-provoking, because at the end one student succinctly said: "that guy [Stacey] is really just using coffee and sugar as a front to further social justice, isn't he?"

That may have been exactly what the four Saanich families envisaged when they banded together in 1997 with the idea of starting a coffee business. Stacey explains their initial motivation: "We saw a lot about globalization that we didn't like, and a lot about the coffee business that we didn't like, and we thought there has to be a better way. We were familiar with the Bridgehead model[2] – the model was good but the coffee was terrible ... it was nasty stuff ... so we started thinking could we start a fair trade business that focused on coffee ... Coffee was a vehicle

131

to get across a message of doing things better than they were usually done in business."[3] The idea of doing things better than they are usually done in business is a concise way of summing up what humanistic management – the focus of this book – is all about. We look in more detail later at how Level Ground Trading fits the humanistic management model.

Returning to the origins of Level Ground Trading, Stacey makes clear that there was a big element of serendipity mixed in: "We decided we really should check with Hugo [a native Columbian and currently LGT President] who had worked for [my wife] Laurie's father and who had farming relatives (in Columbia). We showed up on Hugo's and [his wife] Tracey's doorstep and we told him about this idea right there on the doorstep. He was very excited and said 'come in, come in', and his whole living room was full of Ziploc bags full of green beans. It turned out just the previous month he had said that he wanted to get something rolling on fair trade coffee and he had gone to his local church to find funding for this … to go to Columbia … to get a trade link going with this co-op that [his] grandfather was part of …"[4]

Within 2 weeks, two more families keen to make a difference through fair trade had been brought in to help with financial backing, and the name Level Ground Trading was incorporated. Stacey recalled: "None of us had any history in business … it was all just a learning process."[5] The first lesson came as soon as the first shipment of green coffee beans from Colombia arrived. Level Ground planned to store the product in one family's garage but, surprised by the volume, joked they would have to store it in their living rooms! Now they had the green beans but no commercial roasting machine. Fortunately the group was able to negotiate the after-hours use of a local roaster's equipment. Stacey described the scene: "We would go in from six pm to six am after our day jobs and sleep on the coffee sacks in between roasting."[6] The partners took turns roasting green beans in very small batches to fill the orders they had taken the day before.

And so, Level Ground Trading Ltd was launched, as many small start-up businesses are, through a mix of hope and trepidation, the goodwill of friends and family, and long hours. Orders came from the classic mix of "alternative networks of distribution"[7] used by fair trade organizations around the world – friends, work colleagues, church groups, and "third world" shops. In its first year, LGT sold $50,000 worth of coffee – a significant achievement for a home-based start-up.

Within 2 years, Level Ground had grown enough to move into its own roasting and packaging facility. But by 2003 even the new facility was bursting at the seams, and some office staff had moved into a Volkswagen van in the parking lot to free up space. So the company purchased and renovated a larger facility. After three more years, the space was feeling crowded yet again (there were now 20 staff), but fortunately the upper floor of the building became available to house office staff, which gave the production team a little more elbow room.

In early 2008 the company moved once again, as growth in sales and staff was putting a strain on facilities at the existing site. This time the move was into new custom-designed premises, which the company expects will accommodate future growth. The staff show you around the new site with evident pride – pointing out the paint on the walls, which is free of volatile organic compounds;[8] the recyclable carpet squares in the new meeting and education room; the state-of-the-art packaging and roasting equipment; the eight streams of recycling; the bike sheds; and, most importantly of all, the direct linkages with the farmers and coffee-growing communities whose pictures are on every package of Level Ground coffee.

In ten years the company has come a long way from Ziploc bags of coffee stored in a garage and roasted in tiny batches at night. It has firmly established its brand; it now does business not only with the Fair Trade shops and independent cafés who were its earliest customers, but also with the largest of the big box retailers. LGT has a presence at almost every local community event, and many business events, and many of the local campaigns for social justice are fueled by caffeine donated by the company. Its turnover in 2008 was very close to CAD 5 million. Not a bad track record for young people who began the operation with no knowledge of the coffee business, and few financial resources, but who did have a steadfast vision of a different way of doing business.

Overview/background of Level Ground Trading

Level Ground Trading Ltd. is an established SME, founded in 1997.[9] In 2008, it employed 30 people full-time (30 hours or more per week) and six people part-time. LGT is located in Saanich, BC, approximately 25 km from Victoria – a city of approximately 300,000 people on Vancouver Island. It is a limited corporation, owned by four local families, each owning a different percentage of the company based on their original investment of time and money.

The company mission is "to trade fairly and directly with small-scale producers in developing countries, and to market our products in North America, offering our customers ethical choices." Its vision is "to provide a level playing field on which disadvantaged producers have greater opportunity in the marketplace, in an effort to alleviate poverty in developing countries through trade."

The company is primarily a fair trade coffee importer, roaster and wholesaler, with recent excursions into importing and wholesaling dried fruit and sugar. The coffee is sourced from six countries: Colombia, Bolivia, Peru, Ecuador, Tanzania, and Ethiopia; its Peruvian and Ecuadorian coffees are certified by the Fairtrade Labelling Organization International (FLO).[10]

Since 2002, the company has been importing and wholesaling dehydrated tropical fruit, *Frutos de los Andes*, from Fruandes Ltda, an independent Colombian fruit-drying company started in partnership with LGT. The most recent addition to the product range is *Panela de los Andes Sugar*, organic cane sugar grown by small-scale farmers in Huila, Colombia and processed by Fruandes Ltda.

Total sales (in Canadian dollars) have risen from CAD 50,000 when the company started in 1997 to CAD 606,213 in fiscal 2001 and to CAD 5,000,000 by fiscal 2008.

Embracing humanistic management

As a member of the International Association of Fair Trade (IFAT), LGT exemplifies the notion of generating social benefits rather than focusing on profit maximization. This is not to say that Fair Trade organizations do not strive to be profitable, but rather that they share a greater portion of the profits generated in the value chain with producers than is the case in conventional trade relations. The principles of fair trade are encompassed within the framework of humanistic management in that both are based on a holistic understanding of human nature, supporting genuine human needs and values, and aspiring to enrich peoples' lives as citizens of a global community. To do this, fair trade places the producer at the center of the value chain relationship. As Tiffen and Zadek say: "At the heart of fair trade is that the primary producer comes first, not the product or even the consumer."[11]

The origins of the fair trade movement lie in a range of secular and faith-based perspectives and can be traced back to relief efforts in the post-World War II era. However, the movement is linked historically to an even longer tradition of alternative approaches to social relations of production and consumption. These include the mutual movement of producer and consumer cooperatives, Utopian industrialists, religiously inspired views linking business and social justice, and "alternative lifestyles" based on communalism and "counterculture." These disparate threads share common themes of self-help, development and social justice in production and consumption.

The history of fair trade largely pre-dates the emergence of a broadbased environmental movement and, as a result, tends to focus on producers' well-being rather than environmental concerns. However, since the widely used "FINE" definition of fair trade[12] was agreed in the late 1990s, sustainable development occupies a prominent place:

> Fair Trade is a trading partnership, based on dialogue, transparency and respect, that seeks greater equity in international trade. It contributes to *sustainable development* by offering better trading conditions to, and securing the rights of, marginalised producers and workers – especially in the South.[13]

LGT is a prime example of a modern fair trade organization which has embraced a Triple Bottom Line (TBL) approach, being financially successful while creating social and environmental value for internal and external stakeholders. John Elkington, who is credited with popularizing the term, says: "In the simplest terms, the TBL agenda focuses corporations not just on the economic value that they add, but also on the environmental and social value that they add – or destroy."[14]

Over its 12-year history, the company has won four major awards for its socially and environmentally responsible business practices. Clearly for LGT implementing responsible environmental and social business practices is not an optional extra, but is a deep-seated ethic which informs all that the company does. The company's leadership in these areas has been publicly recognized since the early 2000s.

- In 2003, Level Ground Trading won the *Ethics in Action* award for Overall Leadership in corporate social responsibility.
- This was followed in 2005 by the *EcoStar Award* for waste reduction from the Capital Regional District.
- And then, in 2007, Level Ground Trading was awarded a *WorkLife BC* award for excellence in creating a flexible workplace for a small business, and was also recognized as the *Vancouver Island Small Business of the Year* at the Business Examiner's Vancouver Island Business Excellence Awards.

In relation to the latest award, Stacey said: "We're encouraged that this award acknowledges the way we consider all the triple bottom line components." The following sections examine a number of the company's successes, and the way in which the company exemplifies a humanistic management approach to business.

The Level Ground Trading business model: Direct fair trade

The practice of fair trade encompasses a "fair price" which includes a social premium, fosters long-term relationships between producers and buyers, eliminates middlemen who capture most of the mark-up between producer and consumer, and offers more flexible financial terms to producers, including prepayment and loans. Most fair trade commodities, such as coffee and sugar, reach Northern markets either through importers, roasters, and wholesalers who trade directly with farmers or through the Fair Trade Labeling Organization International (FLO) certification system.[15] The FLO system has set a floor price for coffee (currently around USD 1.50 per pound) to stabilize the market.

Level Ground Trading has chosen to stay primarily outside the FLO registration system. Stacey explains that from the perspective of LGT there is a big difference between LGT's business model of direct fair trade and what he terms "generic" fair trade. He says: "my biggest problem is that the roasters [who buy from FLO] don't do any sourcing so they are into [their own] business development not producer development. It is much easier to do something in your own country."[16] In an effort to expand its market by selling through a variety of smaller supermarket chains, LGT joined the International Association for Fair Trade (IFAT) and displays this logo as a mark of fair trade authenticity. IFAT represents and monitors 100 per cent Fair Trade organizations in the North and South, but does not certify products. LGT relies much more on the "brand equity" it has established over the years and the fact that for some consumers the term "fair trade" has become something of a brand in itself. In the early years consumer trust in Ten Thousand Villages, LGT's main distributor, was sufficient to reassure consumers about the coffee's fair trade credentials. However, because many North American consumers rely on the FLO label as their guarantee of authenticity, LGT has been purchasing FLO-registered beans for two of its coffee lines, from Peru and Ecuador.

Level Ground's approach to fair trade is much closer to the original model of alternative trade developed in the 1960s and 1970s.[17] This model emphasized working closely (LGT calls it directly) with marginalized producers on the basis of long-term economic and social development. LGT had been working with a number of small cooperatives since the business began 12 years ago, prior to the introduction of Fairtrade

Mark Canada (the regional licensing body for FLO in Canada). These producers have not been able to register with FLO, in part because the cooperatives are too small (the minimum size of output mandated by FLO is 40,000 lb of coffee), and because the FLO register is already oversubscribed.

Besides the technical and logistical issues of participating fully in the FLO system, there are also philosophical reasons for staying largely on the outside. The academic literature highlights the possibility of fair trade lifting the "veil obscuring the relations and processes of commodity production"[18] or shortening the distance between producers and consumers.[19] In practice the extent to which the veil is lifted, or distance shortened, varies considerably from product to product and is also dependent on how many links there are in the chain. While many companies who use the Fairtrade product certification route to market do directly source from farmer organizations, others source through importers who may or may not be dealing exclusively in fair trade goods.

LGT promotes itself as a 100 per cent fair trade company, as opposed to the mainstream roasters and distributors who offer fair trade as just part of their product offering. And it is not alone: a number of small 100 per cent fair trade coffee roasters in the USA left Transfair USA to protest against companies appropriating the mantle of fair trade while offering only a very limited amount of fair trade coffee – Starbucks was a frequently cited example.[20] It is, however, a systemic problem inherent in a system in which the commodity is certified. Mainstream sellers of fair trade coffee can buy beans from registered brokers without operationalizing the direct relationships that characterized the origins of the movement. These registered brokers buy from FLO-registered growers, and then sell on to commercial roasters in developed countries.

The main problem that arises from this is the "dehumanization" of fair trade. As Stacey puts it: "If there was a sore spot for me (in fair trade) it would be this ... it would be formulizing fair trade. I thought fair trade was about dialogue ... there are challenges to being really human. The other companies buy from brokers not from individual co-ops, so they don't have to check the farmers."[21] This is far from the idealized notion of fair trade lifting the veil of production.

LGT has taken specific steps to put into practice the idea of shortening the distance between producers and consumers by putting a picture of the farmers (or family members) from the cooperatives it buys from on every coffee package. LGT argues it can tell the consumer exactly where the coffee he or she is drinking comes from, not only by dealing with the farmers directly but also through a project to map its supply chain using GPS. Stacey says: "We have tied ourselves in with photos, and farmers and stories and GPS locations. That's where I think FT loses the opportunity for dynamic change ... we are dumbing it down for consumers. By telling them nothing, we let them think they know everything [but it is a] generic feel good factor for your customers [with] no traceability or way of quantifying change in the community where the coffee comes from."[22] LGT also pays the individuals for the right to use their images on the packaging. And in one notable case a picture of a female coffee farmer has replaced the picture of a parrot on the Cafe Pangoa package.

If a desire to foster and maintain direct human trading relationships is one strong element in LGT's philosophy, another is to sell only single origin coffee through retail points of sale. The only blended coffee sold by LGT is an espresso blend sold to cafes. So why is this a big deal? Stacey sums it up when he says: "In the coffee business you always blend so that there is no big difference in taste. Blending allows you to be really versatile and you always have stock. Single origin means that you are committed ... it makes you not very agile ... it means you can't respond as quickly ... particularly for the mainstream which needs predictability. We only sell from origin."[23] By not selling coffee of blended origins, LGT stays true to its philosophy of direct fair trade: the customer will always know where the coffee comes from, even if this means increased logistical costs and lower sales to big retailers.

Creating social benefits for producers

One of the three pillars of the Triple Bottom Line is the social impact a business has on its stakeholders. A guiding principle of the fair trade movement has been to use trade to foster social development among its producer partners. The fair trade price, which is traditionally well above the market price, creates a social premium that is used in local development projects. LGT has worked closely with producers to channel the social premiums into development initiatives.

Famicafé

Hugo negotiated the company's first foray into direct fair trade with a cooperative of small-scale coffee farmers in Antioquia, Colombia – a trading relationship that survives to this day. From interviews and visits with community members Hugo heard that the farming families' greatest desire was to see their children go to school. Hugo found a group of dedicated teachers and community members who joined together to form Famicafé (Coffee Families Foundation). Famicafé was registered as a Colombian non-profit, non-governmental organization with a mission of "improving the lives of families in the coffee growing region of Colombia through education, job creation and organic farming initiatives." In its first year, six students were provided full scholarships to high school. These original students all completed high school with top marks and are now attending university and technical colleges on Famicafé scholarships.

In 2007 LGT's purchase of ten shipping containers of coffee from Colombia and its relationship with Famicafé resulted in:

- 118 school scholarships and 14 university scholarships for children in the coffee-growing region.
- Funding for Hogar Pro-Juventud, a boarding house for rural students attending high school in Andes, Colombia.
- Joint educational projects with Hogar Juvenil Campesino and 32 rural schools.
- Support to coffee farming families in crisis through a benevolent fund.

Although the Famicafé model is not replicated in other countries where Level Ground does business, the company is committed to supporting producer partners in a range of ways and will explore options with producers as resources allow.

Level Ground Trading as a fair business incubator

Another key role played by fair trade organizations has been as "midwife" in the birth of new ventures and products that diversify the economic base of their producer partners.[24] From his many visits to Colombia, Hugo saw a need and desire for this in the region where LGT sourced its coffee. Overall coffee trading remains a highly volatile business, and most producers sell only a small portion of their overall production on fair trade terms, as supply exceeds demand.

One idea was to export dried fruit, sourced from the trees that shade the coffee trees. In 2001, Level Ground Trading donated funds to purchase a commercial dehydrator and sponsored a Colombian agronomist to come to Canada to learn food-drying techniques. Together, LGT and local small-scale farmers established an independent Colombian fruit drying company, *Fruandes Ltda*, in Bogota. While primarily Colombian-owned, Fruandes has a four-way ownership structure, with Hugo Ciro, on behalf of LGT, owning about 20 per cent of the company.

In keeping with fair trade principles, this company provides both economic and social development: it is creating a new market for fruit; pays a fair price to small-scale farmers; and works with a local relief and development agency to provide employment for displaced women from the Cazuca township. These women are generally landless from displacement, without a husband or partner, living in a squatters' region around Cazuca, which Stacey describes as being "a horrible place to live and raise kids."[25] All employees of the fruit-drying company receive fair wages (20 per cent above national standards), health benefits, and school tuition for their families.

By 2005, Fruandes Ltda appeared to have established a solid business footing in Colombia, employing up to 45 employees over the course of a given year (ten to 12 full-time and the rest part-time). In terms of impacts:

- Three employees have since completed their high school education and three are currently working towards completing their high school education.
- One employee is currently enrolled in a business administration degree program.
- Three employees have successfully purchased homes, allowing them to move out of Cazuca.

Despite these successes, during 2008, according to Stacey, Fruandes was "going through really tough times…it's on life support right now. Hugo has been too involved in Fruandes [and] as Hugo has stepped aside…Fruandes has fallen apart. It made some bad moves into the European market and ate up a lot of money, and in so doing has not served [LGT] well."[26] However, in keeping with the fair trade tradition of long-term partnerships, LGT is working with Fruandes to keep the operation going despite the fact that "price is pretty high and quality is inconsistent." If Fruandes failed, as Stacey points out, the loss would be the social capital created in the venture, not the financial capital: "If we didn't sell Fruandes dried fruit it would not affect our bottom line, [it] makes up 2 per cent of our offering but we are 90 per cent of Fruande's customer base…coffee has carried fruit for sure and carried this business."[27] Going into 2009, LGT will continue in its efforts to establish Fruandes Ltda on a more independent footing and to bridge the gap during this restructuring as inventory of the product runs out.

Creating social benefits for employees

LGT's employee benefit programs were recognized when the company received an *Ethics in Action* award in 2003 and a *BC WorkLife* award in 2007.

Green transportation

On an ongoing basis, staff who regularly cycle, bus, or carpool to work are paid a monthly green transportation bonus. Stacey says: "people want to work at LGT because we pay nine cents a km if you [use green transportation] to work – not because they want the money but because it is a value they believe in."[28]

Fair share bonus

LGT has implemented a bonus scheme to improve the accuracy with which orders are filled. The quality bonus has recently been radically restructured on the principle that, when the company does well, so should the employee. Stacey explains: "Mistakes are very, very expensive. Filling orders is typically an entry level job – but we want to get people to take ownership of the role."[29] This scheme targets a 1.5 per cent error rate and works through both carrots and sticks: $1 is paid for every order correctly filled with the correct package size and correct product, and $40 is deducted for every wrong order. Based on the average number of orders being filled per year, the employee can earn an additional $3,000 per year by paying more attention.

Retirement savings schemes

The company will match an employee's contributions to a registered retirement savings scheme (a special tax-free savings vehicle in Canada), up to 2.5 per cent of salary. For someone earning $40,000, the company will match up to $1,000 of contributions. LGT has also partnered with a Mennonite-owned financial adviser to offer employees financial planning in paid work time.

Flexible working hours

At any one time, five or six people (out of a staff of 36) have some kind of flexible arrangement for starting or finishing. The main reasons are family responsibilities and education timetables. The arrangement does not mandate core time – each case is individually organized. Laurie Klassen, who manages human relations at LGT,[30] explained the company's motivation: "This approach creates sustainable employment and therefore reduces turnover, and it works for everyone because our staff are willing to flex with the needs of the business and will put in extra effort when needed."[31] Stacey agreed: "These are staff who will give you everything when they are in the building ... they know they are getting a break. They have the best work performance."[32]

An environmental ethic: thinking "outside the bin"

Level Ground Trading is guided by an environmental ethic, resulting in a holistic approach to environmental sustainability. Across its operations, LGT works to reduce waste and environmental impacts, even where these actions do not meet the business case of "eco-efficiency." The company's effort was recognized through an *EcoStar Award* in 2005 for waste reduction.

EnviroTotes

In 2005, LGT launched EnviroTotes, reusable containers that hold 5 lb of coffee, for commercial customers on Vancouver Island. Full EnviroTotes are delivered to a customer and the empty ones from the previous delivery are picked up. The EnviroTotes program grew by almost 80 per cent over 2 years, so that now 40,000 lb of coffee are sold (on an annual basis) locally without any packaging being thrown away.

Post-consumer reclamation

In 2007, LGT started to collect and recycle empty coffee packages from individual customers. The company will organize 100 reclaim sites in major centers through BC, Alberta, Saskatchewan, Manitoba, and Ontario. For example, packages can be returned to Ten Thousand Villages stores, the major outlet for LGT coffee across these provinces. The packages are returned to LGT's Victoria facility and then, via a local recycling partner, taken to a "waste to energy" facility in Greater Vancouver.

"Level Ground Trading always strives to do what's best socially and environmentally," says Rich Farr, Level Ground marketing manager. "So it makes sense to us to take responsibility not only for the coffee we sell but also for the package we sell it in."[33]

Consumers unwilling or unable to take the packages back are informed that, if the poly plastic liner is separated from the foil of the coffee package, it can be recycled in the "blue bin" curbside household recycling programs that operate in many Canadian and US cities.

Facility waste

On a weekly basis, LGT generates less than one small bag of waste that goes to conventional landfill. Prior to its waste reduction initiatives, LGT faced the same perverse incentives as other businesses: the cost of waste disposal was essentially the same whether the waste container (in the form of a large metal bin) was full or empty. "Value" is achieved under these incentives by filling the bin.

To accomplish this low waste goal, LGT has carefully examined its waste streams and identified ways to reduce packaging and other waste coming into the facility. The company has also instituted extensive composting and maintains 12 different streams for recycling: metal, soft plastic, hard plastic, Styrofoam, food-contaminated Styrofoam, packing peanuts, gable top cartons, foil products, paper, cardboard, glass, and refundable drink containers. The program extends to allowing staff to bring household waste in these categories for recycling at the company's expense. Many of these waste streams are not catered for in conventional household recycling programs, and staff have proved keen to become part of this initiative.

Trade show waste

In the fall of 2007, LGT started to use biodegradable disposal coffee cups at large events and trade shows. These same cups are also custom printed with the LGT logo and sold to café accounts as of 2008. This initiative is part of a goal of zero waste to landfills when managing shows and events. The Ecotainers™, as they are called, consist of an outer paperboard shell made from wood grown and harvested according to Sustainable Forestry Initiative guidelines, which is bonded to a compostable corn-based inner liner. Clean cups can be recycled with regular paper recyclables.

Conclusions: Building a community at work

The idea of doing business differently lies at the heart of both fair trade and the emerging school of humanistic management. Both support genuine human needs and values and aspire to enrich people's lives as citizens of a global community. Level Ground Trading is, in many ways, an example of a new-style fair trade company that pays as much attention to environmental issues and the well-being of its employees and local community as it does to the marginalized coffee farmers in the South who are its original reason for being. This evolution, we would suggest, is critically important. Ethical and fair trade consumers now want to know that the products an organiza-tion markets cause as little harm to the environment as possible while ensuring that economic benefits are fairly shared through the sup-ply chain. Level Ground's employees and the community of Greater Victoria in which it operates are also absolutely essential components of doing business in a humanistic way.

At the same time as it has been building this "community at work," Level Ground Trading has experienced steady growth in sales. But, more importantly, LGT has been creating value, not just profit. For example, LGT continues to market clearly identifiable "origin" coffees rather than blended coffees, even though the latter would simplify its supply chain and guarantee its revenue stream. Further, LGT has remained faithful to its producer partners over a very long term, even when they suffer problems in quality and delivery that impact on LGT's business. The same is true in its relationship with retailers, continuing to supply Ten Thousand Villages, its original fair trade outlet. The company is also very active in supplying local charities and social organizations with free coffee. Stacey says: "all the local charities drink Level Ground cof-fee; I think we filled 100 per cent of requests this year."[34]

The same is true when it comes to environmental initiatives. LGT has implemented programs that require financial investment in proc-esses and practices that is not balanced by eco-efficiency. If it were, LGT would be operating according to the logic of the "business case" for sustainability – the "win–win" scenario of investing to save money. One example is the company's willingness to recycle household waste that employees bring in to work. Using the recyclable Eco-tainers is another example of the company's commitment to sustainability.

One simple explanation for a focus on social and environmental ben-efits rather than financial return is the shared Christian values of the four families who came together in the beginning. However, Stacey has said: "our values could also be interpreted as hard working too...we have people who champion what we do and they have no Christian affiliation and others that do. There was no question our passion was justice, not coffee. Coffee was a vehicle to get across a message of doing things better than they were usually done in business."

Perhaps the key success factor in the business has been its ability to build a strong organizational culture based on values of developing and sharing social and environmental benefits. Melé[35] has argued that humanistic management centers "on building up a community of per-sons embedded with an organizational culture which fosters character [sic]." One way to reinforce the notions of community in the company is through the monthly team meeting, referred to as a "huddle." Stacey explained that: "Everyone is supposed to be here for huddle – it's our day to connect – we applaud the big things and the small things. The last five to ten minutes is a producer focus – so Hugo puts up images, something that connects us to farmers. I know this can feel like an inconvenience but this is about the farmers."[36] The huddle is used to inculcate a strong culture that relates business activities to the raison d'être, how the process improves the lives of producers.

LGT has also found over time that employees are much more likely to be in tune with these values because they are so explicit. People are coming forward to work there because they share the values, and those who do not share them strongly are likely not to find themselves fitting in and tend to leave – human (and humane) relations are a cornerstone of the business.

Notes

1. Personal communication, December 22, 2004.
2. Bridgehead was the fair trade arm of Oxfam Canada, named for the notion that alternative trade formed a "bridge of people" between Southern producers and Northern consumers.
3. Personal communication, November 20, 2008.
4. Personal communication, November 20, 2008.
5. Personal communication, November 20, 2008.
6. Personal communication, November 20, 2008.
7. Low and Davenport, 2005b.
8. Volatile organic compounds have been associated with adverse health effects and contribute to poor indoor air quality when they release gases into the environment.
9. Industry Canada uses the term SME to refer to businesses with fewer than 500 employees. A small business has fewer than 100 employees (if the business is a goods-producing business) or fewer than 50 employees (if the business is a service-based business), and would be likely to have less than $50 million in gross revenues. In the EU, fewer than 250 employees is considered medium-sized and fewer than 50 is small.
10. FLO is an international NGO that oversees the certification of growers and importers for their adherence to standards of fair trade. See www.fairtrade.net.
11. Tiffen and Zadek, 1998.
12. So named for the four major coordinating groups within the movement – FLO, IFAT, NEWS, and EFTA – who agreed this definition.
13. BAFTS, 2004a (emphasis added).
14. Elkington, 2004.
15. Perhaps confusingly, when products are certified via FLO they are referred to as fairtrade (note the compound word). In this case study we use the term fair trade, which is usually reserved to describe the movement as a whole, to encompass the model of direct fair trade that has been championed by the likes of Level Ground Trading Ltd, among others, outside the FLO system.
16. Personal communication, November 20, 2008.

17. See Kocken, 2003; Low and Davenport, 2005b.
18. Hudson and Hudson, 2003, 407.
19. Raynolds, 2000, 299.
20. Rogers, 2004.
21. Personal communication, November 20, 2008.
22. Personal communication, November 20, 2008.
23. Personal communication, November 20, 2008.
24. See also Low and Davenport, 2005a.
25. Personal communication, November 20, 2008.
26. Personal communication, November 20, 2008.
27. Personal communication, November 20, 2008.
28. Personal communication, November 20, 2008.
29. Personal communication, November 20, 2008.
30. Her official title is Manager of Human Resources, but we conceive the role/ practice to be much closer to managing human relations.
31. http://www.levelground.com/worklifebc_award
32. Personal communication, November 20, 2008.
33. http://www.levelground.com/reclamation_stations
34. Personal communication, November 20, 2008.
35. Melé, 2003, 82.
36. Personal communication, November 20, 2008.

Bibliography

BAFTS (2004). FINE Criteria for Fair Trade. http://www.bafts.org.uk/about-fairtrade [accessed October 3, 2010].

Elkington, J. (2004). Enter the triple bottom line, in Henriques and Richardson, J. (eds) *Triple Bottom Line: Does it Add Up?* London: Earthscan.

Hudson, I. and Hudson, M. (2003). Removing the veil? Commodity fetishism, fair trade and the environment. *Organisation and Environment,* Vol. 16, 413–430.

Kocken, M. (2003). Fifty years of fair trade: A brief history of the fair trade movement. http://www.gepa3.de/download/gepa_Fair_Trade_history__en.pdf [accessed November 1, 2004].

Low, W. and Davenport, E. (2005a). Has the medium (Roast) become the message? – the ethics of marketing fair trade in the mainstream. *International Marketing Review,* Vol. 22, 494–511.

Low, W. and Davenport, E. (2005b). Postcards from the edge: Maintaining the "alternative" character of fair trade. *Sustainable Development,* Vol. 13, 143–153.

Melé, D. (2003) The challenge of humanistic management. *Journal of Business Ethics,* Vol. 44, 77–88.

Raynolds, L. (2000). Re-embedding global agriculture: The international organic and Fair Trade movements. *Agriculture and Human Values,* Vol. 17, 297–309.

Rogers, T. (2004). Small coffee brewers try to redefine fair trade. *Christian Science Monitor.* http://www.globalpolicy.org/socecon/trade/2004/0413fairtradecoffee.htm [accessed December 2, 2004].

Tiffen, P. and Zadek, S. (1998). Dealing with and in the global economy: Fairer trade in Latin America, pp. 163–188, in Blauert, J. and Zadek, S. (eds) *Mediating Sustainability: Growing Policy from the Grassroots.* Bloomfield, CT: Kumarian Press.

11
The Best Inputs for Maximizing Your Output: Humanistic Practices at Micromatic Grinding

Rakesh Kumar Agrawal

> It's not easy being difficult. Difficult to please. Difficult to com-
> promise. Difficult to persuade. Sometimes indeed, difficult to
> do business with. And at all times very difficult to find fault
> with. Yes it is always difficult for us. Taking the easy way out,
> compromising here, adjusting there is always tempting but
> we've chosen never to take the short cut.
>
> Poster in a meeting room at Micromatic Grinding

Mr N. K. Dhand, the managing director of Micromatic Grinding
Technologies Ltd (MGT), looked up pensively as the clock struck four in
his small cabin. In another half an hour, he would be in a "No-Agenda"
meeting with some of his employees. It was called a no-agenda meeting
because that is exactly what it was. Anyone was free to share anything
in the meeting, be it complaints about the flavor of the tea being served
in the company's premises, a philosophy about life and love, the vision
of the organization, or fears of recession. The MD would be listening,
and sometimes sharing his views with some 10–15 officers and workers,
many of whom had joined only a few months ago.

As he thought about the meeting, his thoughts went back to his early
struggles in establishing and building an enterprise based on certain
principles – principles that he thought should be the basis of any organization. Times had been very difficult, but he had never believed in short
cuts – short cuts in delivering quality, short cuts in complying with government regulations, or short cuts in dealing with his people. His personal spiritual discipline had taught him the power of personal integrity,
respect for work, and respect for people – values which were reflected in

the humanistic management style at Micromatic Grinding. A humanistic approach – which affirms the dignity and worth of people – cannot work if there is no genuineness of intent and action, genuineness that can only be ensured by following certain ethical principles and values– principles that are self-evident but often neglected in practice. At MGT, this manifested itself through a practical emphasis on ethics, an emphasis

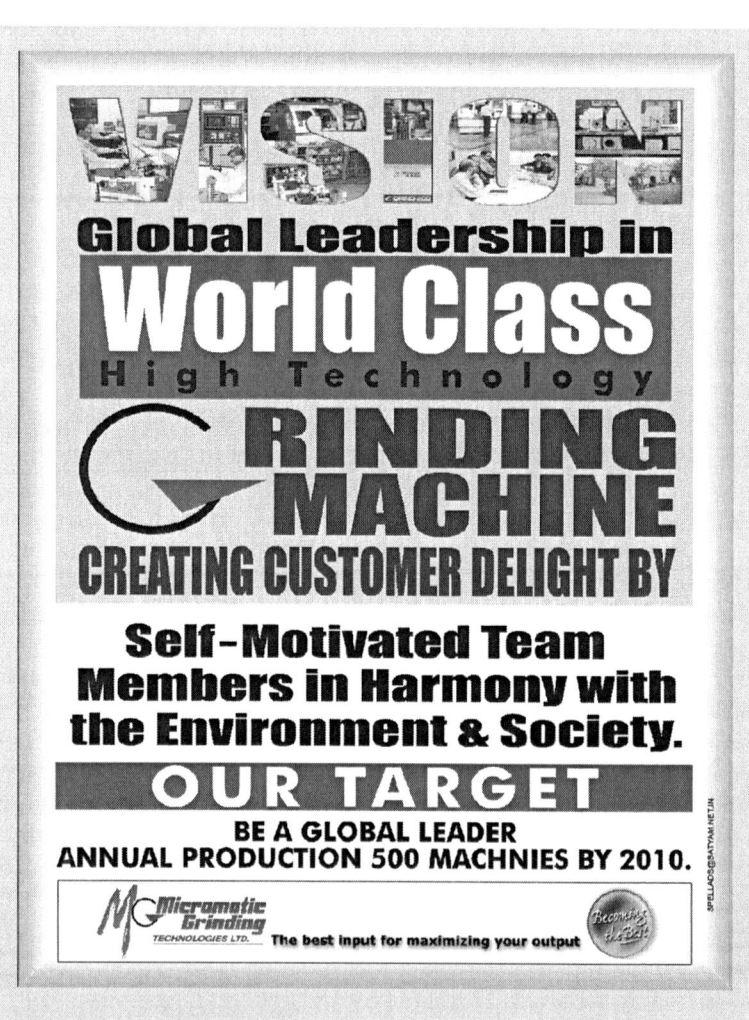

Exhibit 11.1   Vision of MGT

on sensitivity towards employees and other people whom the company came into contact with, and an emphasis on service to society.

Yet Mr Dhand knew that it was not only humanistic principles that had made his organization successful. He had also stressed "Being the

---

Exhibit 11.2 MGT's mission

MISSION
We will

Meet customer expectations by
Establishing a center for high technology, TPM friendly & aesthetically designed reliable machines
On – time delivery
Effective sales & service network for exports & domestic marketing
Quick response

Improve Personal Quality through
Developing positive attitude & motivating colleagues for co-operation and team work
Understanding and satisfying internal customer needs
Creating tension free & enjoyable work place environment
Improving our quality of life & living standards
Performance evaluation system

Continuously train and retrain ourselves by
Acquiring multiple skills to enable anyone accomplish as many different tasks as possible
Improving workmanship to make zero defect machines
Up-grading our competence for higher productivity
Making 'Paperless' working through IT

Offer machines & services at competitive prices by
Implementing costing system to reduce input costs, inventory & operating expenses
Eliminating non-value added work, wastage, rejections, & rework
Reducing cycle time through jigs / fixtures & standardization

Improve Product Quality through
Consistency in workmanship and output quality
Standardization of assembly processes
Quality & reliability' process

Adopt process – based working for
Doing everything "Right First Time"
Improving internal systems by 5 'S', Suggestion scheme, KANBAN etc.

Establish effective Vendor Partnering through
Supporting them to improve quality, cost and delivery
Long term relationships with vendors and suppliers as co-creators of value

Commitment to Society
Work towards improving the community around us keeping environment in mind.

Best" – best in terms of quality and best in terms of customer satisfaction. He knew that without a professional approach the company would not have reached its position as the number one machine tools company in India (see Exhibits 11.1 and 11.2 for MGT's vision and mission statements).

A history of Micromatic Grinding

In 1973, two engineer entrepreneurs, N. K. Dhand and V. S. Goindi, set up a partnership firm under the name of Micromatic Machines. While N. K. Dhand had a bachelor's degree in mechanical engineering from the University of California, Berkeley, V. S. Goindi was a machine tool design engineer belonging to a family with strong Gandhian beliefs. Both belonged to families who had run their modest trading businesses quite ethically and so wished to start their enterprise in an ethical manner.

The company began as a modest tool room or job shop for the engineering industry at Ghaziabad, an upcoming industrial town in the outskirts of Delhi, the capital of India. Yet its aim was to get into the manufacturing of machine tools. It produced its first precision cylindrical grinding machine in November 1977. In 1979, its cylindrical grinder won two first prizes at the International Machine Tool Exhibition – IMTEX – in Mumbai, one for the best design and the other for the best product.

In 1982, the partnership firm was converted into a private limited company with a new name, "Parishudh Sadhan Yantra Pvt. Ltd." The company's product range expanded over the years to cover a range of high-tech cylindrical grinders. Its domestic market share also increased to almost 30 percent and registered a turnover of Rs 24 million in 1990. A new company – Parishudh Machines Pvt. Ltd – was formed in 1987 as a prelude to planned independence, which came into effect on April 1, 1990. The two companies finally split vertically to allow each company to grow in its chosen line and manner.

In fact, the way the split was managed is quite interesting. One of the partners was assigned the task of division into two equal halves, and the condition was that the other partner would choose which half he wanted to have. Since the person dividing the assets was not going to be the chooser, he had the unenviable task of ensuring not only that both the halves were really equal in all respects, but also that neither half lacked any important inputs.[1] The split resulted in two independent companies: Parishudh Machines Pvt. Ltd, the new company headed

Exhibit 11.3 Highlights in the growth of MGT

Year	Sales (Rs Million)	Net profit after tax (Rs Million)	Employee Strength (nos.)	New products introduced
1986–1987	11.9	0.3	72	First CNC Cylindrical Grinder
1987–1988	17.6	0.5	85	
1988–1989	20	0.8	98	
1989–1990	23.8	0.8	110	Centreless Grinding Machine
1990–1991	30.2	1.2	117	
1992–1993	41.8	1.5	126	
1993–1994	47.3	2.6	131	Stroke and length match grinding machine for fuel injection parts
1994–1995	58.9	4	138	Heavy-duty cylindrical grinding machine
1995–1996	96.7	6.5	145	Piston ring profile grinding machine
2002–2003	187.3	15.9	189	Low-cost high-performance CNC grinder model "ecotech 650"
2003–2004	198.1	15.1	191	Internal grinder with auto indexing turret I grind 450
2004–2005	341.7	34.2	193	Heavy-duty CNC cylindrical grinder model "*h*-GRIND 360"
2005–2006	413.7	46.1	204	Joint new product development project, viz. Small "Cam Lobe Grinder" with JTEKT (Toyoda) – Japan
2006–2007	521.9	53.7	217	Universal Grinder FLEXI 65 and Crankshaft Journal Grinder RHINO 80
2007–2008	412.1	34.6	240	
2008–2009*	437.4	18	236	(Started a new plant in Bangalore, India in November 2008)

Note: * Provisional and unaudited.
Source: Company records.

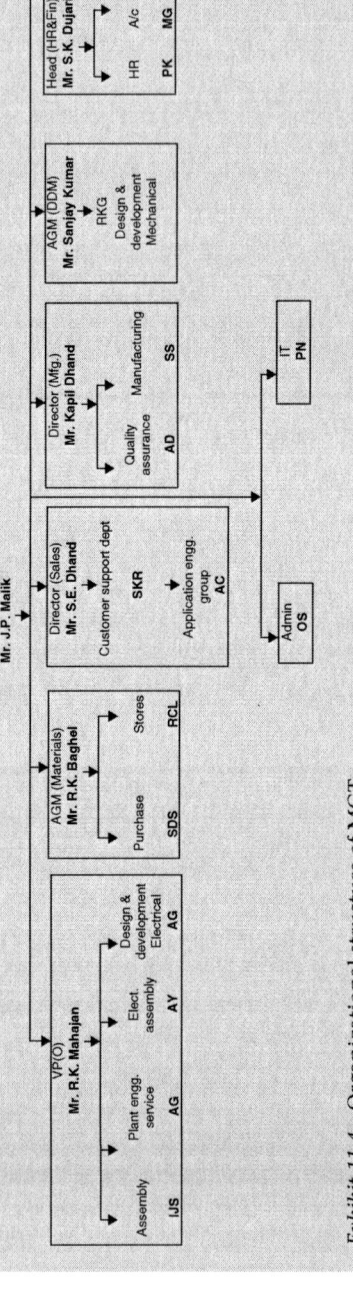

Exhibit 11.4 Organizational structure of MGT

by V. S. Goindi, and Parishudh Sadhan Yantra Pvt. Ltd, the original company headed by N. K. Dhand.

On July 1, 1997, Parishudh Sadhan Yantra Pvt. Ltd became a deemed public company, and it was rechristened as Micromatic Grinding Technologies Ltd. MGT has continued to expand and grow ever since and has attained market leadership in India (ahead of the other company). It currently manufactures a wide range of CNC cylindrical grinders, precision hydraulic grinders and special purpose grinding machines, capturing 40 percent of the market share in India in the cylindrical grinders segment. Its clients include some of the top companies, such as Hero Honda, Yamaha, Mahindra and Mahindra, Bajaj Auto, Tata Motors, Suzuki, Honda, Toyota, and Indian Railways, among others. It has distributor arrangements in Switzerland, Australia, the USA, the UAE, and China. Recently, it has entered into a Joint Venture arrangement with JTEKT Corporation, Japan, for sales and service of Toyoda machines in India, the new JV being named Toyoda Micromatic Machinery India Ltd.[2] Running its operations from three plants, the company now has 236 permanent employees on its rolls, as well as 150 temporary employees. In the financial year 2008, the company's profit after tax stood at Rs 34.6 million. Exhibit 11.3 gives a brief summary of the growth of MGT, while its organizational structure is depicted in Exhibit 11.4.

MGT has formed an unstructured group with five other like-minded companies, creating the largest machine tool group in India, called AceMicromatic Group. There are six companies in total in the group now: Ace Designers Ltd, Bangalore; Ace Manufacturing Systems Ltd, Bangalore; Pioneer Computing Technologies Ltd, Bangalore; Pragati Automation Ltd, Bangalore; Micromatic Grinding Technologies Ltd at Ghaziabad and Bangalore; and the sixth, Micromatic Machine Tools (MMT), the joint marketing company of the group based at New Delhi with offices located all over India (also promoted jointly by Mr Dhand in 1980). MMT is the largest machine tool marketing company in India, with total group sales of approximately Rs 5.5 billion in 2007, and run on similar ethical and humanistic lines.

The philosophy of management

The purpose of business has always been to generate wealth for the promoters, employees and shareholders – and a passionate pursuit of growth ensures that the business objectives are met. However, the preoccupation with growth at times tends to push other elements into the background and as long as the ends are good, the means appear justified. It is our firm belief that wealth earned by unethical means invariably entails the utmost exertion, fear, anxiety, and many times delusion and grief. (N. K. Dhand)[3]

The results of blindly pursuing growth and wealth creation are visible in the current economic meltdown and the consequent hardships brought to many in the world by the financial industry. (N. K. Dhand, in a personal interview with the author)

These remarks of Mr Dhand aptly sum up the management philosophy at Micromatic Grinding. At the foundation of the core values of MGT is the commitment to ethical business practices with a people focus – both within and outside the organization (Figure 11.1). While many organizations concentrate on and even advertise the external superstructures of the business, such as products, technology, customers, and profits, without working on the basic principles, MGT has been careful not to ignore the base of ethics and humanism. Without either neglecting or getting caught up in the superstructures, the company has put a lot of energy into building and protecting the foundations on which the superstructures are built. In practice, these foundations have five arms: honesty, integrity, equity, fairness, and justice – cultured through

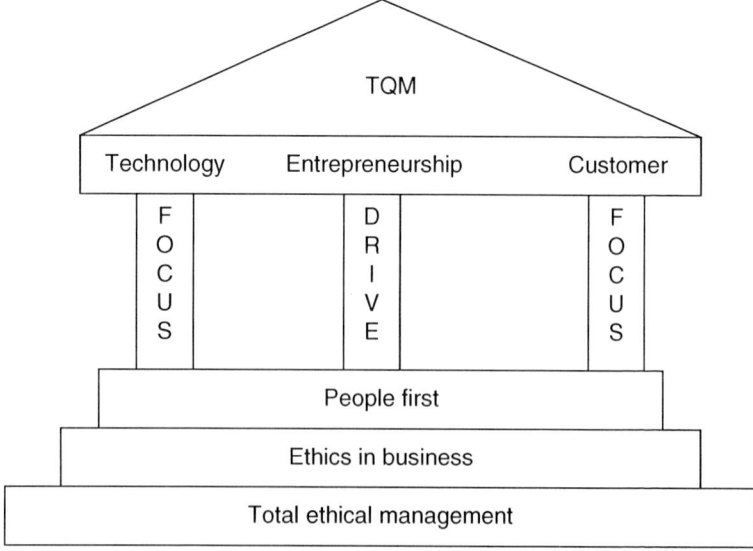

Figure 11.1   Management philosophy at Micromatic Grinding

Exhibit 11.5 Organizational values of Micromatic Grinding

Organizational values
We are bound by...
- Respect for team members and all stakeholders,
- Ethical and selfless behavior,
- Hardworking, teamwork, honesty, integrity, humility, and positive attitude of people,
- Excellence and speed in everything we do,
- Process based working
- Clear, timely, open, and transparent communication,
- Timely appreciation and recognitions,
- Continuous improvement, enhancement of knowledge, skills competencies, and self development,
- Clarity of roles, responsibilities and accountability,
- Involvement of people in decision making,
- Customer driven innovation to delight customers,
- Vendor partnering.

humility in leadership, the outcome of which is trust. While these values were not stated explicitly earlier in the organization's manual, they have emerged naturally from the leadership style and management philosophy at MGT.

Exhibit 11.5 lists the organizational values at MGT. While it is easy to claim that an organization is bound by certain values, it is an altogether different story to live by them and make them an integral part of an organization. At Micromatic, practicing these values is the norm rather than the exception.

The practices

"Honesty" in operations

Honesty in the financial workings of the company is the most visible and important aspect of MGT's business. The company does not generate or distribute any money through unethical means. In its formative years the company faced many moral and ethical predicaments, which haunt the people in MGT even today. But, for the company, sticking to its principled stand was more important than paying some fast money to get work done, although it proved quite costly at times. For example, the company has scrupulously maintained only one set of accounts as a firm policy. They never pad their expenses. They have never over-invoiced purchases or sales. Sometimes, they have even lost valuable orders from customers, mostly government organizations, for this very reason.[4]

There are many instances in its history when the easy way out seemed rationally justified, but, as a business organization, MGT has chosen to be guided strictly by the core values and the principles of ethics in business, walking the talk even at times when its very survival was dependent on conforming to convenient action. For example, the company chose not to have a power connection from the Electricity Board in a plant built in 1997, chiefly because it was very difficult to get the sanction and the power connection without paying extra money to officials (in fact, it was almost as expensive as generating power from one's own installed diesel generators). Due to the increase in diesel prices during the last 10 years, however, MGT decided to apply for a power connection in 2007. It took more than 20 months to get the connection as the company chose not to compromise its values.

In another case, there was a delay of over 18 months in getting Rs 2 million from the office of the Joint Chief Controller of Imports and Exports for the Cash Compensatory Support due to the company for the Rs 10 million worth of exports they had made to the UK in 1991–1992. During the delay MGT officials made numerous representations, frequently in person, to explain their principled stand to all officials concerned. Others told them that they were impractical, not to say foolish, to allow this delay while paying 24 percent overdraft interest to the banks. The company persevered, and their strong belief in their values and practices was able to see them through.

In 1998 the company acquired a plot of land for expansion purposes. Normally, all such deals have two payment components. Since MGT maintains only one set of accounts, it chose to pay an additional Rs 2 million towards capital gains tax on behalf of the seller.

There were other difficulties too. A policeman once came to arrest them with a non-bailable warrant for petty mistakes, such as not displaying the "holiday list" or "timings of shifts," because a certain disgruntled factory inspector had taken the case to court. MGT officials showed patience and persistence till good sense prevailed.

During the initial years, facing such situations required the moral and emotional support of others. The company was fortunate to have the additional support and guidance of a few like-minded companies and people. Dr Jagmohan Garg of Garg Associates and Mr Sudhir Mittal of Sukruti Vidyut Udyog, Ghaziabad, both promoters of industrial units nearby, sometimes physically accompanied Mr Dhand or MGT officials to make joint representations to the authorities, where they underlined the genuineness of the cases and MGT's viewpoint.

Application of the same principles can be seen in MGT's dealings with customers, who are assured of quality products delivered on time, and with suppliers, who believe that MGT will make all payments on time.

"Integrity" in communication

The company has always maintained a policy of free communication with the employees from the topmost to all lower levels. Whether it is happy news about a prestigious order, or bad news about postponement of payment of bonus due to cash flow problems, there is always direct communication. Internal communication is not restricted to fixed formal channels but is encouraged to be free and open. Upward communication is encouraged through active listening.

Work Samiti and Staff Committee Meetings (group meetings) are held every 2 to 3 months, at which every employee, down to the lowest level (a carefully designed representation method uses rotation to ensure participation by all), is encouraged to attend. People are free to bring up any issues (except salaries!), including any new projects being planned or launched. Every employee is free to raise objections.

Whenever there is an important point to be conveyed, whether it is good or bad news, the top management gathers everyone informally on the shop floor and puts the news across. This has been institutionalized since 1990 in the form of a 'General Meeting' on the second Monday of every month. All the department heads, besides the MD, communicate in a free atmosphere, sharing all the important news, developments, and happenings, both inside and outside the company.

The process of culture-building has been given a renewed thrust through a 1-hour "No Agenda" meeting of eight to 10 people, held at intervals with the MD, in which employees can initiate and "talk about any topic on their mind." These are "Truth" and "Self-awareness" sessions. The statements are recorded on a panaboard (in Hindi if required), and afterwards a copy is distributed to all. Employees express their sentiments about a range of issues, including their own reflections about life, process improvements that are required in some unit, how to achieve teamwork, and even the bad smell of the tea being served! See Exhibit 11.6 for one such record.

In fact, at MGT, encouraging every individual to communicate freely and openly is recognized as an effective way of showing respect for individuals. In addition, it avoids all the troubles related to inevitable loss

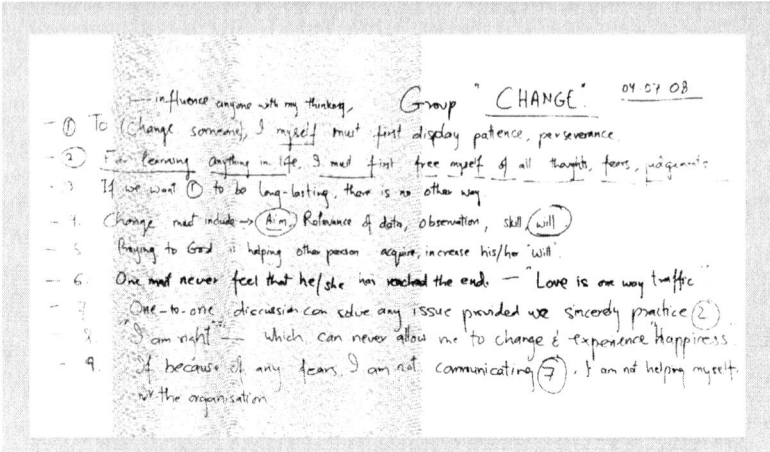

Exhibit 11.6   Statements recorded on a panaboard during a "No Agenda" meeting

of communication down the line, which often result in distortion of the facts and unfortunate interpretations at all levels. It also provides a *personal touch*, which the MD believes is most vital for important matters such as reinforcing the value system of the company. Of course, it puts a direct responsibility on the top management to "Tell It, As It Is."[5]

This integrity in communication is also the hallmark of interaction with outsiders, especially government departments, where the company persists in its stance of no bribes or graft money and chooses to spend time explaining its position to these bodies until the message sinks in.

"Equity" through respect

Perhaps the most important aspect in developing the culture at MGT has been to treat every person in the company as an individual who must be respected, irrespective of the nature of the work he does in the company. The respect factor is not in direct proportion to the individual's position in the hierarchy. Everyone has the right to express himself, and it is the duty of all seniors to listen to him. The person at the lowest level, if not satisfied with his immediate supervisor, can go to the highest level and enjoys the "right to be heard."[6]

The culture of honesty and respect has had its positive fallout in a culture of caring. On one occasion, the sister of a contract worker needed a blood transfusion after an accident. Scores of volunteers responded to a simple appeal. This was later openly appreciated, reinforcing the values emphasized by the company. Such genuine appreciation is another way of showing respect. Words of praise and appreciation are not withheld, and neither are rewards, giving a boost to people's sense of self-worth. And these are not isolated incidents. Respect and care for one another is a norm at MGT.

For example, 25 years ago, Mr Anil Agarwal, a young engineer in the design department, was trying to make ammonia prints. The bottle burst, ammonia entered his eyes, and he lost his eyesight. While many companies terminate the services of such employees after treatment, MGT sponsored his treatment for more than 10 years. Mr Agarwal still continues to work with MGT in the stores department.

Mr Amit Gupta, a senior engineer at MGT, notes the sense of caring that percolates down from the top to all levels. When the highest levels show so much care for others, both verbally and non-verbally, it is unlikely that others will not follow suit. In his opinion, this pro-individual approach has led to a higher degree of cooperation and lower levels of frustration than are prevalent in other companies.[7]

"Fairness" in sharing success

With the cost of living going up every day, we must appreciate and do whatever best possible to distribute the profits generated amongst the employees, who have contributed significantly in bringing those profits in the first place. I am sad to say that so much emphasis is laid upon dividend paid to the shareholders, but hardly any reference is made to the profits shared with the employees. (N. K. Dhand)[8]

Entrepreneurs' expectations of their employees often differ from their expectations of an owner when they were employees – they forget what it is like to be an employee. They tend to believe that success has been achieved solely due to their own efforts, forgetting the hard work put in by other colleagues and employees. At MGT, the management believes in fairness in sharing success with the employees.

So when success comes, as it so often does in an organization like MGT, the rewards are not confined to a chosen few. Micromatic Grinding has maintained an average level of 15–25 percent of net profits to be distributed among the employees as incentives and other benefits. This is in addition to the regular 20 percent bonus granted in recognition of the fact that profits are generated through teamwork. MGT has designed a scheme whereby a percentage of income beyond a certain limit (revised at the beginning of every financial year) is shared with the employees. To illustrate, in the coming year, 1 percent of the turnover beyond

Rs 380 million is to be distributed amongst the employees. This will be enhanced to 2 percent if the turnover exceeds Rs 420 million. While the share of bonuses and profits is linked to salary, the maximum salary for calculating an individual's share is also pegged (currently at Rs 0.12 million per annum). A significant portion, therefore, is distributed at the lower end of the hierarchy.

"Justice" to professionals and society

As well as fair sharing of success and encouraging free, frank, and open communication, Micromatic undertakes a number of initiatives that help in building a just society, both within and outside the organization.

"Professionalism" vs. "Family hierarchy"

In India, a potential area of friction in most family-held companies, both small and large-scale, presents itself when the next generation takes over at the helm, passing over the professionals who have helped to build up the enterprise. It is natural for the professionals to feel dejected, when, notwithstanding their competence, they see no chance of attaining top positions. MGT has clearly announced that this will not be its policy.[9] This has helped to maintain high professional standards in the company. Merit, performance, ethics, integrity, and honesty are the key recognition parameters for career advancement. Although both sons of Mr Dhand work in the organization, Mr J. P. Malik, a professional who joined the organization in 2003, is presently the joint managing director and second in command in the company.

Social justice for workers

Industrial workers in north India are generally first-generation rural migrants from poor or lower-class backgrounds. Large and public-sector companies provide many welfare facilities for these employees. However, little thought is given by small and medium enterprises (SMEs) to the social needs of their workers, who may find it difficult to cope with day-to-day problems such as timely and proper medical care, housing, school admissions, and so on. The staff and management are better equipped to solve these problems because of their education and social background. Micromatic, while admitting that it cannot solve all their problems, does show genuine interest in assisting these poor workers, guides them towards possible solutions, and also helps them financially, wherever possible, through well-thought-out schemes. Some of these schemes initiated by MGT are:

- There is a statutory provision in India for 1.75 percent deduction from wages as employees' contribution towards Employees State Insurance (ESI) for medical care, employers' contribution being about three times the amount. However, the reality is that ESI facilities are generally very poor, so no one even wants to visit the ESI dispensary. Irrespective of whether or not the employee is part of ESI, Micromatic provides a medical scheme for all employees, by which 75 percent of the medical expenses are borne by the employer. This scheme is totally voluntary and was started by the company about 30 years ago when there were only 20 employees. MGT also provides additional financial assistance for medical treatment, if required, depending upon the severity of the situation.
- The company offers low-interest housing loans, in addition to vehicle and marriage loans, to all employees on the basis of seniority of service as determined by number of years of service with the company, and not based on the position within the company alone. The amount may be small, but it is very important to the employee. The company views these small gestures as an appreciation of the employee, reflecting an understanding of the grim economic realities faced by employees in the lower-income group.
- Some workmen and technicians are taken on foreign tours to international machine tool exhibitions. This is quite unlike other organizations, where only senior managers and executives have the privilege of going on foreign tours.
- All employees have the opportunity for upward mobility. Many employees join at lower levels because they never had the opportunity to get higher education and training in their early life. The company tries to rectify the situation by offering opportunities for learning and education.[10]

It must be appreciated that these schemes were not initiated in response to demands by the employees in any bargaining process, but were offered voluntarily by the management of MGT. While some of these schemes, such as loans, might be offered in comparative SMEs, they are generally intended to placate the employees and do not result from adherence to a humanistic philosophy of management. Other schemes, such as medical assistance and foreign travel for workmen, are unique to MGT.

"Humility" in leadership

Many organizations make lofty claims to humanism and a service attitude to society. However, Mr Dhand feels[11] that it is not possible to "walk the talk" in the face of hardships if a person lacks humility – humility that has been cultivated through higher spiritual motivations in life.

> One cannot live by principles unless the belief comes from within, for it is what is truly inside that provides the wisdom and power necessary to actually live by the principles. I have focused on cultivating spiritual knowledge and discipline – a practice I have been regularly following since the past 15 years. My conviction is in the principles given in Gita.[12] When one has ahankar,[13] one cannot understand the nuances of humanistic management. Higher goals in life and surrender to universal laws break this ahankar, developing higher qualities of sensitivity, compassion, and lack of a sense of ownership, even while performing one's actions. (Mr N. K. Dhand, in a personal interview with the author)

The impact

And what are the rewards of these practices? Walking the talk of honesty and respect for human beings has enabled the company to win the *trust* of its employees. The relationship has matured into one of mutual faith, the most important asset of the company, which cannot be easily replicated by competition. So now, if the company has a cash flow problem and the employees are informed, they believe the management. In such a trusting atmosphere, there are no industrial relations problems due to employee unrest. This trust has led to other gains, both economic and non-economic.

The cool fire of rightsizing

This trust was put to test at a critical phase of MGT's history, when the company had to resort to rightsizing during a downturn in business (1998–2002). Mr Dhand was initially quite concerned and perplexed about this step, which again was a very painful decision. Yet the trust built up over the years made the process smooth.

The decision on downsizing was not taken by a handful of people behind closed doors; rather, all the employees of MGT were involved in the process. Continuous, clear, and transparent flow of information about the fortunes of the company was maintained. Detailed information about the company's reduced orders and margins of profit was made available to everyone. Frequent meetings were held to discuss measures being taken to tackle the crisis, at which all could speak up and be heard with respect. Other cost-cutting measures were tried, and their impact was openly discussed. The top 10 people of the company took a 10 percent deduction in their salary as a measure of sacrifice in the greater interest. Finally, when it became clear to the employees that there was no alternative to reduction in staff, stress was laid on sacrifice and a Voluntary Retirement Scheme (VRS) was offered by the company. VRS was regarded as a sacrifice by the individual for the company's long-term viability.

Keeping in tune with the humanistic philosophy of MGT, VRS was handled very sensitively and gradually, and people's reactions, even the emotional and negative ones, were empathically considered. All support and counseling were provided to those leaving, including assistance in finding alternative employment. Guidance was available to those interested in setting up their own private ventures. A number of people were advised to set up subsidiary businesses and assisted in a significant way by being given old machinery at nominal prices. Contracts for services and for supplying parts were given to people who had been laid off. The parting was not like that of a contractual separation; it was parting as friends. MGT kept in touch with the old employees and was still taking an interest in them a few years after the layoff. Even now, relationships between the company and the former employees are maintained. Former employees continue to be invited to MGT functions and to personal events such as weddings.[14]

Financial success

The company has been steadily growing and expanding, and has never seen a loss-making year since its inception. These principles have not only made MGT a profit-making company throughout its entire 35-year history, but have also made it the number one company in its field in India, with nearly 40 percent market share. In fact, MGT is setting up a new plant in Bangalore, as well as another subsidiary company for sheet metal manufacturing in Ghaziabad. The same humanistic principles are being adopted by the directors in charge of these projects, with no interference from the current MD, and they are prepared for the pain and pleasure of sticking to humanistic principles and values in the new projects.

Mr Dhand believes that while ethical principles and humanistic management styles provide the foundation on which everything else rests at Micromatic Grinding, they are not sufficient for the success of a business enterprise. As the business model shows, the role of quality, product development and customer satisfaction cannot be denied. MGT has been awarded a certificate of merit by the National Productivity Council of India, is an ISO 9001 certified company, and has an R&D laboratory certified by the Department of Science, Government of India.

> MGT has a strong focus on ensuring a strong value proposition for the customers – approximately 10–15% better value than the nearest competition. (Mr N. K. Dhand, in an interview with the author)

Efficiencies

MGT's very adherence to principles actually ensures process efficiencies and intangible gains in the long run. Trust between the workers and management, and amongst the workers themselves, is possibly the greatest intangible for any business today. Employees are motivated and want to contribute their best. No man-hours have ever been lost due to agitation or strikes. All these help the managers and workers to focus on production, on R&D, and on customers.

Employee satisfaction

Over 100 new employees have been recruited in the last 3 years. Although salaries at MGT are lower than those offered by other companies, employees prefer to stay at MGT. The attrition rate in the company is only about 6–7 percent, compared with an average of 12–15 percent in similar industries.

This satisfaction and bonding with the company were evident in this author's interviews with employees. Mr Sanjay Singh, Assistant General Manager (Design), had left the company in late 1990s (for higher pay) but rejoined MGT in 2005, primarily for the family feeling and clean working at MGT. In the words of Mr R. A. Yadav, Assistant Manager (Assembly): "*sukh dukh mein sab saath rahte hain* [We are one in times of happiness and distress]." No wonder the employees of MGT have not felt the need to form a trade union.

External reputation

Despite difficulties in the initial years, by persistently sticking to its principles, MGT has built a reputation outside the organization – with customers, with suppliers, and even with the government authorities.

All payments by MGT to suppliers are timely, and if there is any delay the suppliers appreciate that this must be because of some genuine difficulty, and continue their supplies. It is now well known in government offices that MGT will not pay any "facilitation fee," and the word is spread by office bearers. If a new officer comes to a department, he is warned by other employees not to expect anything from MGT, so the work is not delayed as much as previously. Thus, in the long run, the company has saved resources.

Coping with the current recession

MGT has not remained unaffected by the recent recession. Yet in the financial year 2008–9 the company increased its turnover by more than 6 percent and made a profit of Rs 18 million, largely because of orders it had received earlier. The real test will come in the current financial year, as the orders are slowly dwindling. The company has shifted to a 5-day working week since January 2009, and has also made salary cuts at the top level, a strategy which was accepted by all management and staff. The MD personally took a salary cut of 20 percent; the salaries of those in the senior management team were reduced by 10 percent, while other managers' salaries were cut by 5 percent. The workers' salaries have not been touched.

A great learning

However, not all service initiatives have been welcomed. Around 3 years ago, MGT started a solid waste management activity in a few sectors of Raj Nagar, an upmarket colony of Ghaziabad, with the assistance of an NGO, Exnora, from Chennai in south India. Dustbins were provided to residents for separating biodegradable from non-biodegradable waste at source. These were then taken to a separate central facility where the waste was sorted and 90 percent of solid waste sold for recycling. However, the regular sweepers' community from the adjoining Raispur village refused to be involved, as they felt under threat of losing their monthly income. They attacked the rickshaws carrying the waste under the new scheme. It was an important learning for MGT that there is a lack of trust in our society and that such initiatives cannot succeed unless they first work to build up faith, and unless the people affected are assured of a better working life. These sweepers were used to working for only a few hours every day. While some of them would have lost some immediate part-time income, they had been offered full-time employment under the scheme and would have benefited in the long term. Yet they preferred the old ways of working instead of the normal 8 hours under the new system.

The company has now, therefore, started working on building trust, with the same community from Raispur village, before launching any such new initiatives again. This is being done with the help of an NGO, Gram Niyojana Kendra (GNK), which has sufficient expertise and experience of working in this area. The purpose is to build alternative sources of income for these families before weaning them away from past habits and menial tasks, which have formed their sources of meagre, or no, income until now:

- For example, a tailoring and beautician's course has been started to assist girls and ladies of the community in earning an additional income for the household.
- In November 2008, MGT began, again through GNK, to train people for geriatric care, selecting ladies from the same area. This will enable the trainees to earn up to Rs 5,000 (about USD 100) per month, a significant amount for uneducated middle-aged ladies with no other possible source of earnings to support their families. About 50 of these trainees are already fully employed.

Conclusions

There have been other companies that have started with similar ethical principles, but have not been as successful. One of the companies started operations at around the same time as MGT. It doggedly stuck to honesty and ethics, but appeared not to care about its employees. Without understanding others and their needs, the owner expected others to accept and follow his values and beliefs in an authoritarian way. Although this company started off well, it lost its market reputation over the course of time. Another company deviated from its ethical practices when the son of the owner–manager started to influence its functioning. This company witnessed many strikes and often had to deal with labor issues. These examples illustrate that ethics should not be treated in isolation from humanistic principles. A dogmatic adherence to ethics is yet another source for developing *ahankar* (false ego) that makes one forget the humanistic purpose of all activities.

In this sense, Mr N. K. Dhand has been a wise and competent leader – a leader who sensibly practiced what he professed. He adopted a holistic style of ethics and humanism to build up the unique culture at

MGT. But questions remain. Will the culture survive after his exit? Will his successor be willing and able to continue along similar lines? Even now, some concerns are being raised about the quality of the new recruits, who have very high aspirations and are not so eager to accept the ethical principles of working. Retention of these recruits has also become an issue, as the market is providing many opportunities. And what about the economic recession? Will the downturn in the economy affect management practices at MGT? Will it affect the future of the company, and, more importantly, the future of its employees? Mr Dhand was aware that the company had not received a single order for CNC machines, which formed the greatest volume of sales, in the last few months.

Most employees are of the opinion that the humanistic approach has become part and parcel of the cultural fabric of MGT. It is more like a habit. The processes at Micromatic Grinding are tuned to preserving the value-based culture. Yet, in interviews with the author, a few employees feel that no successor will be able to reach the maturity levels of Mr N. K. Dhand. They feel comfortable and secure with Mr Dhand, but not with others. However, others say that it would be very difficult, if not impossible, to change the culture of MGT. Any efforts by a successor to change the value system will be met by stiff resistance, for it has become a part of discipline, part of people's behavior. Even if possible, it will take a long time for any significant changes to be visible.

Mr Dhand looked forward to the meeting ahead – another session of free and open exchanges between the MD and the employees. He was not worried – yet concerned – another quality he had developed by virtue of his personal spiritual engagement.

It is important to understand humanistic principles and ethical values in their true spirit!

Acknowledgements

The author would like to express his gratitude to:

(a) Mr N. K. Dhand, MD of Micromatic Grinding Technologies Ltd, Ghaziabad, for permitting the writing and publication of the case, and also for the deep personal interest he took in sharing his humanistic principles of management.
(b) Mr S. J. Dujari, head (Finance and HR), and Mr Prashant Kumar, assistant manager (HR), who provided much of the assistance

required in collecting data and arranging for the author to conduct personal interviews with the employees of MGT.

(c) Dr Archana Tyagi, adjunct faulty (OB/HR) at the University of Business and International Studies, Geneva, and formerly professor at the Institute of Management Technology, Ghaziabad, for first introducing the author to Mr N. K. Dhand and MGT.

(d) The management, staff, and workers of MGT, many of whom took time for interviews and shared their views with the author about the culture at MGT.

Notes

1. Dhand, 1998.
2. JTEKT Corporation (formerly Toyoda Machine Works) is a $12 billion machine tool and auto-component manufacturer, and number one cylindrical grinding machine tool builder in the world. It is a rare feat for MGT, one thousandth the size of JTEKT Corporation, to have entered into a joint venture arrangement with this manufacturer.
3. Dhand, 2002, p. 93.
4. Dhand, 1998.
5. Ibid; Sharma, 2007.
6. Dhand, 2002.
7. Sharma, 2007.
8. Dhand, 1998.
9. Dhand, 2002.
10. Dhand, 1998.
11. Such internalizations in the case are based on feelings and beliefs revealed by the respondents during personal interviews with the author.
12. *Bhagavad Gita*, which is the holy text for many Hindus.
13. False sense of ego – wherein one regards oneself as the master and the doer of action, instead of an "instrument" of the Divine.
14. Sharma, 2007.

Bibliography

The case draws upon personal interviews with the management and employees of Micromatic Grinding Technologies Limited, as well as documents and material provided by MGT. Some of these are referenced below:

Dhand, N. K. (1998). *Business and Ethics*. Lecture delivered by Mr N. K. Dhand at IIM Ahmedabad, December 14 (handout).

Dhand, N. K. (2002). Business and ethics. *IIMB Management Review*, Vol. 14 (4), 93–96.

Sharma, M. (2007). The role of communication in building organizational culture: The case of Micromatic Grinding, pp. 609–618, in Kaul, A. and Gupta, S. K. (eds) *Management Communication: Trends and Strategies*. New Delhi: Tata-McGraw.

Tyagi, A. and Singh, B. D. (2005). Translating core ethical values into business climate: The case of Micromatic Grinding Technologies Ltd, pp. 271–286, in Sahay, B. S., Stough, R. and Sardana, G. D. (eds) *Cases in Management*. New Delhi: Allied Pubs. Pvt. Ltd.

Various brochures and corporate documents of Micromatic Grinding Technologies Ltd.

Website: www.micromaticgrinding.com

12
Mondragon: Could Something Like This Be in Our Future?

Terry Mollner

My first visit to Mondragon was in 1979. I had been searching the globe for years for a modern company that had moved beyond the common wisdom of the day. My initial reaction to Mondragon was utter amazement. I had never expected to find such a mature and comprehensive example. They are now the largest corporation in the Basque Country and the seventh largest in Spain. They are also the world's largest worker cooperative. However, they are different from the worker cooperatives of the past in one very significant way: their highest priority is not the workers; it is the common good of us all.

Let me give you a short description of the Mondragon Cooperatives. Then I will share what I believe are some of the major lessons we can learn from their more than three decades of stunning success.

The inspiration behind the Mondragon Cooperative Corporation (MCC) was a Catholic priest who in his own way understood the difference between immature and mature behavior. Therefore, he very self-consciously invited some young men to join with him in creating democratic organizations based on giving priority to the common good. The particular highest priority was the creation of more worker-owned jobs for others... not primarily the financial success and social fulfillment of the members of the cooperatives.

His first assignment upon leaving the seminary in 1941 was to be an assistant pastor at the Catholic Church in the small town of Mondragon, which is high in the Pyrenees Mountains of northern Spain. Mondragon is in the Basque region and Father Don Jose Maria Arizmendiarrieta was Basque. This was just after the Spanish Civil War had been won by General Francisco Franco and his fascist party.

Franco had had a difficult time defeating the Basques, who had sided with the freely elected democratic socialist government against the fascists. The democratic socialists had promised that, if they won, the Basques would be able to separate amicably from Spain and create their own nation. As a result, after the war Franco treated the Basque country like an occupied nation. He even outlawed the Basque language. As you can imagine, this forged a strong bond among the Basques, on top of the deep solidarity that already existed within Basque society.

The rainfall in the Pyrenees is such that there has never been a drought. Thus, the Basques have never had to migrate. They have lived in those mountains for the whole of recorded history. Also, their farming and village life has been based on consensual democratic policies for as long as they can remember. At the same time, they have always been dominated by other people. These conditions, plus a unique language and common religion, have forged a deep feeling of family among the Basque people.

So Father Arizmendi, not only a devout Catholic but also a staunch Basque, set about meeting the needs of his parishioners. There was a need for education and jobs. He first started a high school, then the first worker cooperative with five of the boys he had become especially close to as they were going through his school. Since Mondragon was a small town, very far off the beaten path, the people in Mondragon had not only the solidarity of history but also the immediate experience of being prisoners in a prison camp. In this setting, as is usually true of oppressed and imprisoned people, it was natural for Mondragonians to give priority to their solidarity as Basques – the common good of the group – over their individual self-interests: a very fertile soil, within which Father Arizmendi could grow not only businesses but an entire society that gave priority to the common good.

The philosophy of Father Arizmendi

To this fertile mix Don Jose Maria added his view of mature human behavior. Mondragon gives priority to the non-material (call it "agreements" or "mind" or "spirit" or "relationship"). The common good is given priority over a particular good. Or, to put it another way, people come before things.

What is the mature relationship among people? If we let go of our fear of using the word in a business setting, we all know from our personal experience that the one-word answer to this question is "love." But how does love play itself out in the structuring of a business enterprise?

From my research on Arizmendi, I have concluded that he observed that friends (mature people) behave differently around "things" than enemies (immature people). If we are friends or lovers and we have an apple which we both want, we probably will split the apple as evenly as possible and share it. If one of us has not eaten all day and the other just has had a full meal, the latter will take the smaller piece and give the larger half, or even the whole apple, to the former.

Friends behave almost as if they had only one mind and one body. With little effort they share resources appropriately as easily together as they make decisions alone.

Enemies, on the other hand, behave in the opposite manner. If we are enemies and we have an apple, one of us might try to gobble it down while the other is not noticing. Or, if the other is too smart for that, we might agree to share it by cutting it in half. Then we would both try to take the bigger piece, even if one of us had just had a full meal.

Enemies behave as if they had two separate minds and bodies. This is because they think "things" are most important. There being only so many things around at any one time, they try to acquire as many of them as they can. Life for them is a process of competing and taking.

The difference between friends and enemies lies in the fact that the relationship among friends can be timeless and spaceless. For instance, if we make a mistake with a friend, apologize and are forgiven, it can be as if it never happened. Yet it did happen. A human relationship can be timeless and spaceless; things, on the other hand, exist in time and space. *If the relationship is truly mature*, I believe Father Arizmendi would have argued, *there can be an absence of conflict around things.*

Arizmendi simply extended this relationship of the feeling of oneness known by all in friendships and between lovers into the relationship with all things, even with those who see themselves as our enemies – like Franco and his Guardia Civil soldiers, who were nearly always in view when moving about town.

Arizmendi pointed out that they were powerless to decide what people were thinking.

Thus, rather than confronting them, which would be acting as if they could, Arizmendi separated what people were doing from the language and belief system within which they were doing it. "Let's do what we want to do and then simply talk about it in their language and ideas," is the kind of thing Don Jose Maria might have said. "Since in their world view they think we are prisoners, by not confronting them they will think we have accepted our role as prisoners. Oh, we will confront them politically but in all other areas we will be free to do exactly what we want right under their noses. They will think political freedom is the only game in town and we know it isn't. Thus, with them we will act like it is not only most important but also the only important issue. They will be happy and we will be happy without confrontation in all other areas of life." Using this strategy they were able to be happy and prosperous. They were also able to build a society of their own design; this is what was most important to them on a day-to-day basis. They also knew it would outlast the political disagreements.

Stated another way, they discovered that they had the choice of whether or not to give their power to the soldiers. Don Jose Maria convinced them that they could keep their power and use it to build wonderful lives together. His non-violent or loving method of dealing with an oppressor did not even necessitate confrontation. (This makes me think that perhaps Father Arizmendi took non-violent political action to another stage of maturity beyond where Mahatma Gandhi had taken it ... to post-confrontation.)

The lesson here for managers is that in one way or the other we all have an explanation for how life makes sense. They will surely differ, but we all agree that it makes sense to do one thing rather than another at all times. We also each have an explanation of how our thinking all fits together into a whole. This means we all have a sense of our responsibility to that larger whole as well as to ourselves. When we discover that by giving priority to the whole we can have both the needs of the whole and the part fully met, we have moved up to the higher layers of human maturity. This is where we give priority to the common good; throughout history this has usually been described as "moral behavior." If managers genuinely ask all to give priority to the common good, not just of the team but of us all, there is no better basis for uniting people in productive activity. Each of us has our explanation of why it makes sense to give priority to the common good, the whole. By speaking to it we tap this natural unifying force. In a publicly traded corporation where Wall Street has determined that the highest priority is the financial interests of a few, the shareholders, it can be difficult to even give priority to the other local stakeholders, the customers, suppliers, communities, environment, and so on, much more the common good of us all. However, in a context of accepting whatever prison walls exist, as the Mondragonians did, it is still always possible to give priority to the common good wherever and however we can. That is being realistic, and that realism helps neutralize the power of those walls and allows the intuitive priority of the common good in us all to be tapped.

The history of Mondragon

In 1943 Father Arizmendi assisted the students in his youth group to start a cooperative technical high school using funds donated by the community. There were parents, students, teachers, administrators, and community members on its Board of Trustees. He became head of the school. He taught his philosophy to his students, and to many in the community through his evening adult study group classes and conversations in bars, as the way up and out of their predicament. He was not charismatic – people fell asleep during his sermons – but he was sure of his views, consistent, and persistent. The question for which he is most remembered is, "How can we do this in a way which works fully for those in the enterprise and those in the community rather than for one more than the other?" He never let them believe that it was necessary for someone to win and someone to lose. Giving priority to the common good *within an acceptance of conditions as they are until they can be changed for the better* allows all to win.

By 1954 five of his original 11 youth group boys who had gone to college had worked their way up to management levels at the large industrial company in town, the Union Carrejera. However, they became frustrated in their efforts to apply Father Arizmendi's ideas. So they left and formed a new company (Ulgor) where they could implement his teachings. They raised funds from local townspeople, just as they had when they had started the technical school. In 1956 they opened a small paraffin stove factory with 24 people. When butane gas arrived in Spain, they converted to butane stoves and caught the industrial wave entering Spain. Within one year, they had 117 owner–workers and had bought two nearby foundries.

Today, the "Mondragon Cooperative Corporation" is an association of 150 cooperative enterprises, more than 100 of which are owner–worker industrial cooperatives. In 2006 they contributed 3.8 percent towards the total GDP of the Basque Region. Beautiful, clean, and modern factories stretch out along the valley for several miles and are scattered throughout the Basque Region of northern Spain. More than 20 percent of sales are for export, and they now own factories in other parts of the world. They are not cooperatives; this is a concern to many who study them. Many believe that this reveals that their priority is no longer the common good of us all, but rather that of the Basque people. Some of us think Father Arizmendi is continually rolling over in his grave because of this loss of original priority. They argue that people outside the Basque Country do not have the same natural inclinations toward cooperation as are nurtured in their society; yet they treat their workers extremely well in these factories. As someone who has assisted in the development of worker cooperatives and micro-loan programs in the USA, I would have to agree that the high priority on individual freedom here and in many other areas of the world makes it extremely difficult for cooperatives to be successful.

There are more than 50,000 members, whose jobs are virtually guaranteed for life. In downturns, pay cuts are preferred over lay-offs. If workers are laid off, they are given preference in the hiring at other cooperatives. And during the deep European business recession of the late 1970s and early 1980s, when 20 percent of the employees in the surrounding economy lost their jobs, the cooperatives increased employment by 36 percent! They tend to be consistently expanding.

The association of cooperatives is governed by a 650-member cooperative congress, its delegates elected from across the individual cooperatives. The annual general assembly elects a governing council, which has day-to-day management responsibilities and appoints senior staff. For each individual business there is also a workplace council, the elected president of which assists management with the running of the business on behalf of the workers.

More than half of the Mondragon companies are focused on industry, producing the full range of consumer and industrial goods, ranging from plastic rulers to bicycles to robots. Collectively, they are Spain's top producers of industrial machinery and major home appliances – refrigerators, stoves, washers and dryers, machine tools, and so on. In addition, the Mondragon enterprises lead the way in heavy construction, furniture production, farming, and high technology. Spain's first producer of computer chips was a Mondragon firm. Its supermarket arm, Eroski, is the largest retail food chain in Spain and the third largest retail group in Spain.

Co-op members have a broad health insurance plan for their families, a private unemployment program which pays 80 percent of take-home pay if an owner–worker is ever laid off, and a pension program, separate from their accumulation of profits, paying 60 percent of their salary on the last day of work until death. Upon retirement, most members are also offered a plot for a vegetable garden if they don't happen to have one where they live.

They have their own cooperative bank, The Caja Laboral Popular (The Bank of the Working People). As might be expected, all the members and businesses do their banking with their own bank.

I believe that the major lesson here is that all the needs of employees and their families can be met in the private sector rather than by relying on government. They have proven that it can be done. Good government programs should not be duplicated, but they also do not need to be relied upon.

Mature entrepreneurship

I was amazed when I learned that the Entrepreneurial Division, which provides venture capital for developing new cooperatives, has close to a 100 percent success rate! In other words, nearly every cooperative it has capitalized has succeeded. By contrast, venture capitalists in the United States consider a 20 percent success rate respectable, with 80 percent of all new businesses failing within the first 5 years.

The secret of Mondragon's success is that they have a unique approach to business development which virtually guarantees success every time. It not only assumes every new business will succeed, but it also makes a commitment to the business until it does, and it backs this pledge with highly skilled staff at the corporation's Entrepreneurial Division (ED). Managers can learn from this when building teams to carry out projects.

They only begin with a group of people who are already friends, never with one individual. They view these natural bonds of friendship as the bedrock upon which the new firm is built. Then the ED and the founding group agree to stay together until the business is profitable. The members of the founder group put up twice the membership fee others will invest and the ED loans the business the rest of the capital at approximately 13 percent. If the business has difficulty, the ED loans any additional capital at 8 percent. If more trouble, 0 percent. If still more trouble, the Bank will donate capital to the business. In other words, *the riskier the loan the lower the interest rate!* Eventually, even if they have to switch managers or even their product line, the business becomes successful and is able to repay much if not all of the loans, although the bank often uses a portion of its profits to reduce the size of the loans of all of its cooperative businesses.

You may think this is a very unusual relationship. However, it is not as foreign as you might think. The ED is simply relating to these new businesses in the same way as any large company relates to a new division it has created to produce a new product. The only difference is that the ED itself is a division of the one conglomerate called the MCC, and this is its particular task. The circle defining our "we" has simply been extended by all beyond the new corporation to include not only the ED but the entire community.

Unlike conventional businesses, which rank their priorities capital–product–managers–workers, Mondragon ranks its priorities in exactly the opposite order: workers–managers–product–capital. People are given the highest priority and "things" the lowest.

Because capital is mainly stored labor and since the entire community is behind the creation of any business, nothing – not even capital – is ever abandoned. As long as the community is willing to put labor into the formation of a business, there will be capital available. This way the ED never has defaulted loans, interest rates can be lower for riskier loans because the ED will never abandon the business (so it's better not to overburden it), the owner–workers get guaranteed jobs for life, the community gets a stable commercial sector, and the consumers get high-quality, inexpensive products. Everyone wins. This is all the result of thinking in the more mature way Father Arizmendi taught them and having different priorities as a result.

In Mondragon, the venture capital to finance new businesses comes from the savings accounts of bank depositors! This is virtually never done elsewhere. Does this scare depositors? Apparently not. The Caja Laboral Popular is one of the fastest-growing and most successful banks in the world, with a branch in nearly every Basque neighborhood and more than two million depositors. As of 2007 it had USD 20 billion in total assets. To assure that the businesses remain strong, the seasoned business experts at the ED monitor the performance of every cooperative on a monthly basis. They are quick to recommend action if any difficulties emerge.

Mondragon's commercial and community businesses

The MCC has not limited its activities to business and banking. Its total approach includes the needs of workers, their families, and the surrounding community. They have participated in nearly every realm of community development. They have built over 40 cooperative housing complexes, many incorporating grocery stores and other retail shops. They have created the equivalent of private day care, grade school, high school, and higher education facilities. The Mondragon educational system includes over 40 schools and the University of Mondragon with over 4,000 students. In addition, there is a student cooperative, which allows working students to fully cover their tuition and living expenses for their private high school and college while offering the experience of running their own cooperative. Looking at all these benefits, it is no wonder that people brought up in the system usually stay. To support this, children of members go to the head of the line of those seeking positions in Mondragon cooperatives.

In a study carried out in the early 1990s, the profitability of the Mondragon cooperatives was found to be twice that of the average corporation in Spain. Of even greater significance, worker productivity in the cooperatives is higher than in any other organization in Spain. While much of their success in this area is the result of Mondragon's innovative management approach, it can also be attributed to their aggressive use of high-technology production methods, such as robotics. And, casting all conclusions about management performance aside, in a study by the Anglo-German Foundation for the Study of Industrial Society the management was found to be among the most aggressive and innovative ever seen by the Foundation's staff. Also, the members were found to be highly motivated and personally fulfilled by their jobs.

In light of the MCC's extraordinary success record, it should come as no surprise that the MCC became the Basque's model for the future. What is surprising is that the cooperatives were built in spite of suffering over 40 years of repression under General Francisco Franco – a testament to the wisdom of Father Arizmendi. The Spanish dictator died in 1975, but the Basques were not granted local autonomy until 1982. Then, in the 1989 meeting of the Basque National Congress, Mondragon's "third way" was adopted as the official economic policy of the new Basque nation. This may be the first nation in modern times to commit itself to the development of cooperative economics.

The structure of a Mondragon enterprise

Having articulated his philosophy, Father Arizmendi asked his young students and the men and women in the bars and drinking clubs: "If these ideas are true, what kind of an organization does it suggest?"

First, they realized that if they wanted to have a "loving organization," they could not define seemingly opposite roles, for example workers and owners, as the responsibility of different people, as if these roles could be separated. After all, are we not all both full co-owners and co-workers of the planet at all times before we are anything else?

To have easy and freely chosen one-mindedness, it is best if the owner and the worker in a business are the same person. If I am the person who decides what movie to go to and you are the person who goes to the movie, that will seem ludicrous to us. In this example, we easily can see that to separate the *choosing* and the *doing* from one another in time and space (into different bodies) brings fear into the relationship. We will each fear that the other will not be sensitive enough to our needs and wants. The potential for conflict is great.

If I am the chooser *and* the doer, however, I have no fear at all. I know I will be sensitive to my needs and wants, so the relationship between the chooser and doer, both being in me, is peaceful. This inner peace is the result of my freedom; the capitalist in me is happy.

If you and I are going to a movie together and we both are the chooser and the doer, then our relationship can be timeless and spaceless. If we are lovers and you want to go to movie A and I want to go to movie B, we will talk about it. If you want to go to movie A more than I want to go to movie B, we will decide to go to movie A. *We will both be happy – yet in the material world I did not get anything I initially wanted while you got everything you first wanted.* We are happy because we freely acted as if we had one body and mind. The limitations of the material world are fully accepted; we could only go to one movie together. There is peace in the relationship. This peace is the result of solidarity; the democratic socialist in us is happy.

Then Father Arizmendi rose above and beyond the current immature capitalism and democratic socialism by identifying this as not only the loving relationship between the roles of owner and worker but also between the enterprise and everyone outside the enterprise. The individual freedom of others is honored and the good of all is given priority. Thus, this democratic enterprise is also unlike most other democratic workplaces, which explains why it is so successful when most other cooperatives have, more often than not, struggled or failed. In a "mature cooperative" all share the same top priority – the common good. In an immature cooperative, each has a different highest priority – each individual's self-interest. Conflict, not cooperation, is still the basis of the philosophy. Thus, as at Mondragon, Father Arizmendi's mature world view will eventually allow a plethora of democratic workplaces to emerge and flourish within a free market economy.

So, the first rule of a mature cooperative is that the chooser and the doer – the owner and the worker – must be the same person. This merger of roles must go beyond titles and become the actual inner and outer (operational) experience of each member.

Not only does each worker invest in the business by working all day, but also, for the business to succeed, the worker must also become equally invested as an owner. Mondragon believes there is only one thing that will assure this investment as an owner, and that is risking capital (stored labor). Everyone knows what ownership is. It is being at risk if something which is ours gets damaged or lost. People can be fully invested in something without being financially at risk. However, Mondragon wants everyone in the community to be equally invested to be members. So they need to make sure everyone becomes invested 100 percent as an owner. To ensure this, every member is required to loan the cooperative a substantial sum (without collateral) which is the equivalent of the lowest annual salary (about USD 30,000).

New members do not have to possess this capital on day one. They simply sign a note and it will be withheld from their salary over time with no interest attached. Membership, thereby, is open to all, regardless of financial circumstances. If the business goes bankrupt the next day, however, the owner–workers will still need to pay off the loan to the bankruptcy courts. In other words, even though the capital was not loaned on day one, the owner–worker is fully at risk and invested as an owner from the beginning.

The rest of the structure of a Mondragon cooperative is equally insightful, as it provides interesting perspectives on human nature. Only members of the cooperative can be on its Board of Trustees. This assures adult–adult psychology patterns. Many owner–worker cooperatives in the past have invited non-members, such as helpful lawyers and financial investors, to be on their boards, resulting in parent–child psychological patterns.

Each board has two main committees: the Management Council and the Social Council. The manager is an owner–worker who is hired as manager for a 4-year term. During that time the manager cannot be told what to do; he or she can only be demoted. This unique aspect of the Mondragon design is based on the recognition that management is a specialty skill. So Mondragon hires skilled managers and then gets out of their way and lets them do their jobs. This has solved perhaps one of the greatest problems of all other owner–worker cooperative experiments.

In past efforts, managers were suspect because the workers had come from capitalist enterprises where the hierarchy was used as a power tool. As a result, managers often did not have specialized training, and, even if they did, the other owner–workers used their influence to demand changes in management's business plan without sensitivity to the sophistication of its design. Because of these tendencies toward ineffective management, it has been widely believed that democratic ownership could never compete in a capitalist society.

Mondragon has solved this problem by identifying the essence of hierarchy. They discovered that its essence is *efficiency and not power.* A hierarchical division of labor is the most efficient way for a group of people to do a complex task; and, *if the relationships among the people are of the timeless and spaceless variety described earlier, then hierarchy is only an efficiency system.*

Thus, Article 4 of the Social Statutes of Ulgor (the first cooperative), as written by Father Arizmendi, reads: "Work is the means adopted for attaining a higher level of satisfaction for human aspirations and demonstrating collaboration with the other members of the community to promote the common good. To ensure that it is contributed freely, productively, and in a manner that makes everyone's collaboration viable, the members shall respect its discipline, namely a hierarchy..."

At the same time, the Social Council provides the equivalent of a union *within* the cooperative structure and also serves as a forum to provide workers the opportunity for full participation in management.

Every division of 20 to 50 owner–workers in each business conducts at least a monthly work-group meeting to discuss any issues that have arisen. Each division has a representative who will meet with all the other representatives in the Social Council. The Board of Trustees delegate to the Social Council all the issues with which unions are normally concerned: job descriptions, salary scales, fringe benefits, safety, and so on. The Social Council is also responsible for donating 10 percent of any annual company profits to charity. (This compares very favorably with the average American corporate contribution to charity of less than 2 percent.)

Management and the Social Council representatives are part of each division group. There could also be a member of the group who has been elected to the Board of Trustees. Through this system every owner–worker can be involved in managing every aspect of the enterprise. During these meetings, the owner–workers can discuss anything they choose. Whether an owner–worker becomes enthusiastic about management issues or traditional union issues, his or her substantial capital investment keeps the commitment – as an owner and a worker – both 100 percent present in his or her mind. All owner–workers have one share of voting stock. This keeps them all equal in power. Thus, their relationship within themselves and among each other, as well as with the rest of society, is the pattern of "one-minded cooperation" for the common good.

The structure of the cooperative reflects this one-mindedness. The capitalist system's equivalent of management and union are each present and distinct in the MCCs; however, they are both inside the "*us*" of the cooperative, and are subservient to the Board, which assures their total integration and coordination. If the board ever fails in this task, the general assembly of all the owner–workers, which wields the ultimate power within each cooperative, can overrule the board.

Each cooperative elects representatives to the Cooperative Congress. The Congress in turn elects the board of the secondary cooperatives, such as the bank, the research institute, the entrepreneurial division, and the insurance and social security institutions. The main focus of the Cooperative Congress in Mondragon is the creation of owner–worker jobs to expand the opportunity for people to participate in the cooperative economy. There probably is no better service to themselves either, when you take a hard look at it. Job creation gives the current owner–workers greater job security and allows them to be enthusiastic about automation. They are very aggressive in robot development. They recognize that it both eliminates repetitive and dirty jobs and increases productivity, which is important in an international marketplace.

At the same time, they view owner–worker job creation as the best service to the community at large. Once a person has an owner–worker job in a Mondragon cooperative, best efforts are made to guarantee it for life. Thus the person's family will never be dependent upon public assistance but will continually contribute to the needs and development of society. Therefore, every act of each owner–worker every day is experienced as providing for one's self and serving society, both simultaneously and both 100 percent. The for-profit versus non-profit personality split with which we are so familiar in our society is absent in the attitude of the Mondragon member. When you walk through a factory, you feel as if you were visiting with someone in their kitchen or working at a church fund-raising event; and yet their productivity is the highest in Spain.

Finally, the uniqueness of Mondragon is demonstrated in the way profits are distributed by a cooperative. Fifty percent is distributed among the owner–workers based on salary scale and the number of years with the cooperative. However, these profits are not given out in cash. They are allocated to the owner–worker's *internal capital account* and regarded as a loan from the member to the company. Each year, just before Christmas, the member receives, in cash, the 6 percent interest paid annually on his or her internal account. Thus, the owner–worker's investment in the cooperative increases and the cooperative reinvests the worker's profit to create more cooperative economy jobs.

The business receives capital without collateral, normally the most difficult and expensive capital to borrow, at a low interest rate.

Ten percent of the annual profits are donated to charity and the remaining 40 percent are retained in the *collective internal account*. If the cooperative ever ceases to exist, this collective account will be donated to charity, because it is regarded as the portion of profits that is collectively owned and managed for the common good. So, even the profits escape the time and space material axis by seeming to go in two directions at the same time. The owner–worker has the use of his or her portion of the 50 percent because it can be used as collateral at the bank for a loan which will be at an interest rate only a point or two over the 6 percent it is earning. Yet the cooperative has the use of the capital at the same time.

As you can see, there is great power in a mature understanding of the nature of human relationships. By giving priority to the common good we can capitalize on the fact that all humans naturally prefer to give it priority. This can allow for a very high level of self-conscious collaboration and co-creation, for easy and high productivity, for using hierarchy as primarily an efficiency system instead of a power system, and for uniting the priorities of a worker, an owner, and the community into each action by each participant. This results in enhanced personal fulfillment, great morale, and financial and social security.

Mondragon's five guiding principles

Don Jose Maria prepared the first by-laws and social statutes that extended his world view into every aspect of the agreements upon which the business was based, making sure to leave no opening for an easy unraveling into the immature method of operation. This is evident in the five guiding principles upon which the company operated for more than a year before he could break it down into specifics in the by-laws and social statutes:

1. Solidarity
2. Individual economic contribution
3. Labor contribution by all members
4. Democratic government
5. Progressive expansion to incorporate other workers

"Solidarity" was their word for "the common good." It was given the highest priority. The original by-laws and social statutes created by Don Jose Maria have been used by every subsequent cooperative.

The significant difference that is Mondragon is the way the founders looked at the situation in the first place. They started from a different place. Everything else was a result of that.

The people at Mondragon believe they are all in business together – the owner–workers, consumers, bank depositors, and community. They arrange it so that each owner–worker business is ultimately successful, the owner–workers will have jobs they can control for life, the businesses will avoid wasteful crisis management, the bank depositors will feel secure about their savings, and the community will not have to worry about disruptive plant closings or absentee owners. Finally, they have the joy of knowing that they all share the same top priority in all they do: the common good. This allows the feeling of a safe, known, and loving context for the sorting out of all relative differences.

Many today are now coming to agree that cooperation is a fundamental aspect of human nature. Competition, compromise, agreement, and love can be seen as forms of cooperation: the different ways cooperation can operate. Competition is not possible without a cooperative context: without a context of agreement it is not possible to have competition. If no one cares who gets the last piece of blueberry pie, there is no basis for competition. If two people want it, competition, compromise, agreement, or love are the possible ways of deciding who gets how much. Without the agreement that who gets it is important, competition would not be possible. Without agreement not to kill or steal, to drive on one side of the road, and so on, it would not be possible to build a factory, produce a product, distribute it, and collect payment day in and day out in a free market economy. A basketball game is not possible without the cooperative agreement called "the rules." Cooperation cannot be escaped. When this is understood by managers in any situation, they can master the skill of harnessing the natural life force flowing through every human being as Don Jose Maria did. In a few words, it is quite a simple philosophy: "Freely agree to accept the facts of your situation, give priority to the common good, and enjoy the adventure of co-creation together."

As we mature, I believe that Mondragon, and organizations that may not be structured as cooperatives but are based on the same understanding of human maturation, are our inevitable future. Mondragon has revealed the path to it. Now that we know the way, that it works, and is far more enjoyable than other ways, it is up to us to choose to walk it.

13
Novo Nordisk – Making a Difference in Diabetes Treatment

Patricia Palacios, Michael Pirson, and Bradley H. Bader

Introduction

A stormy wind can be disastrous in nature. It can tear off the branches of trees, rip off the leaves of plants, and uproot seedlings, leaving the fields as empty spaces of lost hope. Yet, despite the stormiest winds, there remains the possibility that a seed that was once blown away can find new soil, grow, and then blossom, marking the beginning of a new journey to growth. Novo Nordisk, the world's leading manufacturer of insulin, has blossomed with its ethical approach to business in an industry that has been struck by a stormy wind. With the turn of the twenty-first century, many of the global players in the pharmaceutical industry have not only experienced a decline in profits and rising costs, but have been heavily criticized for their unethical practices. By placing corporate social responsibility at the center of its business practices, Novo Nordisk has shone a light into the pharmaceutical industry, demonstrating how responsible businesses can be profitable. Today, Novo Nordisk has a net income of over USD 462.8 million and more than 27,000 staff members employed in 81 countries.[1]

In addition, Novo Nordisk holds a leading position in the diabetes health care industry and in the areas of homeostasis management, growth hormone therapy, and hormone replacement therapy. The company has been highly recognized not only for its scientific advances in medicine but also, and mostly, for its humanistic approach to business.

A long history of learning

Novo Nordisk passed several milestones in their learning journey before their humanistic approach to business became an integrated part of their strategy. The beginning of their learning journey began more than 85 years ago when, in the 1920s, Dr August Krogh, a Danish Nobel Prize winner in physiology, and his wife, who had late-onset diabetes, heard about diabetic patients being treated with insulin in Canada. After hearing the groundbreaking news, they immediately traveled to Canada in hopes of prolonging her life. What had begun as a race for a cure to treat diabetes soon became the underlying mission of the Nordisk Insulinlaboratorium that Dr Krogh and his wife established in Denmark in 1923.

Like the other players in the pharmaceutical industry, Novo Nordisk began as a traditional for-profit company, where the main focus was centered on increasing operational efficiency and in developing innovative products to capture a greater market share. In order to better respond to the demands of the market and the fierce competition, mainly from Eli Lilly, their strongest rival in the diabetes health care industry, the company went through a series of mergers and eventually formed Novo Nordisk in 1989.[2] After their foundation, Novo Nordisk enjoyed several decades of profitable growth fueled by their medical advances in the diabetes health care segment and industrial enzymes.

Despite continuing growth, a series of events led the company to radically rethink their business practices and management style. A first crisis occurred in the 1960s. Novo Nordisk had just introduced a new production method for developing enzymes. Since the production process entailed several risks, the company was soon criticized by several NGOs and the press. Novo Nordisk was attacked for introducing a production process that had severe implications for employees' health; many employees had already developed allergies caused by the dust that was generated in the production process.[3] Soon many consumers stopped buying detergents that contained these enzymes, fearing the possibility of developing allergies. As a consequence, Novo Nordisk's enzyme sales fell dramatically and the company was forced to fire employees. In order to reduce the risk of employees developing allergies during the production process, Novo Nordisk developed dust-free enzyme preparations. After the US Food and Drug Administration concluded in 1971 that the enzymes presented no risks to consumers, the company was relieved to see sales rise again.

Another incident occurred in the year 2001, when the company, in liaison with other medical firms, raised the issue of protecting intellectual property rights with the South African government. Again, they encountered severe criticism, as the public accused them of placing profits first at the expense of the health of the economically disadvantaged.[4] What had seemed to be a period of blossoming growth was soon struck again by a stormy wind. Not only did Novo Nordisk experience declining sales, but the public's growing mistrust threatened the very existence of the company. In response to the criticisms, Novo Nordisk established the World Diabetes Foundation in 2001 and engaged in dialogue with various stakeholders to define a new pricing policy.

Their shift to a multi-stakeholder dialogue approach is reflected in their stakeholder business models, which have changed over the years, as can be seen in Figure 13.1.

From a customer-driven stakeholder model in the 1970s to a stakeholder management model in the 1990s, the company was placed in the middle of all its stakeholders. In the current model, the reflective paradigm, the company is no longer in the middle, but is situated within a web of cooperating stakeholders with dynamic relationships.

This shift in mindset is also reflected by the way the company responded to the criticisms they had encountered back in the 1960s and in the year 2001: besides merely focusing on introducing innovative products that could bring substantial financial gains, they adopted the Triple Bottom Line in the mid-1990s to emphasize the importance of integrating all three dimensions in their business decisions: being economically viable, socially responsible, and environmentally sound.[5]

However, Lars Rebien Sorensen, President and CEO, together with Mads Øvlisen, chairman of Novo Nordisk and Henrik Gürtler, felt that integrating these issues into their core strategy would be difficult

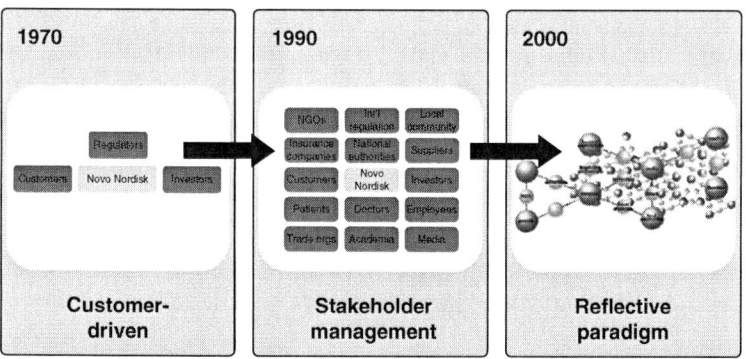

Figure 13.1   Paradigm shift

Source: Novo Nordisk's Stakeholder models, A case for stakeholder engagement, DnB NOR Seminar, Slide 5, 2008.

with the management style that governed the company. At that time, Novo Nordisk's management style was extremely hierarchical: decision-making was centralized at the company's headquarters in Denmark, leaving very little room for engagement by the foreign subsidiaries. In addition, they had found in the past that every time they introduced a new management initiative it would gradually fade away without being fully implemented. It became evident, therefore, that the company needed not only a new management style but, primarily, one with organizational systems that would ensure that Novo Nordisk's strategic goals were implemented across all business units and at the operational level.

The Novo Nordisk Way of Management (NNWoM)

In 1997, the Novo Nordisk Way of Management (NNWoM) was introduced and designed to provide an optimal balance between corporate control and decentralized decision-making.[6]

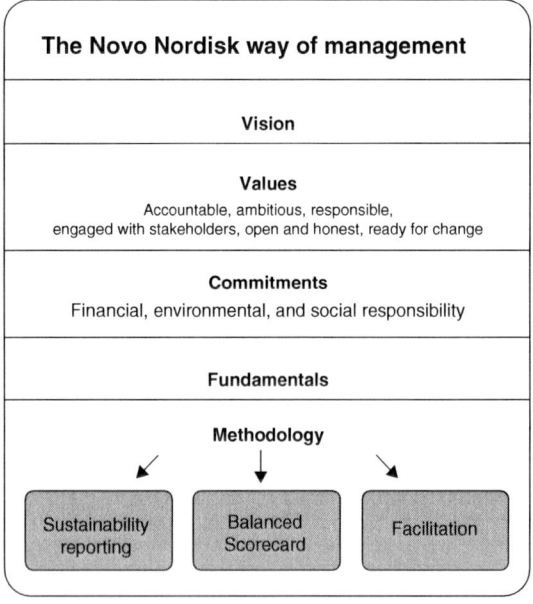

Figure 13.2   The Novo Nordisk way of management
Source: The Novo Nordisk way of management, Novo Nordisk website 2009.

Three elements formed part of the Novo Nordisk Way of Management (Figure 13.2): the vision, the charter (values, commitments, fundamentals, and follow-up methods), and the global company policies. Underlying the vision of becoming the world's leading diabetes care company were their values of being accountable, ambitious, responsible, engaged with stakeholders, open and honest, and ready for change. All these values reflected a culture that was centered on putting people first. The value of engaging stakeholders derived from their belief that everyone could be a change-maker in the lives of their patients and society. Novo Nordisk considered that each of its stakeholders, including their employees, had an important role to play in reaching their vision of eradicating diabetes. Therefore, all their efforts should be centered on their key stakeholder: the patient.

A combination of being ambitious, working with stakeholders, and being open, responsible, and honest was considered key to success in reaching their vision. The fundamentals represented a set of 11 management principles that were established to foster the collaboration and sharing of best practices, a quality mindset, and a focus on business objectives and their customers.[7] To ensure that the Novo Nordisk Way of Management was fully integrated in all their business practices, the company developed a methodology consisting of three elements: *facilitation, sustainability reporting,* and *balanced scorecard*. These elements were considered crucial to making the vision and mission meaningful.

Facilitation

Facilitation consists of a group of experienced managers across the different business units (the facilitators), all of whom are certified auditors and usually work in pairs, visiting a business unit for a period of 3 years. They assess whether or not the company-wide minimum standard requirements or "ground rules" as specified in the Novo Nordisk Way of Management are met. At the same time, they are responsible for correcting identified non-compliance with these requirements and for facilitating the sharing of best practices across the organization.[8] The facilitation process comprises three stages. In the pre-facilitation phase, the scope of the facilitation is identified and material to support the process is developed. The second phase is the facilitation itself, during which facilitators visit the unit and where needed develop an action plan for improvement. The post-facilitation process is considered the monitoring phase, in which the facilitator follows up on the agreed action points and reports to executive management on the achievements made.[9]

Example: Health care in Russia

In 1997 the Health Care Organization in Russia, headed by Henry Itameri, underwent facilitation. Two facilitators, Per Christian Gemow and Peter Frank Holding, were sent to Moscow to monitor compliance with the Novo Nordisk Way of Management. Although the 60 employees of the Russian Health Care division spent time reviewing the fundamentals before the arrival of the facilitators, they were rather skeptical about the benefits of this exercise. To their surprise, by engaging in an open dialogue with the facilitators, they were able to pinpoint several improvement areas:

- **Need for better customer service**

One of the most significant contributions of the facilitation was demonstrating to the Russian health care division that their customer service had not been as good as they had thought it was. The employees were surprised at the results of a customer satisfaction survey, wherein 40 of their largest customers had participated. There was a clear indication that customer service needed to be improved and that a systematic process for following-up on customer satisfaction was missing.

- **Need for better control of distribution**

Part of the low customer satisfaction was attributed to the delivery system. Despite the fact that stock management and delivery operate under very difficult conditions in Russia, customers demanded the same quality standards used everywhere else. In order to gain a better control of their distribution system, the team worked with the facilitators on ISO 9000 certification.

- **Need to pinpoint responsibilities within the organization**

A fundamental pillar of the Novo Nordisk Way of Management was fostering a culture of engagement. The facilitators indicated that there was substantial need to pinpoint responsibilities throughout the different departments, as it was often assumed that activities would be handled somewhere else in the organization. By implementing a system where all departments were asked to provide their area of responsibility in writing, the facilitators did not only foster engagement by bringing transparency into the departments' organizational lines, but also operational efficiency in their activities.

After working extensively with the facilitators, the employees of the Russian Health Care division agreed that facilitation had been a valuable asset to the organization.

To further strengthen a culture that fostered the sharing of best practices among employees, the facilitators encouraged the managers to enter their best practice solutions into a database called FACIT.[11] All employees had access to this database system, and it was often used for performance reviews for business unit managers. The results of the facilitation process were exemplary: within the first 2 years after its inception, it was estimated that 98 percent of the changes introduced had been implemented.[12] Several years after its introduction, many of the employees agreed that this organizational system and the FACIT database were valuable tools for enhancing the communication flow and strengthening the working relationships across the different business units.

Sustainability reporting

Similarly to the facilitation process, Novo Nordisk considers sustainability reporting an integral part of ensuring that their corporate values are integrated in their entire business practice. While many organizations today have developed reports that demonstrate the economic, social, and environmental impacts of their business activities, few have been as effective as Novo Nordisk. For 11 consecutive years, Novo Nordisk's Annual Report was awarded "best non-financial annual report" by the Danish association of state-authorized accountants, FSR, and the business daily, *Børsen*, in 2007.[13] Since 2005, the company has been ranked as one of the 100 most sustainable companies in the world, and was awarded second place in 2004 by the United Nations Environment Program for its ability to identify and manage social and environmental issues as reflected in its sustainability reports.[14]

One of the main factors contributing to their success is the way they present their reports. Unlike many other companies, who have two separate reports (financial and social), Novo Nordisk have integrated their financial and their sustainability report into their annual report in order to anchor their Triple Bottom Line approach.[15] This approach to social reporting has enabled them to communicate and stay true to their values by demonstrating the importance of all three key areas of their Triple Bottom Line. At the same time, this method has also allowed them to explore the interactions between financial and non-financial objectives and to understand how these two objectives impact the organization as a whole.[16]

Another component that has accounted for their success has been the way they have implemented systems to increase transparency and to help them define the material issues that should be included in their reports. In an effort to keep up with the increasing demand for information raised by stakeholders, many companies have added more information in their reports, thereby increasing their length.[17] Ernst & Young found, in a survey they conducted with selected firms from the Financial Times top 500 ranking European companies, that too much emphasis was placed on completeness, or the aim of trying to cover all topics, without considering the importance and relevance of these issues to stakeholders.[18] The result has often been an information overload and a lack of transparency, making it difficult for stakeholders to select the information they were looking for. With the learning curve (see Figure 13.3), Novo Nordisk not only defines at an early stage the material issues that are of interest to its stakeholders, but also maintains an open dialogue with its stakeholders for suggestions on how to improve its performance.

Recognizing that not all the issues are of equal importance to all of its stakeholders, Novo Nordisk has provided a website with a very simple search and sorting mechanism to enable its stakeholders to quickly and effectively find the information they seek. Acknowledging the fact that there is a trend in the divergence of information needs among the stakeholder groups, the company has also introduced several different reports to better satisfy the new demands. Whereas the annual reports are designed to meet the information needs of shareholders, financial analysts, and other corporate stakeholders, the online reporting system

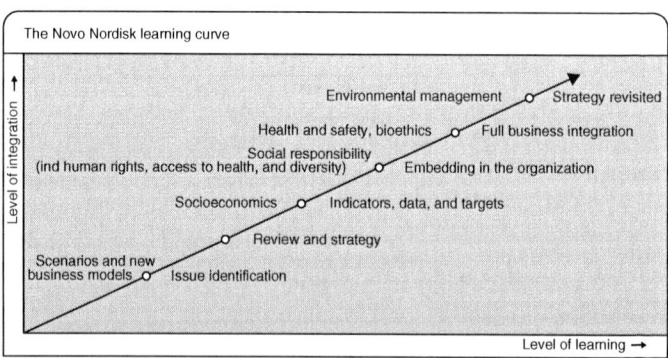

Figure 13.3   The learning curve

Source: The learning curve, Novo Nordisk's Sustainability Report 2002, p. 13.

is mainly for those stakeholders with an interest in specific topics, and particularly those related to sustainability issues.[19]

Balanced scorecard

In order to evaluate its Triple Bottom Line performance, Novo Nordisk has been using the balanced scorecard system since 1996. The scorecards are used to evaluate performance in the following four main areas: customers and society, finance, business processes and people, and organization.[20] Each of these four areas is broken down into a list of objectives, and by using key performance indicators the company measures its performance against them. The scorecards, however, are not kept at the senior management level, but are also cascaded down to the operational level to ensure that every manager follows up on progress and improvement measures.[21]

Stakeholder engagement

Introducing a methodology to ensure that the Novo Nordisk Way of Management formed an integral part of their corporate strategy was a fundamental step the company took to create empowerment within their organization. However, in order to make greater leaps towards improving the treatment of diabetes, management considered that collaboration had to come not only from within the company itself, but also externally. To emphasize the importance of stakeholder engagement the company established the Stakeholder Relations Department in 2002. Among other tasks, this department was responsible for engaging with stakeholders to reconcile dilemmas and to find common ground for more sustainable solutions, as well as for driving and embedding long-term thinking and the Triple Bottom Line mindset throughout the company.[22]

Focusing on the patient behind the disease

As can be depicted on the Figure 13.4, for Novo Nordisk the diabetic patient is the key stakeholder of the company and is therefore centered in the middle. The outer layers represent the remaining stakeholders, positioned according to their level of proximity to the patient.

By focusing on the patient behind the disease, Novo Nordisk has distinguished itself greatly from many of the global players in the pharmaceutical industry. For Novo Nordisk, focusing on the patients behind the disease means not only providing them with the best

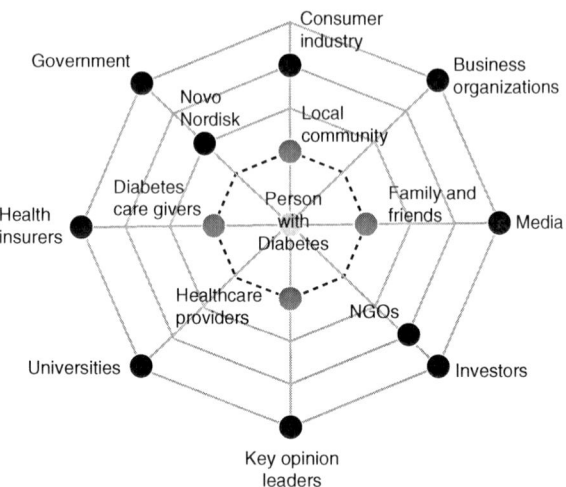

Figure 13.4   Focusing on the patient behind the disease

Source: Interactive Stakeholder Model, *Sustainability Report 2001*, p. 17.

treatment possible – as many of the pharmaceutical companies do – but also giving them the support they need to master their disease in their daily lives and deal with both the medical and the psychosocial challenges it brings.[23] As opposed to many others, Novo Nordisk's two-fold commitment suggests a longer-term strategy to eradicate diabetes.

DAWN (Diabetes, Attitudes, Wishes and Needs) is an initiative that demonstrates the company's commitment to improving both health and quality of life of its patients.[24] In 2001, the first DAWN study was launched, surveying over 5,000 diabetic patients (50 percent with Type 1 and 50 percent with Type 2 diabetes) and 3,000 healthcare professionals in 13 countries. The DAWN study had the following objectives:[25]

- To increase the understanding of patient perceptions surrounding diabetes;
- To develop insights into the attitudes and responsibilities of policy-makers and caregivers;
- To identify areas for improvement in the psychosocial management of diabetes;
- To identify the most important psychosocial barriers and solutions to more effective self-management of the disease across the world;

- To provide doctors, nurses, and policymakers with information to help decision-making and the development of national diabetes care programs; and
- To identify areas where it is critically important to improve collaboration between the parties involved in diabetes management.

The study demonstrated that diabetes care solely focused on medical targets is insufficient. More than two in five diabetic patients reported poor psychological well-being, and many reported having experienced emotional stress related to their diabetes. The results of this study made it evident that there were significant needs that had not been addressed. With these findings, Novo Nordisk established the DAWN program to provide an important platform for dialogue to increase awareness and improve diabetes care for their patients. By engaging different stakeholders, they could not only learn from their experiences, but also gain new insights that could eventually transform into innovative solutions.

Engaging employees in making a difference in diabetes treatment

Management felt that much of the success in making a difference in diabetes treatment would be attributed to the efforts of their employees. For this reason, Novo Nordisk launched "TakeAction!" in 2003 at their yearly international meeting for top managers. Of the 300 managers who attended the meeting, 210 signed the commitment sheet, agreeing to proactively seek ways to make their actions reflect the Triple Bottom Line.[26] All participating managers were encouraged to urge their team members to sign the commitment sheet. Every member who signed the commitment sheet received a pin, and when all the team members had received pins the team was awarded a "TakeAction!" plaque. Within 1 year of launching the initiative, the TakeAction! team had received signatures from 7 percent of all employees worldwide.[27] To further enhance the sharing of best practices, and as a way of establishing a systematic feedback loop by which employees could send in their suggestions and insights, the TakeAction! internal team developed a website that was available to all employees on the company's intranet.

Novo Nordisk supports TakeAction! initiatives with two main programs: the sponsor program and the volunteer opportunity in Tanzania.[28] Employees can choose either to provide donations to support children with diabetes in Bangladesh or El Salvador, or to become part of the volunteer program in Tanzania, where they get the opportunity to collaborate with a local diabetes center in Dar es Salaam.[29] By providing employees with the opportunity to travel to a developing country and to work with diabetes patients and the clinic's staff, the company can motivate its employees by actively engaging them in making a difference to society.

Within the first year of being launched, the TakeAction! initiative had already demonstrated remarkable results and proved to be a very effective tool towards enhancing employee engagement: in a poll that was run in October 2003, 65 percent of the 657 respondents indicated that they had either participated in TakeAction! initiatives or were planning to.[30] In addition, the TakeAction! internal team had received positive feedback from many employees, expressing the value added that they felt with the launch of the initiative. These formidable results were also reflected in the annual employee surveys (eVoice). Throughout the past years, the majority of employees have indicated that they feel their job contributes to the success of Novo Nordisk and that results within the social and environmental areas are important to the future success of the company.[31] In addition, employees have the opportunity, through web-based questionnaires, to rate the company on an annual basis in terms of the company's reputation. Out of 100, Novo Nordisk received a score of 83.5 on average, which is considered excellent.[32] The company has been recognized as a great place to work for, not only internally but also externally. Novo Nordisk has received several recognitions, among the most recent an award for obtaining 57th place among Fortune's 100 best companies to work for.[33]

Public and private partnerships: Balancing profits with public health needs

Mobilizing staff to make a difference in diabetes treatment was crucial to having a motivated and dedicated workforce within the organization. However, blooming on ground covered with the remains of torn branches and trees was going to be challenging. Rebuilding trust in an industry that had been under extreme scrutiny for many years seemed like an endless fight against a stormy wind. The industry's deteriorating image has been growing over the years, as many feel that the massive profits the industry makes are not matched by their contributions to the public good. This imbalance has led many to believe that the pharmaceutical industry has forgotten its central role in society. Michael Santoro, a professor in ethics in the pharmaceutical industry, maintained that: "... the pharmaceutical industry needs to understand that its own survival and well-being depend on the survival and well-being of the patients it serves ... Improve health care and profits will follow."[34]

Access to health has been one of the areas that have tremendously afflicted the image of the pharmaceutical industry. According to a poll conducted in the United States by the Kaiser Family Foundation, 58 percent of the respondents mentioned that they have least trust in the pharmaceutical companies when it comes to fair pricing.[35] Considering that diabetes poses a great threat in developing countries, as the number of patients has increased significantly over the years, the efforts of a company or an organization alone are insufficient to tackle a challenge of this sort. To this end, many academics and professionals in the field have arrived at the conclusion that the establishment of public and private partnerships is necessary to address public health challenges. Michael Reich, professor at the Harvard School of Public Health, maintained that: "Partnerships can produce innovative strategies and positive consequences for well-defined public health goals, and they can create powerful mechanisms for addressing difficult problems by leveraging the ideas, resources, and expertise of different partners."[36]

For Novo Nordisk there are three basic keystones that influence the delivery and quality of diabetes treatment in the developing world: *drivers* (local champions, government's political will, economic resources), *diabetes awareness and education*, and *infrastructure*.[37] By establishing public and private partnerships with several governmental authorities and institutions, Novo Nordisk has been able to offer insulin to the public health systems in the least developed countries at prices that are less than 20 percent of the average price in North America, Europe, and Japan.[38] At the same time, Novo Nordisk has been working with the ministries of health and various organizations in the underdeveloped countries to help them raise awareness and provide education on diabetes. In 2008, Novo Nordisk launched a series of pilot projects in five countries: Cameroon, the Democratic Republic of Congo, Guinea-Conakry, Mozambique, and Tanzania. The aim is to work with the ministries of health in these countries and to find better distribution processes to allow better access to insulin for the disadvantaged. Despite the virtues of the partnerships, Novo Nordisk still has no guarantee that the reduced price will reflect the final price on the pharmacist's shelf. At the same time, although the company has been able to sell insulin at reduced prices to more than 34 of the least developed countries, while securing reasonable profits, it is still unable to sell to 14 of the least developed countries due to political unrest and the inability to establish partnerships with these countries.[39] Although it is clear that Novo Nordisk still has a long way to go in making diabetes treatment more accessible to the economically disadvantaged, by staying true to its values the company has gained the credibility of many of its stakeholders and the public. These factors are reflected in several reputation studies. According to the Reputation Institute, while the pharmaceutical industry as a whole received a score of 66.24 out of 100 in 2007, Novo Nordisk, with a score of 79.09, was ranked substantially higher.[40]

Conclusion

Novo Nordisk's business model has proved to be successful. From 1999 to 2008, revenues more than doubled from USD 3.03 to USD 8.93 billion, while net income also increased by more than 300 percent (see Table 13.1).

Table 13.1   Revenue and income increases

Millions USD	1999	2000	2001	2002	2003
Revenues	3,030.10	2,576.20	2,846.80	3,181.20	4,040.90
Net Income	348.7	382.2	462.8	517.2	739.6

Millions USD	2004	2005	2006	2007	2008
Revenues	4,866.30	5,671.70	6,499.10	7,682.10	8,930.30
Net Income	840.3	985.2	1,082.30	1,565.00	1,890.80

Source: Morningstar, Novo Nordisk, 2009.

As can be seen below, there were several factors contributing to Novo Nordisk's success. By building organizational systems to implement the Novo Nordisk Way of Management, management succeeded in having an engaged workforce, gaining the trust of its stakeholders, and making a difference in diabetes treatment. Above all, the company has demonstrated itself to be a learning organization that has been open to change and has proactively responded to challenges.

> *Success Factors*:
>
> - Learning organization open to change
> - Organizational systems that facilitate the sharing of best practices and compliance with the corporate culture
> - Engaged workforce
> - Reputation for being transparent
> - Establishment of public and private partnerships

Despite their success and their contributions in the treatment of diabetes, the battle still remains. The International Diabetes Foundation (IDF) estimates that by the year 2025 there will be a total of 380 million patients with diabetes, coming mainly from the underdeveloped and developing countries.[41] Novo Nordisk is still facing the challenge of finding better ways of lowering the price of their treatment to increase the access to health care in many underdeveloped countries. At the same time, they are trying to keep up with the demands of educating healthcare professionals and raising the awareness of people to prevent them from developing this chronic disease. Despite several challenges, the company has shed light on how responsible businesses can be profitable. Although many times in its journey the company has been hit by stormy winds, it has been able to learn from its greatest challenges and find new opportunities to blossom.

> *Lessons learned*:
>
> - Becoming a humanistic company is often a learning journey
> - Even when you start out as a traditional company that puts profits first, a transition is possible when:
>   - Leadership is committed to a humanistic vision
>   - Mechanisms are developed that ensure a cultural change towards a learning organization (examples: facilitation, sustainability reporting and the balanced scorecard)
>   - Employees are empowered
>   - Stakeholders are systematically included in the strategic process (e.g. public and private partnerships)

Annex 13.1   Milestones in Novo Nordisk's history

1923   Nordisk Insulinlaboratorium founded.
1925   Novo Terapeutisk Laboratorium founded.

1951   Novo establishes the Novo Foundation with the object of supporting scientific, social, and humanitarian causes and to provide the best possible protection for the company.

1980   The Nordisk Insulinlaboratorium is restructured and becomes Nordisk Gentofte.

1989   Nordisk Insulinlaboratorium, the Nordisk Insulin Foundation and the Novo Foundation merge to become the Novo Nordisk Foundation. The objectives are to provide a stable basis for the Novo Group companies' operations and to support scientific causes.

1989   Novo Industri A/S and Nordisk Gentofte A/S merge to become the world's leading producer of insulin.

1994   Novo Nordisk is the first company in Denmark – and one of the first in the world – to publish an environmental report.

1999   Novo Nordisk publishes its first social report.

2000   Novo Nordisk is split into three separate companies, operating under the umbrella of the Novo Group: Novo Nordisk A/S, Novozymes A/S and Novo A/S.

2001   Novo Nordisk establishes the World Diabetes Foundation with the purpose of improving diabetes care in developing countries.

2002   Novo Nordisk signs the United Nations Global Compact, a platform for promoting good corporate principles and learning experiences in the areas of human rights, labour, environment, and anti-corruption.

2004   Novo Nordisk's articles of association are amended to specify that the company will "strive to conduct its activities in a financially, environmentally, and socially responsible way."

2005   The Novo Nordisk Haemophilia Foundation is set up in response to the significant need to improve hemophilia treatment in the developing world, underlining the company's social responsibility within hemophilia care.

2006   Novo Nordisk signs an agreement with the World Wide Fund for Nature (WWF) that commits the company to reduce its carbon emissions by 10 percent by 2014, compared with 2004. Novo Nordisk is the tenth company in the world to join the WWF Climate Savers initiative.

Source: Novo Nordisk Website, 2009.

Annex 13.2   Fundamentals

Fundamental 1   Each unit must share and use better practices.

Fundamental 2   Each unit must have a clear definition of where accountabilities and decision powers reside.

Fundamental 3	Each unit must have an action plan to ensure improvement of its business performance and working climate.
Fundamental 4	Every team and employee must have updated business and competency targets and receive timely feedback on performance against these targets.
Fundamental 5	Each unit must have an action plan to ensure the development of teams and individuals based on business requirements and employee input.
Fundamental 6	Every manager must establish and maintain procedures in the unit for living up to relevant laws, regulations, and group commitments.
Fundamental 7	Each unit and every employee must know how they create value for their customers.
Fundamental 8	Every manager requiring reporting from others must explain the actual use of the reports and the added value.
Fundamental 9	Every manager must continuously make it easier for the employees to liberate energy for customer related issues.
Fundamental 10	Every manager and unit must actively support cross unit projects and working relationships of relevance to the business.
Fundamental 11	Everyone must continuously improve the quality of their work.

Source: Novo Nordisk Website, 2009.

Notes

1. Morningstar (2009). *Novo Nordisk A/S*. http://quicktake.morningstar.com/StockNet/Income10.aspx?Country=USA&Symbol=NVO [accessed May 17, 2009].
2. See Annex 13.1.
3. Morsing, M. and Oswald, D. (2005). *Novo Nordisk A/S – Integrating Sustainability into Business Practice*. Copenhagen Business School & London Business School. p. 5.
4. Ibid.
5. Elkington (2009). *Enter the Triple Bottom Line*. http://www.johnelkington.com/TBL-elkington-chapter.pdf [accessed 28 October 2009].
6. Morsing, M. and Oswald, D. (2005). *Novo Nordisk A/S – Integrating Sustainability into Business Practice*. Copenhagen Business School & London Business School. p. 7.
7. See Annex 13.2.

8. Morsing, M. and Oswald, D. (2005). *Novo Nordisk A/S – Integrating Sustainability into Business Practice.* Copenhagen Business School & London Business School. p. 8.

9. Ibid., p. 9.

10. Source: Novo Nordisk (A): Global Coordination Case IB-20A, pp. 24–25, Stanford Graduate School of Business.

11. Kamper, A., Podolny, J. and Roberts, J. (1999). *Novo Nordisk (A) – Global Coordination.* Stanford Graduate School of Business. p. 13.

12. Ibid.

13. CorporateResponsibility.Net (2009). *Interview: Novo Nordisk about Their Award Winning CR Reporting.* http://www.corporateresponsibility.net/2008/07/24/interview-novo-nordisk-about-their-award-winning-cr-reporting/ [accessed May 10, 2009].

14. Morsing, M. and Oswald, D. (2005). *Novo Nordisk A/S – Integrating Sustainability into Business Practice.* Copenhagen Business School & London Business School, p. 9.

15. CorporateResponsibility.Net (2009). *Interview: Novo Nordisk about Their Award Winning CR Reporting.* http://www.corporateresponsibility.net/2008/07/24/interview-novo-nordisk-about-their-award-winning-cr-reporting/ [accessed May 10, 2009].

16. Gribben, C. and Olsen, L. (2003). *An Anchor – Not the Answer: Trends in Social and Sustainable Development Reporting.* Ashridge Centre for Business and Society. http://www.ashridge.org.uk/Website/IC.nsf/wFARPUB/An+Anchor+%E2%80%93+Not+an+Answer:+Trends+in+Social+and+Sustainable+Development+Reporting, p. 16 [accessed May 10, 2009].

17. Ibid., p. 9.

18. Ernst and Young (2007). *Keep the Balance Steady: Survey on the Quality of Sustainability Reports 2007.* www.ey.nl/download/publicatie/Keep-the-balance-steady-EN.pdf, p. 2 [accessed May 10, 2009].

19. Novo Nordisk Website (2009). http://www.novonordisk.com/ [accessed May 5, 2009].

20. Ibid.

21. Morsing, M. and Oswald, D. (2005). *Novo Nordisk A/S – Integrating Sustainability into Business Practice.* Copenhagen Business School & London Business School, p. 12.

22. Ibid., p. 5.

23. Novo Nordisk Website (2009). http://www.novonordisk.com/ [accessed May 5, 2009].

24. DAWN Website (2009). http://www.dawnstudy.com/documents/article_page/document/about_dawn.asp [accessed October 28, 2009].

25. Ibid.

26. World Business Council for Sustainable Development (WBCSD) (2004). *Case Study: Novo Nordisk: Take Action! Make the Triple Bottom Line your business.* http://www.wbcsd.org/plugins/DocSearch/details.asp?type=DocDet&ObjectId=MjA3OTU, p. 1 [accessed May 10, 2009].

27. Ibid, p. 2.

28. Ibid.

29. Ibid.

30. Ibid., p. 4.

31. Novo Nordisk Website (2009). http://www.novonordisk.com [accessed May 5, 2009].
32. Ibid.
33. Great Work Place to Work for Institute. *Fortune's 100 Best Companies to Work for in 2009*. http://www.greatplacetowork.com/best/list-bestusa-2009.htm [accessed May 26, 2009].
34. Santoro, M. and Gorrie, T.M. (2005). *Ethics and the Pharmaceutical Industry*. New York: Cambridge University Press, p. 368.
35. Kaiser Public Opinion Survey. *Views On Prescription Drugs and The Pharmaceutical Industry*. http://www.kff.org/spotlight/rxdrugs/index.cfm [accessed May 26, 2009].
36. Reich, M. R. *Public-Private Partnerships for Public Health*. Harvard Center for Population and Development Studies. Cambridge: Harvard University Press.
37. Novo Nordisk Sustainability & Annual Reports 2001, 2002.http://www.novonordisk.com/investors/download-centre/default.asp, p. 25 [accessed May 5, 2009].
38. Novo Nordisk Website (2009). http://www.novonordisk.com/ [accessed May 5, 2009].
39. Ibid.
40. Reputation Institute (2009). *Reputation Institute Report Global Rep Trak Pulse 200* http://www.slideshare.net/cfoglini/reputation-institute-free-report-global-rep-trak-pulse-2007 [accessed May 27, 2009].
41. Changing Diabetes Barometer (2007). www.novonordisk.si/Images/content_images/Barometer_eng.pdf, p. 11 [accessed October 21, 2009].

14
SEKEM – Humanistic Management in the Egyptian Desert

Clemens Mader, Gerald Steiner, Friedrich M. Zimmermann, and Heiko Spitzeck

The change agent: Ibrahim Abouleish – his life and vision

Ibrahim Abouleish was born in 1937 in Cairo, Egypt, where he grew up. Aged 19, he moved to Graz, Austria to study technical chemistry and pharmacology at the Graz University of Technology. In Austria he married Gudrun Erdinger and founded his family with two children, Helmy and Mona. After university, Ibrahim worked in leading research positions with pharmaceutical companies in Austria. During this time he regularly visited his family in Egypt, but initially did not notice the profound social changes that were happening back home. That was until a trip he made together with his family in 1975. This trip opened his eyes to the changes Egypt had undergone over the previous 20 years under the presidency of Nassar. He recalls in his own words:

> The once cheerful population seems to have sunk into a deep depression. The cities are dirty and there are terrible rubbish dumps everywhere. Under the reign of Nassar all businesses had been nationalized, even the restaurants... I experience agriculture as a catastrophe. The farmers were forced to use a certain amount of artificial fertilizer per hectare of land. Illiteracy was on the increase. More than 40 per cent of children did not go to school because they had to work to support their families.[1]

Back in Austria, Abouleish started to search for solutions, and especially investigated alternative approaches to agriculture in science and anthroposophy.[2] He was sure that he could do something to improve the situation back home in Egypt if he had enough time to plan and prepare (Abouleish, 2005). Together with the expert Georg Merckens, he made several research trips to farms in Austria and Italy to learn more about biodynamic farming. During his travels, his thoughts on an alternative, more humanistic and holistic approach to agriculture matured: "As well as the farm it would need several economic projects, a school and different educational institutions and offer cultural projects and medical care."[3] His first priority was to educate people, as education and a qualified workforce were the main missing aspects of the Egyptian economy. In 1977, Dr Abouleish and his family packed all their belongings into three VW vans and moved to Egypt. There he founded SEKEM, a desert community 60 kilometers northeast of Cairo, the capital of Egypt. The nearest small town, Bilbeis, is about 20 km to the North. By founding this community in the desert, he wanted to prove that even there productive land could be claimed by biodynamic agricultural methods and to demonstrate that sustainable development is possible.

However, establishing a farm on its initial 70 hectares of desert land turned out not to be as easy as expected. Abouleish was busy making arrangements with Bedouins, who claimed the land, as well as involving people from surrounding communities who were skeptical about their new neighbor and his European family. After drilling wells with the help of local workers, Abouleish planted about 120,000 trees to prevent sandstorms encroaching from the desert and to provide shade. This laid the cornerstone for SEKEM. Abouleish endured over the years, built good relationships with his neighbors, and was rewarded in 2003 when he was named "Outstanding Social Entrepreneur" by the Schwab Foundation.

Abouleish's approach to decision-making helped him significantly in obtaining the support of the community as well as in making the

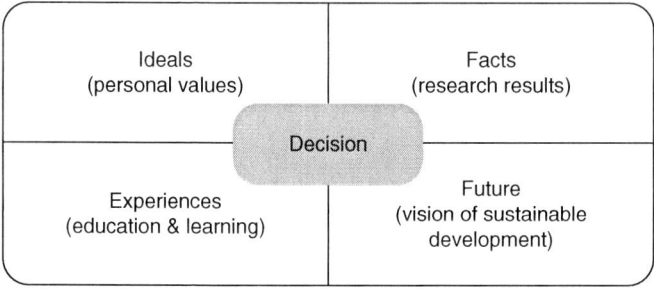

Figure 14.1 Principles of decision making by Dr. Ibrahim Abouleish (Mader, 2009)

right business decisions. He uses four interconnected principles for his decisions (Figure 14.1) (Interview: Dr Abouleish, 2008):

Ideals: At the core of Dr Abouleish's ideals is the idea that business is a deeply human activity and can be used as an instrument to foster human well-being. In a human community people need to trust each other, support each other's needs and development, and work together towards a higher goal than corporate profits.

Experiences: Abouleish's personal experiences during the education he received in Austria, as well as during his travels in Europe, gave him confidence that a more human approach to business is not only desirable but also feasible. His experience taught him that he could put a great deal of faith in people.

Facts: Research has been part of Abouleish's life. From his studies in Austria to his work in pharmaceutical research (he registered patents for several pharmaceutical products), he saw how facts drive value and business success. Upon his return to Egypt, significant research activities framed the development of new products that could be sold and that could generate revenue. Today the Heliopolis University is doing research related to the products of SEKEM companies, as well as in social development, through investigating work models and poverty alleviation.

Future: The future is reflected in the ideal of sustainable development in Egypt. Business can be used as an instrument to support and finance development programs and to provide education and development opportunities for people (Abouleish, 2005).

SEKEM – a humanistic approach to business

Ibrahim Abouleish founded SEKEM in 1977 upon his arrival in Egypt. SEKEM is a transliteration of a hieroglyph that means "vitality coming from the sun." This is reflected in the mission and vision of SEKEM:[4]

The SEKEM Initiative aims to meet the challenges of our time by contributing to the all encompassing development of man, community and earth.
THE SEKEM VISION

1. The development of biodynamic agricultural methods suitable for Egypt's climate, agricultural conditions and all the crops planted in Egypt.
2. The development and production of a variety of consumer products and services according to the real needs of the consumer, always bearing in mind that these products must be of highest quality, reliable

in efficacy, taste and convenience based on responsibility towards our environment.

3. The "human" orientated marketing of the above products shall be conducted in a socially conscious manner based on cooperation, association and brotherhood instead of egoism, competition and war.

4. All employees should have continuous access to personal development, education and training in order to achieve their fullest self-realization. They should have the unconditional right to freely express their opinion and ideas.

5. The social frame and the social conditions of cooperation between the employees should be clear, well-defined regulations and principles allowing the establishment of a healthy society.

6. The support of and cooperation with organizations which aim to actively participate in the social and cultural development of Egypt (schools, kindergartens, continuous education, hospitals, etc.).

7. To spread the SEKEM idea throughout Egypt and to enable other projects to apply the SEKEM concept successfully as a basis for the development of Egypt's future generations.

This mission encapsulates the humanistic values of SEKEM. Several closely related, but independent, components work together to achieve this mission:

(1) Economically profitable and responsibly managed enterprises: the SEKEM Holding Company embraces several agro-industrial–manufacturing and technological companies; each is managed as a separate specialized business.

(2) Supporting sociocultural–human development holistically: The SEKEM Development Foundation (SDF).

Figure 14.2 provides an overview of the SEKEM network's configuration.

Economically profitable and responsibly managed enterprises

In 2006 SEKEM group reported a turnover of EUR 17.5 million and profits of EUR 1.34 million. Growth was close to 25 percent in each of the years between 2005 and 2007. Future growth is expected to be close to 30 percent in the coming years.[5] Seventy percent of all SEKEM's products are sold in Egypt and the remaining 30 percent are exported to Europe and the US.

In 2008 SEKEM Group reported a turnover of EGY 196 million (~ € 24 million) and investments of EGY 77 million (~ € 9.6 million), which

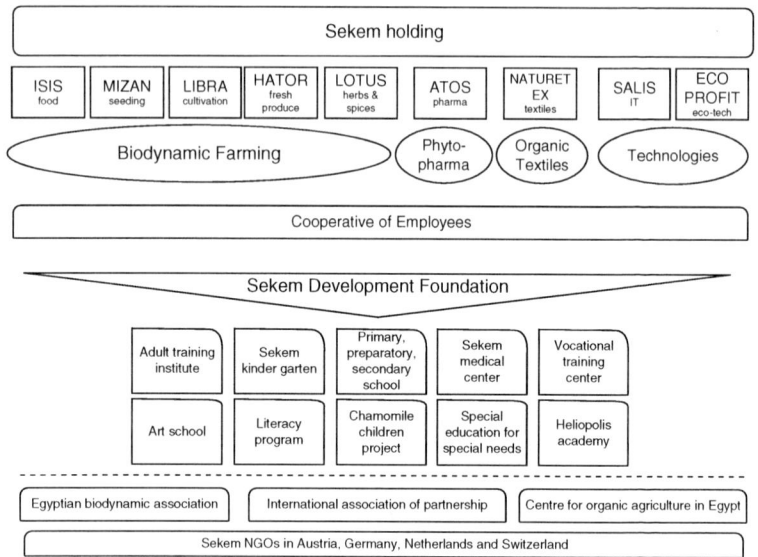

Figure 14.2   Structure of SEKEM network (Mader, C., 2009)

were split equally between purchase of land and further development of existing farms.[6]

Initially, the commercial activities of SEKEM focused on biodynamic agriculture. Over the past three decades, the organization has expanded into several business areas. At present SEKEM is focusing on three product lines: phyto-pharmaceuticals, foodstuffs cultivated biodynamically, and textiles made from organic cotton. The number of product lines and other activities included has continuously increased. In chronological order, these developments were:

While being economically profitable, SEKEM puts humans, and not profits, at the heart of management. The group has a special relationship with its employees, its suppliers, and its customers and is careful to stick to the principle of fairness. How this translates into practices is explained in more detail below.

Employees   SEKEM employees are organized in a cooperative, bound to the mission of the company. The Cooperative of SEKEM employees (CSE) clearly spells this out in its mission statement:

> The cooperative of SEKEM employees seeks to develop work models that ensure respect for dignity and humankind and guarantee the

Table 14.1 Year, company, main business activity

Year	Company	Main business activity
1979	SEKEM	Organic herbs and spices
1986	ATOS	Natural Pharmaceutics
1990	COAE	Certification for Organic Agriculture in Egypt
1993	LIBRA	Fostering the cooperation between farmers
1994	NATURTEX	Organic cotton textile products
1994	EBDA	Egyptian Biodynamic Association offering consulting and training
1996	HATOR	Packaging of fresh produce
1996	Nature Best Shops	Sales of organic food and textiles
1996	IAP	International Association of Partnership – a business partner network
1997	ISIS	Manufacturing of foodstuffs
2005	SEKEM Europe	Marketing in Europe
2005	MIZAN	Organic seeds
2005	LOTUS	Production of herbs and spices
2005	SALIS	Information Technology firm on software engineering
2006	ECOPROFIT	Renewable energy (wind and solar power)
2009	SEKEM Energy	Renewable Energy Consultation, company based in Austria

equality of everyone in the community. It aims to raise consciousness of the concepts of humanity and sustainability and the importance of sharing and mutual trust among the employees of all SEKEM companies.[7]

To build trust and to exchange views, all employees meet once a week in an open theater on the farm. Abouleish uses this opportunity to speak with all his employees about recent global developments, achievements, or challenges. Furthermore, employees meet within their specific company every morning before work starts and form a circle in which they welcome each other. At these meetings employees have the opportunity to co-create SEKEM's policies and strategies and actively engage with the organization.

The CSE fulfills a number of specific tasks:

- It is responsible for employing new workers at SEKEM. In the recruiting process rights and responsibilities of the workers are openly discussed. Furthermore, social workers document the family situation, state of health, and level of education. On this basis, a development and support program for each employee is formulated. Employees pay a small monthly contribution into a social fund, which is used for the development of employees, as well as for covering costs such as hospital charges or wedding ceremonies.

- It is responsible for the health and working conditions of the workers. In addition to workplace safety programs, preventive events and education are also provided.
- It is responsible for improving the living conditions of the employees. Such improvements include, for example, measures enhancing the current infrastructure through paving roads, installing phone lines, or establishing post offices. Supported by the European Union, SEKEM has also built a water treatment plant, giving villages access to clean drinking water at home.
- A social worker of the CSE is responsible for determining the goals employees have to fulfill – goals that each employee can set individually. Once a month the social worker and employee will assess whether the goals have been achieved. If the employee has not achieved the goals, a training or support program may be agreed upon.

All these responsibilities of the CSE make it clear that employees at SEKEM are not viewed as a simple human resource, but as human beings who aim to realize themselves in their work and who have others to care for. HR at SEKEM does not stand for human resources but human relations.

Partners in the Supply Chain   SEKEM applies the same approach to its partners within the supply chain, mainly farmers. To give one example, SEKEM guarantees fair prices and long-term cultivation contracts to farmers. This protects farmers from rapidly changing world market commodity prices and ensures their livelihood throughout the year, while giving them a positive perspective on their future. A visible result of this fair approach to famers is the fair trade certifications for SEKEM's fresh produce, herbs, rice, and cotton, as well as ready-made garments.

To foster interaction between farmers, producers, and traders, the International Association of Partnership (IAP) was founded in 1996 and has become a forum for all people interested in organic farming. Through providing consultation and education as part of the cooperation between SEKEM and the farmers, SEKEM communicates consumer needs and expectations to the farmers and thereby ensures that the farmers efficiently meet consumers' expectations.

The eye on the customer – Quality Management The biodynamic and organic movement is receiving more attention and recognition in world markets and has to assure equal quality delivery around the world. In order to assure the same level of quality at its various international locations and to be competitive with other international organic brands, SEKEM started to certify its companies according to international standards in 1997. Atos, Naturtex, and Hator are ISO 9001 and all manufacturing and packaging plants are ISE 14001:2004 certified. Furthermore, products are expected to meet international quality standards such as the International Demeter Guidelines, European Community Regulations for Organic Agriculture (EC regulation 2092/91), European Pharmacopoeia, and ISO 9001:2000, as well as the Hazard Analysis Critical Control Points Certification. Products exported to the US and Switzerland are certified according to the National Organic Program (NOP) and the BioSuisse program.

Holistic sociocultural human development

Profits are usually reinvested, not only in SEKEM enterprises, but in its social facilities and educational programs (see also Figure 14.2) (GLS, 2007). In 1984 SEKEM established the SEKEM Development Foundation (SDF) in order to holistically improve the quality of the lives of employees and their families, as well as rural inhabitants in areas surrounding the SEKEM facilities. Today the SDF portfolio includes activities in formal education, informal and adult education, vocational training, health and medical care programs, community development, performing and visual arts education, and poverty alleviation.

> In implementing these activities, the emphasis is not only on improving the level of living of the people, but also on enhancing their moral and cultural awareness through the integration of arts and sciences into their daily lives. It is believed that this integrated approach would lead to the comprehensive and sustained development of the individual, the community and the local environment.[8]

Among the numerous programs which SDF is supporting are the following:

Chamomile Children Project

The Chamomile Children Project is targeted towards children dropping out of school. It enrolls 80 children and offers both education and limited employment for children between the ages of nine and 14, who usually come from underprivileged families and were either school dropouts or deprived of the opportunity to attend school.

Vocational training

The vocational training center offers training in the following fields: industrial mechanics, electricity, computer maintenance and electronic technology, mechanical repairs, carpentry, agricultural machinery, textile production technology, general administration, and plumbing. Over 1,000 students have graduated from the center since it opened (1997–2006). The center encourages both men and women to join the training. Moreover, the center keeps a list of various factories which intend to hire new graduates from the center. The graduates are recognized in the labor market for their good reputation and for being well trained, hard-working, and disciplined.[9]

Heliopolis University

"Right from the beginning, when SEKEM's agriculture started in the desert, when the first plant extracts were being developed and the first herbal teas cultivated, research has been an essential and intrinsic part of the SEKEM story" (Heliopolis University, 2008). The Heliopolis University for Sustainable Development was acknowledged by the Egyptian government in August 2009 and is the next logical step in the fulfillment of the educational and research vision of SEKEM. Currently, SEKEM is conducting applied research projects in five research centers:

- Medical Research;
- Pharmaceutical Research;
- Organic Production Research;
- Social Research, and Community Development; and
- Visual and Performing Arts Development

Regional Centre of Expertise on Education for Sustainable Development Cairo

In December 2008, SEKEM also became part of the United Nations University network of Regional Centres of Expertise on Education for Sustainable Development (RCE Cairo). Thus, SEKEM became part of a global network of 66 RCEs (October 2009), all focusing on sustainable development in research and education. The aim of the RCEs is to build up a regional network of institutions seeking to conduct cooperative sustainability projects and to exchange good practices globally.

Summary and key findings

What can be learned from the SEKEM case? How could other organizations apply some of the SEKEM practices and ideas?

First, we would argue that humanistic management needs strong
leadership from the top and, ideally, from the very beginning.
Ibrahim Abouleish took the initiative to improve the dismal state of
the local communities and their economic environment in Egypt.
His aim was to create an organization that fosters the quality of life
and protects human dignity. He opted to found a business organization that works towards this goal and reinvests profits into its
mission.

Second, there are some organizational features that might help
other organizations working towards life-conduciveness and sustainability. SEKEM is built on strong stakeholder engagement and participatory governance. Abouleish and his team reached out to the
communities, listened to their problems, and tried, successfully, to
create win–win relationships instead of founding a business with no
relation to its surroundings. SEKEM also created the necessary discursive infrastructure to make sure stakeholders have a voice in the
decision-making processes. Indeed, it is hard to tell whether SEKEM
is a group of companies or a social movement for sustainable development in Egypt. By overcoming differences of opinion between different stakeholders and working towards a shared goal everybody really
subscribes to, SEKEM was able to have systemic impact. For example,
through research and harvest results SEKEM was able to prove to the
Egyptian politicians that the farming of cotton in Egypt without
the use of pesticides is indeed economically feasible. In this way,
the consumption of pesticides could be reduced significantly. Today
less than 10 percent of the previous amount of pesticides is in use.
By 1999, almost 80 percent of Egyptian cotton was being cultivated
organically, and production had increased by almost 30 percent per
acre (EBDA). Due to this alternative and, as we argued, humanistic approach to management, SEKEM received the Right Livelihood
Award in 2003. This award, better known as the Alternative Nobel
Prize, was given for its "... 21st century business model which combines commercial success with social and cultural development."[10]
The prize is traditionally awarded the day before the Nobel Prize ceremony and has recognized outstanding social organizations, people,
and entrepreneurs worldwide. We look forward to the SEKEM example inspiring other organizations, and such organizations eventually
receiving similar honors.

Notes

1. Abouleish (2005).
2. The term anthroposophy is of Greek origin, meaning human wisdom or the knowledge of the nature of man. Modern anthroposophy builds on the work of Rudolf Steiner.
3. Abouleish (2005).
4. SEKEM (2008).
5. GLS (2007).
6. SEKEM Europe GmbH (2009).
7. SEKEM Development Foundation (2006).
8. SEKEM Development Foundation (2007).
9. SEKEM Development Foundation (2007).
9. Right Livelihood Award (2009).

Bibliography

Abouleish, I. (2005). *SEKEM A Sustainable Community in the Egyptian Desert.* Edinburgh: Floris Books, p. 221.

Egyptian Biodynamic Association (2008). *Organic Cotton Cultivation.* EBDA.

GLS (2007). Report der GLS SEKEM Fonds GbR. Bochum.

Heliopolis University (2008). Information Document Heliopolis University (under establishment), International Affairs.

Kogut, B., Shan, W. and Walker, G. (1993). Knowledge in the network and the network as knowledge: The structuring of new industries, in Grabher, G. (ed) *The Embedded Firm: On The Socio-Economics of Industrial Networks.* London: Routledge.

Mader, C. (2009). *Principles for Integrative Development Processes Towards Sustainability in Regions.* Dissertation. Graz: University of Graz.

Mair, Johanna and Schoen, Oliver (2005) *Social Entrepreneurial Business Models: An Exploratory Study.* IESE Business School Working Paper No. 610. Available at SSRN: http://ssrn.com/abstract=875816 [accessed September 9, 2009].

Merckens, K. (2007). *Annex VII Interim Narrative Report: A Comprehensive Poverty Alleviation Intervention in Rural Sharkeya, Egypt.* Verein zur Förderung Kultureller Entwicklung in Ägypten e.V.

Right Livelihood Award (2009). SEKEM/Ibrahim Abouleish (2003), http://www.rightlivelihood.org/sekem.html [accessed March 2009].

SEKEM Development Foundation (2006). Human Development at SEKEM. SEKEM Development Foundation.

SEKEM Development Foundation (2007). SEKEM Development Foundation Achievement Report. SEKEM.

SEKEM Europe GmbH. Hintergrundinfo July 2009. SEKEM.

SEKEM (2008). www.SEKEM.com [accessed October 2008].

Sosik, J.J. and Dionne, S.D. (1997). Leadership styles and deming's behavior factors. *Journal of Business and Psychology,* Vol. 11 (4), 447–462. Human Science Press.

Spitzeck, H., Pirson, M., Amann, W., Khan, Sh. and von Kimakowitz, E. (2009). *Humanism in Business.* Cambridge: Cambridge University Press.

15
What Is Your Calling? SEMCO's Invitation to Participatory Management

Carlos Largacha-Martínez

> The conflict between advanced technology and archaic mentality is, I believe, a major reason why the modern workplace is characterized by dissatisfaction, frustration, inflexibility, and stress.
>
> Ricardo Semler

> There is no way to treat employees as responsible and honest adults unless you let them know and influence what is going on around them.
>
> João Vendramim

Introduction

Imagine that you just sent your resume to Semco. You have been called for an interview. Once you arrive at the company, nobody is waiting to receive you. You start asking other people because there is no receptionist at the front desk either. Then you ask for the Human Resources Department, but there is no such thing at Semco. As a next step, you ask for Mrs Obrigada, the person who contacted you, and the answer you receive is even more wearisome: "She is here but I don't know where. Since we restructured 5 years ago, these are *Non-Territorial Offices*[1] and every day, no, even more often, we choose any free place to work." So what do you do? You start wandering around, without knowing that Management by Wandering Around (MWA)[2] is one of the management practices at Semco.

You bump into a bulletin board. Maybe there you will find some information about your interview. You see the financial report of the last semester posted in a brief and easy-to-read format. To your amusement, you see all the financial information displayed, even those parts that are normally not made transparent,[3] such as the salaries of all the 4,000+ workers of the 12 business units. Next to the report you see a call for an internal workshop for shop-workers with the title: "How to understand financial reports in order to have a clear position on how much wage and how much of the profit-sharing plan you want to receive." Wow! Suddenly, you hear people talking loudly, so you walk towards the noise. On your way you become aware that there are no doors or walls separating the workplaces, only plants and flowers, and, as you get closer to the group whose discussion you overheard, you are noticed by one of the ladies. She asks you "What do you think?" "Well," you say, "I was not invited, but let me help you a little. Show me your strategic master plan." "What?" everybody asks. "We haven't had a plan for more than 25 years." "Okay, maybe you have a different name for it," you interrupt them – now is the moment to impress them, you think – and ask: "Let's organize this. Who is the boss here, what is the goal of the meeting, and what are the procedures and policies implied?"

First, silence. Then someone says, "at Semco we don't have 'bosses,' and nobody is in charge of this meeting. At Semco, we don't have a 'goal' for this meeting. We are part of an initiative called 'Out of your Mind!'[4] Finally, at Semco we don't have policies for this type of meetings or for almost any other task. As Ricardo Semler, our Chief *Enzyme* Officer – CEO, and major stock-owner – says, *'our policy is no policy.'*[5] As João Vendramim argues, 'we don't control people, just processes'."

Now, you are the one gazing speechlessly. Suddenly, someone is running all over the place, calling your name. You hesitate to raise your hand. Once in the garden with hammocks at Semco, and after apologizing for being late to your "interview," Mrs Obrigada asks you: "Tell me, what is your Calling?" After that question, would you think: "I should leave? This is too much for today?" And, if you decided to stay, and even more challenging, would you know what to answer? Do you know what your calling is? Before deciding what to do, let me give you some more stories about Semco and how this company has become one of the most sustainable, democratic, participatory, humanistic *and* profitable companies in Brazil.

Although this chapter summarizes a lot of inspiring information about Semco, Ricardo Semler[6] wrote about his book *The Seven-Day Weekend* that "what you are about to read is a combination of a political manifesto, a business case history, and an anthropological study...I warn you, it's messy, inefficient, and hugely rewarding...[with the goal of] finding a balance between work and private passions." At Semco they see themselves as a business case of *"participatory* or *democratic* manage-ment." For me, they have a lot of the elements required for best practice in "humanistic management." In order to have that, I think you need to have three basic elements: 1. *Alterity*, or dignifying the other in eve-rything that you do; 2. *Non-ideological stances*, or, that the corporate *space* is always under scrutiny; and 3. *Social obligations*, which broadens corporate social responsibility frameworks, including human sustain-ability, which permanently actualizes being human. All of which are based on my quantum humanism.[7]

Brief history

Semco, which comes from "Semler & Company," was founded in 1952 by a European immigrant, Mr Antonio C. Semler. After working for more than a decade for DuPont in Argentina, Antonio started working on a "patent for a centrifuge that could derive separate lubricating oil from vegetables,"[8] but it was with marine pumps that he seized the oppor-tunity for steady growth; this arose from a Brazilian military National Shipbuilding Plan. However, in the 1980s the marine pumps business was in a slump, threatening Semco's survival, since it represented 90 percent of their business. At this point, Antonio's son Ricardo Semler came onto the scene. Ricardo, a lawyer, was working as an intern as well as in other positions at Semco. He "became convinced [that] Semco's only chance of survival was to broaden its product line,"[9] while his father had an expansion plan worth USD 1 million within the marine industry.

But that was not the main problem; Ricardo and Antonio had substan-tially different views on how to manage the company. Because of these contradictory views, Ricardo thought that he should leave the company. He remembers his thoughts while at Semco: "How can I spend the rest of my life doing this? How can I stomach years of babysitting people to make sure they clock in on time? Why is this worth doing?"[10]

Antonio took the sudden decision to make Ricardo the major stock-owner, and left on a 3-week trip. He appointed Ricardo, at the age of just 21, as CEO, with the power to make all major decisions. The following day, in less than 8 hours Ricardo "had fired 60 percent of Semco's top management."[11]

Clearly, Ricardo's mindset had also changed during this transition of allowing Semco to become a democratic company. In the 1980s Ricardo was very pleased, since at Semco "Everything seems so professional. No one could get in or out of our plants without showing an ID card.

Our pride and joy was our new budget system. The numbers were ready on the fifth working day of every month, all in color-coded folders."[12] What a different picture compared with Semco today. Summarizing, Ricardo states:[13]

> Semco has no official structure. It has no organizational chart. There's no business plan, no goal or mission statement, no long-term budget. The company often does not have a fixed CEO. There are no vice presidents or chief officers for information technology or operations. There are no standards or practices. There's no human resources department. There are no career plans, no job descriptions or employee contracts. No one approves reports or expense accounts. Supervision or monitoring of workers is rare indeed. Most important, [and this truly *is* the most important] *success is not measured only in profit and growth* [emphasis added].

The lesson here is that at Semco almost everybody knows that their democratic–participatory approach is only halfway there, and there is still much to be learned and to be achieved. Humbleness, thus, is part of having a humanistic management approach. As João Vendramim, Semco's former Counselor, argues, "This has been a long journey. We still need some years to have all the participatory practices functioning in the whole company." Bear in mind that I am talking about a conglomerate that grows between 20 and 40 percent annually, with USD 212 million revenues in 2004, and an employee turnover of less than 1 percent, while being a top player in every niche it occupies.

Ricardo has been invited to give speeches at very prestigious universities such as Stanford, Harvard, MIT, the London School of Economics, and INSEAD. The first book about Semco, *Maverick*, was on the bestseller lists in 12 countries, selling more than one million copies.[14] This is not to mention that Ricardo Semler has been Businessman of the Year twice in Brazil, as well as Latin American Businessman of the Year during the 1990s, and Semco was also nationally awarded in the 1990s for labor relations. They received so much media attention – including a BBC documentary – that for the twenty-first century, Joao argues, "It has been Semco's position to keep a low profile by trying to stay out of media for some time. We have declined many requests for visits and so on."

Semco has four major business platforms: industrial equipment, technology, services, and new ventures. Semler[15] argues: "We've moved from industrial manufacturing to services to high technology without giving up any earlier businesses." Currently they have 12 business units that are highly diverse, with "a minimum common denominator" embedded in a "hidden synergy that satisfies three basic criteria:" complexity, premium players, and unique niches.[16] As Ricardo Semler puts it, "all of our business units are highly engineered, premium providers, and market leaders in each niche. We haven't ventured into any of them by chance." By November 2008, João Vendramim describes the structure as follows:

> Today Semco has two Business Units in the Industrial area, which are: *Semco Equip. Industriais* and *Semco Equip. de Refrigeração*, the first one making Mixers and the other Cooling towers. One Joint Venture – *Pitney Bowes Semco*, (Equipment to handle document and postal services). *Semco Manutenção Volante*, still in the same building had its control sold to ISS. *ERM, Cushman & Wakefield*, and *RGIS* which were already in different buildings while under Semco control had the ownership sold to the partners. Semco has partnership interests in *Tarponinvest*, that deals with financial operations and at *Brenco* a new start-up investment on bioenergy. Regarding the number of people involved I should say that it is about the same size (if not larger) in the service companies (ERM, CW, RGIS) although Semco is not in control anymore. Brenco alone (bioenergy is around 1000 people); *J.Controls* was discontinued – the Joint Venture portion of our partner was acquired by Semco; contracts were reallocated among other units. I don't know how you want to consider it but the total number that was around 3000, today would be more than 4000; all of the Business Units are successful, running well – making money; disregarding who owns them.

The synergy that Semco is looking for can be seen at one of its clients, Wal-Mart, which "has gradually become a customer of four of our units – we count their inventories, manage their cooling towers, administer their buildings and warehouses, and conduct environmental site investigation and remediation."[17]

Although he is the major stock-owner of the private equity company, Ricardo Semler *can't make decisions* (see Colvin, 2001; Fisher, 2005; Shinn, 2004; Vogl, 2004). At least not in the traditional sense of corporate decision-making processes. Before clarifying this idea and explaining their democratic approach, let me briefly present what type of business Semco is. Again, we are in trouble, since Ricardo argues that: "If you ask me to describe [Semco]...in conventional business terms, I'd have to admit that I have no idea what business Semco is in."[18] Furthermore, "Our 'architecture' is really the sum of all the conventional business practices we avoid."[19]

Renunciation: Semco's foundation for being humanistic

Reviewing some sources[20] about the meaning of the antonym of renunciation, you can find words like: domination, hegemony, manipulate, rule, influence, restriction, oppress, monitor, inspection, command, authority, and, obviously, power. How in any people's mind can you manage a business and try to be humane by *command and control*? What is more frustrating – and enlightening at the same time – are the antonyms for control: weakness, helplessness, powerlessness![21] Thus, if you don't control and exert power you are weak and only inspire helplessness. What a depressing picture. That says a lot about the Western mainstream mindset. There is one critical success factor that is at the core of being humanistic. It was mentioned when Ricardo Semler answered Lisa Creffield's question:[22] "[If it is so successful] why are people not adopting your methods, what's holding them back?" Ricardo argued: "Basically, because it takes a leap of faith...and the way we do things [at Semco] means giving up control, and people apparently don't give up control easily when they are in power. So it is very difficult to adapt because people have no real personal motivation to take that leap of faith." This explains why some of the articles' titles about Semco

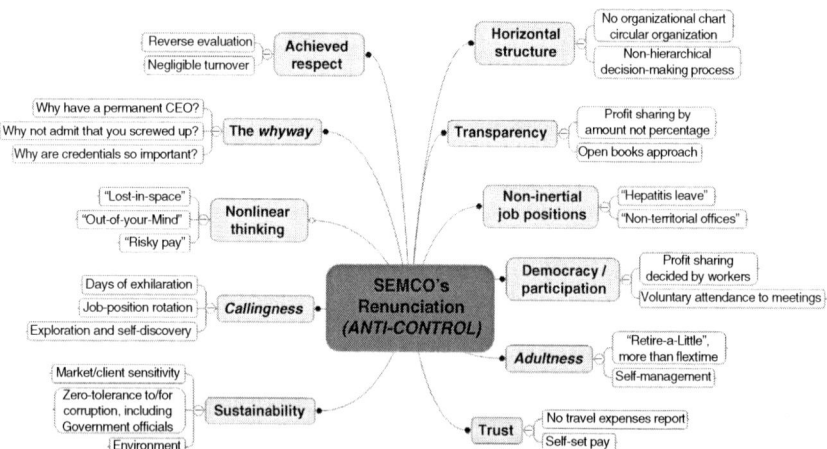

Figure 15.1   SEMCO's renunciation
Source: Graph and analysis done by the author.

and Ricardo Semler are: "The Anti-CEO," "Ricardo Semler Won't Take Control," "The Anti-Control Freak."[23, 24]

The best practices – or critical success factors – that have brought Semco where it is now are: transparency, non-inertia, trust, sustainability, participation, adults as adults, tapping into the reservoir of talent, non-linear thinking, horizontal structure, the *whyway* and achieved respect (Figure 15.1).[25]

Asking why – or the *whyway* management practice – is a management pillar at SEMCO, allowing its stakeholders to ask why. A deeper why. A challenging why. A disruptive why, if you wish. As Ricardo Semler[26] states: "Ask it all the time, ask it any day, every day, and always ask it three times in a row." But why is it so hard for corporations to let workers ask why? Because, Semler argues, it forces top managers to "give up control," which for Semler is an "absolute necessity."[27] Letting workers ask why is about sharing control, being democratic, and being participative. Semco is against the "blind, irrational authoritarianism" that permeates the majority of business organizations.[28]

For Ricardo Semler[29] "our insistence [is] that workers seek personal challenges and satisfaction before trying to meet the company's goal." They want to give people room for exploration and self-discovery. "Once employees feel challenged, invigorated, and productive, their efforts will naturally translate into profit and growth for the organization."[30] Thus, *asking why* in Semco is a profoundly human experience. The opposite would be a "huge waste of human potential" whereby people "simply learn to live with boredom without drawing on their true talents."[31] These are some examples of the *whyway* written by Ricardo Semler: "Why not retire at age forty, go back to work at sixty? Why hire the best and the brightest? Why are credentials so important? Why not shrink? Why grow at all? Why not admit that you screwed up? Why are financial reports impossible to decipher? Why have a permanent CEO?"

Regarding the next salient management pillar, or critical success factor, *achieved respect*, a brief reflection is necessary first to acknowledge its deep connection with renunciation. There are two types of respect: ascribed respect and achieved respect. In an organizational setting, the ascribed respect is the reverence tacitly received by a given job-position, a given role played by an employee. Consequently, what happens in the majority of companies is that the power ascribed to the job position forces subordinates to "respect" that person. At Semco, things do not work that way. At Semco they have constructed a setting where achieved respect can flourish. This means that a person in a given position, through his or her actions, behaves in ways that honor the power and respect his or her subordinates have given him or her. "Only the respect for the leader creates it" is part of the *Introductory Booklet* – or Survival Manual – given to new employees, which constitutes the only written set of rules.[32]

For example, that explains why they use "reverse evaluation," in two ways. First, a person is interviewed by his prospective subordinates when applying for a job, and second, if chosen, the subordinates will evaluate him on a regular basis in order to determine whether he can continue working in that group, or even at the Company. As Ricardo Semler[33] puts it, "power and respect cannot be imposed in connect-the-dot fashion."

Theft is something that happens at plants. Semco decided to manage this issue differently, in a more humane way, based on *trust and adultness* rather than mistrust. It is simple: if you treat humans like human beings, they will respond as such. Semler[34] argues that "workers are adults, but once they walk through the plant gate companies transform them into children." Semler[35] claims: "we don't make our employees ask permission to go to the bathroom ... we get out of their way and let them do their jobs." Thus, he decided to end searches at Semco, and a sign was put up at the gate saying: *"Please make sure as you leave that you are not inadvertently taking anything that does not belong to you."*[36] The rationale is a humane one. Why put *all* workers through humiliating searches when no more than *3 percent* of workers take advantage of the trust given? Thus Semler affirms: "I would rather have a few thefts once in a while than condemn everyone to a system based on mistrust."[37]

Adults as Adults, or *Adultness*, can be seen in the words of one of Semco's workers, called Zeca. Since at Semco there are no time-schedules, no nine to five, he spends long lunches with his girlfriend. Zeca states that "Only because I work at Semco ... nowhere else could I do that without feeling guilty." Also Zeca loves tennis, and happily followed Brazilian tennis player Gustavo Kuerten playing Roland-Garros matches on TV during "working hours." "He didn't ask permission," Semler highlights, and "He didn't miss a match, and his work didn't suffer either. On the contrary, pursuing his hobbies or his girlfriend allows him to create balance in his life."[38] Another telling story about adultness and time management reveals that RGIS, one of Semco's business units, was committed to inventorizing a client on the day of the soccer World Cup finals. I would bet that any *command & control* company in any country where soccer is important would not have been able to get the work done – and in Brazil soccer is almost a religion.

Well, Semco did it and the competition didn't, so the following week RGIS had won another client.

Semler[39] assumes that "what people call participative management is usually just consultative management. There's nothing new to that...it is only when the bosses give up decision making and let their employees govern themselves" that we can talk about true *democratic–participative management.* Over the last 25 years Semco employees themselves have created many committees that have proposed ideas and actually implemented them. Spontaneous groups formed to discuss changes, and Semler[40] highlights that "the strength of these groups was their diversity. They included factory workers, engineers, office clerks, sales reps, and executives." No one is forced to assist.

For example, these committees and groups have been working on reducing inventories. By letting workers choose their actions, some business units at Semco rotate their inventory 17 times per year, compared to an industry average of three times per year.[41] Also, when they were deciding on the place for a new plant, Semco hired buses, closed the factories and everybody went to see four prospective new sites. They decided on the one least appealing to the top managers.[42] But that is democracy. In the long run, the results confirmed that this is a good path to take, as Semler[43] asserts "human nature demands recognition."

Democracy and participation without transparency are not real. So Semco had already decentralized power and decision-making, but they had to take it further by including financial information, status, and salaries. They opened all their books – similar to the Open-Book methodology,[44] *eliminated* the organizational chart and elitist job positions, transforming a 12-layered organizational chart into a three-circled one – Counselors, Partners, and Associates.[45] Within these circles, there are triangles, representing the Coordinators, which are like junior managers floating around the business units – between six and 12 triangles for each one. Semler remembers that "the circles and triangles and trendy new names signified the most radical changes we had yet contemplated at Semco,"[46] giving it a more *horizontal structure.*

Regarding the salary structure, discussions with employees took place, based on four criteria: "what they thought they could make elsewhere; what others with similar responsibilities and skills made at Semco; what friends with similar backgrounds made; and how much money they needed to live."[47] Based on these participatory approaches, people at Semco set their own salaries. Also, they set up the profit-sharing plan – SemcoPar – when, after discussions and negotiations with the workers, agreement was reached on sharing 23 percent of

Semco's profits among the whole workforce – almost double the average of 8 to 12 percent present in Corporations.[48,49] In addition, the plan works so that the lowest-paid employees benefit disproportionally, as they receive a higher profit-sharing bonus in relation to their salary than higher-paid employees, which is, again, in sharp contrast to traditional companies where bonuses generally disproportionally benefit those employees who are already the top earners in the organization. At the end, authoritarian profit-sharing "doesn't create employee involvement."[50] Profit-sharing that does is about the distribution between employees as much as it is about the overall sum or percentage figure that is being distributed.

Semco has zero tolerance for corrupt practices.[51] Profit maximization and/or market rationality do not form part of Semco's raison d'être. As stated, there has to be a balance between workers' "callings" and Semco's *sustainability*. For example, Semco applies *diseconomies of scale*. They found that a group of more than 150 people generated alienation and low social cohesion, and so they split their factories.[52] This increased their costs, but generated productivity, innovation, and humaneness. By doing this, Semler argues, "people who worked in them [the smaller units] would feel human again. In a small factory, it is possible... *To belong*."[53] It is interesting to see the correlations between Semco and what Charles Handy writes regarding the "Federal Organization." In his experience, and based on organizational research, a federated corporation can be as big as it wants but it must be divided into organizational units – a federation of businesses for Semco – of no more than 120 to 200 people, so that everybody can know each other.[54] As well, Handy argues that hierarchical and centralized control will inevitably fail in the twenty-first-century company.[55] Semler believes that "the old way of doing business is dying, and the sooner it's dead and buried the better off we all will be."[56] Very similar to what is happening right now at Cisco, and what Peter Drucker and Charles Handy state about reducing control as the twenty-first century's new paradigm.

Ricardo Semler works towards *days of exhilaration* for Semco's workers. Thus you must tap into what he calls the "reservoir of talent" ... [or] some refer to it as a "calling".[57] *Callingness* is salient in Semco's participatory approach. Some examples can be seen in Ricardo Semler's ideas toward this critical success factor:[58]

- Most [workers] cannot figure out how to reconcile living with making a living.

- For a company to excel, employees must be reassured that self-interest, not the company, is their foremost priority.
- Stress levels are highest where balance is lowest. Workplace stress reflects the difference between expectation and reality.
- We always hope that on their own, people will discover their true calling. Most of the [workers in the world] are not answering a calling.
- Why is it that church groups, amateur choirs, or chess teams have such a high degree of commitment, but companies have to train, retrain, motivate, and remotivate all year around?

The space given to this case only allows me to summarize other initiatives highlighting some interesting structural possibilities that Semco has created over the years in order to give flexibility to employees – including factory workers. For example, *Lost-in-space*, during which newcomers at Semco spend a year getting to know all business areas with no responsibilities; *Hepatitis Leave*,[59] their version of *sabbaticals*; *Job rotation*, at a rate of at least 25 percent per year; *Risk salary*, according to which workers bet 25 percent of their salary on the possible profit of that semester – if the latter is good, they have a great return but if it is not good, they lose the bet;[60] *Teams*: Semco does not have year planning or strategic 5-year planning, only semester plans, and for each semester you have to "apply" for the job, waiting for a Counselor, Partner or Coordinator to accept you in the team, composed of no more than 12 people – this is also where people set their own salary; *Up'n' Down Pay*: depending on peoples' lives and phases, you can decide how much time you are going to work; *Retire-a-little*, similar to the last one, but allows you to retire while working and *redeem* the time not worked in the future.[61]

Transferring Semco's anti-model

The reader could be asking: How can I apply some of these ideas to my company or workplace? "Patience," João Vendramim argues. "This is a process, a long one. It took us 20 years," he admits. Although Ricardo Semler highlights that "Semco practices have been adopted at schools, hospitals, police departments, and large and small companies around the world," he does not think there is a "model" to follow. That would limit your creativity and put at risk the *whyway*. You must start making changes and allow people to propose anything that pops into their minds. "The type and size of the organization is irrelevant,"[62] Semler argues. "Semco isn't a model … Semco is an invitation."[63] When Ricardo Semler gives talks about Semco and its proven success, he normally hears comments like "Mr. Semler, before answering other questions, can you please tell us what planet you're from" (Semler, 2004, p. 7), or "This story of yours is all very interesting … [but nothing is] applicable … at my hospital and pharmacies."[64] Regarding the last phrase, when answering the owner of the pharmacies, who is a doctor, Ricardo Semler asked some questions: who decides where the medicines are placed, or by whom and how are workers' schedules done? After some questions and answers, Ricardo convinced the doctor to give him control of the smallest of his pharmacies, representing 1 percent of his sales and three employees. The doctor agreed and gave Ricardo full control. The first thing Semler did was to give his book to the three employees, meet with them, and tell them that the owner had given "them the freedom to try anything they desired."[65]

During the first 6 months they changed several things and made some innovations: for example, they changed schedules to fit in better with their leisure time; repositioned medicines based on demand, not alphabetically as the doctor had said it was "easy to find" – and supposedly the best way; reduced inventory costs by creating a numbered inventory of medicines – the inventory was done during the night when few customers arrive; diversified the pharmacy with items related to medicines, such as bandages, sunscreen, and the like, and "last I heard," Semler asserts, "the employees had proposed a profit-sharing plan and the doctor was spreading the Semco gospel at his hospital."[66]

The lesson that can be learned from the last story is that, since Semco comes from *another planet*, nothing seems possible within a traditional mainstream corporate paradigm. Once the doctor experienced the positive outcome himself, he expanded his paradigm. Thus, the *invitation* is for you to try it in small units or projects in your company. Have faith, patience, and, most important, be mentally and spiritually prepared to renounce control – that will be the hardest, I bet. Don't try to convince your boss or peers by "speaking" theoretically, since their paradigms will not allow them to comprehend[67] what you are saying – unless they are not traditional and/or narrow-minded.

Ricardo Semler advises us that even in "the most hidebound of environments … with perseverance and courage, Semco-style management can flourish," and that was what happened in "Brazil's imperious [and highly traditionalist] Federation of Industries of the State of São

Paulo." In a similar fashion as in the pharmacy, he was positioned as an officer of the Federation's technology department, the "youngest director in the Federation's history."[68] He experienced a lot of resistance, but some of the industrialists supported him. During the first days at the Federation he started to feel what bureaucracy really meant. Nothing could be done, moved, or signed without his consent. So Ricardo changed that, allowing an executive – Joyce Leal – to sign documents. Later, he changed their contract to part-timers so they didn't have to use time cards, without reducing their income, but allowing them to manage their time. The result was higher productivity and motivation.

Then, Ricardo ordered them to tear down their cubicles and started to form a team, since they "had only a vague idea of what their colleagues were doing."[69] Some workers were transferred to other departments since they were not able to handle so many changes. That allowed Ricardo to pay Joyce more, as well as others that stayed. "After a few months," Ricardo remembers, "I no longer signed any papers." Following his leadership style of "Managing without Managers,"[70] he "started coming in only once a week, then every other week, then once a month." To cut a long story short, the result was that his department became the best one, and Ricardo was elected Vice President of the Industrialists' Federation.

Conclusion

It is not easy to end this chapter, since there is so much more to say about SEMCO – for example, gender equality programs ("Semco-Women"), alliances with civil society, respect for the environment. Also, there are plenty of examples of frustrations, things that did not work, and ideas that never saw the light. For example, Joao told me that when they were deciding which factory to buy and where it would be located, since this democratic approach was still new workers "were not ready" to propose an aligned vision of it. The result was rather costly, since they had to move the factory again the following year.

It is not easy to accept Semco's approach even if you really like it. As Ricardo Semler argues, "Unfortunately, our society conditions us to accept boredom from an early age."[71] That explains, besides their corporate social responsibility programs, why Ricardo created Semco's foundation, the Lumiar Institute,[72] in order to "deprogramme adults." Hence, the best way to end this chapter is to read a story that shows how far this can go and the big social benefits that such humanistic companies produce. Ricardo Semler wrote that one day a worker's wife arrived at Semco, and

> She was puzzled about her husband's behavior. He no longer yelled at the kids, she said, and asked everyone what they wanted to do on the weekends. He wasn't his usual, grumpy, autocratic self. The woman was worried. What, she wondered, were we doing to her husband? We realized that as Semco changed for the better, he had, too.[73]

I have been researching Semco for the last 2 years. I know that I want to help other workers and companies to be humanistic. That is why I proposed to João Vendramim the creation of a branch of Semco's foundation – *Lumiar* – in Colombia, where I live right now, since that is my calling. What is yours? Would you know what to answer in your so-called *interview*?

Notes

Author: Carlos Largacha-Martínez, PhD, clargacha@ean.edu.co. I want to acknowledge and thank João Vendramim, former Counselor at Semco and retiring consultant, for his time in several phone conferences we had in order to improve and align this case study. As you have read in this chapter, a Counselor is something similar to a Vice President, since at Semco there are no hierarchies or job positions.

1. Amaral and Pozzebon, 2005.
2. Management by Wandering Around, popularized at Hewlett-Packard (Semler, 1993, p. 70).
3. Within this initiative people voluntarily assist in meetings where you can propose any idea that you have, even if it is crazy, without feeling that somebody can tell you "Are you nuts, or out of your mind!" Visit http://semco.locaweb.com.br/en/content.asp?content=4
4. "We make public virtually all information, from salaries to strategies and productivity statistics to profit margins" (Semler, 1993, p. 335).
5. Semler, 2004.
6. Semler, 2004, p. ix.
7. Largacha-Martínez, 2006.
8. Semler, 1993, p. 10.
9. Ibid., p. 17.
10. Semler, 2004, p. 10.
11. Semler, 1993, p. 22.
12. Ibid., p. 31.
13. Semler, 2004, p. 8.
14. Ibid., p. 18.
15. Ibid., p. 12.
16. Ibid., pp. 12–14.
17. Ibid., p. 16.

18. Semler, 2004, p. 7.
19. Ibid., p. 9.
20. For instance, Webster's New Collegiate Dictionary (1953); Roget's II. The New Thesaurus (1980).
21. Roget's 21st Century Thesaurus, 3rd ed. [accessed October 30, 2008 at www.dictionary.com].
22. At the World Business Forum, 2007.
23. These elements, as well as the foundation, renunciation, are from the author's viewpoint. However, they occur throughout Ricardo Semler's writings, specifically in the Glossary of his book *Maverick*.
24. See Colvin, 2001; Fisher, 2005; Shinn, 2004; Vogl, 2004.
25. You can find these articles at Semco's website, http://semco.locaweb.com.br/en/
26. Semler, 2004, p. 17.
27. Ibid., p. 5.
28. Semler, 1993, p. 4.
29. Semler, 2004, pp. 8–9.
30. Ibid., p. 14.
31. Ibid., p. 45.
32. Semler, 1993, p. 300.
33. Ibid., p. 196.
34. Ibid., p. 67.
35. Ibid., p. 59.
36. Ibid., p. 68.
37. Semler, 2004.
38. As cited by Semler, 2004, p. 33.
39. Semler, 1993, p. 83.
40. Ibid., p. 87.
41. Ibid., p. 132.
42. Ibid., p. 127.
43. Ibid., p. 109.
44. Boyett and Boyett, 1999.
45. Semler, 1993, p. 190.
46. Ibid., p. 192.
47. Ibid., p. 200.
48. Semler, 1993, p. 139.
49. "We began with Semco's total profits the revenues minus expenses. Then we agreed that 40 percent would be deducted for taxes, 25 percent for dividends to shareholders, and another 12 percent for reinvestment, the minimum the company needed to continue to prosper. That left 23 percent" (1993, p. 139).
50. Ibid., p. 138.
51. Semco states about corruption: "More than a few government inspectors who set out to extort Semco have ended up in jail. This has caused us plenty of trouble with the government inspectors all over Brazil, but it's worth it rather than send a signal to our employees and customers that we tolerate dishonesty". *Maverick*, p. 330.
52. Semler, 1993, p. 125.
53. Ibid., p. 118.
54. Handy, 1994, p. 141, as cited by Boyett and Boyett, 2000, p. 298.

55. Ibid., p. 295.
56. Semler, 2004, p. 5.
57. Ibid., p. 39.
58. Ibid., pp. 39–64.
59. The name came out when they asked themselves: What would happen if you got hepatitis?
60. Teams at Semco set their own sales goals each semester and can bet 25 percent of their salary on the team achieving their self-set goal. Achieving the goal will result in a bonus payment, but the downside is that failing to meet the self-set goal, having placed a bet, will lead to a partial loss of that money.
61. Semler, 1993, pp. 329–335; Semler, 2004, pp. 51–54.
62. Semler, 2004, p. 13.
63. Semler, 1993, p. 290.
64. Ibid., p. 275.
65. Ibid., p. 276.
66. Ibid., p. 277.
67. Kuhn, 1996.
68. Ibid., p. 278.
69. Ibid., p. 279.
70. You can see this idea developed in the e-paper *Managing without Managers*, Harvard Business Review, October 25, 2008.
71. Semler, 2004, p. 45.
72. See http://www.lumiar.org.br/english/index.html
73. Semler, 1993, p. 7.

Bibliography

Amaral, Cecilia Gurgel do and Pozzebon, Marlei (2005). *Non-Territorial Offices at Semco*. Richard Ivey School of Business. The University of Western Ontario.
Boyett, Joseph and Boyett, Jimmie (1999). *Lo Mejor de los Gurús*. Barcelona: Ediciones Gestion 2000.
Colvin, Geoffrey (2001). The anti-control freak. *Fortune*, Vol. 144 (11), November 26.
Creffield, Lisa (2007). Middle East business information site AME, http://www.youtube.com/watch?v=rXXpTDl_65M [accessed September 2009].
Fisher, Lawrence (2005). Ricardo Semler won't take control. *Strategy + Business*, Vol. 41, 1–11.
Kuhn, Thomas (1996). *The Structure of Scientific Revolutions*. 3rd ed. Chicago, IL: University of Chicago Press.
Largacha-Martínez, Carlos (2006). *Theorem f. A Holistic-Humanistic Model of Development*. Dissertation. University of Miami. Coral Gables.
Restrepo, Andrés (1989). *La Empresa Escuela de Compartir*. UNIAPAC de Colombia, Bogotá.
Semler, Ricardo (1993). *Maverick: The Success Story Behind the World's Most Unusual Workplace*. New York: Warner Business Books.
Semler, Ricardo (2004). *The Seven-Day Weekend: Changing the Way Work Works*. New York: Portfolio.
Shinn, Sharon (2004). The Maverick CEO. *BizEd*, January/February, pp. 16–21.
Vogl, A. J. (2004). *The Anti-CEO*. The Conference Board Review Article, May/June.

16
Triple Bottom Line Management at Sonae Sierra

*Pedro Teixeira Santos, Miguel Pina e Cunha,
Arménio Rego, and Miguel Pereira Lopes*

Introduction

Sonae Sierra is one of the five largest shopping and leisure center developers in Europe, but it is number one when it comes to corporate responsibility. The company has focused its attention not on the quantity or size but on the quality of its work, striving to always stay ahead and be seen as the best specialist in the sector in Europe. Sonae Sierra's commitment to sustainable practices has been long-lasting. Since its foundation in 1989, social and environmental responsibilities have played a part in the organization's strategic decisions. This case study aims to guide you through Sonae Sierra's evolution and achievements, while providing some examples of best practices at the company and making clear the advantages of investing in a triple bottom line.

Sonae Sierra: A profile

Sonae Sierra is an international company specializing in shopping and leisure centers (www.sonaesierra.com). It is currently operating in seven countries – six in Europe and one in South America (Brazil) – where it owns and manages 47 centers. These centers correspond to a gross lettable area of 1.85 million square meters, which means that the company rents out to tenants roughly the area of 250 soccer pitches. Sonae Sierra has 12 other projects under development. It directly employs 789 people and is currently celebrating 8,162 contracts with tenants. The impact caused by the development and management of these shopping centers is significant: on the environment, on society, and on the economy.[1]

The company was founded in 1989 in Portugal and is jointly owned by Sonae SGPS (Portugal) and Grosvenor (UK), with 50 percent each. Although initially dedicated to engineering and other services related to real estate development, Sonae Sierra changed paths and became specialized in shopping centers, responding to the increase in demand for diversity and choice of consumption. By 1991 it had opened the first Portuguese shopping center. Since then, Sonae Sierra has grown and has been divided into four separate businesses: Sierra Investments, Sierra Developments, Sierra Management, and Sierra Brazil. These businesses share the same corporate services – which include finance, legal, human resources, environment, communication, safety and health, and back-office services – and are supervised by an executive committee and board of directors which clearly set corporate responsibility as a vision and mission for the company.

Sonae Sierra aims to become the best sustainable international specialist in shopping and leisure centers, and its mission is "to create value for its shareholders, through the shopping center business, while taking into account its social responsibilities towards other important stakeholders, as well as its environmental responsibilities," as it believes this balance is crucial in order to ensure a sustained development of the company.

Where did it start?

The company's vision was strongly influenced by one man, the former CEO of Sonae SGPS (Sierra's holding group, see www.sonae.pt), Belmiro de Azevedo. Described as a "liberal with social concerns,"[2] he began early on to understand the importance of sustainable development[3] and responsible practices. He embarked on group-wide initiatives concerning community and employee relations beginning as early as 1985. Sonae SGPS's concerns with sustainability were strengthened when in 1995 the company became one of the founders of the World Business Council for Sustainable Development (WBCSD), a world organization that provides a platform for companies to investigate sustainable development and share information, experiences, and best practices.[4] In 2004 it signed the United Nations Global Compact – a strategic policy initiative for businesses that are committed to aligning their operations and strategies with ten universally accepted principles in the areas of human rights, labor, environment, and anti-corruption[5] – and in 2005 signed the World Safety Declaration, which is concerned with improving safety at work.[6]

Companies within the group were invited to explore corporate responsibility (CR) as a competitive advantage. Corporate responsibility can be viewed as a company's contribution to sustainability, meeting the needs of the firm's stakeholders (such as shareholders, employees, clients, communities, etc.), without compromising its ability to meet the needs of future stakeholders as well. Definitions of corporate social responsibility tend also to present it as "a concept whereby companies integrate social and environmental concerns in their business operations and in their interaction with their stakeholders on a voluntary basis. Being socially responsible means not only fulfilling legal expectations but also going beyond compliance and investing 'more' into human capital, the environment, and the relations with stakeholders" (European Commission, 2001, p. 8).

Several initiatives were undertaken, such as diverse forums on the environmental and social impact of the businesses in order to diffuse the best practices throughout the companies of the group, environmental guidelines were implemented, and companies were urged to initiate corporate responsibility reporting. These initiatives slowly trickled down and ingrained themselves into the entire group as part of their culture and identity. To quote from Belmiro de Azevedo's lecture in the leadership forum at the London Business School in 2006: "A company cannot be simply a money making machine. In addition to giving the maximum return on investment to shareholders, businesses have to earn the respect of the societies in which they operate, preserving social cohesion, protecting the environment, and ensuring the long term sustainability of the planet on which we live."[7]

What was done at Sonae Sierra?

Sonae Sierra understood the importance of corporate responsibility, but a long path had to be followed in order to ensure that this view would be adopted and that this aspect would become an integral part of its identity and culture. When it comes to implementing such a vision, it cannot be merely a top-down decision. As Elsa Monteiro, head of Institutional Relations, Environment, and Communication put it, "the employees are the ones who run the business and are ultimately responsible for the implementation of the sustainable policies. They are also responsible for sharing their experiences and best practices, while the tenants and business partners are responsible for providing appropriate feedback."[8] As such, several measures to promote stakeholder engagement were put in motion. Sonae Sierra "borrowed" environmental and social guidelines from Sonae SGPS, initiated corporate responsibility reporting, set up internal forums to diffuse best practices, held stake-holder training sessions, set up tenant satisfaction surveys and visitor surveys, and defined a framework for evaluation and monitoring.

As a consequence, Sonae Sierra managed to publish its first environmental report in 2000 and a second in 2002. These reports illustrated some practical examples and the progress of environmental indicators and achievements in energy and water savings and waste management. An example illustrated in the 2002 report was the Greenlight project, which consisted of substituting 8,770 magnetic light bulbs for electrical ones in a Lisbon shopping center parking lot. The results for this project were as follows: investment, EUR 125,000; reduced energy use, 400,830 KWh/year; cost savings, 23,810 €/year;[9] CO_2 emission avoided, 200 tons/year. Sonae Sierra also issued an internal quarterly environmental newsletter – to raise awareness and encourage best practices amongst employees – up until 2004, when they responded to Sonae SGPS's request to strengthen sustainability strategies and publish corporate responsibility reports.

As a response to the call for corporate responsibility reporting by Sonae SGPS, Sonae Sierra officially adopted a triple bottom line view of business (Elkington, 1997) and used the Global Reporting Initiative[10] (GRI) Sustainability Reporting Guidelines as a way to properly evaluate and monitor the progress made, equating the social, environmental, and economic areas, to ensure sustained development. Sonae Sierra believes that its long-term business success is dependent upon outstanding

Table 16.1 Areas of impact

Economic impact areas	Environmental impact areas	Social impact areas
• Local economic benefits • Job creation • Financial impact on key stakeholders	• Climate change (energy consumption/efficiency, greenhouse gas emissions and other gas emissions) • Water use and emissions to water • Waste production and management • Land use and biodiversity • Materials use and responsible procurement	• Tenant satisfaction • Community relations • Visitor satisfaction • Nuisance (noise, dust, traffic) • Accessibility • Crime prevention and security • Employee satisfaction • Training and skills • Safety & Health • Responsible procurement

Source: Sonae Sierra Corporate Responsibility Report, 2007, p. 4.

performance in relation to all three. In order to clarify this view to its stakeholders, Sonae Sierra identified some key areas of impact that fell into the different categories. Table 16.1 shows the breakdown of the three pillars.

Again, the major obstacle here was stakeholder engagement and education: the ecocentric view of business (Cunha et al., 2008; Shrivastava, 1995), whereby the philosophy of the company is anchored in the natural environment, was far from established. Another problem that arose in the reports was the quality of the data. The quality depends on the response of the tenants and employees, which may or may not be accurate. Several training sessions were held in order to coach them on how to properly provide data, but even today this is a major difficulty when it comes down to assessing the veracity of the data.

The bottom lines

An organizing template for Sonae Sierra's sustainability approach was the notion of a triple bottom line, introduced by John Elkington in his book *Cannibals with Forks* (Elkington, 1997). This idea refers to a focus simultaneously on economic prosperity, environmental quality, and social justice. In this section we discuss how this philosophy was operationalized at Sonae Sierra.

Economic prosperity

Sonae Sierra has grown steadily throughout its existence, constantly delivering better financial results. Sonae Sierra's EBITDA grew to EUR 156.2 million in 2007, a 5 percent increase from 2006; and its net profit grew to EUR 300.1 million in 2007, an 11 percent increase from the previous year.[11] Today the company is affected by the negative climate now prevailing in the property markets of most of the developed countries where Sonae Sierra operates, implying a reduction in the value of the corresponding real estate property. However, the company losses were mitigated by valuation gains in Brazil, a market that was not affected by the crisis.

But economic value goes far beyond that which is created for the shareholders. Sonae Sierra is only directly responsible for 789 employees, but it is indirectly responsible for a much larger pool of job creation during the management phases, such as the shop staff (totaling 62,400 people) and the outsourced cleaning and security staff (totaling 10,200 people).[12] It is their policy to positively impact the societies where they operate. Their new project in Brazil alone, which opened in spring

2009, is expected to create around 3,000 jobs. Furthermore, they are responsible for creating business for their suppliers and retailers, and pay a significant amount of taxes (EUR 78 million in 2007[13]). They also have an impact on local communities, having donated a total of EUR 512,796 in 2007.[14] Sonae Sierra has a tremendous economic impact on the areas in which it operates, sometimes singlehandedly revitalizing local economies.

Environmental quality

Sonae Sierra made a commitment to be environmentally certified in all its shopping and leisure centers. It developed an internal environmental management system (EMS), based on the ISO14001 and certified by Lloyd's Register Quality Assurance, to promote a rigorous approach to project development and management. Sonae Sierra's internal management system did, however, present some deep-rooted challenges for the company, forcing them to question some assumptions and really stand their ground. The EMS is far more demanding than the legislation, and in many cases more demanding than the country's culture, presenting no clear competitive advantage. This poses the question of how to adapt to different markets. Tiago Vidal, corporate communications manager, pointed out while talking about Sonae Sierra's expansion into Romania that: "Our CR parameters are much stricter than those that are imposed, given the country's culture and legislation. This gives the opportunity for our competitors to embark in projects which we cannot because of our business model."[15] The question of "how to develop a company culture where CR is looked upon as an integral part of the business strategy while taking into account the complexities posed by a multicultural management" was raised. The investment in sustainability also has a cost of 3–5 percent more in the development phase than it would otherwise. At a time when access to credit is limited, this extra development cost may act as an impediment to entering new projects. On the other hand, it is this slack between the internal requirements and the legislation that gives Sonae Sierra its competitive edge. By looking toward the future, it can anticipate any alterations in legislation and minimize "surprises" (Cunha et al., 2006). It is also these strict demands that define the company – they are its identity and culture.

Sonae Sierra's answer to all these doubts was clear. It is in the difficult times and in adverse conditions that they define themselves more than ever as a sustainable company. Although difficulties may arise, it is their belief, and part of the company's strategy policy, that equating the short and the long term is crucial for Sonae Sierra's present success and will continue to be so in the future.

Social justice

Sonae Sierra took action in each of the areas of impact in a number of ways. The most salient in the social area was the "Personae" program. This multi-awarded program (awards include the ECO award from American Chamber of Commerce in 2006 and the Dupont Safety Award for Visible Management Commitment in 2007) seeks to achieve a zero injury culture, and ensures responsible practices in the shopping and leisure centers. The program's target audience is cross-sectional, ranging from contractors, to tenants and support staff, to visitors. Over the course of the past 4 years since the project was implemented, more than 70,000 people have been involved with the project to some degree.

To implement this project, Sonae Sierra developed Safety and Health norms and procedures for stakeholders, activities, and the premises. These norms and procedures were diffused through the company by means of forms and educational pamphlets, as well as seminars, workshops, behavioral safety preventive measures, and training for evacuations and emergency response. Additionally, *Quick Wins* – a practical guide to observing low-cost, quick-fix nonconformities in the workspace, and the corrective measures that should be applied – and *Safety Tips* – communicating practices that should be followed in different situations, from using the stairs to preventive driving techniques – were distributed.

Sonae Sierra's CEO Alvaro Portela commented, while receiving the Dupont Safety Awards, that: "We are very pleased with this recognition of our success through felt leadership and focusing on each individual's behavior, rather than relying solely on a team of safety professionals."[16] The "Personae" program was also the basis for the Sonae Sierra Safety & Health Management System, which allowed the company to earn its place as the first European company in the shopping and leisure center industry to receive certification for Safety and Health – the OHSAS (Occupational Health and Safety Assessment Series) 18001. The Personae program promotes a proactive approach to accident prevention, creating a sustainable "inside-out" safety culture by empowering individuals to effect positive change on the organization at large, while enhancing reputation among the different stakeholders and promoting external recognition.

In 2005 Sonae Sierra's Board decided to define the main aspects of ethical behavior that should be adopted by its businesses in order to ensure social equity. This led to an ethical code of conduct, which includes the following principles:

- Respect for the dignity and rights of each individual;
- Respect for individual identity, independent of race, gender or religion;
- Strict compliance with the law;
- Acting with honesty and integrity;
- Promoting a balance between personal and professional life; and
- Commitment to the community.

These principles are expected to ensure that ethical principles and business integrity are maintained in Sonae Sierra's relationship with its employees, customers, suppliers, partners and society.[17]

With the intent of guaranteeing a greater degree of satisfaction to its stakeholders, and in line with its code of conduct, Sonae Sierra has recently appointed an ombudsman. The ombudsman is "a knowledgeable facilitator between the company and its stakeholders, fostering their mutual respect and preventing any abusive conduct from the company and or any of its employees."[18] The ombudsman will thus be the entity responsible, alongside the employees themselves, for ensuring that the code of conduct is followed. The anticipated improvement in satisfaction levels is expected to encourage better internal and external professional relationships among the company and its stakeholders.

Other social contributions include supporting community programs such as *Bem querer mulher* in Brazil – an initiative supported by the United Nations Development Fund for Women (Unifem). The objective was to raise awareness of female victims of domestic violence. Sonae Sierra offered space for the campaign stations, and lectures were given inside the shopping centers on issues such as health, self-esteem, violence, and other issues related to the feminine universe.[19]

Another example of Sonae Sierra's outreach to the community is the field trips made to the shopping centers by local schools. These field trips have the goal of teaching children about issues related to sustainability, safety and health. Sonae Sierra coordinated 291 school visits in 2007.

What changes were made to the governance structure?

Although we have already seen that the implementation of a strategy such as this cannot be a top-down decision, it is always important to have the support of top management. In 2002 Sonae Sierra structured itself into seven CR working groups, each focusing on a particular

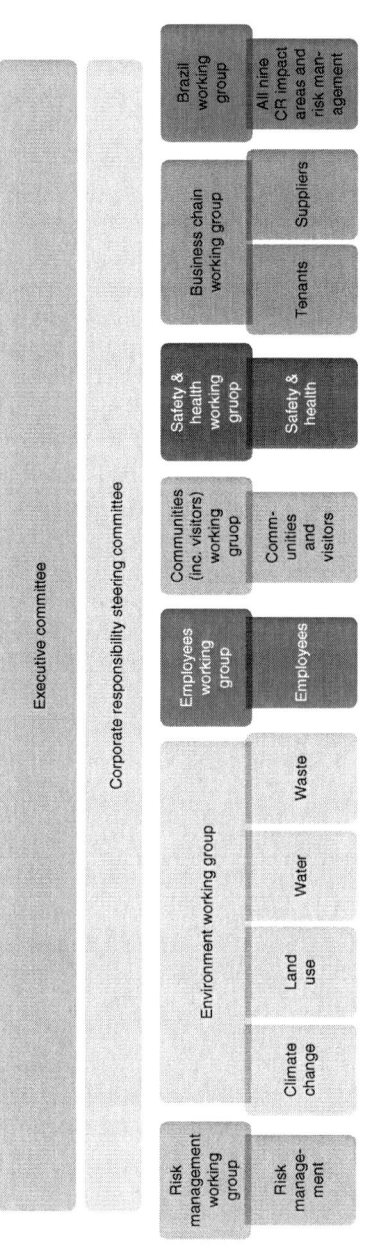

Figure 16.1 Corporate responsibility governance structure

Source: Sonae Sierra Documents – Corporate Responsibility Report 2007, p. 15.

aspect of corporate responsibility – risk management, environment, employees, communities, safety and health, the business chain, and the Brazil working groups. Although these groups already provided support to each area and allowed close contact between employees and top management, Sonae Sierra decided that it was necessary to have a more coordinated, cross-sectional view of what were the CR needs. In 2006 they created a CR steering committee, constituted by the heads of each CR working group – of which four are members of the executive board – and chaired by its CEO, Alvaro Portela. The aim of the steering committee is to oversee the organization's identification and management of issues related to economic, social, and environmental performance; and to provide a clear vision for the company's CR strategy – setting and reviewing policies, approving long-term objectives, short-term targets, and budgets for each working group. This change in the governance structure reinforced the importance of the CR strategies to Sonae Sierra's business model (Figure 16.1).

What were the results?

External recognition

Sonae Sierra has won multiple prizes in the CR domain and has been named the best developer in Europe on more than one occasion (see Table 16.2). This external recognition is the confirmation that Sonae

Table 16.2   2007 and 2008 awards

Awards 2008	Awards 2007
Global RLI Awards • RLI Developer of the Year **Construir Awards** • Best Real Estate Developer **AECC** • Best Social Solidarity action Una Sonrisa contra el hambre' **Liquid Real Estate** • Best Developer in Western Europe • Best Retail/Shopping Company in Italy • Best Developer, Best Retail/Shopping Company, and Best Property Manager in Portugal **Green Thinker Award** • Best Sustainability strategy	**Dupont Safety Awards – Visible Management Commitment** • Personae Project **European Property Awards** • Best European Retailer/ Leisure Developer **ICSC** • ICSC ReSource Award

Source: http://www.sonaesierra.com/en-GB/aboutus/awards/currentyear/default.aspx [accessed October 8, 2010].

Sierra is moving in the right direction. While receiving an award for best developer in Europe, the company's CEO commented: "This award brings us a special satisfaction, since it demonstrates that the work carried out by the Sonae Sierra team in the development of shopping and leisure centers is acknowledged by the main European specialists in the sector as a company that specializes in shopping center development, we know that our passion for innovation forces us to set a path for the future for shopping centers that anticipates the citizens' demands."[20] This external recognition has brought many advantages to the organization. It has reinforced the sense of belonging and pride amongst stakeholders, resulting in improved employee retention and attraction, increased motivation, and worker satisfaction (Willard, 2002). The recognition also motivates employees to continue to make an effort to act in a corporately responsible manner in order to ensure that the company continues to succeed. It has also created a higher demand among clients – the tenants – which choose Sonae Sierra's shopping centers to operate in because of the increase in client and societal awareness and demand for responsible business in our flat, hot, and crowded planet (Friedman, 2008). Finally, it has heightened the possibility of finding potential investors and partners. This is crucial for Sonae Sierra's international expansion, whose strategy relies on international investors and local partnerships.[21]

Key performance indicators

Sonae Sierra draws out clear targets for its CR policies. Examples for 2008 include: the reduction of greenhouse gas emissions by square meter of gross lettable area; improving the results of the employee satisfaction survey by 10 percent in the areas of working conditions and work–life balance; and investing 5 percent of shopping center marketing budget in community-related initiatives.[22] Using guidelines from the GRI, key performance indicators (KPI) were developed in order to monitor the progress of its policies. In 2007, they successfully achieved 71 percent of their CR targets. Table 16.3 depicts the developments that Sonae Sierra has made in some key performance indicators in the past 3 years.

Identity and culture

Sonae Sierra has managed to create a strong culture centered on corporate responsibility. The intense reporting initiatives, creating an appropriate governance structure with the involvement of top management, and the creation of forums to share experiences and diffuse best

Table 16.3   Evolution of the key performance indicators from 2005 to 2007

Global average indicators	2005	2006	2007
GHG emissions of the owned and managed portfolio (tCO$_2$–e/m^2 GLA)	0.138	0.132	0.121
Elecricity efficiency (KWh/m^2 mall + toilet area)	704	685	651
Water efficiency (liters per visit)	3.8	4.0	3.9
Waste recycling rate (%)	27	34	38
Tenant satisfaction index	2.8	2.8	4.6*
Community investment (charitable donations made by shopping centers and collected by visitors) (€)	n.d.	n.d.	9,629
Total number of man hours of safety & Health training provided	n.d.	3,219	5,185

Notes: n.d. = no data.
*A new methodology was used in 2007 and a different scale (1 to 6), so the year-on-year results are not comparable.
Source: Sonae Sierra Corporate Responsibility Report, 2007 (Summary), p. 7.

practices, were crucial for this evolution. Compensation schemes based on CR key performance indicators were also set up. Elsa Monteiro clarified that "caring about CR is not only an act of good faith, it is part of the company, and as such, the company recognizes and compensates their workers accordingly."[23] Some other simple measures were taken. For instance, when you walk around the Sonae Sierra offices you are immediately drawn to the colorful signs which remind you to turn off the lights or to recycle. The distribution of the Al Gore documentary, "An inconvenient truth," was Sonae Sierra's Christmas present in 2006, in order to raise awareness and alert employees to the change they can make as a whole. Tiago Vidal, corporate communications manager, commented that this present "allowed for a better understanding of the effort and investment that Sonae Sierra is making toward the environment, and alerted our individual conscience of the contribution that each one of us must make as citizens in order to minimize our impact on climate change."[24]

All these factors created a great sense of unity and purpose, which reflects on the employees' motivation and satisfaction levels. Again, it also attracts and retains talent that wants to belong to a company that behaves in a responsible way, caring about itself and its surroundings.

Improved efficiency

When dealing with CR practices, one of the great challenges is to find new and attractive ways to do business. There are two aspects of Sonae Sierra's business approach that are critical for this to take place. First, Sonae Sierra's long-term approach allows it to make investments that are attractive in the long term but may not be the most appropriate in order to obtain short-term profit. Second, it also takes environmental and social costs into consideration. So, even though to one company it may not seem like a good investment, this is because they are taking into account different costs. This gives Sonae Sierra a great zone of maneuverability to explore new solutions. There are many occasions when solutions found are profitable – even in the short run – and also have a positive impact on the environment and society. Used water, treated through a self-owned waste water treatment plant for toilets and irrigation, is one example. The investment was recovered within 1 year, and from that point on it will lead to lower running costs, while reducing the impact on the environment. In order to stay at the forefront of this movement, Sonae Sierra has to constantly investigate new possibilities and assure that there is a constant diffusion and exchange of information. For this purpose, Sonae Sierra is a member of various associations that seek to find eco-efficient solutions, such as the World Business Council for Sustainable Development, of which Sonae SGPS is a founding member. Elsa Monteiro outlined: "It is a challenge for the market as a whole to find new technologies, to see to what extent the new technologies available are in fact efficient, and to make them available at a reasonable market price."[25] Sonae Sierra is part of the core group for Energy Efficiency in Buildings, which is concerned with making buildings self-sufficient – that is, achieving zero net energy – by 2050. This challenge becomes of special importance when we see that buildings are responsible for 40 percent of the carbon dioxide emissions in Europe. But being an innovator also carries its own risks. Valuable resources may be put into projects that end up being unsuccessful or need further adjustments.

Finding more efficient solutions also means reducing costs. This gives Sonae Sierra an advantage over its competitors. It can become internally more competitive because it has higher margins, or it can be more competitive externally by lowering prices. Sonae Sierra has followed a market-oriented pricing strategy, while exploring corporate responsibility as a differentiation advantage.

Lower risk

One big issue with the shopping and leisure center industry is the colossal investment needed to develop each shopping center. For instance, the recently opened shopping center in Italy required investments of EUR 102 million. Any adjustments that are needed are always less expensive if they are made in the planning phase. Although there is an increase in development costs from 3–5 percent, the potential increase in costs if an adjustment had to be made later on would be much higher – not mentioning the fact that this cost will be recovered during the running of the center. Another characteristic of shopping centers is their long life cycle, stretching for over 25 years. But when would an adjustment be necessary? Sonae Sierra is preparing itself for if and when the laws eventually change. Being years ahead of the legislation allows these buildings to be sustainable in the long run, reducing costs and risks. The company also bears in mind the needs and demands of its clients. A recent study on sustainability, commissioned by the Real Estate Publishers and the International Council of Shopping Centers, based on phone interviews with property executives responsible for 250 retail companies representing 48,000 stores from 27 countries, has shown that the number of retailers with corporate responsibility policies has increased from 28 percent in 2007 to 41 percent in 2008. If the current trend is maintained, sustainability will be a key decision factor for tenants in the future.

Conclusion

Sonae Sierra's proactive attitude towards sustainable practices – inspired by the vision of the CEO of Sonae SGPS (Sierra's holding company) since its conception in the late 1980s – seems to have laid out a prosperous business model. The investment in corporate responsibility and management to create a culture based on these principles was a success, and expresses the possibility of the "necessary revolution" (Senge et al., 2008) in terms of the relationship between organizations and the natural environment. By understanding the interdependent relation it had with its stakeholders, Sonae Sierra was able to create win–win situations – there has been a reduction in the ecological footprint, an increase in the positive impact on society, and an increase in business volume and profits. The key factor was developing this strategy and culture in such a way that the whole organization was part of, and responsible for, the change. The involvement and commitment of top management was evident through company policies and the redesign of corporate governance structures, but the important thing was to involve everyone at every level through education, recognition, and empowerment. Many challenges did in fact arise, but the company has stood firm in its beliefs and values. Sonae Sierra has approached these challenges not as obstacles, but as part of the path to achieve a greater degree of humanism and respect, while creating a greater sense of identity, contribution, and purpose.

Notes

Miguel Cunha gratefully acknowledges support from Fundação para a Ciência e a Tecnologia (PTDC/GES/70167/2006).

1. The data in this paragraph refer to 2007.
2. In Expresso: http://clix.primeirasedicoes.expresso.pt/ed1344/e014.asp
3. *"Sustainable development seeks to meet the needs and aspirations of the present without compromising the ability of future generations to meet their own needs."* Citation from: "Our Common Future, Report of the World Commission on Environment and Development, World Commission on Environment and Development, 1987." Published as Annex to General Assembly document A/42/427, Development and International Co-operation: Environment August 2, 1987: http://www.un-documents.net/wced-ocf.htm [accessed January 2009].
4. For more information see the WBCSD website: http://www.wbcsd.org
5. http://www.unglobalcompact.org/AboutTheGC/index.html
6. For more information see: http://www.worldsafetydeclaration.com
7. Sonae SGPS Corporate Responsibility Report 2006, p. 15.
8. Interview with Elsa Monteiro, Head of Institutional Relations, Environment and Communication, Lisbon, July 2007.
9. Sonae Sierra deems a payback period of less than 10 years in an environmental investment to be acceptable.
10. For more information see: http://www.globalreporting.org
11. For more information see: http://www.sonaesierra.com/enGB/ourfigures/financialreports/currentyear/default.aspx [accessed October 8, 2010].
12. http://www.engenheiros.pt/cis2007/comunicacoes/Pedro_Rodrigues.pdf [accessed January 2009]
13. Sonae Sierra Corporate Responsibility Report, 2007, p. 114.
14. Sonae Sierra Corporate Responsibility Report, 2007, p. 81.
15. Interview with Tiago Vidal, Manager of Corporate Communications, Lisbon. February 2008.
16. Sonae Sierra Documents: http://www.sonaesierra.com/en-GB/pressroom/news/2007/584/Sonae_Sierra_wins_2007_DuPont_Safety_Award.aspx [accessed October 8, 2010].
17. For more information see Sonae Sierra's Code of Conduct: http://www.sonaesierra.com/en-GB/behaviorcode.aspx [accessed October 8, 2010].

18. http://www.sonaesierra.com/en-GB/corporateresponsibility/sierraombuds-man.aspx [accessed October 8, 2010].
19. http://www.bemquerermulher.com.br/bqm_sonaesierra.htm
20. Sonae Sierra Documents: http://www.sonaesierra.com/en-GB/pressroom/news/2007/577/Sonae_Sierra_internationally_acknowledged_as_the_best_company_in_the_Shopping_Centre_sector.aspx
21. These conclusions have been drawn by Sonae Sierra from the feedback and close communication that Sonae Sierra maintains with its stakeholders, and have been backed up by its increased growth and financial results.
22. Sonae Sierra Corporate Responsibility Report, 2007.
23. Interview with Elsa Monteiro, Head of Institutional Relations, Environment and Communication, Lisbon, July 2007.
24. Interview with Tiago Vidal, Manager of Corporate Communications, Lisbon. February 2008.
25. Interview with Elsa Monteiro, Head of Institutional Relations, Environment and Communication, Lisbon, July 2007.

Bibliography

Cunha, M. P., Clegg, S. R. and Kamoche, K. (2006). Surprises in management and organization: Concept, sources, and a typology. *British Journal of Management*, Vol. 17, 317–329.

Cunha, M. P., Rego, A. and Cunha, J. V. (2008). Ecocentric management: An update. *Corporate Social Responsibility and Environmental Management*, Vol. 15 (6), 311–321.

Elkington, J. (1997). *Cannibals with Forks: The Triple Bottom Line of 21st Century Business*. Oxford: Capstone.

European Commission (2001). *Promoting an European Framework for Corporate Social Responsibility*. European Commission.

Friedman, T. (2008). *Hot, Flat and Crowded*. New York: Allen Lane.

Savitz, A. W. (2006). *The Triple Bottom Line*. San Francisco: Jossey Bass.

Senge, P., Smith, B., Krushwitz, N., Laur, J. and Schley, S. (2008). *The Necessary Revolution*. London: Nicholas Brealey.

Shrivastava, P. (1995). Ecocentric management for a risk society. *Academy of Management Review*, Vol. 20, 118–137.

Sonae SGPS (2007). Sustainability Report 2006.

Sonae Sierra (2003). Environmental Report 2002.

Sonae Sierra (2005, 2006, 2007). Corporate Responsibility Report 2004, 2005, 2006.

Willard, B. (2002). *The Sustainability Advantage: Seven Business Case Benefits of a Triple Bottom lIne*. British Columbia: New Society Publishing.

17
Can Business and Humanism Go Together? The Case of the Tata Group with a Focus on Nano Plant

Radha R. Sharma and Shoma Mukherji

Founded by visionary Jamsetji Tata in 1860, the Tata group has always been driven by a spirit of nationalism[1] and welfare of the community. "Improving the quality of life" is one of the guiding principles of Tata Group, one of India's largest business conglomerates with revenue equivalent to about 2.8 percent of the country's GDP in 2006.[2] The group currently has 98 companies encompassing seven business sectors – materials, engineering, energy, chemicals, services, consumer products, information systems and communications – across six continents. The group has all along had responsible leadership integrating ethical considerations into the company's decision-making, and managing the firm with personal integrity and widely held organizational values of compassion, high ethical standards, community development, and welfare of people in general, which are the principles of humanism. Successfully combining the dual challenges of "doing good" and "doing well" over a span of 140 years is what makes the Tata group truly stand out.

Jamsetji: The Pioneer of Tata Group with nationalism and humanism

Jamsetji Tata was a visionary industrialist inspired by nationalistic principles. He believed that India had to gain political freedom along with economic self-sufficiency and industrialization.

Born in 1839, he studied at Elphinstone College, Bombay, and started his professional life in a solicitor's office. Marriage and the birth of his son increased his financial responsibilities and he joined his father's textile business. Jamsetji left for England in 1864 to represent his firm, which was exporting large quantities of cotton to Liverpool. During a business visit to Manchester, in 1867, he attended a lecture by Scottish historian and sociological writer, Thomas Carlyle. Carlyle's thesis that "the nation which gains control of iron soon acquires the control of gold" made a deep impression on Jamsetji. He dreamed of making steel for the country for its technological power, and was also interested in hydroelectric energy. He carried samples of coking coal and iron ore from India to Germany for testing. British licensing laws, at that time, discouraged private mining. Limiting metallurgy and mining checked production of firearms and ammunition by locals, thereby preventing the possibility of rebellion.[3] Jamsetji, however, kept track of minerals in India by saving all press clippings. He was willing to wait for the right opportunity. In 1868 he set up Tata & Sons, and was a man of substantial fortune by the time he attained the age of 50.

Major Mahon's report of 1899 stating that the time was ripe for establishing an iron and steel industry in India led to the then Governor General, Lord Curzon, relaxing the rules for mining licenses. Jamsetji visited England to meet Lord Hamilton, the Secretary of State for India, and expressed his desire to set up the steel industry under Indian management. Moved by Jamsetji's enthusiasm and nationalistic principles, Lord Hamilton agreed to policy changes. Jamsetji visited the world's largest ore markets in Cleveland, USA, studied coking processes in Alabama, and garnered support from Julian Kennedy, a leading metallurgical consultant, and Charles Page Perin, one of the best surveyors in the industry. His efforts bore fruit when the first ingots rolled out of Tata Iron and Steel Company (TISCO) in 1912, but Jamsetji had passed away in 1904 and did not see his dream turn into reality.

Jamsetji always believed that progress of enterprise was inextricably linked with the welfare of people. Wealth generation was a means to an end, for the increased prosperity of India. Successive generations of the Tata Group leaders have always held the belief that no success in material terms is worthwhile unless it serves the interest of the nation and is achieved by fair and honest means.

Tata values and business philosophy

Humanism is concerned with the advancement of humanity, applying rational thinking and analysis. It develops a code of behavior that frees humans from the supernatural and the unreasonable, but still places mankind in the appropriate universal context (Gunasekara). The concept recognizes human beings as a part of nature and holds that values – be these religious, ethical, social, or political – have their source in human nature, experience, and culture. Jamshetji, in a letter written to his son Dorabji Tata in 1902 (excerpts given below), long before the site of the TISCO plant was found, laid the foundation of the Tata way of humanism.

> Be sure to lay wide streets planted with shady trees, every other of a quick growing variety. Be sure that there is plenty of space for lawns and gardens. Reserve large areas for football, hockey and parks. Earmark areas for Hindu temples, Mohammedan mosques and Christian churches.[4]

Founder Jamsetji Tata's humaneness was evident in his unwavering belief that "in a free enterprise, the community is not just another stakeholder in business, but is in fact the very purpose of its existence."[5] He offered half his fortune, consisting of 14 buildings and four landed properties worth INR 3 million (in 1896), to the British government if they would make a contribution equal to his gift and pass an enactment to found a university. The dream became a reality only in 1905, a year after his death, when the British Government agreed to establish the Indian Institute of Science at Bangalore. Fountainhead of India's scientific and technological endeavor and mother of many national laboratories that grew after independence, the institute continues to be a center of excellence in scientific research.

At Tata Steel there has been a separate division for Community Development and Social Welfare since 1956, providing pre-primary education programs for bustee (slum) children, awareness for society-building, education and youth leadership development, vocational training, health, hygiene, overcoming addiction, and a socio-economic program. The rural development program focused on family planning, counseling for family disputes, family life education, and tribal and Harijan (under the Indian constitution called scheduled caste) welfare programs.

The American Psychological Association has developed general principles of Humanistic Psychology: competence, integrity, professional and scientific responsibility, respect for people's rights and dignity, concern for others' welfare, and social responsibility. The Association of Humanistic Psychology (AHP), founded in 1962, is a worldwide community of diverse people promoting personal integrity, creative learning, and active responsibility in embracing the challenges of being human in these times. "As the world's people demand freedom and self-determination, it is urgent that we learn how diverse communities of empowered individuals, with freedom to construct their own stories and identities, might live together in mutual peace."[6] The core values upheld by AHP are:

• a belief in the worth of persons and dedication to the development of human potential;
• an understanding of life as a process, change is inevitable;
• an appreciation of the spiritual and intuitive;
• a commitment to ecological integrity;
• recognition of the major problems affecting our world; and
• responsibility and hope for constructive change.

The abovementioned values have all along been manifest in the actions of the Tata Group. The Tata Council for Community Initiatives coordinates the CSR activities of the group companies. Though each company undertakes CSR initiatives under its own steam, the umbrella organization provides homogeneity of policies and ensures that the Tata values of volunteerism, innovation, continuous improvement, and creativity are adhered to.

Developing the Tata way

Dorabji Tata, Jamsetji's eldest son, succeeded him and ensured the fulfillment of his father's dreams. The business grew from three cotton mills and a five-star hotel (The Taj, Bombay) to include India's largest private sector steel company, three electric companies, and one of India's leading insurance companies. Leveraging the nationalist (*swadeshi*) spirit which ran high during that time, Tata Iron and Steel Company Limited decided to tap the Indian capital market and issued shares on August 26, 1907. A total of INR 23.2 million (USD 511,111) was raised through issuance of ordinary, preference, and deferred shares, to set up a plant with a rated capacity of 72,000 tons per annum, 14 percent of India's total steel requirement. Work on the plant began in 1908 and the first ingot was rolled out on February 16, 1912.

Sir Dorabji Tata was fond of sports and became the President of the Indian Olympic Association. He financed the Indian contingent to the Paris Olympics in 1924. He was instrumental in setting up the Lady Tata Memorial Trust to advance study into diseases of the blood. He also established the Sir Dorabji Tata Trust, the funds of which were used for learning, research, disaster relief, and other philanthropic purposes. Jehangir Ratanji Dadabhoy Tata (JRD) played an active role in establishing Tata Memorial Hospital, a super-specialty cancer hospital and research center, with the triple objectives of treatment, research, and education. He was also instrumental in setting up the Tata Institute of Fundamental Research, under the stewardship of Homi Bhabha, who went on to guide India to become self-reliant in the field of atomic energy.

JRD became Chairman of Tata Sons, the holding company of the Tata Group, at the age of 34. Under his stewardship, till 1993, the number of companies in the Tata Group grew from 15 to over 100 and the assets grew from INR 620 million (USD 1.37 million) to over INR 100,000 million (approximately USD 2.22 billion). Blending humane business practices with political savvy and a pioneering spirit, JRD is remembered as one of India's most important and influential business leaders. He insisted on maintaining high ethical standards and refused to bribe anyone in any way for business growth. He strengthened existing businesses such as steel, power, and hotels, and pioneered the Group's initiatives in the airline business, chemicals, commercial vehicles, computers and software services. Inspired early by aviation pioneer Louis Blériot, JRD took to flying and got the first pilot license issued in India. In 1932 he founded India's first commercial airline, "Tata Airlines," which in 1946 became Air India, now India's national airline.

JRD, besides being a great leader, had the rare ability to create leaders. He chose Russi Mody, an employee at Tata Steel, to succeed him in 1984 and himself remained Chairman Emeritus. Mody enhanced marketing operations and started an export cell. He also gave the company the legendary "G" blast furnace, which was equipped with a sophisticated monitoring and control system and an up-to-date automation system, enabling production of high-quality hot metal at the lowest cost. In 1945 JRD commissioned Tata Engineering and Locomotive Company (TELCO) with the objective of making locomotives for the Indian Railways. Known as Tata Motors now, it is among the world's top ten manufacturers of commercial vehicles.

J. R. D. Tata, Chairman of the Tata Group from 1938 to 1991, was conscious that in a country as diverse as India the task of social progress cannot be undertaken by the Government alone. He firmly believed that "the aim of an industry should be to discharge its overall social responsibilities to the community and the society at large, where industry is located."[7]

Ratan Tata took over the reins of the Tata Group in 1991 when India embarked on globalization and allowed large-scale entry of multinationals. In the four decades since India gained independence from British rule, indigenous industry had thrived under protective laws. With the opening up of the economy, these industries faced unprecedented competition from global players. The Tata group not only dealt successfully with the changed environment, but also emerged as a force to be reckoned with in new business areas. The group's turnover rose from INR 106,270 million (USD 23,615 million) to INR 494,560 million (USD 109,902 million) with a contribution of 2.4 percent towards the country's gross domestic product in just over a decade. "If you can't be in line, please leave," was Ratan Tata's first message to some group heads, as "nobody is bigger than the brand." Identifying China as the main competitor, he commissioned a strategic review and emphasized that there was need for thinking big and shifting gears to become a global heavyweight rather than a stodgy regional player. Tata Motors has emerged from an India-centric truck-maker to a global auto firm as a result of his visionary leadership, determination, and focus on the big picture. The launch in 2007 of the world's lowest-cost car, Nano, agreement on the acquisition of two of the most upmarket brands (Jaguar and Land Rover) less than 3 months later, the imminent launch of a "world truck" (Daewoo) out of Korea, expansion in the capacities of three existing plants (Jamshedpur, Pune, and Lucknow), and building three new plants (Pantnagar, Singur, and Thailand) at new locations – all these are happening simultaneously.

Time magazine featured Ratan Tata in its 2008 list of the World's 100 most influential people. Tata was hailed for unveiling his tiny Rs. one lakh[8] car "Nano." He was awarded an honorary doctorate from the London School of Economics and was listed among the 25 most powerful people in business named by *Fortune* magazine in November 2007. On August 29, 2008, the Government of Singapore conferred honorary citizenship on Ratan Tata in recognition of his abiding business relationship with the island nation and his contribution to the growth of high-tech sectors in Singapore.

Concern for all the stakeholders

Jamsetji's philanthropic principles were rooted in his belief that India has to harness its finest minds to overcome poverty. With this in view he established the JN Tata Endowment in 1892. This enabled Indian students, regardless of caste or creed, to pursue higher studies in England.

This beginning flowered into the Tata scholarships, which flourished to the extent that by 1924 two out of every five Indians coming into the elite Indian Civil Service were Tata scholars.

The greater achievement for JRD was not the expansion of the group, but an expansion on the ideals and ethics of the principles of the Group's founder. He said: "The wealth gathered by Jamsetji Tata and his sons in half a century of industrial pioneering formed but a minute fraction of the amount by which they enriched the nation. The whole of that wealth is held in trust for the people and used exclusively for their benefit. The cycle is thus complete; what came from the people has gone back to the people many times over."[9] This is evidence of humanistic work – compassion for community and the welfare of people in general, irrespective of diversity, without any expectation and with an exemplary humility.

JRD was instrumental in setting up the Tata Administrative Service and the Tata Management Training Center at Pune with a view to modernization of science and technology. The philosophy of humaneness remained unshaken even when Jamsetji met with political challenges. JRD avowed: "The Tata philosophy of management has always been and is today more than ever, that corporate enterprises must be managed not merely in the interests of their owners, but equally in those of their employees, of the customers of their products, of the local community and finally of the country as a whole."[10] In the globalized economy Tata's humanism is benefiting people across nations where the group has its operations. The following will throw light on how the values of humaneness have been combined with business growth.

Linking business growth with humanism

Tata Iron and Steel Company (TISCO), founded nearly 100 years ago, was a pioneer in the Indian steel industry. Steel prices were regulated during the socialist phase of India's economy. When deregulation happened in 1991, TISCO, instead of caving in, emerged as one of the most efficient steel producers in the world through a focused program to adopt cutting-edge technology, increase yield, and reduce costs across the value chain. It had accomplished all of this while earning a reputation as one of the most sought-after firms to work for. It has assiduously pioneered many employee welfare measures, being responsible for the 8-hour working day in 1912, long before the USA or Europe; free medical treatment in 1915; leave with pay in 1920, 25 years before it became a law in India; a provident fund for employees in 1920, 32 years before it was legalized in India; maternity benefits in 1928, and a pension scheme in 1989.[11]

In 1957, TISCO set up a joint consultative worker–management council to handle employee grievances. In 1980, it became the first Indian company to conduct a social audit of its activities. Today the company runs hospitals, schools, and a college and provides services including water, power, landscaping, street sweeping, and civil construction at its base at Jamshedpur, later named as Tata Nagar.

Scions of the Tata family continued with the tradition established by Jamsetji and invested substantial fortunes in trusts for the good of the community. The Sir Ratan Tata Department of Social Sciences was established at the London School of Economics in 1912. Naval Tata, a contemporary of JRD, who was at the helm of affairs of a number of Tata enterprises, lamented: "despite the progress of science and technology in recent years, there are more millions living in misery than ever ..."[12] As a spokesman for Afro-Asian countries at the International Labour Organization, Naval Tata brought India to the forefront of labor matters in global forums. He spearheaded expansion of Tata Power at a time when electricity generation was almost exclusively the government's preserve.

The Tata group has evolved a collective commitment to maintain stronger connections between their values and first-in-class business practice, not by putting either one ahead of the other, but by establishing strong linkages between them. "From health and education to livelihoods and women-children welfare, from tribal hamlets in Jharkhand and the rural outback of Gujarat to the high ranges of Kerala and disadvantaged villages in Andhra Pradesh – the community work being undertaken by the companies and trusts of the Tata Group touches a multitude of Indians across the land."[13] A substantial part of the profits of many of the companies in the Tata group is channeled back to the people through major philanthropic trusts. As a result, great national institutions have come into being in the areas of science, medicine, atomic energy, and the performing arts. Tata BP Solar Ltd looks at ways of bringing affordable power to villages that presently are not connected to a supply.

The Tata Council for Community Initiatives (TCCI), currently headed by Kishore Chaukar, coordinates the varied and widespread community development activities of Tata companies.

The various Tata companies were spending money but making people dependent on the scheme. TCCI was set up to coordinate and integrate the various social projects undertaken within the Group, institutionalize the processes, and focus on building self-reliant communities rather than simply doing charity. Every Tata company adopts an Article of Association on social responsibility. TCCI then helps them evolve policy statements, recognize the core competency, and develop activities accordingly. For example, the core competency of the Taj Group of Hotels is hospitality. This can be used to teach slum women baking and help them make some money. In Hyderabad, Tata Teleservices gets together all Tata companies in that region to send volunteers to teach maths and computer skills to the local needy children. TCCI has, in collaboration with the United Nations Development Program (India), crafted the Tata Index for Sustainable Human Development, a pioneering effort aimed at directing, measuring, and enhancing the community work undertaken by group enterprises.[14]

The Tata group's sustained integration of social benefit generation with commercial success, described above, has been widely applauded. As a result of its endeavors, the company enjoys a great reputation, long-lasting commitment from talented individuals, very good labor–management relations, and decades without strikes. Cynics, however, have commented that ultimately the array of non-core activities began to negatively affect the core steel business. During the last few years Tata Steel has had to restructure and redesign its social welfare programs in order to refocus on its corporate strategy. However, restructuring too was done in a humane way, ensuring proper redeployment and resettlement of the employees affected by restructuring. When Tata Steel had to shed 32,000 workers to remain competitive, it offered a redundancy package not easily found in the corporate world. It promised to pay workers who opted for redundancy a frozen salary until retirement age – even if they found another job.[15]

Nano: A common man's dream car

The thought had come to Ratan Tata, Chairman of the Tata group, about 6 years ago in 2002, on his way to his office in Tata Indigo (a Tata Motors product), when he saw a family of four riding on a two-wheeler scooter. A man drove the scooter, with his wife at the back holding a baby in her arm and a young child standing in the space in front of the father's seat. Humanism, a core value at Tata, gave him the idea that Tata Motors could come up with a low-cost people's car which would be fuel-efficient and meet all safety standards and emission norms. Initially, people were apprehensive that a cheap car would lead to greater pollution and congestion on the roads. But Ratan Tata, having inherited the Tata values, planned for a better tomorrow for his countrymen.

In an interview, Ratan Tata clarified that the car was not priced at INR 1 lakh (USD 2,220); to quote: "I was interviewed by the British newspaper *Financial Times* at the Geneva Motor Show and I talked about this future product as a low-cost car. I was asked how much it would cost and I said about INR1 lakh. The next day the *Financial Times* had a headline to the effect that the Tatas are to produce an INR100,000 (USD 2,220) car. My immediate reaction was to issue a rebuttal, to clarify that that was not exactly what I had said. Then I thought, I did say it would be around that figure, so why don't we just take that as a target. When I came back our people were aghast, but we had our goal."[16]

A top caliber team of 500 people was formed under the leadership of Girish Wagh. It took 5 years for this team to convert the dream into reality and to unveil the prototype of the NANO – the high-tech small car – at the Auto Show, 2007, in New Delhi, the capital of India. The four-door vehicle, powered by a 33-horsepower, 634-cc engine with mileage of approximately 20 kilometers per liter, was designed to meet Euro IV norms that would seat five passengers. During the unveiling, Ratan Tata reiterated that the "Nano" would cost INR 100,000 (USD 2,220) as promised 4 years ago, despite costs having gone up. "Promise is a promise," he stated. He decided to locate the Nano plant at Singur, an economically backward village in West Bengal.

The Nano car, the result of a series of path-breaking innovations, harnessing the latest technological advances, is a symbol of the group's continuous commitment to applying the best in business in the service of the people. It is powered by a two-cylinder rear wheel drive engine with capacity of 623 cc. The lean design strategy has minimized weight, maximizing performance per unit of energy consumed. The higher fuel efficiency ensures that the car will have low carbon dioxide emission. Its contemporary mono volume design maximizes interior space by pushing the wheels to the corners and placing the power train under the rear seat. Made of all sheet-metal body, it has a strong passenger compartment, with safety features such as crumple zones, intrusion-resistant doors, seat belts, strong seats and anchorages, and the rear tailgate glass bonded to the body and its tubeless tyres further enhance safety. These features are not commonly found in the low-cost car segment in India.

The political climate at Singur

West Bengal, a state in Eastern India, has been governed by the Communist Party of India since 1977. The first chief minister, Bidhan Roy, founded large industrial plants in Durgapur, Asansol, Kalyani, Howrah, and Calcutta, making it one of the most industrialized states in the country during the 1950s. A flight of capital started in the 1960s during the violent anti-state Naxalite uprising, gaining momentum in the 1970s during an era of militant trade unionism and disruptions by the Bangladesh War. When Buddhadev Bhattacharya became Chief Minister in November 2000, the economic situation in the state was quite grim. Unemployment in urban areas, a serious crunch in technical and medical education facilities, and a near-breakdown of health services had become serious issues. Bhattacharya's integrity and progressive outlook helped him win the assembly election for his party for the seventh time. He was determined to attract investments in new industries and IT-related services and put Bengal on the global industrial map again.

Ratan Tata took a risk when he decided to base the Nano project at Singur. The Communist party in India exhibited concern for the downtrodden and was known for its anti-industry stance. Tata, however, was impressed with Bhattacharya's sincerity and understood that he was keen to host Tata Motors' new plant as it would have a ripple effect of attracting greater investment for rapid industrialization. In line with the Tata philosophy, he was keen to be a part of the industrial rejuvenation of the state. The industry minister, Nirupam Sen, along with the concerned agencies, was proactive, supportive, and willing to match any incentive offered by other states. The location had to meet specific requirements of physical characteristics, logistics, and costs laid down by the expert team. Singur, 45 km from Kolkata, standing alongside an arc of the Durgapur expressway near the Ratanpur crossing with National Highway-1, met these requirements and was found to be suitable for the new plant. In May 2006, the West Bengal Government decided to acquire 997 acres (645 acres for the mother plant, 290 acres for a vendor part to host ancillaries), for Tata Motors' new project. Nearly 6,000 families, including agricultural workers and marginal peasants, were to be affected by loss of livelihood. Long before the plant's construction started in January 2007, Tata Motors had chalked out and begun to implement a plan in association with the state government to integrate the community with the project, as it had done at the other sites at

Pune, Jamshedpur, and Lucknow. The objectives of the plan were to a) enhance employability of men in the community; b) create employability for women; and c) improve health and education facilities.

Adjacent to the main Nano plant, it was planned to develop a vendor park for about 56 different ancillary companies to supply parts to Nano, with the option that these ancillary companies could supply parts to other firms as well. In line with the nationalistic philosophy of the Tata group, Ratan Tata believed this would provide an opportunity for West Bengal to emerge as a cluster for auto and auto component-related manufacturing.

Manik's new world

Manik Patra pulled on his green and blue uniform, hurrying to cross the boom gate of the Nano plant in the next 15 minutes. The Shift Supervisor would be annoyed if he was late again. Manik was beginning to learn the meaning of time schedule and punctuality, since he had joined as an apprentice at the Tata Motors plant at Singur in West Bengal.

Singur had transformed during the past 2 years. Instead of the swaying yellow paddy, one saw a spanking new plant as one crossed the Durgapur highway. Life had metamorphosed for Manik during the past 4 months. He remembered dropping out of school after Class 8 to help his father in the paddy field. Manik's father, as a sharecropper, had had to toil hard to make ends meet and needed a helping hand for the fields. But now Manik was an apprentice in the paint shop at the plant and was acquiring new skills. With a decent salary, two square meals was no longer a problem for the 12-member family. Manik's father, like several erstwhile farmers, had found employment as a laborer with Shaporji Pallonji, the building contractor at the plant site. His brother, Jeevan, had recently joined a school set up by the Tatas in the vicinity and would ride pillion on Manik's bicycle to reach the highway, from where he made it on his own to the new school.

Community gearing up for the sunrise at Singur

Life had changed completely for Manik's neighbor, Shiuli Das. Six months ago she had not even heard of Tata Motors, but she had seen those Tata trucks on the highway when she went to work in the paddy fields. In March 2008 Shiuli was among a group of 25 women selected for training at the Institute of Catering and Hotel Management in

Kolkata. Now they ran a canteen which supplied food to the construction workers at the Nano plant site. Manik's school friend Namita had joined the sewing group, which had undergone training and now made uniforms, gloves, and other items required by the workers. Manik's sister-in-law, Rupa, was one of the group of 30 women trained by Tata Yazaki Autocomp. They were now busy making important components for the world's lowest-cost car – integrated modular wiring harness (to provide power to the vehicle), high-tension cables (for carrying heavy currents from the battery to other parts of the vehicle, exclusively used for petrol variants), connectors, and terminals.

Tata's focus on the employability of youth led to the comment: "What we would like to see ideally, in the India of tomorrow, is 10 young graduates getting together out of an Indian Institute of Technology (IIT) and saying, they would like an enterprise of their own instead of having to work for somebody. We would like that enterprise to also sell the vehicle in that area. We would like the service engineer to be trained by us that could perhaps serve the customer. He could use the spare parts of this enterprise to service the customer."[17]

Manik's childhood friend Robi now had no time to waste. He and another 178 young men like him, who had been just sitting around after finishing the school leaving examination, had now been selected for the 4-month intensive training program at Ram Krishna Shilpa Mandir. Life was now full of promise for these men, who were now working as electricians, fitters, turners, and welders at the plant. Another 350 people from the nearby villages were being trained for similar jobs. Haran Das had formerly been a teacher at the primary school at Singur where Manik started his education. He was now in the Tata-sponsored program at NIIT (National Institute of Information Technology, a well-known software development and training institute), learning computers. Soon he would be part of the workforce at the plant, like the 250 other young men in the program. Another of Manik's friends, Naveen, had registered with the West Bengal Industrial Development Corporation, hoping to hear of some employment opportunities. He was now part of a group of young men and women undergoing 15 months' hands-on training at Tata Motors' facilities to become multi-skilled.

A long line of men made their way to the factory every morning to work as loaders, construction workers, and laborers. During the induction program, Gautam Saran, a senior manager from the Tata CSR team, had explained that the Tata philosophy and guiding principle had always been to change the lives of the people, not just by way of recruiting locally, but by drawing up a long-term sustainable program.

The Tata group has always focused on enhancing employability of men in the community, creating employability for women, and improving health and educational facilities.

Clouds gather at Singur Nano plant

A call came just as Ratan Tata was disembarking from the Falcon jet. He had inherited his mentor JRD's love of flying, and often flew the corporate jet himself. As he was preparing to land at Mumbai airport he could see the majestic Taj Mahal hotel across the Gateway of India. On the other side, at Trombay, he could see the Tata Power plant, which supplied 80 percent of Mumbai's electricity. On the crisscrossing streets below he could see the miniature Tata cars, trucks, and buses. Billboards advertising various Tata products – tea, watches, cosmetics, cellular services – came into view. As a person, Ratan Tata is perceived as a reserved personality, but his professional business dealings, assertive stance, and out-of-the-box thinking surprise many.

Tata was slightly worried this morning in August 2008. He had placed his best people at Singur to ensure that the Nano would roll out as promised in October 2008. But Mamata Banerjee, the leader of the opposition political party, Trinamool Congress, had been organizing protests and strikes throughout the past 2 years against the acquisition of land by Government for the plant at Singur. Tata had depended on the Chief Minister of the ruling party to have the matter amicably settled with the local population. Of the 12,000 families affected by land acquisition, 10,000 had willingly accepted the compensation already. Banerjee, for her own political reasons, was encouraging people to retract and demand the return of 290 acres of land earmarked for the ancillary industries by Tata Motors. As this was an integrated project, the mother plant and vendor park had to be together, and for cost efficiency and business reasons this was not acceptable to Tata Motors.

Girish Wagh, the lead manager of the Nano project, who was on the phone line from Singur, informed that two security guards at the Ratan Tata Nano plant had been badly beaten up and were in hospital. The Trinamool Congress had set up a blockade and was not allowing workers to enter the plant site. When some senior managers had tried to reason with the agitators they had been physically threatened. The situation had become very volatile.

Ratan Tata was not smiling now. About INR 15,000 million (USD 333.33 million) had already been invested in the project. Besides, the national and international media were following the developments of the Nano plant and its aim of producing the world's lowest-cost people's car and promoting prosperity and employment in an industrially laggard state. The deadline for putting the car on the road was just about two and half months away. Ratan Tata had to find a solution to this complex political and socio-economic business situation soon. There was no way that the safety of his employees would be compromised.

A strange sight greeted Manik, the new apprentice at Nano plant, as he was about 500 meters away from the plant gate. There was a multitude of people waving green flags and brandishing sticks, and they seemed to be pushing back the other workers who were at the gate already. There was a posse of policemen standing at a distance, looking at the people. Just across the main factory gate, a podium had been erected and a lady seemed to be giving a speech.

Headlines and wide coverage were appearing in the national dailies about Singur, otherwise an unknown village, because of "Nano," the people's car, the Tatas' involvement, and, of course, democratic freedom. Because of the Tatas' legacy, most people believed that the Tatas would not do anything that would harm a community anywhere. Newspapers did their own research and reported that acquisition of most of the land for the project had been smooth and the landholders were satisfied with the compensation received. A small number of absentee landholders, illiterate farmers, and Trinamool Congress supporters refused to accept the compensation offered. Another point that emerged was that most of the landholders had never bought the disputed land. Agricultural land was doled out by the ruling party to their party supporters in the name of "land reform." The opposition's assertion that the land was extremely fertile was debatable, reported the papers. The landholders had not experienced significant levels of agricultural output efficiency or prosperity, and this was the reason why most of the community there was welcoming the Nano plant.

Ratan Tata met the Chief Minister, West Bengal, who influenced the Governor to mediate and pacify the raised temper of the opposition leader. Work had been suspended since September 3, 2008, leading to business loss and delay in project implementation. The other option, of shifting out of Singur, would amount to a loss of INR 15,000 million (USD 333.33 million) invested in the plant and machinery, besides the additional investment in training and other facilities. Staying on at Singur would involve risk to the life and safety of employees. No assurance had been given by the ruling party or the opposition that there would be no agitation in the future.

Turning point at Singur: People first

Various states began to offer a red carpet welcome to Ratan Tata, as they knew that locating the Nano plant in their state would bring prosperity and growth along with community development in line with the Tata legacy. Tata waited patiently until all negotiation efforts had failed for political reasons, and made the final announcement on October 3, 2008. He finally chose the safety of his employees and commitment to customers over the heavy investment in plant and machinery, and decided to shift the Nano plant to Sanand, near Ahmedabad in the state of Gujarat. This state was the *karmbhoomi* (workplace) of Mahatma Gandhi, the father of the nation, and has historical links with the Tata group.

The rollback process began, and machinery and other materials that could be shifted were loaded for transport to Sanand. However, the training institutes/centers and schools are there to stay. The community development initiatives will benefit Singur for years to come. The people who acquired skills at Singur have received offers from Ratan Tata to work at the new site. Those unable to move would be able to find new avenues of employment with the acquired skills.

Manik Patra picked up his bag, touched his parents' feet (the Indian way of paying respect to parents), and set out for the Durgapur highway, where the Tata bus was waiting to take him to Kolkata. There he planned to board a train for Gujarat, the new location of the Nano plant. He turned to his neighbor, Tushar, who had chosen to join the agitation against the Tatas. "What have you gained? Even if you get the land back, you cannot cultivate anything. So many will be jobless in our village. I am going to Gujarat. What will happen to you?"

Conclusions

Business growth and humanism can go together. The Tata way has been to go beyond making profits, to ultimately improve the quality of life within the community, by alleviating poverty and suffering and making a difference. The group has evolved a collective commitment to maintain stronger connections between their values and first-in-class business practice – not by putting either one ahead of the other, but by finding mutually beneficial bridges between them.

Value theories investigate the positive and negative connotations applied by people to things and concepts, the reasons they use in making their evaluations, and the scope of applications of legitimate evaluations across the social world. Most companies can claim to have "values." The challenge, however, is to ensure that these values are understood by the employees and that they are part of everyday behavior and work culture. Responsible leadership means integrating ethical considerations into company decision-making, and managing on the basis of personal integrity and widely held organizational values. As initially stated, successfully combining the dual challenges of "doing good" and "doing well" over a span of 140 years is what makes the Tata group a true business leader.

Michael Porter, while working on *The Competitive Advantage of Nations*, realized that "viewing economic and social issues as separate agendas was not only wrong but counterproductive. A successful economy depends on people who feel safe at work, who are healthy, and who have a sense that if they work hard, they will have the opportunity to do better."[18]

"If people are going to claim a value and not actually track it, they have no right to make that claim. An investor needs more than a picture of a smiling face from a program for inner city youth; you need to be able to track how your intervention is going to keep a kid from moving into the juvenile justice system."[19] This is what the Tata group upholds. The basic purpose is to effect a transformation.

The Tata case shows that a firm combining humanism with business growth will be sustainable in the long run. The group has been able to achieve business growth without compromising stakeholder interests, yet has remained unshaken from its focus on the community. It has demonstrated that focus on humanism ultimately builds brand reputation, which promotes investors' confidence, employees' loyalty, customers' trust, and the community's goodwill.

The Tata group started as a family business and has emerged as a conglomerate of 98 firms by virtue of ethical and professional management. The people at the helm have shown that, first, leaders have to lead by example, and, second, they have to create the environment for development of future leaders. For sustainable growth, the values of the corporate have to be identified, institutionalized, and carried forward by future leaders. The overriding concern for people, be it employees or the community as a whole, and adherence to humanistic principles facilitate inclusive engagement and sustained growth.

Lessons learned

Sustainable growth of business is possible, keeping in view the interests of its stakeholders.

The Tata way has been to go beyond making profits, to ultimately improve the quality of life within the community. The group has evolved a collective commitment to maintain stronger connections between their values and first-in-class business practice – not by putting either one ahead of the other, but by finding mutually beneficial bridges between them.

Focus on humanism builds brand reputation, which promotes investors' confidence, employees' loyalty, customers' trust, and the community's goodwill. The Tata group has always focused on alleviating poverty and suffering of the community as a whole and engaging in a variety of programs. A firm combining humanism with business growth is sustainable in the long run, and this has been proved by the Tata group over a span of 140 years.

A company can survive for over 100 years when it innovates, focuses on quality, is adaptive to the environment, and enjoys customers' trust. The critical success factors for sustained growth are: i) principles of humanism; ii) responsible leadership; iii) professionalism; iv) institutionalization of corporate values; v) integrating ethical considerations into a company's decision-making; and vi) concern for all the stakeholders.

Note on humanism

Humanism should develop an attitude of compassion to those in a state of suffering from whatever cause that leads to the suffering, and seek to engage in action that alleviates this suffering. The only relevant spheres of action for humans are humanity in a collective sense, individual human beings, and the physical environment (nature) in which they operate.[20]

Notes

1. The terms "nationalism" and "patriotism" were perceived differently before Indian independence, and an individual's contribution to community development and the welfare of people in general (irrespective of caste/cultural/gender diversity) without any expectation was perceived as humanistic work.
2. www.nation.lk
3. Lee, 2008.
4. Lala, 1993.
5. Branzei and Nadkarni, 2008.
6. O'Hara, 1992
7. http://www.tatatiscon.co.in/csr.php [accessed October 11, 2010].
8. 1 lakh = 100,000.

9. http://blogs.ibibo.com/prabu/JRD-TATA-A-life-Extraordinery
10. Branzei and Nadkarni, 2008.
11. Elankumaran et al., 2005.
12. www.tata.com
13. www.tata.com
14. Branzei and Nadkarni, 2008.
15. *The Independent*, 2007.
16. *Economic Times*, January 11, 2008.
17. *Autocar Professional*, January 15, 2006.
18. http://www.news.harvard.edu/gazette/2000/12.07/01-michaelporter.html
19. Emerson, 2003.
20. http://www.uq.net.au/slsoc/manussa/coreprin.htm

Bibliography

Branzei, O. and Nadkarni, A. G. (2008). The Tata way: Evolving and executing sustainable business strategies. *Ivey Business Journal*, March–April.

Elankumaran, S., Seal, Rekha and Hashmi, Anwar (2005). Transcending transformation: Enlightening endeavours at Tata steel. *Journal of Business Ethics*, Vol. 59, 109–119.

Emerson, J. (2003). http://www.gsb.stanford.edu/news/bmag/sbsm0305/ideas_emerson_social_innovation.shtml [accessed February 24, 2009].

Gunasekara, V. A. The core principles of secular humanism. *Manussa Tracts on Humanism No. 1.* http://www.vgweb.org/manussa/humdocs.htm [accessed June 30, 2008].

http://www.domain-b.com/companies/companies_t/tata_group/20040728_leader.html [accessed August 15, 2008].

http://www.nation.lk/2007/03/11/busi8.htm [accessed August 15, 2008].

http://www.news.harvard.edu/gazette/2000/12.07/01-michaelporter.html [accessed February 24, 2009].

Jain, V., Malik, S. and Cruickshank, J. (2006). The emerging threat of Asia's corporate tigers. *Strategy & Leadership*, Vol. 34 (4), 19–24.

Joseph, G. (2008). A rationale for stakeholder-based management in developing nations. *Journal of Accounting & Organizational Change*, Vol. 4 (2), 136–161.

Lala, R. M. (1993). *Beyond the Last Blue Mountain.* New Delhi: Penguin Books.

Lee, J. (2008). History of metallurgy and mining in India. http://www.zum.de/whkmla/sp/0910/florida/florida1.html [accessed February 24, 2009].

The Independent (February 1, 2007). From Parsee priests to profits: Say hello to Tata. http://www.independent.co.uk/news/world/asia/from-parsee-priests-to-profits-say-hello-to-tata-434575.h [accessed February 23, 2009].

18

TerraCycle – A Business Founded for Societal Benefit Generation

Heiko Spitzeck

Introduction

Have you ever wondered how to turn manure into money? A small company in the US has found a way of doing just that. TerraCycle uses worm castings – the technical term for worm poop (feces) – to produce organic plant food. This is not only good business, but also good for the environment, as it reduces the amount of waste going to landfill and sustainably uses resources that our planet provides.

History

The business idea was conceived by two Princeton University graduates inspired by a box of worms. When Tom Szaky and Jon Beyer discovered that worm castings could be used as plant fertilizer, the students became aware that this could be the way to realize their dream of setting up a company that "could be financially successful while being ecologically and socially responsible."[1]

However, it was not easy to find the right input mixture to nurture the worms. An initial trial with the waste of Princeton's Dining Services turned out to be unsuitable. Nevertheless, they stuck with the idea, discovering the right mixture half a year later. This mixture is now used by worm farmers across the US to produce worm castings. The castings are bought from independent worm farmers around the country and then brewed in big tanks at TerraCycle's Trenton, New Jersey, facility. TerraCycle concentrates on the liquefying process, as liquid fertilizers have higher margins than non-liquid forms and are more easily used by the public.

The company's initial product lines were plant fertilizers and potting mixes. Thereafter it expanded its portfolio beyond products made from castings to repellents, composters, window and kitchen cleaners, fire logs and bags. Wherever possible, TerraCycle recycles materials in the production process. The strategy turned out to be successful and sales have grown from $70,000 in 2004 to $4 million in 2007 and $7.5 million in 2008, while the estimates for 2009 are $15 million.[2]

TerraCycle not only takes worm castings and makes organic plant food, but also uses recycled soda bottles and other recycled containers to package its products. Although the company purchases most of its recycled packaging from professional suppliers, it also reimburses charities and schoolchildren for sending in their recyclables. The so-called "Bottle Brigade" encouraged people to recycle their waste and send it to the company. In return, TerraCycle donated 5 cents per bottle to a charity of the supplier's choice.

The case for humanistic management

The first reason for TerraCycle to qualify as an example of humanistic management lies in its business model. The company uses organic waste to feed the worms and uses recycled plastic bottles to provide packaging. Other recyclables, such as plastic shopping bags and juice pouches (plastic bags), are used to produce tote bags, pencil cases, and even shower curtains. The business model aims to reduce the amount of waste going to landfill.

The second reason lies in the company management's resistance to a mainstream business model. The litmus test for humanistic management is whether they have the right priorities.[3] TerraCycle has demonstrated that its environmental and social agenda is not a nice side effect or marketing campaign, but is built into the company's purpose. In 2003, the founders participated in the Carrot Capital business plan contest, a competition run by a New York venture capital company aimed at finding the best and brightest collegiate and graduate students in businesses. To their own surprise, TerraCycle won the contest and was offered $1 million in seed capital to finance the expansion of the business. However, Tom Szaky and Jon Beyer decided to turn down the offer, as Carrot Capital wanted to take the company towards a mainstream business model and away from the students' environmental agenda (e.g., by using chemical fertilizers instead of natural ones, like worm poop). They walked away from that prize and secured over $1 million in financing from angel investors. A first breakthrough came in May 2004 when Home Depot began selling TerraCycle products online. Today, the company supplies Whole

Foods, Wal-Mart, Home Depot, Target and other major retailers in the US and Canada.

The third reason for TerraCycle to qualify as an example of humanistic management is that it aggressively applies its motto, "better, greener, cheaper," to its diversification strategy. Following this paradigm, TerraCycle signed a contract in July 2008 with Kraft, an international food company, to sew, fuse, or weave its juice pouches and cookie wrappers into products such as shower curtains, umbrellas, pencil cases, totes, lunchboxes, and backpacks – a process known as "upcycling."[4] The term "upcycling" was coined by William McDonough and Michael Braungart, authors of Cradle to Cradle: Remaking the Way We Make Things. Upcycling is a process in which waste materials are used to provide new products. It is generally a reinvestment in the environment. Similarly, TerraCycle uses old wine barrels from the Kendall-Jackson winery to produce rain barrels and composters.[5]

While all three reasons clearly relate to environmental issues, and TerraCycle is obviously an example of eco-capitalism, there is a strong link to humanistic management. Green businesses are necessary to maintain or enhance the health of our planet, on which all human life depends. If companies apply humanistic values like fairness and due care regarding sourcing and marketing, but use natural resources unsustainably, our common future is in peril. If green companies deal unfairly with employees and do not care about their value creation for other stakeholders, they might sustain the basis of their existence, but would diminish the quality of life. Humanistic management combines both – maintaining the basis that enables life as well as fostering the quality of life.

From the above, we argue that TerraCycle is a convincing business model, which maintains the natural environment necessary for human life. TerraCycle would not be considered a humanistic business if it did not have considerable social strengths as well.

First, TerraCycle encourages local, small-scale businesses, as the company shares its value chain with independent worm farmers. Worm farms are easy to set up, but have to be managed well in terms of organic waste fed to the worms, maintaining the right temperature and the worm population.

Second, to source bottles and containers, TerraCycle encourages citizens to collect and send in their packaging for reuse. Via diverse brigades,[6] (for example, the bottle brigade, energy bar wrapper brigade, yogurt cup or cork brigade), citizens and community groups are encouraged to collect their recyclables and either bring them to a collection point or send them in. In the case of juice pouches, collectors earn 2 cents per item to donate to a charity of their choice. This fosters a culture change and raises awareness about the waste issue in general, while supporting worthwhile causes like environmental and educational concerns.

Third, the company relies on various student interns for its production process and management. During its first 3 years of operation, Tom Szaky bought a house close to the head office where interns would also live in a community – receiving room and board – while working for the company. Academics would call this approach "experiential learning"[7] or "action learning,"[8] as students enter into a learning-by-doing relationship. The following student quote is a typical summary of their experience:[9]

> My internship with TerraCycle completely changed my career goals. I had no business experience prior to working with TerraCycle and, frankly, little interest in business. To me, business was synonymous with people wearing suits and sitting in stuffy offices. TerraCycle's unique business plan and entrepreneurial environment proved to me how wrong I was. Perhaps the best part of my experience with TerraCycle was the freedom to take ownership of ideas and projects. Throughout my internship I helped launch a new product, make TerraCycle's first international sale, develop a new marketing campaign, and hire, train, and manage a team of interns at my university. Steve Kurz – Cornell University

Fourth, TerraCycle's "Annual Worm Poop Factory Graffiti Jam" features live painting done by over 50 graffiti artists from as far as Washington DC, Texas, Virginia, and upstate New York. TerraCycle opens its doors to the public and invites children from community summer programs, local musicians, and local food vendors to enjoy an event that both beautifies the neighborhood and raises community spirit. The purpose of the Jam is to offer urban artists a constructive outlet to express themselves, while showcasing a more positive side to urban art.[10] Some of the products offered by TerraCycle, like the Urban Art plant pots made of recycled e-waste such as computer or fax machine cases, spray-painted in unique designs, are also designed by local artists.

While TerraCycle appears to be a clear case of eco-entrepreneurship, the company simultaneously takes good care of its social impact. In sum, it is an example of what humanistic management can look like in practice – inspiring managers and entrepreneurs to follow the company's good example.

The business case for humanistic management

"What's interesting about garbage is it's a commodity that people are willing to pay to get rid of, and that paradigm is what really drove TerraCycle to where it is today," says CEO Tom Szaky in an interview.[11] While other companies pay for their input factors, TerraCycle gets paid for them. The company generates income from sales as it does from waste management for its suppliers – a double leverage for profitability. In its eco-capitalist position paper, TerraCycle calls this "The Power of Negative Raw Material Cost."[12]

On the more qualitative side, TerraCycle has received extensive public recognition for its business. CBS Evening News commented on the unusual business idea: The "story is a *reminder about following your dreams. The pot of gold may require dealing with a ton of crap.*"[13] Other reports about the company appeared in The New York Times, The Wall Street Journal, The San Francisco Chronicle, Toronto Star, The Globe, and The Mail. Red Herring Magazine named TerraCycle one of the 100 most innovative companies in 2004. TerraCycle won the New Jersey 2006 Business of the Year Award as well as the Home Depot Environmental Stewardship Award in 2005. Extensive media coverage, as well as the winning of the environmental awards, helped shape the company's public image as one of the greenest start-ups in the US. Since TerraCycle's business model addresses the concerns of people around the world, the company attracts free media attention. This public recognition makes the company especially appealing to partners such as Wal-Mart or Kraft Foods, as it helps them "green" their own profile legitimately.

The broader context

Through its business model, TerraCycle demonstrates the benefits of a positive business-in-society relationship.[14] This relationship can be either antagonistic or mutually beneficial.[15] Humanistic management supports the foundation of a mutually beneficial relationship.[16]

In an antagonistic relationship, businesses take advantage of regulatory gaps and pursue a purely economic agenda. This leads to a pattern of crises, as businesses overstretch themselves to reach their economic targets at certain time intervals. They then act against the values or concerns of other societal actors such as governments or civil society organizations. Governments, for example, normally follow a regulatory approach to resolve a crisis caused by corporate actors. Some of the most prominent examples are:

Table 18.1   The crisis ... and the consequences

The crisis		...and the consequences	
1929	Stock Index Crash in New York due to massive speculative trade. The "Stock Exchange" institution lost public trust.	1933–1934	Securities and Exchange Act The SEC is established as a regulatory body governing the stock exchange.
1970	Penn Central, the biggest rail company in the US, collapses due to mismanagement and board failure.	1977	Stock Exchange Commission and NYSE Rules Listed companies have to institutionalize an audit committee composed of external directors only.
1975–1984	62 percent of the Fortune 500 companies involved in one or more corruption scandals.	1991	Federal Sentencing Guidelines If established, an internal code of ethics in combination with internal control systems can reduce the costs of litigation.
2001	Enron scandal	2002	Sarbanes–Oxley Act Extensive regulation to assure compliance and good governance within corporations.
2008	Global financial crisis triggered by US subprime mortgages' default.	2008	Banks such as Fortis, Glitnir, Bradford & Bingley and the Royal Bank of Scotland are partly nationalized.

Similarly, other civil society organizations could also become critical about business behaviour, and non-governmental organizations could start campaigning,[17] or consumers could start boycotting actions.[18] In essence, the business in question loses its customers' trust[19] and faces great difficulties in overcoming the antagonistic relationship. Examples of such cases are Shell and the Brent Spar affair[20] or Nike and child labor.[21]

In a mutually beneficial relationship, businesses take co-responsibility for societal challenges. A precondition for this is to know what the current challenges are and to address them with an entrepreneurial spirit.[22] As the TerraCycle example demonstrates, there are profitable ways of doing so. A look at the challenges TerraCycle's business model tries to address helps one understand the value that the company generates for society.

Our global society faces increasing challenges regarding the resources used for the production of goods and services. Different global institutions have pointed out that the current use of resources is not sustainable in the long term. The World Wildlife Fund's (WWF) Living Planet Report shows that current production and consumption patterns equal an ecological footprint of 1.3 planets.[23] In other words, humanity is not living from the returns of natural capital (which would be sustainable), but from the capital base itself. Figure 18.1 illustrates that even a scenario of "moderate business as usual" is expected to push resource consumption to the level of 2.5 planets by 2050.[24]

The resource equivalent of the current lifestyle in developed regions like Europe or the US requires resources of between three and six planets. This is why several international initiatives such as the UN Global Compact have incorporated environmental sustainability as one of their core objectives.[25]

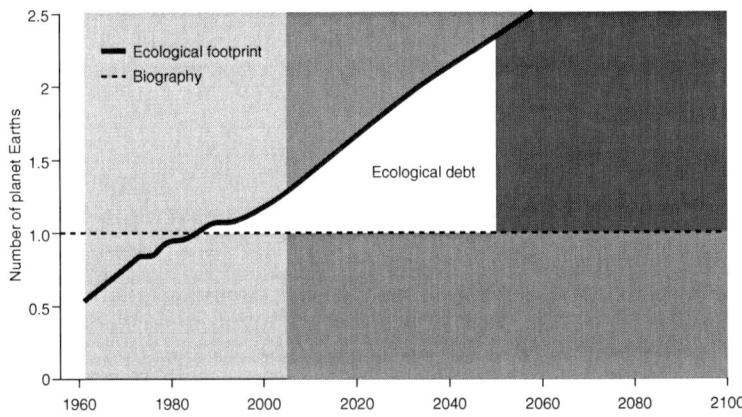

Figure 18.1   Business-as-usual scenario (1961–2100)

Resources are used to produce goods and services, which, after use, end up in landfills around the globe.[26] The UK, for example, produces more than 434 million tons (478 million short tons in the US) of waste every year. This rate of rubbish generation would fill the Albert Hall in London in less than 2 hours. On average, each person in the UK throws away seven times their body weight (about 500 kg) in rubbish every year. To deal with this issue, the UK government has issued a landfill directive encouraging waste avoidance and recycling. Landfill tax is regarded as a key mechanism in enabling the UK to meet the demanding targets set by the landfill directive to reduce the amount of biodegradable municipal landfill waste.[27] As of April 1, 2008 the standard rate of landfill tax is £32 per ton, up from £24 previously. The UK Government's 2007 budget announced annual increases in the standard rate of landfill tax of £8 per ton from September 2008 until at least November 2010, by which time it will have reached £48 per ton.

A more efficient use of resources could help to reduce resource consumption as well as reducing waste going to landfill. International as well as national government agencies call for businesses' greater awareness of the challenges of resource use and waste generation. Companies that are purely driven by economics may perceive this as the public sector taking a high moral tone and implementing unwanted regulation; consequently management could limit its response to minimal compliance. This compliance and risk management perspective, however, ignores the synergies between environmental consciousness and sound business. This is where humanistic business models like that of TerraCycle can create win–win solutions, as they address societal challenges in a profitable way. This is the desired business model for the twenty-first century, in short: business that is good for humanity.

Conclusion

TerraCycle could be considered the most aggressive business model for recycling and using waste as an input factor. The company is even using the model to diversify into different product groups. On the business side, this generates income from suppliers, as TerraCycle basically acts as their waste collector and upcycler. It generates income from the sale of environmentally friendly products and generates a green media profile at no cost. On the societal side, TerraCycle's business model addresses resource consumption and waste generation challenges in a socially responsible and entrepreneurial way. The win–win logic is obvious: the more successful the company, the better for people and the planet.[28]

Other companies could learn from TerraCycle to take a closer look at their waste management and to check whether some of their waste could be used as an input factor either in their own production process or in other companies' manufacturing. Likewise, some of the waste generated by other companies might be used as an input factor; for example, substituting some of the packaging currently used by recycled containers.

Additionally, looking at waste could open new business activities, such as producing bags from recycled plastic. Some companies, such as the retailer Marks & Spencer in the UK, use their natural waste for the production of biogas. Others, such as the flooring company Interface, have developed a closed-loop system in which worn-out products are reassembled and reused.

Since the price of landfill waste is on the rise, the business case for more environmentally friendly behavior might be created sooner than expected. Companies with a humanistic mindset are definitely quicker to see and enter into these markets than companies with a reactive attitude.

Notes

1. Quote taken from http://www.terracycle.net/story.htm [accessed October 15, 2008].
2. LoGiudice, Vincenzo (2008). TerraCycle and Kraft looking to revolutionize industry. *New Jersey Business*, 54 (10), 48.
3. Spitzeck et al., 2009.
4. Bounds, Gwendolyn (2008). On other fronts: TerraCycle breathes new life into old wrappers. *The Wall Street Journal*, July 2, 36.
5. DeBare, Ilana (2008). Kendall-Jackson barrels get new, greener identity. *The San Francisco Chronicle*, May 27, D1.
6. http://www.terracycle.net/brigades/ [accessed December 10, 2008].
7. Kolb, 1984.
8. Revans, 1980.
9. Taken from http://www.terracycle.net/careers/intern_testimonials.htm [accessed January 9, 2009].
10. This paragraph has been taken from http://www.terracycle.net/graffiti.htm [accessed January 15, 2009].
11. Interview with CEO Tom Szaky in LoGiudice, Vincenzo (2008). TerraCycle and Kraft looking to revolutionize industry. *New Jersey Business*, 54 (10), 48.
12. http://www.terracycle.net/revolution_4.htm [accessed January 15, 2009].

13. Holguin, Jaime (2004). Turning "Poop" into Gold. CBS Evening News, December 15, 2004. Available at: http://www.cbsnews.com/stories/2004/12/15/eveningnews/main661329.shtml [accessed March 1, 2009].
14. Epstein, 2000; Jones, 1983.
15. Beloe et al., 2004, p. 7.
16. Ulrich, 2009.
17. Livesey, 2002; Sethi, 1994.
18. Hertz, 2001.
19. Pirson and Malhotra, 2008.
20. Livesey, 2001.
21. Zadek, 2004.
22. Grayson et al., 2008.
23. WWF, 2008.
24. WWF, 2008, p. 22.
25. Beloe et al., 2004.
26. Annie Leonard's "Story of Stuff" provides a good and simple illustration of the value chain from resource extraction to waste. See www.storyofstuff.com [accessed October 10, 2008].
27. See www.defra.gov.uk/environment/waste/topics/landfill-dir/pdf/landfilldir.pdf [accessed October 25, 2008].
28. As with all companies, one could object to some issues, for example, that TerraCycle uses factories in the Maquiladora belt in Mexico for some production processes, thus increasing its carbon footprint through transportation and using cheap labor with all the implications this holds.

Bibliography

Axelrod, R. (1984). *The Evolution of Cooperation*. New York: Basic Books.

Beloe, S., Elkington, J., Kavita, P.-M., Thorpe, J., Zollinger, P. and Kell, G. (2004). *Gearing Up – From Corporate Responsibility to Good Governance and Scalable Solutions*. London: SustainAbility.

Elkington, J. (1994). Towards the sustainable corporation: Win-win-win business strategies for sustainable development. *California Management Review*, Vol. 36 (2), 90–100.

Epstein, E. M. (2000). The continuing quest for accountable, ethical, and humane corporate capitalism: An enduring challenge for social issues in management in the new millenium. *Business Ethics Quarterly*, Vol. 10 (1), 145–157.

Grayson, D., Lemon, M., Slaughter, S., Rodriguez, M. A., Jin, Z. and Tay, S. (2008). *A New Mindset for Corporate Sustainability*. Cranfield: Doughty Centre for Corporate Responsibility.

Hertz, N. (2001). Better to shop than to vote? *Business Ethics: A European Review*, Vol. 10 (3), 190–193.

Jones, T. M. (1983). An integrating framework for research in business and society: A step towards the elusive paradigm?' *Academy of Management Review*, Vol. 8 (4), 559–564.

Kolb, D. A. (1984). *Experiental Learning: Experience as The Source of Learning and Development*. Englewood Cliffs: Prentice Hall.

Livesey, S. M. (2001). Eco-identity as discursive struggle: Royal Dutch/Shell, Brent Spar, and Nigeria. *The Journal of Business Communication,* Vol. 38 (1), 58–91.

Livesey, S. M. (2002). Global warming wars: Rhetorical and discourse analytic approaches to ExxonMobil's corporate public discourse. *The Journal of Business Communication,* Vol. 39 (1), 117–148.

Pirson, M. and Malhotra, D. (2008). Unconventional insights for managing stakeholder trust. *MIT Sloan Management Review,* Vol. 49 (4), 43–50.

Revans, R. (1980). *Action Learning: New Techniques for Management.* London: Blond & Briggs.

Sethi, P. S. (1994). *Multinational Corporations and the Impact of Public Advocacy on Corporate Strategy.* Boston, MA: Kluwer Academic.

Spitzeck, H., Pirson, M., Amann, W., Khan, S. and von Kimakowitz, E. (2009). *Humanism in Business.* Cambridge: Cambridge University Press.

Ulrich, P. (2009). Towards a civilized market economy: Economic citizenship rights and responsibilities in service of a humane society, pp. 143–155, in Spitzeck, H., Pirson, M., Amann, W., Khan, S. and von Kimakowitz, E. (eds) *Humanism in Business.* Cambridge: Cambridge University Press.

WWF (2008). *Living Planet Report 2008.* Gland.

Zadek, S. (2004). The path to corporate responsibility. *Harvard Business Review,* Vol. 82 (12), 125–132.

19
Wainwright Bank and Trust Case Study – Humanistic Management in Practice

Christine Arena

Introduction

It's Election Day, 2008. America's stock index scores its worst perfor-mance in 21 years, with the Dow plummeting 2,400 points over a period of 1 month. A credit crisis that started by squeezing financial institutions such as Lehman Brothers, Merrill Lynch, Citibank, and Bank of America spills into the mainstream, hampering banks' ability to lend and consumers' ability to borrow. Meanwhile, a ripple effect spreads to the rest of the world economy, causing similar turmoil on stock markets from London to Hong Kong. Collective fears center on a looming global recession. With so much at stake, many corporate chiefs are understandably on edge today. And yet Robert Glassman, Founder and Co-chairman of the publicly traded Wainwright Bank & Trust Company, isn't fazed. And neither is his board. That's because, unlike other banks requiring massive federal bailouts in order to offset mistakes of the past, Wainwright's strong financials and unique man-agement philosophy enable it to play up its strengths and better plan its future.

With over $1 billion in assets, 40,000 accounts, and over half a mil-lion transactions per month, Wainwright is far from being the largest bank in the country. But its recent performance serves as an impressive contrast to a volatile industry plagued by a collapsed subprime market and diminished consumer confidence. According to Wainwright's third quarter 2008 results, average assets increased by $87 million, or roughly 10 percent from the year before. Its average outstanding loan balances grew by about 15 percent, while residential real estate loans spiked an impressive 31 percent. The Bank also saw nice growth in its commercial real estate and commercial loans. "All this turmoil in the financial markets has continued to create opportunities for us to capture additional market share, especially in our residential real estate products," Glassman explains. "We are pleased that there continues to be a market for our products and approach."

The "approach" of which Glassman speaks is key. In fact, Wainwright sells the very same products that you can find at any bank – checking accounts, savings accounts, loans, and so on. That's not what drives the company's performance. It's *how* the company sells its products, how it conducts business overall, that sets it apart from its peers. For over two decades Wainwright Bank has been a step ahead of its industry with a socially progressive agenda and humanistic approach to management, both of which represent an ever important second bottom line to the company. "One platform sustains the other," Glassman explains. "Our business success is fueled by the difference we make in our community."

Wainwright's business approach is as atypical as its end results. To date the Bank has issued over $700 million in loans to community development projects like affordable housing and HIV/AIDS services, and also has experienced virtually no defaults on those loans. Wainwright also has the highest level of customer loyalty and the lowest rate of employee turnover in its industry. Overall, the Bank doesn't look or behave as its Wall Street competitors do. Wainwright establishes a sense of openness and decency in all of its dealings, and its stakeholders and shareholders evidently love that.

Business as unusual

To fully appreciate the extent to which Wainwright's humanistic management philosophy protects shareholder interests and sets the Bank apart from its peers, you have to first consider the current state of the market. In October, 2008 former Federal Reserve Chairman Alan Greenspan characterized the banking industry's troubles by saying: "We are in the midst of a once-in-a century credit tsunami." He acknowledged he was "shocked" when the system "broke down," but also predicted that the nation would emerge from the current credit crisis with a "far sounder financial system."[1]

Those comments irked House Representatives, including committee chairman Representative Henry Waxman, a Democrat from California, who chastised Greenspan, along with SEC chairman Christopher

Cox and former Treasury Secretary John Snow, for a lack of oversight. Waxman blamed the three for failing to prevent the credit crisis and for refusing to take responsibility for it. "The list of regulatory mistakes and misjudgments is long and the cost to taxpayers and the economy is staggering," he said. Greenspan responded by conceding that he "made a mistake" in presuming that banks themselves were more capable than regulators of protecting their finances. But he also reiterated his support for the $700 billion Wall Street bailout approved by Congress, which allows the US government to buy back bad mortgage investments from troubled lenders.[2] Theoretically the bailout is intended to thaw the credit freeze by freeing up capital, thereby allowing banks to offer new loans. But has it? And also, did it adequately address the underlying systemic issues that caused things to go awry in the first place? Wainwright's Glassman isn't so sure.

"The current meltdown is based on the extension of credit, but credit in itself isn't the problem," he explains. "The problem is how credit was passed from one party to the next with no ethical oversight under the veil of normal business activity." Glassman uses the subprime debacle as an example: "Each player along the way – from the originator, to the mortgage broker, who sold the mortgage to an investment bank, who then created a pool of mortgages for sale to investors, and ultimately the rating agencies who were supposed to protect the investors – had no continuing stake in the transaction and certainly no concern for the well being of the underlying homeowner."

By contrast, Wainwright keeps a vested interest in all of its transactions. It has historically declined to repackage and resell its loans to third parties, and also provides customers with useful tools for building enduring financial success, thereby increasing customers' ability to repay the Bank. For instance, in 2001 Wainwright launched an online service for nonprofit clients called CommunityRoom.net, which, among other things, offers free hosted web pages and the ability to accept online donations. According to Glassman, over 200 of the Bank's 500 nonprofit clients have joined CommunityRoom.net and donations generated through this channel totaled $1.1 million in 2007.

Wainwright prides itself on a string of similar products designed to promote financial stability among Bank clients and also serve worthy causes. Wainwright's Green Loan, launched in 1999, provides homeowners with a discounted home equity loan rate for energy-efficient home improvements. Its Equal Exchange CD provides a competitive interest rate while allowing deposits to act as collateral for lines of credit issued to Equal Exchange, a Fair Trade coffee merchant providing third world farmers with a livable income. Overall, community development lending is a significant part of Wainwright's business strategy.

Currently over 50 percent of Wainwright's commercial loan portfolio is committed to financing projects such as homeless shelters, food banks, affordable and special needs housing, HIV/AIDS services, immigrant services, inner-city schools, community health centers, and breast cancer research, among others. "The majority of our customers are aware their deposits help fund these loans," says Glassman. "We attract new customers because they want their money to support local community development, and once with us, become fiercely loyal."

Customer loyalty is a great asset to any bank, especially in a largely undifferentiated industry with fungible products and services. In this respect, Wainwright does stand out. But what's perhaps even more noteworthy is the rate of repayment the Bank manages to achieve. Over the past 20 years Wainwright has invested $700 million in community development loans, and not one has ever failed. "Not a single client has entered into default," says Glassman. That's not only atypical; it is radically unsettling to the banking world's prevailing mindset.

"The general assumption among most bankers is that community development loans are unprofitable, risky, and just another form of charity," says Glassman. "But nothing could be further from the truth. Our community development loans are not discounted and are market priced like any other commercial loan." Indeed, it's not the product itself that makes the difference. It's *how* the product is structured and serviced. Rather than catering to pre-prescribed bank terms, Wainwright's loans are designed to meet the needs of individual borrowers. The Bank has found that allowing flexibility dramatically increases the probability that loans will be paid back. That's a key reason why Wainwright remains solvent and continues to grow.

At a time when many mortgage brokers have gone bust and most of the larger commercial banks have decreased or altogether halted lending activities due to problems with capital levels or deterioration in the quality of their loan portfolios, Wainwright remains well capitalized. It is still actively lending to small businesses and homebuyers. In fact, according to *American Banker*, one of the industry's most widely read daily news publications, Wainwright's home mortgage portfolio business experienced growth of 31.8 percent in 2007, making it one of the fastest growing community banks in the nation. "Wainwright Bank is a powerful example of a bank that does well by doing good," said David Longobardi, editor in chief of *American Banker*. "It epitomizes how a banking company can operate in support of a set of social or political principles, while also remaining profitable."[3]

As of January 2008 Wainwright's financials remain strong. The Bank ended the fourth quarter with a 5 percent increase in net income, from $1.17 million in 2007 to $1.23 million in 2008. For the year, the Bank's assets surged 15 percent to $1.06 billion, while deposits increased 16 percent to $717 million in 2008. Furthermore, Wainwright's net interest yield rose to 3.20 percent in the fourth quarter, compared with 2.97 percent for the same 3-month period in 2007. While Wainwright's solvency and growth earn it praise in local financial journals, wider communities also see the value of its double bottom line. Sustainablebusiness. com considers Wainwright to be one of the world's top 20 sustainable stocks. The Social Investment Forum sees it as one of America's top ten "green" banking firms. And, among its community, Wainwright is portrayed as "a bank that gives people strength," "a bank that keeps its promises," and "totally fearless when it comes to (its) beliefs."[4]

People clearly love what Wainwright does differently, though the Bank does not pursue every market segment equally. Glassman and his colleagues realize that it does not matter whether all the public loves the company. What matters is that the *right* people love the company. Wainwright knows that it will never please everyone, so it does not attempt to waste its energy with fruitless efforts, for instance shamelessly pandering itself as everybody's "favorite bank" or as the industry's "best citizen." To succeed in humanistic management is to remain wholly authentic and unpretentious, while also putting people's needs ahead of industry norms.

Putting people first

Robert Glassman thinks more executives should forget about fluffy concepts like "good values" or "doing the right thing." Instead, they should just listen more and respond better. That means closely examining what stakeholders' deepest needs are, and what issues are most worth fighting for. It also means taking opportune and substantive positions and backing the positions up in ways that are totally genuine, tangible, and financially productive. Wainwright does this really well.

The Bank takes a stand: "One of the most unique aspects of our business, especially considering we're a publicly traded company, is our advocacy of social justice issues on behalf of our clients and employees," says Glassman. "Because of the progressive causes we champion and support in various ways, and the recognition we receive for that, we've created a certain amount of what we call 'cultural capital'. And as controversial as some may be perceived, we're not afraid to stand up for these issues even if we stand alone."

Wainwright has stood alone on multiple fronts, as the Civil Rights movement of the 1960s has been a major influence in the creation of the Bank's progressive social agenda. In 1996 Wainwright was the only publicly traded company in the United States to testify before Congress in support of the Employment Non-Discrimination Act, which would have outlawed discrimination against gays in the workplace. More recently the Bank stood in opposition to an anti-gay constitutional marriage amendment in Massachusetts, and has also been a signatory to social justice initiatives, including the endorsement of a living wage in Massachusetts.

Some wonder why a Bank would take such risky positions. Glassman explains: "Over the years we have seen the same voices of intolerance arrayed against the civil rights movement, the women's movement, gay rights and the civil liberties of people with AIDS. For us, the rights of these groups are all connected threads that weave the fabric of a just society."

Along these lines Wainwright translates the concept of humanistic management to a model of social inclusion that penetrates all levels of the organization. "Employees, customers and communities have an equal place at the table alongside our stockholders," explains Glassman. "We believe each of these constituencies is best served when all are served." As such, Wainwright has consciously created a corporate culture that stresses individuality and promotes equality. "We have set up an atmosphere where our people don't have to conform to some corporate notion of what a bank should be," says Glassman. "They can be comfortable with who they are and feel free to express themselves."

At Wainwright a "free" work environment is one where all are provided with the same opportunities for professional advancement, regardless of race, color, religious creed, age, sex, marital or family status, sexual orientation, genetic information, ancestry, national origin, physical or mental handicap, membership in the United States Uniformed Services, or any other characteristic protected by law. That amounts to true diversity. According to Glassman, Wainwright's Board of Directors consists of nine outside members, two of whom are African American, two are female and one is openly lesbian. Among the Bank's 166 employees, 60 percent are women and 10 percent are openly gay, including two senior vice presidents. Minorities comprise over 30 percent of the total population of employees, while 22 languages are spoken at the Bank.

"There's also the recognition that employees have lives outside the bank," says Glassman. In addition to providing 3 weeks' paid vacation and four sick days annually to all full-time employees, regardless of their position (the industry average for a teller trainee is 1 week's vacation), Wainwright provides free life insurance, generously subsidized health and dental coverage, health club membership, and public transportation reimbursement. And, recognizing a 401(K) plan will likely be the primary source of income for an employee in retirement years, all employees are automatically enrolled in the Bank's generous retirement savings plan and must opt out if they do not wish to participate. According to Glassman, only one employee has opted out to date, as the Bank annually matches 100 percent of the first 4 percent of an employee's salary saved, and 50 percent of the remaining amount saved up to the maximum allowed by law.

With all the benefits, liberality, and inclusion, who wouldn't want to work at Wainwright? Indeed, Glassman notes that such perks help keep the talent pool flowing and costs down. "Since we're a small company with limited resources, employment candidates generally find us," he says. "While there is no formal requirement a job applicant must support the Bank's progressive social agenda to be employed, many enthusiastically do and in fact seek to work at Wainwright because of it."

There are other benefits, too. Employee turnover is a key issue in the banking industry, as it can translate to a loss of valuable customer relationships. It is thus interesting to note that the United States banking industry's average annual voluntary employee turnover rate is estimated at nearly 23 percent, while the average cost of turnover is said to be roughly 25 percent of an employee's annual salary.[5] In light of this, Wainwright has managed to keep its turnover rate significantly lower than the industry average, with a 9 percent turnover rate in 2007. According to Glassman, the Bank credits its overall commitment to social responsibility and a double bottom line. "This concept has become so embedded in the Bank's products and human resource practices that a clear and resonant brand image has emerged, one that is recognized and valued by employees and customers alike," he says. "Day to day decisions are made with the support or enhancement of the brand in mind."

Wainwright's strong brand resonates in valuable ways – from affecting human resource policies to inspiring people to willingly contribute to the Bank's success. For instance, in 2006 Wainwright's facilities department unilaterally decided to install automatic light switches and low-wattage fluorescent bulbs throughout company headquarters, and to completely switch to recycled products. Glassman notes that this was not a response to a mandate from senior management, but rather a voluntary, collaborative effort by motivated people who strongly support the bank's commitment to the environment. Another recent example is the Bank's response to an increase in customer requests suggesting the Bank offer electronic monthly statements to reduce paper and energy usage. The Bank is reportedly working on this capability and will soon be launching it.

Wainwright considers reciprocal relationships a key to success and a cause for innovation. For instance, when a customer closes a Wainwright checking account they receive a survey from the President and CEO asking why the account was closed. According to the Bank the response rate to the survey is consistently over 40 percent, with 97 percent of the responses favorable. Eighty-five percent of those who do respond indicate that they closed their account not because they are dissatisfied, but because they moved from the Boston area, while many express a wish that the Bank had a presence in their new home city.

Socially responsive companies

If Wainwright's success story proves anything, it's that the vague and lofty notion of "corporate social responsibility" is dead. The best, most successful firms do not concentrate on what it means to be perceived as socially responsible. Instead they focus on the simple notion of being *strategically responsive*. Rather than ignoring employee and customer feedback, strategically responsive companies listen and learn. As opposed to resisting or procrastinating, they rise to the occasion. Instead of struggling to comply with regulations, they use changes in the marketplace and the global climatic system, and among the needs of stakeholders, as a means of accelerating growth and performance. The world's most responsive companies do not worry as much about putting their values on paper as they do about producing actual, measurable *value* – socially, environmentally, and financially. At the end of the day, this is what matters most. This is the legacy that companies leave behind.

"Embracing a business model that considers social benefit as well as profit does not preclude the strength of either," Glassman insists. "The success of Wainwright Bank is proof of this." Indeed, looking to the future, Glassman sees a clear trend toward what he calls "conscious capitalism," as more stakeholders (including shareholders) demand that corporations view their business through a wider lens and better acknowledge and address their true impact. Ideally, says Glassman, "this [concept] will become so ubiquitous as to no longer be considered an alternative way of doing business. It will become the best way of doing business. It is plausible that companies who fail to recognize this will eventually cease to exist."

The clear business trend toward greater strategic responsiveness – whether it is labeled "social responsibility," "humanistic management," or "conscious capitalism" – will eventually affect every company, regardless of size or industry. Therefore it becomes increasingly important that current and future business leaders look to success stories of the past in order to make informed future decisions. In doing so, many will find a string of attributes that the greatest, most "humanistic" companies tend to share. These five common threads are no random coincidence. They represent a higher order – a skill set and mindset not commonly taught in business schools, and yet increasingly necessary for enduring the constantly changing economic tides:

1. *Higher Purpose: Beyond making money for shareholders, what in the world is the company here to do?* Truly humanistic companies are purpose-driven, meaning that they have identified a core reason for being that enables them to succeed. Whatever their particular purpose is, it serves stakeholder interests and also drives most everything the company does, from the products it sells to the way it treats people and the planet. For instance, as demonstrated above, Wainwright Bank has a clear higher purpose, which is to "provide equality and financial empowerment." This purpose is relevant to stakeholders in that it helps to meet unmet socio-economic needs and also keeps the company competitive. Every product, service, and policy that Wainwright institutes – from flexible personal loans to green CDs and progressive outreach efforts – is an extension of its higher purpose. Therefore, the better Wainwright fulfills its higher purpose, the more value it generates overall.

2. *Relentless Innovation: Is "good enough" ever enough?* In humanistic companies the answer is decidedly "no." That's because humanistic companies are always raising the bar and constantly looking for new, enterprising ways of fulfilling their purpose. Such companies are never content to rest on their laurels. Glassman explains: "Despite all that we do, we don't consider ourselves the perfect corporate citizen. There is still so much work to be done." Even as Wainwright succeeds by all the traditional measures, Glassman feels a little restless, as if he ought to be doing more. Therefore he and his management team are

always regrouping, rethinking and revising their strategic approach. This plays back to the old business adage that self-satisfaction and complacency invite competitive disadvantage, whereas healthy self-criticism allows continual advancement.

3. *Authenticity: How does a company foster unswerving love and devotion from its stakeholders?* Glassman insists the answer isn't expensive marketing gimmicks or even philanthropic efforts, but rather an authentic state of being: "If we can't project an internal commitment to social justice, then we're not going to be perceived as credible externally," he says. "The sense of openness and decency toward our employees generates benefits for the customer and also a sense among our wider constituency that we are the real deal. We are exactly what we appear to be." Humanistic companies like Wainwright don't have to fabricate elaborate means of conveying a certain image for themselves because that image is intrinsic. It is who they are and what they are. These companies remain true to their core, which is a key reason why the right people steadfastly support them.

4. *Intuition: How does a company best decide where to go next?* The most ingenious and humanistic firms do not follow tradition, remodel old models, mimic competitors' moves, or look to focus groups for answers or inspiration. Instead they liberally draw on a skill that is underutilized in the mainstream business world: *intuition*. The most significant business breakthroughs at Wainwright were based on a keen internal sense of what was right. As Glassman explains, he and his team "just knew." They just knew that many of the risks facing the banking industry could be easily mitigated through more transparent, responsive, and flexible products. They also knew that the goal of promoting equality and empowerment would be better served by taking an aggressive stand on controversial issues and also promoting an internal environment that rejected stringent management hierarchies and strict employee codes of conduct. On many occasions Glassman and his team have leapt into the void, proven to be unafraid of the unknown – and succeeded. When a leader's sense of intuition is strong, the possibility for what can be achieved is limitless.

5. *Collaboration:* What's at the core of the fundamental shift in business? If there is one attribute that best characterizes the humanistic leadership mindset, it's collaboration. People at truly collaborative organizations such as Wainwright are empowered and engaged. They co-labor successfully, reach agreement, resolve differences, and produce results that are the envy of the industry. Glassman and his team

use collaboration as an efficient means of engaging stakeholders and promoting innovation. As noted above, the company constantly listens and learns. It provides stakeholders with useful mechanisms for feedback and then uses the feedback to deepen relationships and beef up offerings. As Glassman proves, collaboration does not mean abdicating power, but rather sharing it. He knows that the more stakeholders are involved in ongoing decisions, the more buy-in and traction those decisions will ultimately gain.

Truly humanistic companies, or "High-Purpose Companies," thrive because without them society would be worse off. Since they are designed to help meet unmet human needs, they grow *invaluable* to people and *worthy* of success. That ultimately boils down to a new supply and demand model – one that honors a multitude of factors beyond just short-term economics. The businesses that do grow invaluable to people tend to do so because they stand for something greater than the products they sell or the money they generate for shareholders. They embody something that is meaningful, substantive and necessary, not frivolous or easily replicated. In such companies, the concept of a higher purpose is so integral to the fabric of the organization that, if you removed that thread, the company would start to unravel.[6] Indeed, the idea of "providing equality and financial empowerment" has had such an effect on Wainwright's people, products, process, and performance that without it Wainwright might be just another bank.

Theoretically, could Wainwright temporarily increase its stock price and maximize shareholder returns by cutting more corners and taking a less purposeful route? Possibly, yes! Although Wainwright has managed to strike an unprecedented balance between purpose and performance, there are certainly ways in which the company might improve margins by reducing its emphasis on "humanistic" initiatives – for instance, cutting social outreach efforts or limiting employee benefits to levels commensurate with the industry average. But again, as mentioned above, moves like these could cause a steady erosion of the company's core value proposition, which could in turn diminish the company's market share. While humanistic management isn't necessarily the most profitable short-term route, it does tend to mitigate certain risks and generate multiple long-term benefits for all stakeholders involved. Therefore this whole issue of whether or not to embrace humanistic management boils down to leadership, and tough decisions.

At a time when everyone seems to be talking "change" and economic, social and environmental issues have reached crisis proportions,

Table 19.1 Humanistic management in the banking industry

Traditional model	Wainwright model
Single bottom line	Double bottom line
Serves shareholders	Serves stakeholders
High reward model (that is private equity)	Steady reward model
Hidden risk	Transparent methods
Lack of ethical oversight	Constant ethical oversight
Exclusive client base (favoring wealthy)	Inclusive client base (favoring social groups)
Product-centric	People-centric
Procedure orientation	Relationship orientation
Preset terms	Customized terms
Hierarchical structure	Collaborative culture
Emphasis on marketing	Emphasis on authenticity
High employee turnover: 28 percent	Low employee turnover: 9 percent
High customer default rates	Zero percent customer default rate
Reeling from market crisis	Seizing market opportunities

business leaders must face difficult questions. They must decide which management style is most needed for what lies ahead: Mandela-like leadership or Attila the Hun? They must think about what they're in the game in order to achieve: a quick turnaround with maximum returns, or a balanced approach with fair returns? And they must consider the importance of legacy. After all, as renowned author Jim Collins asks readers in his bestselling book, *Built to Last*: "Why on earth would you settle for creating something mediocre that does little more than make money, when you can create something outstanding that makes a lasting contribution as well?" Humanistic management does present a challenge – hopefully one that's worth taking (Table 19.1).

Notes

1. Testimony of Alan Greenspan before the House of Representatives Committee on Oversight and Government Reform, October 23, 2008.
2. Commentary of Alan Greenspan and Henry Waxman before the House of Representatives Committee on Oversight and Government Reform, October 23, 2008.
3. Press release, "Wainwright Bank Co-Founder Named 2007 Community Banker of the Year," November 30, 2007.
4. E. Jeanne Harnois, "Bank official brings financial literacy to inner-city audience," *Boston Banner*, Thursday, June 5, 2003; Trinity Creative Communications, "A Bank that Keeps its Promise," The Angle e-Newsletter,

May 2002 issue; Shawn Macomber, "Branching Out in Green," Brookline TAB, September 22, 2005 (http://www.wainwrightbank.com/html/about/news/news/archive.html) [all accessed October 11, 2010].

5. Statistics taken from "The Cornerstone Report: Benchmarks and Best Practices for Mid-Size Banks," Scottsdale: Cornerstone Advisors, September 2007, 1–4.

6. This description of High-Purpose Companies was derived from Christine Arena (2007). *The High-Purpose Company.* New York: Collins Business, 22–24.

20

Zipcar Incorporated: Do We Really Need to Own Our Automobiles?

Janet L. Rovenpor

> You don't have to own a well to get water or a generator to get electricity. Must you own a car (or two or three) to drive? 'You can join a mobility plan, like you join a cell-phone plan. It is self-service, on-demand, pay as you go. And you get different vehicles for different needs,' says Dan Sturges.[1]
>
> Margot Roosevelt

"Wheels when you want them." That was the advertising slogan of Zipcar, an automated car-rental service, founded in 1999. The idea came up during a conversation between two mothers watching their children frolic in a playground in front of a school in Cambridge, Massachusetts. Later, discussions about business strategies continued in a local bistro.[2] German-born Antje Danielson told her friend, Robin Chase, about a company in Berlin that rented cars by the hour. Chase, with an MBA from MIT's Sloan School of Management, was excited about the opportunity to "transform urban transportation."[3] The pair proposed a company that would lease and maintain a fleet of cars, parked near mass transit stops, throughout the Boston area. A client would pay an annual membership fee, reserve a vehicle on the Internet, and rent it on an hourly basis. He or she would be able walk to a convenient location and unlock the door to the car with a digital key. As a courtesy to the next member, the client would return the car, cleaned and fueled with gasoline.

With initial seed money of USD 250,000 from Boston Community Capital, Chase and Danielson launched Zipcar's car sharing service on June 22, 2000. The next month, the company had 100 members who shared nine vehicles parked in Cambridge and other Boston neighborhoods. Funds were increased to USD 1.3 million, which enabled Zipcar to expand into Washington DC and New York City. By October 2001, Zipcar had 1,300 members who shared 60 cars. Initially, the annual membership fee was USD 75; a security deposit of USD 300 was required. Additional charges ranged from USD 4.50 to USD 8 an hour (depending on location) and 40 cents per mile. By December 2008, Zipcar had 250,000 members, 5,500 vehicles in urban areas and college campuses in 26 North American states and provinces as well as in London, England (see Table 20.1).

Zipcar's message was crafted to suggest that car sharing not only saved members time and money, but was also good for the environment. The Automobile Association of America estimated that the average cost of owning or leasing a mid-sized family car (including gas, insurance, and parking) was USD 700 a month.[4] A Zipcar member could take one round trip excursion per day for a month between Harvard Square and Boston's Logan Airport for approximately USD 340 (with time left over for grocery shopping). A member's typical monthly bill for 15 hours of driving amounted to even less, at USD 100 – USD 150 a month.[5] With such savings, car-sharers could easily afford a nice winter vacation – in Florida or Hawaii.

Table 20.1   Zipcar incorporated's growth from 2000 to 2008

	2000	2001	2002	2003	2004	2005	2006	2007	2008
No. of members	130	1,300	5,000	7,200	30,000	50,000	80,000	180,000	250,000
No. of cities served	1	3	3	4	21	28	36	40	50
No. of North American states/ provinces served	1	3	3	4	7	10	13	25	28
No. of vehicles	12	60	N.A.	240	400	900	2,500	5,000	5,500
Revenues (in millions; USD)	N.A.	N.A.	2	4	7	15	40	60	100

Notes: N.A.: Not available.

All data are approximate. They are based on company press releases and published articles. In October 2007, Zipcar merged with Flexcar.

Research indicated that each shared vehicle took between six and 23 vehicles off the roads.[6] The number of miles driven by car-share members dropped on average from 5,295 to 369 per year; between 11 percent and 26 percent of car-share members eventually sold their cars.[7] Car sharing had the potential to significantly reduce air pollution and congestion in major cities. Since fewer cars needed to be fueled by gasoline, the nation's dependency on oil could be reduced as well. White and green signs over Zipcar parking spaces read: "Improving Air Quality."

This case study traces Zipcar's transition in leadership from a founder–entrepreneur model to a professional manager model. It also examines the critical success factors – its use of viral marketing, its forging of partnerships, its merger with a competitor, and its deployment of carefully conceived operating principles – that put Zipcar on the path to profitability. Zipcar's best practices are highlighted so that entrepreneurs can gain insights into how to develop business plans that strive for both profitability and sustainability.

The origins of an idea

Antje Danielson got the idea for starting a car-sharing company in Boston in the late summer of 1999. She ran some preliminary business scenarios, discussed the idea with friends, and asked Robin Chase if she wanted to be her business partner in October or November of 1999. Chase had expressed the desire to explore new interests after having spent time at home caring for her three children. Danielson, a scientist and community leader, foresaw that she would need someone with a business degree to convince others of the merits of her proposal. Zipcar was incorporated in early January 2000, with both women becoming equal shareholders. Danielson was vice president of the company and Chase was president.[8]

When asked about her role, Danielson commented that she "did just about any job required in a start-up, from running financial calculations, to meeting with potential investors and banks, to developing the business, to hiring, and to jump-starting broken-down cars." Most notably, she oversaw the proprietary in-car and car access technology development and worked on community relations.[9] Along with Paul Covell, an MIT student, Danielson developed the hardware side of the reservation system (access system, board computer and wireless transmission). Chase, with the assistance of another employee, handled the software side of the reservation system and database.[10] Chase was charged with the additional responsibilities of financial management and investor relations.

Chase and Danielson wanted to make renting a car as easy as retrieving cash from an automated teller machine at a bank branch.[11] Technology could be deployed to simplify the onerous car rental process. To rent a car from a traditional company, such as Hertz or Avis, an individual contacted several different agencies in order to find the best rate. He or she placed a reservation over the telephone. The renter arrived at the agency's location, stood in line, signed a rental agreement and sped off. The car was returned to the same location and inspected. The renter left with a receipt. If the renter did not return the car at the designated time, substantial late fees were added to the bill.

With a car-sharing service such as Zipcar, an individual applied for a membership online or by telephone. A background check on the applicant's driving record was conducted. If approved, the applicant received a magnetic card by mail. He or she reserved a car, which was parked on a nearby street or in a parking lot, online or via the telephone. The magnetic card unlocked the car.[12] The key for the ignition was found inside the car. Zipcar paid for the gas and the automobile insurance. A gas card was tucked under the driver's front visor. It could be used at a gas station pump, like a credit card, or given to an attendant.[13] Cars were available 24 hours a day and 7 days a week.

When investors began to ask who Zipcar's chief technology officer was, Chase brought in her husband, Ray Russell. Russell, along with an IT team, tweaked the reservation method and system over several years. The advanced technology combined radio frequency identification with wireless communication networks. When a reservation was made online, a message was sent to a small computer hidden inside the car. A member swiped his or her Zipcar card, with RFID technology, in front of a reader on a reserved car's windshield. The car recognized the member and the reservation time. Data were transmitted between the vehicle and the back office reservation system so that Zipcar could remotely monitor the miles driven, determine the time the car was used and check engine functionality such as battery voltage and fuel level. The system detected when a member forgot to turn off the headlights after returning a car. An employee was sent to the location to turn the lights off. This eliminated extra costs and customer inconveniences (the next member would not encounter a car with a dead battery).[14]

Zipcar members agreed to abide by several car-sharing rules. Just like the technology, these too evolved over time. Members were not allowed to take pets for a ride or smoke in the cars. They were not supposed to return a car with less than a quarter of the tank full with gas. They were responsible for paying parking and speeding tickets on time so that the cars would not be booted. A system was developed to penalize members for violations. Fines ranged from USD 20 – USD 65 per violation. Repeat offenders risked losing their membership. According to Chase, very few members were asked to leave. She commented: "When people join, they understand the rules of the game. It's a pretty self-selecting group; they know it's a community-based program, and they feel good about sharing resources. If they do make a mistake, they make it only once."[15]

It was crucial for local organizations and government agencies to buy into the car-sharing concept. City officials in Cambridge, for example, leased three parking spaces in municipal lots to Zipcar for just USD 1 each. They promised to provide 27 more spaces over the next 3 years for the same charge. After that, Zipcar would pay the going rate of USD 180 a month per space. Sommerville offered a parking space for USD 40 a year instead of the business rate of USD 40 a month. "The T," Greater Boston's subway system, donated parking spaces at four Massachusetts Bay Transportation Authority garages for Zipcars. Legislation was considered that would require large real estate complexes and city-owned garages to set aside parking spots for short-term rentals.[16]

Chase's original business plan suggested that the company would break even when it had 70 cars averaging 6 hours of daily use. She hoped to attract city dwellers who had opted out of car ownership because insurance rates were high, traffic was heavy, and parking spaces were scarce. Early surveys indicated that 37 percent of Zipcar members earned over USD 80,000 a year, 95 percent had a college education, and 50 percent were 25–50 years of age.[17] Chase saw herself as a good example of a potential Zipcar member. She lived in Cambridge, Massachusetts and had three children. She often needed a car for several hours during the day when her husband took the family car to work. She believed that the Internet "enabled a large group of people to share a unique resource" – even a car.[18]

In January 2001, Zipcar received USD 1.3 million from BCLF Ventures, Boston Community Venture Fund, Gravistar, the Hub Angels, and other investors. Raising funds from venture capitalists to finance Zipcar's operations was not easy. Chase compared the process to "pushing an elephant through a door jamb. It's not a keyhole, so it is possible, but it takes brute force."[19] The original investor, Boston Community Capital (BCC), shared Zipcar's commitment to the environment. Its mission was to "build healthy communities where low-income people live and work."[20] It invested equity dollars into businesses that created social and financial returns. In 2001, BCC also invested in CASTion, a water purification/recovery business, and SelecTech, a plastics recycling business.

Zipcar's marketing strategies

Chase was responsible for several of Zipcar's innovative marketing ideas. Along with marketing vice president, Nancy Rosenszweig, she built a sense of community among Zipcar members. She sent personal messages to new members; used words such as "family" in company newsletters; and assigned fun names to the cars, such as Beetle Buster and Jetta Judy. The company held potluck dinners and let its members suggest names for new cars added to its fleet. If members felt they belonged to a friendly, close-knit group, like a cooperative, they would be more likely to return cars on time and to clean them. The sense of community was so strong that members who had marketing backgrounds offered their professional services in return for free hourly rentals.[21]

Zipcar vehicles, consisting of Volkswagens and Mini Coopers, projected a cool, hip image. A green colored Z appeared on the passenger's side of the car. They were small and fuel-efficient. Advertisements were placed on urban panels, bus shelters, and subway station displays.

Chase believed that Zipcar had built a "product that is addictive" and would improve the "civic infrastructure."[22] Forty-seven percent of Zipcar members reported that they had delayed or avoided purchasing a car because of the service, while 11 percent said they had sold their cars.[23]

Zipcar enters other large metropolitan areas

Zipcar soon expanded into two other major US cities. In October 2001, it started service in Washington, DC and its suburbs. Residents in Arlington, Virginia received incentives from local government officials to sign up. They were reimbursed for their membership fees. The first 25 commuters who became members also received free 1-month transit passes.

In February 2002, Zipcar placed ten compact Volkswagens for 100 members in New York City. The service was meant for city dwellers who did not own a car but who would like access to one occasionally, perhaps to get out of town on the weekends. The car-sharing concept had a compelling logic. US government surveys indicated that most cars in urban areas were driven only about an hour a day.[24] They sat idle for long periods of time, taking up space while their owners were at home or at work.[25] It was more cost-effective and convenient to rent a Zipcar for an hour.

Scott Griffith replaces Robin Chase as CEO

A change in leadership occurred at Zipcar in 2003. The Board of Directors, which consisted of four outside investors (besides Chase), replaced Chase with Scott Griffith as chief executive officer. Jonathan Seelig, a co-founder of Akamai Technologies and an early investor in Zipcar, became the chair. A board member said: "While we all think Robin did a fabulous job starting the company, the sense at the board level was that we needed a different type of manager for the next stage."[26]

Robin remained a board member and consultant for a short period of time. After leaving Zipcar, she founded two other businesses: Meadow Networks, a transportation consulting firm, and GoLoco, an Internet-based service that enabled drivers and riders to create car pools. Danielson had resigned from the Board of Directors a few years earlier, in the Spring of 2001. She sold a small amount of shares in the summer of 2001.[27] During her career, Danielson held positions at several universities. She was manager of Harvard University's Faculty of Arts and Sciences Campus Energy Reduction Program and Green Campus Initiative. She established a research group on geological carbon sequestration at Durham University, UK and later ran the Tufts Institute of the Environment (TIE) at Tufts University in Medford, Massachusetts. In addition to its primary focus on research, TIE supported campus greening.

Scott Griffith, Zipcar's new CEO, had been the head of two previous startup firms. He managed Digital Goods, a software company that failed in 2001, and Information America, a database company, which he sold for USD 25 million in 1999. Earlier in his career, Griffith had been an executive at Boeing and Hughes Aircraft. Griffith had been following Zipcar's progress for a few years and thought it was a "fascinating idea."[28] He called the process of taking over from Chase "awkward."[29] The venture capitalists, however, believed that the company needed to make the transition from an environmentally friendly cooperative to a lifestyle company with a strong brand.

At Zipcar, Griffith was charged with: (a) achieving profitability in the company's current markets. The Boston operations were profitable but operations in New York and Washington, DC were not; (b) expanding into new markets; and (c) licensing Zipcar's automobile reservations technology to other companies that operated large fleets of vehicles.[30]

As US companies began to develop sustainability strategies to address rising social concerns about global warming, Griffith recognized the importance of Zipcar's green agenda. He continued to promote Zipcar's service as convenient, cost-effective and good for the environment, since for every Zipcar put on the road 20 other vehicles came off, as drivers decided to rent instead of own.[31] The average passenger vehicle emitted 5.5 metric tons of CO_2 emissions each year.[32] So, car-sharing significantly reduced air pollution.

Zipcar improves its business model

Griffith was quick to improve Zipcar's service. Under Chase, Zipcar had used whatever parking spots it could get. Focus group data, however, suggested that people who were familiar with Zipcar, but had decided not to join, felt that the service was inconvenient. The only car available for rental was several blocks away and they were afraid that it would not be available when they needed it. Griffith decided to divide cities into distinct zones or neighborhoods. He filled each zone, one at a time, with cars that were not parked individually, but in clusters located in parking lots and garages. A fleet crew was assigned to each zone. Employees were deployed on foot or on bicycle to handle problems (for example, a car that had not been cleaned).[33]

Griffith increased accountability among Zipcar's city managers. He made them responsible for financial results. He awarded cash bonuses to managers to reach goals set for revenues, profits, car usage, and customer satisfaction. City managers could do their own marketing. This, too, was typically done zone by zone. Advertising throughout an entire city via billboards, bus shelters, and newspapers raised awareness of the Zipcar brand but did not attract new members. Managers could be more effective by blanketing a particular neighborhood. Employees placed brochures in popular ice cream parlors or handed out information cards to commuters as they entered or exited subway stations.[34]

In the Chelsea section of Manhattan, Zipcar launched a promotion with Whole Foods in celebration of Earth Day. For a week, shoppers who spent over USD 100 at the gourmet grocery store could get free rides home in a Zipcar Prius. They could become Zipcar members for a discounted rate of USD 25. In Harvard Square, a Mini Cooper was filled with frozen Ikea meatballs. People who passed by, many of whom were students, were asked to guess how many meatballs were in the car. The winner received a USD 250 Ikea gift certificate, a free 1-year Zipcar membership, and a USD 250 driving credit. An equal amount of packaged meatballs was donated to a food pantry and food bank. In Justin Herman Plaza in San Francisco, local residents and business owners could vent their frustrations with the costs and hassles of maintaining a car in a city by destroying two old, fuel-inefficient vehicles. For USD 1, they could use a regular hammer; for USD 5, they could use a sledgehammer. All proceeds were donated to The Avon Walk for Breast Cancer.

Griffith carefully positioned Zipcar as a "lifestyle" company. Psychographic research conducted by Yankelovich, a consumer research company, identified two types of potential customers: "aspiring achievers," who were concerned with brand and status and who were likely to purchase a car, and "individualists," who were early Internet users and frequent bloggers.[35] Zipcar expanded upon the models that it offered in order to target different neighborhoods with different cars. Residents in Cambridge, Massachusetts were liberal-minded and social activists – they wanted Priuses. Residents in the more upscale neighborhood of Beacon Hill wanted Volvos and BMWs. Flashy logos were removed from more expensive cars, since renters wanted them to impress a date or take out a client. Harvard Square students wanted cool cars, like a Mini Cooper, to run a quick errand. Couples in Back Bay wanted a larger car for weekend trips to Cape Cod.

Sometimes the same Zipcar member needed a different car for a different purpose. A four-wheel drive car could be rented for a ski trip or a pickup truck might be needed to buy supplies at Home Depot. One NYC businesswoman liked to rent a hatchback so that she could transport her designs from a textile studio in the fashion district to meetings in New Jersey. One car that Zipcar members could not rent was a Hummer (not allowed in Zipcar's fleet because of its fuel inefficiency). Car-sharing was smart, flexible, and more convenient than owning a car.

Zipcar routinely surveyed members to learn more about their needs. When it introduced Toyota Prius hybrid cars, members complained about the hourly fee of USD 10. The company listened, and lowered the rate to USD 7.[36] Zipcar also kept track of consumer usage and reminded members of the benefits of the service. After renting a Zipcar, a journalist received a compelling message on her account page: "If you continue spending at this monthly rate, you will save USD 7,247.00 this year vs. owning your own car! That may justify the home entertainment center you've wanted to buy or at least a new computer, printer, and fax machine! We won't tell if you throw in a few CDs or computer games!"[37]

Griffith raised additional funds to fuel Zipcar's growth. USD 10 million in venture capital came from Benchmark Capital in 2005; USD 25 million came from Greylock Partners in 2006; a personal investment was solicited from Thomas Stemberg, the founder of Staples. In May 2006, Zipcar entered Toronto with 50 cars, launching its first expansion outside the US. In November 2006, service was rolled out in London because, in Griffith's words, "London is a beachhead for us to think about a pan-European strategy."[38]

Zipcar targets college students and businesses

Most traditional rental car companies, such as Hertz and Avis, did not typically rent to people under the age of 21 because of the high costs of insuring a risky age group. The Insurance Institute for Highway Safety reported that the crash rate per mile driven for 16–19-year-olds was four times that of drivers 20 years and older.[39] Drivers between 21 and 24 years of age were charged extra daily fees.

Nonetheless, in 2002, Robin Chase targeted college students who did not have cars but who might want to rent one to go on interviews or to run errands. Harvard and MIT provided on-campus parking spots and marketing support for Zipcar. The arrangements were mutually beneficial. Zipcar could increase its membership base and colleges could reduce the number of cars students, and even faculty, drove to campus. According to an operations manager of parking and transportation at MIT, the university was able to add over one million square feet of new office space without a single new parking space because of Zipcar and other transportation options (with savings of USD 9 million).[40]

Before leaving Zipcar, Chase had entered a dialogue with administrators at Wellesley University (her undergraduate alma mater) to see whether it would pay insurance premiums for drivers under 21 years old. Wellesley agreed when Griffith became CEO. Griffith used the data on the good driving records of Wellesley students to convince Zipcar's insurance company, Liberty Mutual, to offer coverage for drivers under the age of 21 with lower than average premiums. With Liberty Mutual's consent, Griffith started service at three more schools; when those programs were successful, Liberty Mutual agreed to extend insurance coverage to young drivers in 35 schools.[41] Zipcar was allowed to market its services on campus, and it got access to inexpensive parking spots. The company believed that early college student adopters would continue using Zipcars after graduation.

Griffith wanted to attract business customers. Employees working in large cities needed cars parked in convenient locations to go to meetings or to pick up supplies. Renting a Zipcar would be cheaper than taking a taxi. In early 2004, the firm launched Zipcar for Business (Z2B). It later signed on 7,500 businesses, including Wells Fargo, PriceWaterhouseCoopers, Genzyme and Ameripath.[42] The strategy enabled Zipcar to increase its vehicle utilization from 9 am to 5 pm Mondays through Fridays without interfering with members who wanted cars after work or on the weekends.

In 2007, Zipcar entered a partnership with Equity Residential, a large owner and operator of apartment properties in the US. Residents received exclusive offers from Zipcar, including USD 75 of driving credit. In a similar arrangement, AKA, an upscale extended-stay chain with nine apartment-style hotels in the eastern US, offered its guests a 1-year complimentary membership of Zipcar.

Zipcar and Flexcar merge

In October 2007, Zipcar merged with its main competitor, Flexcar. Zipcar had 3,500 cars in 35 markets and Flexcar had 1,500 cars in 15 markets. Flexcar, with headquarters in Seattle, Washington, had a strong presence on the West Coast. As a result of the merger, Zipcar added five new cities. The combined company employed 220 employees, had 180,000 members, and served 70 college campuses. Griffith remained CEO while Flexcar's CEO, Mark Norman, became COO. The name "Zipcar" remained. According to Thilo Koslowski, a senior automotive analyst at Gartner Inc., the combined firm's major challenge was to increase awareness of its service among the general population.[43]

Zipcar's focus on social responsibility

Zipcar showed its commitment to the environment. It taught its members about how to change their driving behaviors to reduce their own expenses and carbon emissions. It also promoted a healthy, active lifestyle. Car-sharing members reported a 47 percent increase in mass-transit use, a 26 percent increase in walking rather than driving, and a 10 percent rise in bicycling trips.[44] Zipcar invited 300 individuals to take a North American Low-Car Diet challenge. They were asked to live for a month without their personal vehicles. Combined, participants saved almost 4,000 gallons of fuel and prevented over 75,000 pounds of carbon emissions. Fifty-eight percent of the participants said they planned to continue to live without their own cars; 40 percent reported that they lost weight due to the increased amount of walking and biking.[45]

Zipcar sponsored events to raise money for leukemia and lymphoma, children's hospitals, and bicycling associations. In Washington DC, for example, Zipcar hosted a drive-in movie screening of the "Arctic Tale," a wildlife adventure. Residents who donated their cars to charity got lifetime Zipcar memberships with USD 500 driving credit. Proceeds went to a non-profit organization that promoted bicycling for fun, fitness, and transportation. In San Francisco, the company provided free driving time to Zipcar members if they volunteered to deliver meals and companionship to homebound seniors. Zipcar also offered free rides at predetermined times to commuters from the outskirts of SF to downtown as part of a promotion. Tips for the drivers went to Meals on Wheels.[46]

Zipcar's rental fees and driving plans

In 2009, Zipcar offered different options for different needs. The "occasional driving plan" was for people who needed a car a few times a month. They paid an annual membership fee of USD 50 and an application fee of USD 25. Rental fees depended on a member's location, type of car, and weekday or weekend times. If a member rented a Zipcar in NY or NJ, hourly rates on a weekday started from USD 11 and daily rates on a weekday started from USD 77. Hourly rates on a weekend started from USD 13 and daily rates on a weekend started from USD 115. Gas, insurance, and 180 free miles were included with no extra charge.

The "extra value plan" had no annual fee, but members made a monthly commitment to pay USD 50, USD 75, USD 125 or USD 250. They also paid a USD 25 application fee. Members got discounted hourly and daily rates. In NY and NJ, the USD 50 plan, for example, had hourly rates on a weekday starting from USD 9.90 and daily rates on a weekday starting from USD 69.30. Hourly rates on a weekend started from USD 11.70 and daily rates on a weekend started from USD 103.50. Gas, insurance, and 180 free miles were included. Extra fees were incurred only if a member's use exceeded the USD 50 per month commitment.

Students, faculty, and staff at affiliated colleges and universities had access to much lower annual membership fees (for example, USD 25 or USD 35) and no application fees. Business customers could sign up for special driving plans and rental fees.[47]

Zipcar's future

Zipcar was a privately held company and did not release financial reports. In 2008, *Inc. Magazine* ranked Zipcar number 327 among 5,000 small private companies with revenues of USD 59 million and a 3-year growth rate of 883.3 percent.[48] *Business Week* reported that revenues were expected to reach USD 100 million by the end of 2008.[49] Zipcar won Creative Good's 2008 Copernican Award for putting the customer first.

CEO Griffith began to assemble a strong senior management team. In October 2007, Edward Goldfinger was appointed to the position of chief financial officer. Previously, he had been the CFO of Spotfire (a database management firm), Sapient (an online marketing and consulting firm), and the Latin American beverage business of PepsiCo. In October 2008, Victoria Godfrey was hired as Zipcar's chief marketing officer. She had been CMO of the Princeton Review and had had an earlier career as a vice president at Monster.com. The top management team needed to get ready for increased competition in the rental car business.

Enterprise Rent-A-Car piloted a car-sharing program at Washington University in St Louis. Focusing on business customers, it expanded its WeCar services to Google and REI (a sporting goods retailer). It was in "some stage of negotiations" with ten other organizations.[50] U-Haul, a moving van rental company, launched U Car Share in 12 cities. Like Zipcar, it offered an annual membership and hourly pay or daily usage rates. Customers, though, had to go to a U-Haul location where they picked up one type of car, a Chrysler PT Cruiser. Even Hertz Global Holdings planned to enter the market.[51] Zipcar managers were confident that there was room for everyone in the market. They were not considering an initial public offering or an acquisition by a larger company. According to CFO Goldfinger, "It's early in the life cycle. We're pioneering a new model within the industry. We have a lot of untapped potential."[52]

Concluding remarks

The Zipcar story showed that responsible businesses cannot be created in a vacuum. Solving today's problems – global warming, poverty, and financial crisis – requires a coordinated effort among such players as investors, entrepreneurs, scientists, business leaders, academicians, community advocates, and government officials. Robin Chase and Antje Danielson devoted their respective careers to finding ways to alleviate traffic congestion, reduce air pollution, and create environmentally sustainable college campuses. Their efforts to promote Zipcar as an alternative to car ownership, fortunately, were supported by a community development financier, Boston Community Capital, which gave the cofounders much-needed startup capital.

Government officials did their part by donating parking spaces to Zipcar. Universities came through by picking up some of the on-campus advertising costs, while an insurance company took a risk by offering affordable insurance premiums for young student drivers. Real estate developers believed that they could offer parked Zipcars as an amenity for their tenants. Finally, customers were able to let go of an important status symbol – ownership of an automobile. The overall gain was increased car-sharing and less car-owning.

Many small businesses fail within their first 5 years. Griffith did a good job ensuring Zipcar's survival for the long term. He significantly increased the influx of investor capital, expanded service to other cities, completed a merger with a competitor, fine-tuned Zipcar's marketing and operational strategies, and created partnerships with other businesses. While Chase and Danielson passionately articulated the important social and environmental benefits of car-sharing, Griffith was able to implement them.

As part of a study of the growth and impact of US car-sharing and station car services, Shaheen examined the implications of a leadership shift from entrepreneur to professional manager that occurred at several car-sharing organizations (including Zipcar) between August 2002 and July 2003. She found that the new managers were able to increase member: vehicle ratios from 27:1 to 37:1 and to attract business customers who wanted to avoid the expense of operating and maintaining a traditional corporate fleet. Approximately 50 percent of US car-sharing organizations said they would increase the proportion of hybrid vehicles in their inventory, citing "organizational philosophy" as a primary motivator.[53]

In summary, Zipcar started out as a "new generation of social benefit-oriented business" under the leadership of Chase and Danielson (Table 20.1). It may have evolved into a "traditional business that has integrated social benefit generation into its core strategies" under

304 *Janet L. Rovenpor*

the management of Scott Griffith.[54] Many different types of social entrepreneurs exist.[55]

Notes

1. M. Roosevelt (2005). Clearing the Roads. *Time*, vol. 165, February 21, 50–53.
2. E-mail communication from Antje Danielson dated January 28, 2009.
3. I. Mochari (2001). Deals on Wheels. *Inc.*, vol. 23, February 27, 25–27.
4. W Brown (2008). The little Zipcar deal dwarfs the Big Jaguar sale. *The Washington Post*, March 30, G2.
5. J. Haberkorn (2004). Putting zip into driving. *The Washington Post*, August 17, C10.
6. C. P. Pierce (2007). Earth angels: The entrepreneur – The car-sharing business has made Zipcar cofounder Robin chase a force in the drive to lesson fossil fuel's toll. *Boston Globe*, November 18, 54.
7. Ibid.
8. E-mail communication from Antje Danielson dated January 28, 2009.
9. E-mail communication from Antje Danielson dated January 27, 2009.
10. A US patent was filed covering the methods and systems for an automated car-sharing system on February 16, 2001. See http://www.freepatents online.com/20030034873.pdf [accessed September 30, 2010].
11. S. Tripoli (2000). "Car Sharing." National Public Radio (NPR), Morning Edition, July 27.
12. For a video on how to reserve a Zipcar vehicle, go to: http://www.zipcar.com/how/
13. A member punched in an identification number to prove that he or she was authorized to use the gas card. For a demo on how a Zipcar member filled a vehicle with gasoline, go to: http://www.zipcar.com/gas/play
14. M. K. Pratt (2006). RFID: A ticket to ride. *Computerworld*, vol. 40, December 18, 2006, 21.
15. C. G. Estion (2001), "Zipcar Coming to Washington, DC," Arlington County Commuter Assistance Program, May 12, http://www.commuterpage.com
16. R. Lewis (2001). To unclog roads, city eyes 'car sharing.' *Boston Globe*, November 28, B1.
17. M. Rosenwald (2001). All the (road) rage: urban planners, drivers embrace car-sharing leases. *The Boston Globe*, October 20, p. A1.
18. I. R. A. Breskin (2003). Renting wheels by the hour. *New York Times*, June 22, p. 3.
19. M. Micheli (2002). Weathering the storm. *The Boston Business Journal*, vol. 22, December 27), 1.
20. http://www.bostoncommunitycapital.org/news/files/annualreport.pdf-link.pdf [accessed September 30, 2010].
21. R. Lieb (2002). Big buzz, zero budget. INT Media Group, March 1, http://www.clickz.com/clickz/column/1712065/big-buzz-zero-budget [accessed September 30, 2010].
22. Rosenwald, 2001, op. cit.
23. Ibid.
24. Roosevelt, 2005, op. cit.

25. http://www.freepatentsonline.com/20030034873.pdf [accessed September 30, 2010].
26. S. Clifford (2008). How fast can this thing go anyway? *Inc.*, Vol. 30, March, 94–101.
27. E-mail communication from Antje Danielson dated January 27, 2009.
28. L. van der Pool (2007). Scott Griffith. *Boston Business Journal*, August 24. http://boston.bizjournals.com/boston/stories/2007/08/27/story5.html
29. Ibid.
30. S. Kirsner (2003). New chairman, CEO shifts gears at Zipcar. *Boston Globe*, May 26, D1.
31. S. Salk (2007). Zipcar CEO details company's slow start. *The Northeastern Voice*, May 22, http://www.northeastern.edu/voice/pdfs/052207/p4.pdf
32. A. Frankel (2008). Zipcar makes the leap. *Fast Company*, issue 123, March, 48–49.
33. Clifford, 2008, op. cit.
34. Ibid.
35. M. Beirne (2007). Temporary plates. *Brandweek*, vol. 48, July 9, 30–34.
36. K. Marquardt (2008). 5 keys to Zipcar's success. *US News & World Report*, August 3.
37. Ibid.
38. C. Reidy (2006). Zipcar to debut in London, Gets $25 Million in Capital. *Boston Globe*, November 29, 2006.
39. D. Everson. Zipcar Goes to College. *Wall Street Journal*, August 22, 2007, p. D1.
40. "Zipcar Expands Nation's First Car Sharing Program for Universities with Addition of Seven New Schools," *PR Newswire*, September 6, 2006.
41. Clifford, 2008, op. cit.
42. Company press release, November 2007, http://www.zipcar.com/press/onlinemediakit_gb/zipcaruk_corporate_overview.pdf
43. C. Y. Johnson (2007). Zipcar is expected to join with Rival Flexcar. *Boston Globe*, October 31.
44. Frankel, 2008, op. cit.
45. "Zipcar low-car diet leads to permanent car loss," *PR Newswire*, August 26, 2008.
46. "The Early Bird Catches a Free Ride to Work," *PR Newswire*, May 15, 2006.
47. See http://www.zipcar.com for more information.
48. Transportation. *Inc.*, vol. 30 (September 2008), p. 3.
49. A. Aston (2008). Growth Galore, but profits are zip. *Business Week*, issue 4098 (September 8), 62.
50. S. Nassauer (2008). Enterprise plans to expand car-sharing business in US. *Wall Street Journal*, October 1, D2.
51. Ibid.
52. M. Cole (2007). Trading management Jargon and numbers for a "coolness factor." *Financial Week*, November 19.
53. S. Shaheen (2004). "US carsharing & station car policy considerations: Monitoring growth, trends & overall impacts," Institute of Transportation Studies, University of California, Davis, 2004. http://repositories.cdlib.org/itsdavis/UCD-ITS-RR-03-12
54. Call for Cases: Humanistic Management in Practice, 2008, p. 2.

55. See B. L. Massetti (2008). The social entrepreneur matrix as a "tipping point" for economic change. *Emergence: Complexity and Organization*, vol. 10, 107; G. Vega and R. E. Kidwell (2007). Toward a typology of new venture creators: Similarities and contrasts between business and social entrepreneurs. *New England Journal of Entrepreneurship*, vol. 10, Fall, 15–18.

21
Concluding Remarks

Michael Pirson, Ernst von Kimakowitz,
Claus Dierksmeier, Heiko Spitzeck, and Wolfgang Amann

We live in a world of multiple crises. We struggle to make sense of the financial turmoil and the ensuing bailouts. We witness constantly increasing inequalities between and within countries. While hunger, poverty, and armed conflict often ravage two-thirds of the world's population, the other third struggles with obesity, depression, and the spiritual emptiness that stems from a culture of consumerism. We are acutely aware of the environmental degradation that we cause and which will prohibit future generations from enjoying the comforts of our lifestyle.

Pressed for answers, we want to find solutions, but feel overwhelmed by the enormity of the problems. Issues seem too complex, too impenetrable, and too vast; consequently we often allow ourselves to become lethargic, merely lamenting that nothing can be done. Business seems to be one of the main culprits of the present dilemmas and, unsurprisingly, cynicism about the corporate world has reached unprecedented heights.

It is true that business, or, more generally, the way in which we provide products and services, is contributing to and exacerbating social and environmental crises. However, the *Humanistic Management Network* firmly believes that something can be done, and that it can be done by business.

The cases we have collected in this book are a patent confirmation of our belief that, despite a multitude of adversities, businesses of all sizes, in a variety of industries, and in all regions of the world, can earn healthy profits, making them competitive players in a market environment, while putting people first.

There is more good news. Bringing about positive change is not primarily a question of financial sacrifice. Nonetheless, it might be a deeply unsettling process for many. The change we have in mind is a change in our ideas, a change in the paradigm of what business is, can do, and can achieve in order to be more life-conducive. For such a change to occur in our ideas, we need to question the underlying assumptions that led us to unsustainable business practices. Albert Einstein is credited with the adage: "We can't solve problems by using the same kind of thinking we used when we created them." Consequently, we advocate a new role for business in society, centered on a humanistic management approach as outlined in the introduction to this book. The cases within this book serve as illustrations of how successful businesses around the globe equally respect all stakeholders and deliver value to society at large. The cases selected highlight true business leaders and provide us with a template for the role of business in a life-conducive economy.

In the following, we revisit the 19 case studies to provide an overview and a reminder of the accounts given in this book. We then present general lessons for humanistic management by looking at some characteristics that the described companies share. Finally, we outline a humanistic paradigm of business by comparing it with traditional views on the role of business in society.

Case revision – humanistic management in practice

As Stuart Hart notes, "Capitalism is at a Crossroads," and scholars, practitioners, and policymakers are called to rethink the role of business strategy in light of major external changes (Hart, 2005). As the title of this book suggests, we wanted to present cases of businesses that are managed in humanistic ways by managers who strive towards humanistic objectives. We also wanted to demonstrate that humanistic management is not confined to wealthy nations or to less competitive environments, but that it is a global and universal possibility. To illustrate this promise, we provide examples of various industries, different organizational setups, and a range of organizational sizes.

The first case is that of ABN AMRO Banco Real, a Brazilian bank, whose top management embarked on a humanistic transformation process when faced with a post-merger situation. As the CEO of a very typical bank, Fabio Barbosa examined the possibilities of creating a culture of shared values to better integrate the different banking branches. Exhibiting all the traits of a transformational leader, he reflected on the normative basis of banking in general. Together with his team, he concluded that the new organization needed to be of service to the community, while serving authentic needs; only then would they be able to create a shared culture among the diverse workforce. Many of the community's needs were rooted in the social and environmental problems that Brazil faced. Implementing a transformation could, however, only be accomplished by refocusing the purpose of the bank towards creating social value instead of maximizing its profits. This proposition required profit as a means, but not an end in itself. A new philosophy, "banking with values," has been the crux of the cultural revolution that has taken place in the organization ever since. New products and services have been created, the bank continues to be profitable, and has in turn created high levels of stakeholder trust.

The next case, that of AES, focuses on the unique humanistic philosophy that supported the creation of a US-based energy producer. The founders, Dennis Bakke and Roger Sant, had worked in bureaucratic environments before and knew the stifling effects of such organizational forms. They knew that AES needed to be different in that it had to allow room for personal development and help people flourish. They created a highly decentralized, fundamentally democratic organizational structure, based on the organizational principles of honesty, fairness, responsibility, and fun. The employees are responsible for all of the decisions required to carry out their projects, including the financial budgeting. Receiving that much trust, employees feel empowered and motivated to earn the trust by delivering superior work. Such a decentralized organization can only be managed with a strong unifying purpose, which AES describes as acting as a steward of resources to meet society's needs.

Next we have an example from China. The Broad Air Conditioning case allows us to study how humanistic management is carried out in Asia and in the economy that is soon to be the largest in the world. Broad Air Conditioning views environmental sustainability as a critical problem, and has consequently ignored opportunities to service the fast-growing domestic market for electric home air conditioners. This was a principled decision based on the fact that these air conditioners use the energy they consume inefficiently. Instead, Broad has focused on innovating eco-friendly air conditioning solutions, and within just over 20 years has become the world's largest absorption chiller manufacturer. It has achieved industry leadership by developing innovative products from within a corporate culture that empowers the individual.

In turn, the bracNet case reveals how humanistic management can be harnessed as an innovative development tool, bringing cutting-edge technology solutions to serve the underprivileged. Khalid Quadir, a social entrepreneur par excellence, was convinced that societal value creation could be integrally tied to financial value creation. He succeeded in bringing broadband wireless technology to Bangladesh, aiming to bridge the digital divide. Believing that information access is a very effective and empowering way of promoting development, he created humanistic business models that delivered such services to the rural poor. bracNet serves as a remarkable example of how innovation focused on social sustainability can help people flourish and be financially self-sustaining.

The story of the Canadian paper manufacturer, Cascade Pulp and Paper, highlights how a humanistic management style can become the source of competitive advantage, not because it was introduced strategically, but because it was done on normative grounds. The paper industry is a very mature industry with high levels of competition. Cascades, a large, multi-billion paper manufacturer, uses a unique approach to source used paper and manage decentralized units, which allows it to grow and be innovative at the same time. As is illustrated by many other examples, the decentralized and democratic management approach often seems to provide a better, more humane way of organizing. However, the downside in terms of cost-effectiveness is also discussed.

The dm case presents another story of a humanistic transformation process. It started out as a traditionally managed drugstore chain, but the founder, Goetz Werner, faced continued criticism from his employees. In contrast to many other corporate leaders, Werner actually listened and vowed to change his ways. He embarked on a personal learning journey and took the company along with him. Similarly to AES and Cascades, dm now uses a highly decentralized management approach, in which employees are granted great freedom but also take responsibility for their decisions. With EUR 4.7 billion in turnover and 30,000 employees, dm is a successful model of humanistic management that continuously redefines itself. It is notable that Werner has consistently aimed to influence public opinion with regard to responsible practices. He uses his platform to present innovative policy solutions that maintain human dignity, thus effectively demonstrating a humanistic manager's active social role.

We return to Bangladesh, a hotbed of social innovation, for another example. The Grameen Danone case is a veritable inspiration for a new type of business: a social business that places social value creation before profit creation. Muhammad Yunus, the 2007 Peace Nobel Laureate, enticed the CEO of Danone to co-create a business to eradicate malnutrition. The business would therefore be non-loss, non-dividend, which means that it aims to make no loss, but also does not distribute dividends to shareholders. All the profits are reinvested to further the business's mission of eradicating malnutrition. The case provides additional insight into the operative innovations that need to take place when operating at the base of the pyramid. Benefiting from regional expertise, very small-scale production facilities were created to serve a fresh product effectively, thus contradicting the big-scale production and distribution model. This case is a further innovation in humanistic business models, aiming to serve authentic human needs, while being financially sustainable.

Remaining in Asia, but again focusing on China, the Hongfei Metal Ltd case proves that, no matter where, a corporate leader's vision and perseverance can help transform a traditional business into one that is humanistic and successful. Often ridiculed by his peers because of his concern for his employees and society at large, Mr Li acted on his principles. Despite many challenges, he was often rewarded by the employees' motivation to help make Hongfei successful. Notwithstanding regional cultural differences (such as a shift in emphasis from an individualistic to a more collectivist approach to notions of managerial care and responsibility), the Hongfei example showcases the universal appeal of humanistic values. It also demonstrates the leap of faith that many humanistic leaders are making. They treat people with dignity and invest in human capabilities, based on normative grounds; nevertheless, they are often rewarded with economically positive results.

The Level Ground Trading case pushes the envelope in terms of corporate mission and management style, as the organization is rightly classified as a social activist group, using business to promote justice. Starting with no knowledge about the industry, but with a lot of passion to right the wrongs of coffee-trading, four families in Canada started Level Ground Trading. They did so to make a statement that business could be a force for good, upholding the dignity of coffee producers, who were normally short-changed by large trading houses. In contrast to many fair trade dealers, Level Ground aimed to truly create a community by innovatively establishing relationships between the producers and consumers.

In the case of Micromatic Grinding Technologies, light is shed on the role of the spiritually grounded and enlightened leader who gained credibility by sticking to ethical principles when expedience commanded otherwise. Using various humanistic management techniques, such as profit-sharing and meritocratic advancement, Micromatic developed into a creative community of tool-makers, becoming the market leader in India. The company emphasizes the leaders' humility, which contrasts with typical leadership attributes of strength and dominance, but which is critical to gain genuine respect and trust.

By examining the power of humanistic philosophy, the Mondragon case describes how spiritual teachings influenced one of the biggest cooperative success stories. As a conglomerate cooperative in the Basque region of Spain, Mondragon has defied conventional business wisdom with a highly democratic governance model, with an incentive and pay-out matrix geared towards social equity and communal relationships. Following the teaching of Father Arizmendi, and inspired by regional structures of communal self-governance, Mondragon employed innovative humanistic management approaches with extraordinary economic success. It was a symbol of resistance against the repressive Franco regime and a herald of the current democratic corporate governance. It consists of 120 different companies, 42,000 worker–owners, 43 schools, and one college; does more than USD 4.8 billion of business annually in manufacturing, services, retail and wholesale distribution; and administers more than USD 5 billion in financial assets based on a humanistic business concept animated by the social doctrine of the Catholic Church. It has become a centerpiece of the Basque region's economic and social development.

Returning to a story about humanistic transformation, the Novo Nordisk case illustrates how even in one of the most criticized industries, such as the Pharma industry, business can opt to act as an agent for the world's benefit. Novo Nordisk was originally founded by August Krogh, a Nobel laureate in Medicine, with the goal of finding a cure for his wife's diabetes. Starting out in the 1920s, Novo Nordisk underwent many transitions and ended up a very traditional firm in the 1960s. Then several crises hit and Novo's management decided to listen to its critics and adopted changes. It actively embraced a learning journey towards servicing society's most urgent needs, while respecting the dignity of stakeholders around the globe. Novo Nordisk's example showcases that humanistic transformation does not cost much, except the willingness to actually embrace and implement it. Many companies face similar critics and crises, but rarely adopt and implement any changes.

Conversely, the SEKEM case is a story of a humanistic firm by design. SEKEM is a group of organic agricultural businesses that literally transformed the desert to be life-conducive. SEKEM operates universities and schools to support its operations and contributes to a larger humanistic educational agenda. In 2006, SEKEM reported an annual turnover of USD 23 million and profits of around USD 1.75 million; its growth rate to date had been 25 percent annually, and was projected to rise in the future. While the financial success is telling, the social ambitions are so intertwined with the company's goals that outsiders have difficulty in distinguishing SEKEM from a social movement for sustainable development. SEKEM functions not only as a business, but as a regional development incubator. As such, it is an example of the scalability of ethical management. SEKEM is another case that invites us to rethink the possibilities that business has to solve some of the most important environmental and social problems of our time.

Competing against dm as the example of the most fundamental transformation process, the Semco case reveals how counterintuitive management strategies allow people to flourish at their work.

When Ricardo Semler took over the company from his father, it was a traditional top-down bureaucracy. Ricardo felt that the employees had to be "baby-sat" and controlled, something he hated doing. When he took over, he fired 60 percent of the managers who used a traditional management style, and began the journey towards a people-centered approach. Semler believes that controlling and directing people interferes with human dignity. At Semco, processes are now controlled, not people. Self-directed people are hired and groomed. They decide where the company will go. At this point, Semco operates in eight different industries as a premium provider. All the business units operate at a profit. As such, providing grounds for self-direction was key not only to personal but also organizational growth.

The Sonae Sierra case is not as concerned with a specific humanistic management style as it is with the generation of life-conducive strategies. The case outlines how Sonae Sierra, a real estate management company, started innovating around the triple bottom line, and ended up adopting it as a strategic focus. The case delineates the changes the company introduced to become a corporate responsibility leader in an industry hardly known for active sustainability orientation.

In turn, the Tata Group case sheds light on the controversies that humanistic management can cause. The Tata group was founded to provide India with independent life-conducive industries, such as the steel industry. The founders saw their business as a vehicle for economic emancipation from Britain, and as such always pursued a political goal as well. Tata has a legacy of serving authentic human needs, and the example of the subcompact car, Nano, exemplifies how such an ambition can energize a company and a region. According to Michael Porter, treating social and economic agendas separately is a mistake many companies make. Tata is a great example of how those agendas can be combined to help people flourish and create long-term wealth.

By examining the TerraCycle case, the power of innovative business models can be studied once again. Two young graduate students found a business opportunity that would serve as a model for a sustainable company. Using worms, they transform organic waste into high-end plant fertilizer, which can be sold at premium rates. Being a social and environmental steward is part of TerraCycle's DNA. Early in the startup process, the founders even turned down an offer of USD 1 million because the VCs demanded that they change the company's core strategy to become more mainstream. Despite these challenges, the company enjoys strong growth in revenue and profitability. TerraCycle highlights how entrepreneurial energy, combined with the mission to solve a massive problem, can be the best breeding ground for new and innovative businesses.

Similarly to Level Ground Trading, the Wainwright Bank case demonstrates how social activists can use business to advance social justice. Employing a fundamentally service-oriented business approach, Wainwright Bank supports its communities by providing financial tools for social development. Since responsibility for societal value creation is part of its strategy and day-to-day operation, Wainwright represents business at its best – an approach that many a mainstream banker will find utterly unsettling, yet one that has proven to be more crisis-resistant than many traditional banking approaches.

Closing our selection, the Zipcar case in turn describes how a social and environmental problem can be a business opportunity in disguise. Zipcar is a US-based mobility provider that developed its business model to reduce environmental pollution and serve community-oriented individuals. The case itself deals with the challenges faced by a humanistic business startup in remaining true to its origins when traditional economist investors have a say. So far, it seems that Zipcar has remained true to parts of its humanistic approach by focusing on societal value creation, but that it has made compromises in terms of its community-oriented management approach for the sake of profitability.

Humanistic management – lessons learned

In the introduction to this book we stated that we set out to provide proof of concept. We wanted to demonstrate that businesses can embrace a broader vision when measuring their success and determining managerial tasks by focusing on positive social impact generation with legitimized profit, rather than merely maximized profit. This para-digm shift, which we advocate at the *Humanistic Management Network*, needs to be more than a regulative idea, more than a hypothetical role model for how businesses should act in a perfect world. That alone might constitute an interesting contribution to academic discourse. Proof of concept, however, demands workable and practical alterna-tives to the current mainstream and it must, simultaneously, provide those alternatives under the rules of engagement in economic activities that are shaped by the still dominant management paradigm, which is based on a singular focus on profit maximization as the objective func-tion of the firm.

The key lesson from these cases is, consequently, that these busi-nesses do indeed provide us with workable and practical approaches to humanistic management. We must, therefore, realize that argu-ments aiming to blame practical constraints or inherent necessities to justify unethical managerial practices are flawed. If one company can earn self-sustaining profits while adhering to the guiding principles of humanistic management, then others can do so as well. We have por-trayed 19 of them in this book and we know that there are many more. What these cases share is perhaps indicative of what other businesses can learn from them. The heterogeneity of the accounts in this book makes it likely that these cases' common characteristics are replicable elsewhere.

- Managers from the businesses discussed in this book acknowledge our shared human vulnerability and recognize the resultant need for protection of human dignity. These companies integrate ethical reflection into all business decisions, thereby abrogating conflict between ethically sound business conduct and profit-related aims. They will not pursue business opportunities that may conflict with ethical evaluation. Managers of these companies are also aware that they can make honest mistakes in their evaluations, and thus seek to share responsibilities with internal as well as external stakeholders. In short, they follow the guiding principles of humanistic manage-ment and they do so based on moral insight rather than strategic calculus.
- The companies profiled in this book are steadfastly purpose-based. Their purpose provides the platform needed for the autonomous individual to make decisions for the organization's benefit. The pur-pose is a universally shareable, legitimacy-inducing goal, providing stakeholders with a reason for wanting the company to succeed. In

turn, the company can count on motivated employees, loyal customers, trusting business partners, and a high degree of goodwill from other stakeholders.

- Humanistic management styles as implemented in these cases aim to promote human development, which includes psychological, physical, social, and financial dimensions. Humanistic management is learning-oriented. There is no state of perfection, but only a constant drive to improve and organically evolve.

- The businesses examined in this book provide for decentralized structures, based on trust, allowing their members autonomy while providing a sufficient level of integration to create a community. Humanistic management structures are modeled after democratic systems that create checks and balances, guarding against the imbalances of a corporate control and command structure. They know that trust is reciprocal – one needs to show trust to gain trust – and they have at one stage made a leap of faith, trusting their employees and business partners, and have gained their trust in return. This allowed them to do away with control mechanisms that impede creativity, innovations, and productive interpersonal interactions, and that impose transaction costs.

- Managers in these cases are "servant leaders" and regard themselves as stewards for the greater good. They are often spiritually grounded, self-effacing, and humble. They see their roles as guardians of a culture of dignity and serve as co-developers of a learning community. Humanistic leaders do not see the need to dominate to experience gratification in their career, but derive great satisfaction from being able to share their passions and convictions with their communities. They are grateful for and exhilarated by their ability to contribute to a better world.

Towards a humanistic paradigm for management

The traditional concept of business has been termed "economistic" (Ashley, 1983; Gasper, 2004). Economism refers to an exaggeration of the economic sphere's importance in the determination of social and political relations (Ashley, 1983). An economistic approach thus puts economic motives not alongside but above all other objectives of human action – it aims to establish a primacy of markets. In consequence, it often disregards other concerns, such as moral and cultural viewpoints, as illegitimate in theory and as irrelevant in practice. While it represents a powerful and simple way to think about life, the economistic paradigm is seriously flawed and could prove suicidal. Drawing from the lessons above, we can now try to extrapolate and deduce elements of a humanistic paradigm for business. We do so by juxtaposing the economistic paradigm for the various aspects of management: the perspective of the individual, the business organization, and the view of society at large.

The differing views of the individual

As is clear across all cases, the authentic needs of people are the focal point of business activity. These authentic needs consist of more than mere material necessities. They also include social, psychological, and spiritual well-being. In the traditional, economistic view of management, people's needs are all too often reduced to a need for material acquisition.

In the economistic view, human beings are conceived as utterly self-serving and only interested in maximizing their immediate utility. Economic man (*homo oeconomicus*) is believed to engage only in transactional, short-term-oriented, market-based encounters with others. His engagements are interest-based and other people are a means to an end. His actions are not evaluated for universal applicability and, hence, he is amoral (Dierksmeier and Pirson, 2010). The philosophy of humanism views the individual as a *zoon politikon*, a relational human being – someone who materializes his or her freedom through value-based social interactions. People with whom he or she engages must, even when serving as a means, also be respected as an end in themselves. In the humanistic view, human beings are guided by universally applicable principles and aim at long-term relationships. They are intrinsically motivated to self-actualize and serve humanity through what they do. They do not have fixed preconceived utility functions, but their interests, needs, and wants take shape through discourse and continuous exchange with the outside world. As such, human beings do not maximize their utility, but balance their interests and those of the people around them in accordance with general moral principles (Dierksmeier and Pirson, 2008).

View of the business organization

As we have seen in the cases, humanistic business organizations are quite different from traditional economistic business organizations. They differ, among other things, in their strategy, governance systems, structure, leadership style, and culture.

Business strategy

The bracNet, Grameen Danone, and SEKEM cases illustrate that serving authentic social needs can turn into a profitable business model. The inspiration for these businesses has never been the ambition to create maximum return for shareholders; on the contrary, they were all conceived to provide authentic benefits to many different stakeholders.

From the humanistic perspective, organizations are a vehicle for social relationships, essential to human nature, much more than mere sets of contracts or mechanisms for profit creation. These social relationships manifest themselves both inside and outside the organization. They can only be sustained on normative grounds if they provide long-term value and contribute to human flourishing in general. As witnessed in the Micromatic case, discourse-based social processes are central to the notion of organizing and supporting the creation of mutual goals. The aim of these processes is to achieve a balance and, therefore, any imperative for the maximization of a single interest is rejected. Humanism's universal ambition requires multiple objectives to be integrated and harmonized. Shared value-creation processes are theoretically and practically imperative; a balance between multiple stakeholders and between short and long-term interests is essential. As such, humanistic businesses pursue stakeholder benefit-creation strategies, rather than shareholder value-maximization-oriented strategies.

Many economists and economistically inspired managers would disagree with such a stakeholder-oriented approach to business strategy. They agree with Milton Friedman that the business of business is business; any call for social responsibility is unwarranted. In the economistic view, organizations are a mere nexus of contracts to which people agree when transaction costs are too high for a market-oriented approach. Organizations based on the notions of *homo oeconomicus* are designed to fit the maximization imperative. Organizations in the economistic mold are built to maximize utility in terms of wealth and the need to maximize profit. An optimal way of ensuring utility maximization is for organizational leadership to focus only on shareholder interest. Jensen (2002), for example, argues that there has to be a single objective (shareholder value) for the firm, otherwise one could not purposefully manage it. Stakeholder value-creation strategies are thus deemed impractical.

It is worth noting, however, that some of the most avid proponents of shareholder value maximization, including Jack Welch, former CEO of

General Electric, have now come to the insight that shareholder value maximization is not a good strategy.

On the face of it, shareholder value is the dumbest idea in the world [...] Shareholder value is a result, not a strategy ... your main constituencies are your employees, your customers and your products.

It remains to be seen how many businesses re-evaluate their strategies and follow the path of Novo Nordisk, Sonae Sierra, ABN Amro Real, Semco, and dm towards stakeholder value creation. In many cases, widespread public ownership of the firm and the ensuing pressure from financial analysts are an impediment to such a transformation. It is no coincidence that many of the cases in this volume feature privately held businesses, in which the owner is personally liable, holds a majority stake, and has the ability to implement strategies that counter short-term financial pressures.

Governance

The AES and Broad Air Conditioning cases highlight the role of stewardship. Dennis Bakke of AES pursues the mantra of acting as a steward of resources to meet society's needs. Similarly, the Zhang brothers of Broad Air Conditioning view their enterprise as a conduit for natural, cultural, political, and economic progress. Taking the stewardship role even further, both Wainwright Bank and Level Ground Trading perceive themselves as a social movement to better the human condition by their way of doing business. These business leaders are intrinsically motivated to serve the company and its stakeholders; in contrast to traditional businesses, in which managers are assumed to work in their own interest to the detriment of shareholders. The established governance mechanisms in mainstream business focus on controlling the opportunistic, self-serving manager, so that owners will obtain their rightful profit. In humanistic firms, economistic types of top-down control are usually detrimental to motivation and can backfire (Davis *et al.*, 1997; Donaldson & Davis, 1991; Muth & Donaldson, 1998)). Governance mechanisms need to focus more on strategic support for corporate leaders; a board of directors will only add to the business when it helps management effectively promote their mission.

While top-down control mechanisms are essential to the governance structure of economistic organizations (some organizational theorists call them "remnants of feudalism"), systems of checks and balances are essential in humanistic organizational structures. As we can see in the Mondragon case, democratic control structures, such as stakeholder councils, are in place to prevent systematic abuse. These internal checks and balances mutually reinforce one another to serve various stakeholder needs in a balanced way (see also Gratton, 2004).

Structures

As you might have noticed, a substantial number of businesses presented in this volume differ in their internal structure from traditional businesses; they are often extremely decentralized and focus on self-governance. At Cascades Pulp and Paper, managerial responsibilities are part of each employee's job description. Headquarters is mainly involved in training its employees for these responsibilities. Providing its employees with so much leeway allows Cascades to reap motivational benefits, which have so far provided a competitive advantage and allowed ongoing growth. Similarly, at AES even budgetary responsibility is delegated to the workers. Management believes that people who have direct access to the client and project site know best what to do, and should therefore make the decision. AES headquarters simply serves as a consultant to the local project teams. At Semco, Ricardo Semler is known for his distaste of control and leaves employees to form their teams organically; decision rights are spread throughout the organization in a way that engages the expertise of all employees. At Mondragon, business units are limited to no more than 200 employees, since self-governing capabilities seem to decrease above that number.

In contrast, structures in economistic organizations often serve the profit-maximizing strategy of the firm and are efficiency-oriented. To that end, the organizational structure is centered on economies of scale, hierarchies, top-down decision-making, and financial incentives. While economistic structures rely on a large number of authority levels, humanistic structures reduce authority levels in the organization, support the development of human capabilities, and focus on effectiveness. Financial incentives are used cautiously, because they often undermine intrinsic motivation. However, compensation is structured in a very equitable way. At Hongfei Metal Ltd, employees own shares of the company; at Cascades and Micromatic, gain-sharing programs are in place. At Mondragon, all workers are owners of their respective cooperative, and co-determine their compensation via the workers' council.

Leadership

In several cases we have witnessed the enormous role a leader plays in determining the character of an organization. At Micromatic, the spiritually grounded, self-effacing leader, N. K. Dhand, guided his organization according to ethical principles. AES was created on the founder's philosophy of creating a fun and responsible work environment. dm started its humanistic learning journey because of Goetz Werner's reaction to employee criticism. ABN Amro's leadership used a merger situation to create a novel culture, guided by the principle of banking with values. All these leaders had to earn their stakeholders' trust and inspire them to follow. What Bass and Avolio (1994) term "transformational leadership" fits well in a humanistic view of leadership. Based on moral values, transformational leaders inspire followers, stimulate them intellectually, and engage them emotionally with organizational tasks. They base their influence on the power of the argument rather than the power of a hierarchical position in the organization; they demonstrate care for individual followers and their personal development.

Bass and Avolio (1994) call the economistic type of leader a transactional leader. The transactional leader is primarily involved in ensuring compliance and setting incentives so that the followers deliver. Since the economistic view generally regards the organization as a nexus of contracts, the role of the leader is to constantly negotiate those contracts. This requires the leader to constantly clarify goals and desired outcomes with followers. Nurturing quality long-term relationships is irrelevant, and often a hindrance (for example, hiring and firing is a capacity that requires leaders to be emotionally disconnected from followers). Followers are mainly considered as human resources (not human beings), and a skillful transactional leader is one who maximizes the efficiency of resources.

Culture

Different strategies, structures, and leadership styles unsurprisingly create distinctive organizational cultures. Semco again serves as a vivid example of a human-centered organizational culture that defies all business tradition. There are no bosses, no goals, no plans, and no policies; as Ricardo Semler states, "Our policy is no policy." This flexibility is manifest in many other organizations, such as Micromatic and Cascades.

Humanistic cultures allow constant, organic change and evolution. They are open and participative, not only within but also outside the organization. Broad Air Conditioning, Novo Nordisk, and dm actively engage with outside stakeholders to promote organizational development. In line with the leadership model, humanistic organizations support cultures that are more transformational in nature and create organizational identities based on inter-human relations (relationally) inclusive of a larger group (communal) (Brickson, 2007). They are aimed at promoting human flourishing within, but also outside, the organization.

In contrast, economistic organizations support cultures and organizational identities that are mostly oriented towards the individual (Brickson, 2007). These cultures are often described as transactional in nature (Bass and Avolio, 1994). Consequently, economistic organizations follow rather linear, mechanistic, and closed-loop thought and interaction processes. In addition, as Collier and Esteban (1999) argue, mechanistic organizations attempt to transform the environment "adversarially and competitively rather than seek to respond to it" (p. 176). Uncontrolled change is viewed as a threat, because it interferes with the optimal implementation of the maximization imperative.

View of the societal system

These different paradigms also influence the view of the systemic environment and the responsibilities towards it. In an economistic view, the main function of the corporation is to accumulate wealth, while the main function of the state is to provide security. In this division of labor, the state creates rules to coordinate organizations, and organizational leadership's main responsibility is to obey those rules while maximizing profits. These rules are, however, based on "laissez faire" assumptions so that individuals and organizations can follow their respective utility functions. Any further commitment to societal causes is incompatible with utility maximization at the individual and organizational levels. Talk of responsibilities is generally viewed as systematic interference with liberty. Calls for corporate responsibility and sustainability are only heeded when they are compulsory and part of the legal infrastructure. Voluntary engagement with societal issues, such as equity and intergenerational justice, does not fit the economistic view unless it makes strategic sense in terms of increasing material wealth (Dierksmeier and Pirson, 2010).

In the humanistic perspective, individuals, organizations, and the state all play important roles in helping people flourish. As there needs to be a balance on each level, there is no real division of labor. In the humanistic view, personal morality is linked to responsibility for the systemic consequences. Business leaders accept and assume responsibility for the consequences of their actions on both the systemic and the individual levels. More than that, they view societal ills as a potential business opportunity. SEKEM, bracNet, TerraCycle, Level Ground Trading, and Zipcar present business models that are inherently socially responsible, because strategically they serve a societal need. As Peter Drucker once said, "every social or global problem is a business opportunity in disguise." This integral thinking does not allow a separation of the economic and the societal; it also does not permit a total separation of individual, organizational, and societal problems. Humanistic organizations engage with the outside and view responsibility to stakeholders as elementary for conducting business. Only in that mutual responsibility for individuals, organizations, and the wider system is sustainable human flourishing possible.

The journey forward

As demonstrated by the featured cases of humanistic management in practice, a different way of business is feasible. It is not only feasible, but possibly very liberating. The *Humanistic Management Network* believes that, in order to deal with the current crises, we need nothing short of a revolution in thinking. We argue for a humanistic paradigm to supplant the economistic paradigm. For this to happen, we must realize that our economic activities follow man-made rules and, therefore, it is in our hands to allow those rules to evolve rather than readily accepting the status quo as a given order.

The humanistic management paradigm is centered on three guiding principles: the need for the protection of human dignity, and the need to integrate ethical evaluation into managerial decisions. In addition, the new paradigm appreciates that shared responsibility will be able to produce more life-conducive business activities than individually assumed responsibility can. Humanistic managers assume responsibilities *with*, not for, stakeholders.

Will humanistic business conduct one day replace today's dominant business practices? We hope so. We acknowledge the strength of status quo-conserving mechanisms, but we can also increasingly observe businesses, like those that you have read about in this book, actively changing the ways in which we produce goods and services.

Can businesses that adhere to the guiding principles of humanistic management win the competitive game against strictly profit-maximizing businesses? As demonstrated in this book, we know that they can, and we have also seen that they are supported by loyal customers, engaged and motivated employees, trusting business partners, and much goodwill from other stakeholders.

Yes, it takes managerial vision and guts, it takes great products and strong values, it takes enlightened owners and passionate employees.

But the bottom line is that it can be done, and those who have experienced humanistic management would never want to do business any other way.

Bibliography

Ashley, R. (1983). Three modes of economism. International Studies Quarterly, vol. 27 (4), 463–496.

Bass, B. M. and Avolio, B. J. (1994). Transformational leadership and organizational culture. International Journal of Public Administration, vol. 17 (3/4), 541–554.

Brickson, S. L. (2007). Organizational identity orientation: The genesis of the role of the firm and distinct forms of social value. Academy of Management Review, vol. 32 (3), 864–888.

Collier, J. and Esteban, R. (1999). Governance in the participative organisation: Freedom, creativity and ethics. Journal of Business Ethics, vol. 21 (2–3), 173–188.

Davis, J. H., Schoorman, F. D. and Donaldson, T. (1997). Toward a stewardship theory of management. Academy of Management Review, vol. 22 (1), 20–47.

Dierksmeier, C. and Pirson, M. (2008). Oikonomia Versus Chrematistike: Learning from Aristotle about the future orientation of business management. Journal of Business Ethics, vol. 88 (3), 417–430.

Dierksmeier, C. and Pirson, M. (2010). Freedom and the modern corporation. Philosophy of Management (formerly Reason in Practice), vol. 9 (2).

Donaldson, L. and Davis, J. H. (1991). Stewardship theory or agency theory: CEO governance and shareholder returns. Australian Journal of Management, vol. 16 (1), 49–66.

Gasper, D. (2004). The Ethics of Development – From Economism to Human Development. Edinburg: Edinburg University Press.

Gratton, L. (2004). The Democratic Enterprise: Liberating your Business with Freedom, Flexibility and Commitment. London: Financial Times.

Guerrera, F. (2009). Welch rues short-term profit "obsession", Financial Times. New York.

Hart, S. (2005). Capitalism at the Crossroads – The Unlimited Business Opportunities in Solving the World´s Most Difficult Problems.

Jensen, M. C. (2002). Value maximization, stakeholder theory and the corporate objective function. Business Ethics Quarterly, vol. 12 (2), 235–257.

Muth, M. M. and Donaldson, L. (1998). Stewardship theory and board structure: A contingency approach. Corporate Governance: An International Review, vol. 6 (1), 5–29.

Index

Abed, Fazle Hasan, 68
ABN AMRO REAL, 13–27, 308–9
  "3Rs" eco-efficiency program, 16
  bank of value concept, 14–15
  insolvency rate, 20–1
  leadership development at, 23
  micro-lending by, 21
  product stewardship, 19–21
  sharing of best practices by, 21–3
  staff, 17–19
  stakeholder engagement at,
    21–3
  student lending, 23–4
  success of, 24–6
  sustainability and, 15–17
  vision of, 13–15
Abouleish, Ibrahim, 204–6
Acción International, 21
accountability
  at AES Corporation, 36–8
  at Cascades Inc., 83
AceMicromatic Group, 153
achieved respect, 221–2
action learning, 269
Adultness, 222–3
AES Corporation, 28–41, 309
  business rationale, 29–30
  leaders and people, 35–40
  lessons learned from, 40
  organizational structure, 36–7
  social responsibility at, 32–5
  values and guiding principles, 30–2
Agarwal, Anil, 159
agriculture, 205
alterity, 217
Amigo Real Project, 18
Aristotle, 128
Arizmendiarrietta, Father Don Jose
    Maria, 170–4, 178–9
ascribed respect, 221–2
Association of Humanistic
    Psychology (AHP), 249–50

Atlantic Forest, 16
authenticity, 286
Azevedo, Belmiro de, 232–3

Bakke, Dennis W., 28, 29, 35
balanced scorecard, 193
Banco Real, 13–14
Banerjee, Mamata, 260
Bangladesh
  context, 64–5
  development indicators, 116
  digital divide and, 64–5
  government collapse in, 71
  microfinance in, 103–5
  wireless broadband access in, 62,
    69–73
bank of value concept, 14–15
banking industry
  see also Wainwright Bank and Trust
  humanistic management in, 288
Barbosa, Fabio C., 14
Basques, 170–1, 174–5
Beyer, Jon, 266, 267
Bhattacharya, Buddhadev, 257
biodynamic farming, 205
bonuses, 223–4
Boston Community Capital, 294–5
BRAC, 67–9, 71–2
bracNet, 62–75, 309–10
  beginnings of, 65–6
  challenges facing, 71–3
  e-hut concept, 69–70
  financing of, 70–1
  humanistic business model, 66–7
  humanistic-based partnerships,
    68–9
  lessons learned from, 73–4
  mission of, 62
  value creation strategy, 65–6
Braungart, Michael, 268
Brazil, 14
Bridgehead model, 131

Broad Air Conditioning, 42–61, 309
  company overview, 48
  cultural and spiritual "civic"
    functioning, 51–2
  cultural dimension, 51–2
  environmental impact, 48–50
  environmental protection and,
    50–1, 55–6
  as integral enterprise, 57–8, 59
  knowledge cycle, 53–4
  management philosophy, 51–2
  natural and communal "animate"
    functioning, 48–51
  private (business) dimension, 54–7
  scientific and technological
    "public" functioning, 52–4
  success philosophy of, 54–5
business, new role for, in society,
  7–8, 308
business incubator, 139–40
business organizations, 317–23
business strategy, 318–19
business-in-society relationship,
  270–3

callingness, 224–5
Calvert, 70
carbon, 33
Carlyle, Thomas, 248
Cascades Inc., 76–91, 310
  business overview, 88–9
  challenges facing, 85–6
  company overview, 76–7
  consolidation process, 80–5
  expansion process, 79–80, 84–5
  lessons learned from, 86–7
  management style, 84–5
  production process, 78–9, 84–5
  sustainability initiatives, 87–8
Chamomile Children Project, 211–12
Chase, Robin, 290, 292–6, 299–300
China
  economic development, 43
  energy shortages in, 55–6
  small private firm in (case study),
    119–29
  township-and-village enterprises
    (TVEs) in, 120
Chinese culture, 127–8

Chowdhury, Abdul-Muyeed, 68
circulating fluidized bed (CFB)
  boilers, 33
Cisco, 224
civil society, 271–2
collaboration, 181, 183, 189, 286–7
collectivism, 128
Collins, Jim, 288
communication, integrity in, 157–8
community, social responsibility and,
  34–5
community development loans, 280
CommunityRoom.net, 279
competition, 184
Comte, Auguste, 128
Confucianism, 127–8
conscious capitalism, 284–5
cooperation, 184
corporate misdemeanor, 1
corporate responsibility, 6, 74,
  231–234, 239–242, 244, 313, 322
corporate social responsibility, 10,
  73–4
  see also social responsibility
  at ABN AMRO REAL, 15–26
  at AES Corporation, 29–40
  at Hongfei, 121–7
  at Novo Nordisk, 185
  at Sonae Sierra, 233–46
  Wainwright Bank and Trust and,
    284–8
  at Zipcar, 301
Cox, Christopher, 278–9
culture, 321–3
culture of caring, 158–9
customer loyalty, 280

Danielson, Antje, 290, 292–3, 296
Daoism, 43
Das, Shiuli, 258–9
DAWN (Diabetes, Attitudes, Wishes
  and Needs) initiative, 194–5
decentralized structures, 316
decision making
  Abouleish's principles of, 205–6
  managerial, 1–2
  at Semco, 219–20
DEFTA partners, 70, 72
democratic management, 215–30

developing countries, digital divide
  and, 62–4
Dhand, N. K., 147–50, 153–4, 166–7
diabetes treatment, 194–9
dialogue-based leadership, 97–102
digital divide, 62–4
diseconomies of scale, 224
disintegration, 42–4
dm, 92–102, 310
  company overview, 92–4
  dialogue-based leadership at,
    97–103
  origins of humanistic management
    approach at, 94–7
  principle of individualism at,
    97–100
dormitory labor, 122
downsizing, at MGT, 162–3
Drucker, Peter, 224
DryWash, 19–20

East, 44–5
eco-capitalism, 268
economic man, 317
economic prosperity, 235–6
economic rationality, 10–11
economistic paradigm, 316–17, 322
Ecotainers, 143
Egypt, 204, 205
e-hut concept, 69–70
Einstein, Albert, 308
Elkington, John, 135, 235
Employee Assistance Programs (EAPs),
  125–6
employee benefits, 141–2, 283
employee bonuses, 141
employee engagement
  at ABN AMRO REAL, 17–19
  at AES Corporation, 38
  at Cascades Inc., 82
  at Novo Nordisk, 195–6
  product innovation and, 123–4
employee entertainment, 126
employee satisfaction, at MGT, 164
employee turnover, 283
employee welfare, 125–7
employees
  empowerment of, 97–8, 221–2
  investment in, 121–2

profit sharing with, 223–4
  of SEKEM, 208–10
  sharing success with, 159–60
  social benefits for, 141–2
  social justice for, 160–2
  of Wainwright Bank and Trust,
    282–4
empowerment, 69, 97–8, 221–2
enemies, 172
energy optimization, at Cascades
  Inc., 78–9
enlightenment, 12
entrepreneurial leadership, 124–5
environmental ethic, at Level Ground
  Trading, 142
environmental protection
  Broad Air Conditioning and, 50–1,
    55–6
  at Level Ground Trading, 142–3
  Wainwright Bank and Trust and,
    283–4
environmental quality, 236–7
environmental sustainability, AES
  Corporation and, 33–4
EnviroTotes, 142
equity, 158–9
Escola Brazil Project, 18
"Espaço Real de Prácticas em
  Sustentabilidade," 22
ethical concerns, integrating into
  managerial decisions, 6–8
Ethical Fund, 19
ethical reflection, 4, 6–8
experiences, 206
experiential learning, 269

Faber, Emmanuel, 107
facilitation, 189–91
facility waste, 143
facts, 206
fair trade coffee, 131–46
fairness, 31, 159–60
Famicafé, 138–9
family hierarchy, 160
federated corporation, 224
Federation of Industries, 226–7
Flexcar, 300
flexible working hours, 141–2
Foell, Armin, 94

Franco, Francisco, 170–1
Friedman, Milton, 318
friends, 171–2
Fruandes Ltda, 139–40
fun, 31
future, 206

GAIN, 109, 114
Gates, Bill, 46
Gavelle, Guy, 109–10
geographic diversification, at Cascades
    Inc., 79–80
Glassman, Robert, 277–88
global financial crisis, 277–9
global integrity, 47
globalization, 43, 45, 47
Goindi, V. S., 150
governance structure, 319–20
Grameen Bank, 103–5
Grameen Danone Foods, 103–18,
    310–11
  beginnings of, 106–7
  challenges facing, 113–16
  distribution process, 111–12
  eco-friendly initiatives, 112–13
  mission and objectives of, 108–9
  production process, 109–11
  social goals, 114–16
Grameenphone, 62–5, 70, 72, 75n8
green businesses, 268
green transportation, 141
greenhouse gas emissions, offsetting
    of, 33–4
Greenspan, Alan, 278, 279
Griffith, Scott, 296–300, 302
Groupe Danone, 103–7, 113–16
Gupta, Amit, 159
Gürtler, Henrik, 187

Haitao, Li, 121–9
Handy, Charles, 224
Harsch, Erich, 92, 93
Hart, Stuart L., 22, 308
Health care, in Russia, 190–1
Heliopolis University, 212
higher purpose, 285, 315–16
holism, 44–5
homo oeconomicus model, 100, 318
honesty, 155–7

Hongfei Metal Ltd (pseudonym),
    120–9, 311
human development, 316
human dignity, 4–6, 315
human rationality, 11
human resources, 5
human resources management
  at Cascades Inc., 82
  humanistic and welfare-oriented,
    125–7
  in TVEs, 120
humanism, 44–5, 248–9, 264, 317
  Confucian, 127–8
humanistic management
  see also specific companies
  benefits of, 10
  common threads in, 285–8
  definition of, 4–5
  lessons learned from, 314–16
  paradigm for, 316–17, 323–4
  principles of, 3–10
humanistic psychology, 249–50
humanistic-based partnerships, 68–9
humility, 162

ideals, 206
individual, differing views of the, 317
individualism, 97–100, 101
Indonesia, 31–2
information access, at Cascades Inc.,
    82
information sharing
  at AES Corporation, 38–9
  at MGT, 162–3
innovation, 285–6
  at Broad Air Conditioning, 52–4
  employee involvement and, 123–4
integral enterprise, 44–60
  Broad Air Conditioning (case study),
    47–58
  guidelines for becoming, 58–60
  structure of, 46
integrity, 30, 157–8
internal communications, at Cascades
    Inc., 82
International Association of Fair Trade
    (IFAT), 134
International Association of
    Partnership (IAP), 210

internet access, 62–5
intuition, 286

JN Tata Endowment, 252–3
just society, 160

Kant, Immanuel, 5, 11, 12
Klassen, Laurie, 141–2
knowledge creation, at Broad Air
    Conditioning, 52–4
Koslowski, Thilo, 300
Krogh, August, 186, 312

leadership, 320–1
    at ABN AMRO REAL, 23
    at AES Corporation, 35–40
    dialogue-based, 97–103
    entrepreneurial, 124–5
    humility in, 162
    principles of, over time, 101
legitimacy, 4, 8–12
Lemaire, Antonio, 76
Level Ground Trading Ltd.,
    131–46, 311
    awards won by, 135–6
    business model, 136–8
    community building at, 143–5
    employee benefits program, 141–2
    environmental protection at, 142–3
    as fair business incubator, 139–40
    humanistic management at, 134–6
    mission and objectives of, 131–2,
        133–4
    origins of, 132–3
    overview/background of, 133–4
    social impact of, 138–9
local identity, 47
Longobardi, David, 280–1
Lumiar Institute, 227

Management by Wandering Around
    (MWA), 215
managerial decisions, 1–2
    integrating ethical concerns into,
        6–8
managerial tasks, 5
Marchant, Emmanuel, 103, 109
market rationality, 224
Marubeni Corporation, 70

mature entrepreneurship, 176–7
McDonough, William, 268
mentoring, at AES Corporation,
    39–40
Merckens, Georg, 204
microfinance, 21, 103–5
Micromatic Grinding Technologies
    (MGT), 147–68, 311–12
    atmosphere of trust at, 162–3
    career advancement at, 160
    efficiencies at, 164
    employee satisfaction, 164
    Entrepreneurial Division, 176–7
    equity through respect at, 158–9
    fairness in sharing success at,
        159–60
    financial success of, 163–4
    growth of, 151
    history of, 150–3
    honesty in operations at, 155–7
    humanistic management at,
        147–50, 153–67
    integrity in communication at,
        157–8
    leadership at, 162
    management philosophy, 153–5
    mission of, 149
    organizational structure, 152
    recession and, 165
    reputation of, 164–5
    rightsizing at, 162–3
    social justice for workers and,
        160–2
    vision of, 148
Microsoft, 46
mistrust, 222
Mody, Russi, 251
Mondragon Cooperative Corporation,
    170–84, 312
    commercial and community
        businesses, 177–8
    guiding principles of, 183–4
    history of, 174–6
    mature entrepreneurship at,
        176–7
    organizational structure, 178–83
    overview/background of, 170–3
Monteiro, Elsa, 233, 243
moral legitimacy, 11–12

Nano, 252, 255–8
non-ideological stances, 217
Norman, Mark, 300
normative legitimacy, 4, 8–12
Novo Nordisk, 185–203, 312
    balanced scorecard at, 193
    challenges facing, 199
    employee engagement at, 195–6
    facilitation at, 189–91
    fundamentals, 200–1
    history of, 185–8
    lessons learned from, 199
    milestones, 199–200
    multi-stakeholder approach at,
        186–7
    reflective paradigm at, 187–8
    stakeholder engagement at, 193–8
    success of, 198–9
    sustainability reporting, 191–3
Novo Nordisk Way of Management
    (NNWoM), 188–98

organizational structure, 319–20
    at AES Corporation, 36–7
    at Cascades Inc., 81–2
    decentralized, 316
    at MGT, 152
    at Mondragon, 178–83
    at SEKEM, 208
    at Semco, 223
    at Sonae Sierra, 238–40
Øvlisen, Mads, 187

participatory management, 215–30
patient focus, at Novo Nordisk, 193–5
Patra, Manik, 258, 262
Patrick Brummer and Partners, 70–1
people, utilization of, 5–6
pharmaceutical industry, 185, 196–7
    see also Novo Nordisk
Portela, Alvaro, 237
Porter, Michael, 263, 313–14
post-consumer reclamation, at Level
    Ground Trading, 142
poverty reduction, digital divide and,
    63
pragmatic legitimacy, 9
Prieto, Oscar, 28
private sector, role of, 7

product diversification, at Cascades
    Inc., 79–80
product innovation, 123–4
product quality, 123
professionalism, 160
profit maximization, 3, 6–8, 10–11,
    224
profit sharing, 223–4
    at Cascades Inc., 83–4
publicity, 11–12
public-private partnerships, at Novo
    Nordisk, 196–8
purpose, 315–16

Quadir, Iqbal, 65
Quadir, Khalid, 62, 64–73
quality management, 211

recession, 165, 277
reciprocal relationships, 284
recycling, 78, 142, 268–9, 273–4
reflective paradigm, 187–8
Regional Centre of Expertise on
    Education for Sustainable
    Development Cairo, 212
Reich, Michael, 197
renunciation, at Semco, 220–5
resource optimization, at Cascades
    Inc., 78–9
respect, 4–6, 83, 158–9
    achieved, 221–2
    ascribed, 221–2
responsibility, at Cascades Inc., 83
retirement savings, 141
reverse evaluation, 222
Riboud, Antoine, 106
Riboud, Frank, 105, 114
Roosevelt, Margot, 290
Rousseau, Jean-Jacques, 128
Russell, Ray, 293
Russia, health care in, 190–1

safety, 35
Sant, Roger W., 28, 33
Santoro, Michael, 197
SEKEM, 204–14, 312–13
    employees, 208–10
    founding of, 205
    humanistic management at, 206–11

SEKEM – Continued
  lessons learned from, 213
  mission and objectives of, 206–7
  organizational structure, 208
  quality management, 211
  supply chain partners, 210
SEKEM Development Foundation,
  211–12
Semco, 215–30, 313
  adoption of practices of, 225–7
  critical success factors, 221–5
  history of, 217–20
  lessons learned from, 225–7
  management practices at, 215–17,
  220–5
  organizational structure, 223
  salary structure, 223–4
Semler, Ricardo, 215–21, 224–8, 313
Sen, Nirupam, 257
servant leaders, 316
shareholder value maximization, 7,
  10–11, 318–19
shopping centers, 244
Singur Nano plant, 257–63
Snow, John, 279
social benefits, 3, 138, 141–2
social business enterprise (SBE)
  challenges of, 113–16
  concept of, 103, 105, 106
  Grameen Danone Foods as, 103–18
  increase in, 116
  tenents of, 107
social inclusion, 63, 282–4
social justice
  fair trade coffee and, 131–46
  Sonae Sierra and, 237–8
  Wainwright Bank and Trust and,
  281–2
  for workers, 160–2
social obligations, 217
social relationships, 318
social responsibility, 31, 318, 322–3
  see also corporate social responsibility
society, 42–3
socio-environmental risks, 17, 20
solidarity, 183–4
Sonae Sierra, 231–46, 313
  corporate social responsibility at,
  233–46

  efficiency at, 243–4
  external recognition for, 240–1
  governance structure, 238–40
  identity and culture, 241–3
  key performance indicators, 241,
  242
  profile of, 231–5
  social contributions of, 237–8
  triple bottom line approach at,
  234–45
  vision of, 232–3
Sorensen, Lars Rebien, 187
South, 44–5
staff training and development,
  126–7
  at ABN AMRO REAL, 18
  at AES Corporation, 39–40
  at Broad Air Conditioning, 51–2
stakeholder dialogue, 8, 10, 11–12, 187
stakeholder engagement
  at ABN AMRO REAL, 21–3
  at Novo Nordisk, 193–8
  at Tata Group, 252–5
stakeholder-oriented approach, 318
stakeholders
  benefit-creation strategies, 318
  humanistic management and,
  11–12
  normative legitimacy and, 8–10
Starbucks, 137
Stiglitz, Joseph, 62–3
student lending, 23–4
supply chain partners, 210
sustainability
  at ABN AMRO REAL, 15–17
  at Broad Air Conditioning, 50–1
  at Cascades Inc., 87–8
  at Semco, 224
  at Sonae Sierra, 236–7, 244–5
Sustainability Leadership program, 23
sustainability reporting, 191–3
Szaky, Tom, 266, 267, 269, 270

Tata, Dorabji, 250–1
Tata, Jamsetji, 247–8, 249
Tata, Jehangir Ratanji Dadabhoy,
  251–2, 253
Tata, Ratan, 252, 255–6, 257, 260,
  261, 262

Tata Council for Community
Initiatives (TCCI), 254–5
Tata Group, 247–65, 313–14
    history and development of, 250–5
    humanistic management at, 253–5
    lessons learned from, 263–4
    Nano car and, 255–8
    Singur Nano plant, 257–63
    stakeholders and, 252–5
    values and business philosophy,
    248–50
Tata Index for Sustainable Human
Development, 255
Tata Iron and Steel Company (TISCO),
253–4
Tata scholarships, 253
TerraCycle, 266–75, 314
    business model, 267–8, 270, 273–4
    history of, 266–7
    humanistic management at, 267–70
    internships at, 269
    public image of, 270
    societal context and, 270–3
theft, 222
Toews, Stacey, 131–2, 135–8, 144–5
township-and-village enterprises
(TVEs), 120
Triple Bottom Line (TBL) approach,
135, 138, 187, 193, 234–45

unethical behavior, 1
United Nations Global Compact, 232
upcycling, 268
utility maximization, 318

value creation, 14, 65–6, 73–4, 318
values, 263
Vendramim, João, 215, 219, 225
vocational training, 212
Voice over Internet Protocol (VoIP), 72
volatile organic compounds, 145n8

Wagh, Girish, 256, 260
Wainwright Bank and Trust, 277–89,
314
    company overview, 277–8
    corporate social responsibility and,
    284–8

employees of, 282–4
    environmental protection and,
    283–4
    management philosophy, 278–81
    social inclusion at, 282–4
    social justice and, 281–2
    success of, 280–1
Wall Street bailout, 279
Wal-Mart, 123, 127, 219
waste reduction, at Level Ground
Trading, 143
Waxman, Henry, 278
Weber, Max, 9
Welch, Jack, 318–19
Wells, Christopher, 20
Werner, Goetz, 92–4, 97–8, 100–1, 310
whyway management practice, 221
WiMAX technology, 66, 73, 75n10
Winograd, Terry, 69
wireless broadband access, in
Bangladesh, 62, 69–73
Wolff, Greg, 69
World Bank, 68
World Business Council for
Sustainable Development
(WBCSD), 232
World Safety Declaration, 232

Yin and Yang, 43
Yunus, Muhammad, 103–6, 116, 310

Zhang Yue, 51–2, 53, 55, 56–7, 60
Zidane, Zinedine, 103
Zipcar, 290–304, 314
    business model, 297–9
    college students and businesses
    targeted by, 299–300
    expansion of, 295–6
    future of, 302–3
    growth of, 291
    leadership of, 296–7
    lessons learned from, 303–4
    marketing strategies, 295
    merge with Flexcar, 300
    origins of idea for, 292–5
    overview/background of, 290–2
    rental fees and driving plans, 301–2
    social responsibility and, 301